Dear Alan

Thanks for helping us enjoy
the year so much. All the
best for the future & look
forward to catching up with
you sometime soon.

Brendan & Mike

# Born to Lead

*The Untold Story of The All Black Test Captains*

# Born to Lead

*The Untold Story of The All Black Test Captains*

**Paul Verdon**

Celebrity Books
*Sports & Personality Book Publishers*

FIVE CAPTAINS: Five test captains are present in this photo of the 1949 All Black team that toured South Africa. They are the team captain, Fred Allen (front row, with ball), Alex McDonald (1913, front row, sixth from left), Peter Johnstone (1950–51, second row, fourth from left), Kevin Skinner (1952, third row, third from left) and Ron Elvidge (1949, fourth row, fourth from left).

*Elvidge's father, John is in the back row, eighth from left, wearing an All Black blazer after being appointed an honorary assistant manager during the tour (see Elvidge chapter for details).*

# CONTENTS

This special commemorative Canterbury edition has been proudly published for the supporters of Canterbury rugby.

Commissioned by The Warehouse Ltd exclusively for its valued customers in the Canterbury region, this book commemorates the appointment of Todd Blackadder as All Black captain for the first international rugby season of the new Millennium. In this season when the Canterbury Crusaders achieved three consecutive Super 12 Championships, the year 2000 All Blacks have been strengthened by the inclusion of 11 players from the Crusaders/Canterbury region.

We salute former All Black captains from the Canterbury region:

| | |
|---|---|
| Herb Lilburne   1929 | John Graham   1964 |
| Jack Manchester   1935–36 | Chris Laidlaw   1968 |
| Bob Stuart   1953–54 | Tane Norton   1977 |
| Pat Vincent   1956 | Jock Hobbs   1985–86 |
| Bob Duff   1956 | Justin Marshall   1997 |

ISBN No 1-877252-05-0
Published in 2000 by Celebrity Books
PO Box 33 1071, Takapuna
Auckland, New Zealand

© 2000 copyright Paul Verdon
Cover art, book design and production by **BookNZ**
Printed by PrintLink, Wellington
Celebrity Books is the imprint of The Celebrity Book Company Limited,
Unit 11, 101–111 Diana Drive, Glenfield, Auckland, New Zealand.

# ACKNOWLEDGEMENTS

In the researching and writing of this history the author has been assisted by a host of New Zealand rugby personalities. Without their co-operation and courtesy this book would not have been possible.

The author owes a debt of gratitude to the following:

Bob Luxford, Curator, NZ Rugby Museum

Charlie Saxton

Brent Edwards

Reg Maskell

Dave McLaren

Lindsay Knight

Ron Palenski

Sir Terry McLean

Fionna Hill

Helen Adams

Deborah La Hatte

Dick Cavanagh

The late Neville McMillan

Bob Stuart and JJ Stewart

Jim McKenzie

Bruce Hawkins

The late Russ Thomas

Geoff Miller

Geoff Longley

Bob Schumacher

Andrew Funnell

Paul Neazor

Fran Whild, *BookNZ*

Bill Honeybone, Celebrity Books

The photographs in this book were supplied by the NZ Rugby Museum, with the exception of those on pages 103, 178, 179, 184, 189, 193, 208, 210, 217, 218, 222, 223, 226, 227, 228, 231, 232, 234, 235, 237, 238, 239, 242, 244 and 246 supplied by Photosport, and those on pages 116, 121 and 260 from the Cavanagh collection. The author and publisher have made every effort to trace copyright owners of every photograph and apologise for any omissions.

# DEFINING MOMENTS OF ALL BLACK TEST CAPTAINCY

CARDIFF, DECEMBER 16, 1905
Dave Gallaher, for the only time on the first great tour, is unable to muster his team to victory. Wales wins 3–0. But Bob Deans believed he did score, thus launching the legend of the All Blacks and their battles with Wales.

WELLINGTON, SEPTEMBER 17, 1921
The selectors have caused a sensation by dropping captain George Aitken and replacing him with Teddy Roberts after the first touring Springboks had tied the series 1–1. But appalling conditions contribute to a 0–0 draw.

SWANSEA, NOVEMBER 29, 1924
Jock Richardson, who captained the Invincibles in the three home union tests when Cliff Porter was either injured or could not make the team, buries the Welsh bogey with a 19–0, four-try demolition.

CAPE TOWN, SEPTEMBER 1, 1928
Maurice Brownlie, after ordering a week's holiday for the team and 2-1 down in the series, drives a magnificent All Black forward pack to victory, 13–5. The series is therefore shared again.

PORT ELIZABETH, SEPTEMBER 17, 1949
The worst moment in All Black history as Ron Elvidge, deputising for tour captain Fred Allen, leads his team off after a 4–0 whitewash by South Africa.

CHRISTCHURCH, AUGUST 18, 1956
Bob Duff leads the revamped All Blacks to a 17–10 victory over the Springboks, after kicking maestro Don Clarke makes test debut. Duff's team would then take the series, the first over South Africa.

AUCKLAND, SEPTEMBER 18, 1965
Wilson Whineray, who has led the All Blacks since 1958, captains them to a decisive 20–3 win over the Springboks to take the series and regain the mythical 'world crown'. It is the middle of a golden All Black period, winning all series between 1961 and 1969.

CARDIFF, NOVEMBER 11, 1978
Graham Mourie produces an escape act befitting Houdini when the All Blacks pip Wales, 13–12, after the infamous Andy Haden lineout dive. The win enables Mourie to complete the first All Black Grand Slam in Britain.

AUCKLAND, JULY 25, 1987
David Kirk, deputising for an injured Andy Dalton, leads the All Blacks to a 29–9 win over France to take the first World Cup.

DUBLIN, OCTOBER 27, 1991
The era of captain Gary Whetton and coach Alex Wyllie has almost ended. Australia has just beaten the All Blacks, 16–6, in a semi-final of the World Cup and will go on to win the final.

JOHANNESBURG, JUNE 24, 1995
Sean Fitzpatrick's All Blacks, devastated by food poisoning, have lost the third World Cup final to South Africa after producing easily the most outstanding form of any participant in the lead-up matches.

PRETORIA, AUGUST 25, 1996
Fitzpatrick gains sweet revenge for the previous year and satisfaction for generations of All Blacks when his team takes the first series ever won by the All Blacks on South African soil.

SYDNEY, AUGUST 29, 1998
Australia 19, New Zealand 14 and ignominy for captain Taine Randell as the All Blacks experience something that has never happened in a century of international rugby – losing five tests in a row.

LONDON, OCTOBER 31, 1999
France 43, New Zealand 31 in semi-final of World Cup. The era of coach John Hart is one game from its end. He resigns from the job after the even more embarrassing loss to South Africa in the 3rd–4th play-off.

# INTRODUCTION

## Select group chosen to wear the purple

THE ALL Black test captains have always been a special band. Right from when the soon-to-be tragic figure of William Millton led the first 'New Zealand' team overseas in the 19th century, the captains emerged as men who were surely born to lead.

From its beginnings in 1870, rugby had been dear to this tiny fledgling nation. Hundreds of clubs sprung up in a few short years and both European and Maori races embraced the game.

The hold of rugby on its people never weakened. It reflected the country's aspirations in a way no other sport could compete with. Given the robustness and psyche of the pioneers, and the way they turned rugby into a science, it was inevitable a national team would quickly evolve and just as inevitable it would prosper. The feats of the team, called the All Blacks since 1905, became legend.

But as New Zealanders flocked to rugby as players and spectators, the demands came at a price. The highest expectations were always felt. The nation's confidence hit a low point whenever the side faltered.

But the All Blacks and their predecessors seldom let their followers down. Year in, year out, through the decades of the late 19th century, throughout the 20th century and now into the new millennium, they have forged an international record that none can match.

And while styles and tactics and personnel would alter through the seasons, the consistency would not.

The men who took most on their shoulders to ensure this record remained a proud one were the test captains.

All Black coaches might scheme and plan the downfall of the mighty Springboks or any of the other rugby nations. But it was the captains who had to put those tactics into practice on the field. And often, in the years before World War II, these battleground generals had to do the job without a coach.

Let us look back for a moment to the magic times of the past for examples of the great New Zealand captains.

Charles Marter would write of Tom Ellison

that he 'could not only plan out deep, wily schemes, but personally carry them through to triumphant execution.' A man could learn more in a half-hour's talk and exhibition in the gymnasium with Ellison than he would pick up otherwise in years.

The evidence suggests Gallaher's All Black Originals' leadership style, honed from time spent in the Boer War, was highly effective. He knew how to 'psyche' his team up and on match days would ask each man to spend an hour on his own to 'rest and contemplate the game ahead'. He insisted the team be totally disciplined and pay attention to detail, both on and off the field – very much a forerunner of the captains who were to follow.

When the 1924 Invincibles' tour did not begin as well as its predecessor had, Cliff Porter took the drastic action of calling the players together and putting the position squarely before them. He told them they must draw up rules of conduct if they wanted to succeed. They drew up rules about practices, exemptions, curfews for those playing the next game and other matters. The outlook of the tour changed immediately when the team destroyed the first Welsh club, Swansea …

*Born to Lead* asks the questions and then uncovers or recovers much 'lost' material about the men who led our teams:

How Ellison really felt about those early British referees, how Gallaher sought to stop his old captain from wielding too much power on the Originals tour, how ironman Freddy Roberts escaped death on that tour and how one of the team's most generous men, Jimmy Hunter, turned into a 'pillar of stone' at the end of his sad, long life.

How Porter came to hate his manager and whether the controversial Mark Nicholls was behind the coup that ousted Ces Badeley from the captaincy of the 1924 Invincibles? What did Maurice Brownlie really think of George Nepia? Did you know New Zealand got its first professional rugby coach in the 1920s? Was Charlie Saxton really robbed of the chance to be All Black captain?

Into the more modern era and still the gems are there to be dug out. How JJ Stewart broke the heart of a future All Black captain, how Frank Oliver was asked to captain the 1978 team that became the first All Black Grand Slammers. And how and why he turned it down.

How an extraordinary total of four All Black teams had been unbeaten on tours of Britain yet couldn't achieve what Mourie's men did. Why Andy Dalton decided to seek to have Mourie reinstated even though he could have taken over the captaincy permanently.

How some All Black captains had to drop out of tour contention because they couldn't afford the losses to their farm or business, while other were treated handsomely. Did Gary Whetton conspire to have Buck Shelford dropped? What Shelford thinks happened? How Sean Fitzpatrick was offered an All Black coaching role – before he'd even retired – and why he turned it down? And will Fitzy ever come back?

A remarkable statistic that will surprise readers is that 23 of the All Black test captains came from the South Island and only 22 from the North. Another is that the ratio for All Black coaches is almost the same. These figures hardly reflect the north's much greater population advantage, but may show the great preponderance of rugby knowledge that is handed down in the south like a royal lineage.

*Born to Lead* unravels some of the mystique that lies behind the position of All Black captain. How do the selectors make their choice and what qualities they identify with.

The game's followers have been intrigued by the contention that, until Wilson Whineray's era, there had never been a long-term captain. But was it quite as simple as that? Porter was in fact the first to hold the job for a sustained period, from 1924 to 1930, though his omission from the 1928 tour to South Africa needs analysing. The book examines why this was so and uncovers some interesting statistics to show great captaincy was not limited to the modern era.

Porter also led the All Blacks many times against New South Wales, in games not counted as 'tests' by the NZRFU. But in March 1999 the Australian Rugby Union confirmed the status of all international matches played in Australia by NSW in the early 1920s as official test matches. It said NSW was effectively the Australian

team. Included in the ARU statistics were 15 matches against New Zealand. When this book was published the NZRFU had not reciprocated, leaving the record books of the two countries' performances differing.

These games were approached as 'test matches' by the New Zealand teams and the national selectors and coaches. The author believes it likely the NZRFU will eventually accord 'test status' to these matches. So a chapter on these games is included.

We know some All Black captains had to carry the leadership load virtually unaided. They had no coach. Porter and Brownlie of the 1920s are the classic cases. But there were others.

The NZRFU does not emerge lilywhite in this book. Its treatment of some captains, as with some coaches, sometimes left much to be desired. Badeley's treatment was scandalous, but others also lost their jobs in heartless fashion.

The adage that 'uneasy lies the crown ...' could easily apply to some All Black leaders. Captains have been dropped because they did not conform with the ideas of the manager–coach. Examples studied include Porter and manager Stan Dean in 1924, Frank Kilby and Vinny Meredith in 1935, Ian Kirkpatrick and JJ Stewart in 1974 and Shelford and Wyllie in 1990.

Other captains have been unsentimentally dropped because of form – George Aitken in 1921, Badeley, Porter, Pat Vincent in 1956, and Shelford too.

There are many sad endings recorded in this book. How Fred Allen couldn't bring himself to even think about rugby for several years after tossing his boots into the ocean in despair. How Jock Hobbs felt at missing the first World Cup, when he had earned the right to be in the squad. There is the bitterness of Gary Whetton when given the cold shoulder by Laurie Mains, and many more.

Any book on the captains highlights the strugglers. How Colin Meads found himself in charge of a fledgling All Black team against the best the British had ever produced. Why Stu Wilson remains the only winger to have captained the All Blacks on tour. And what it was like to replace a captain of the mana of Mourie while leading a depleted side.

*Born to Lead* looks too at the short-term

captains who came up trumps. Trying to match Bob Duff's feelings when he defeated the Springboks for the first time in history would be hard. But then Dalton's euphoria at the Springboks' demise in 1981, contrasted with his misery when injury destroyed his World Cup campaign in 1987, probably does just that.

Who is the greatest? Some All Black captains were better than others. It is impossible to objectively compare one era with another, since rugby's evolution depends on ever-changing conditions, rules, tactics and the state of the opposition.

But *Born to Lead* does delve into the pros and cons of why certain captains deserve elevation into an elite group more deserving of the purple. And why the accolade of 'the greatest' might not go to the captain who has perhaps been the public's popular choice.

Some self-effacing captains told the author that running the All Black team was 'like driving a Rolls-Royce' and that 'a donkey could do it.' But depending on the state of maturity of the side, others clearly found constant challenge in extracting hard-won victories with inexperienced or modest personnel.

This book proves, clearly, that some of the best All Black years came when there were great captain-coach partnerships. There has been a succession of these. Perhaps the Whineray–Neil McPhail alliance was the first long-term alliance – and the perhaps the best?

But look at some of the others. The Allen–Lochore union was superb – and unbeaten. Leslie and JJ Stewart have been credited with picking the All Blacks up after some rough years. The Mourie–Jack Gleeson team produced the first Grand Slam and Mourie showed he was able to produce similar on-field magic for Eric Watson and Peter Burke. Coach Wyllie's alliance with first Shelford (unbeaten in 14 tests) and Whetton (12 wins out of 15) produced exceptional results the critics seem to have forgotten.

Today the standing the All Black test captain enjoys in the community remains high, even allowing for the tribulations of the young John Hart-appointed captain, Taine Randell.

This was never more amply demonstrated than when Shelford was dropped a decade ago. 'Bring back Buck' became a popular cry and,

incredibly, is still occasionally echoed around grounds overseas.

Almost all New Zealanders feel some 'ownership' of the All Blacks, even more so now they have to pay out big money to watch them in person or on paid television.

But Shelford's demise took on more significance than the overthrow of a prime minister for some people. Indeed, it should not astonish the reader that many Kiwi boys, given the choice of one day being the prime minister or the All Black captain, would quickly opt for the latter.

In Lindsay Knight's 1991 book, *They Led the All Blacks*, which primarily covered the 1960s, 1970s and 1980s, the author described the All Black captains as 'remarkable characters and personalities' and added that the job 'bestows some sort of mystical distinction' upon the holder.

That was no exaggeration for there is no doubt many of the captains have and will continue to be successful in other fields besides rugby. Two have recently been knighted. Others made their way to the top in business, education, economics, medicine, diplomacy, politics and many other fields. Others became leading rugby coaches and administrators, including at least seven who went on to coach the All Blacks. *Born to Lead* suggests why this phenomenon occurs.

The author can attest to the fact that meeting old All Black captains can still stir the blood. There remains something inspirational present, calling for respect ... there is usually a modesty but also a quiet inner strength.

While Rod McKenzie, in Auckland's Ranfurly Home, was too ill to participate [McKenzie died earlier this year], Jack Griffiths, long retired with wife Jean in Paraparaumu, was his cheery old self.

It cannot be doubted one would follow Whineray through thick and thin, be inspired by John Graham's enthusiasm and energy, be intrigued a mellowing Fred Allen could have been such a 'Needle' and be warmed by the tales of the retiring Ron Elvidge.

Kevin Skinner still has the physical presence, Bob Duff the organised authority of his accountancy calling, Bob Stuart remains a remarkable achiever and Colin Meads is as humble as ever he was.

Lochore, still giving to this country far more

than he ever gained in return, finds time to deal with the chores expected of an outstanding former All Black captain. Kirky's integrity surely had him born to the purple. Leslie and Tane Norton remain friendly, unpretentious men, all too ready to assist.

The more introspective Chris Laidlaw may not be the fire-eater of old but shows he cares deeply for his country. Dave Loveridge hasn't forgotten any of the lessons his work ethic taught him about rewards two decades ago. Stu Wilson's sense of humour readily lifts an interviewer.

Dalton is an obliging but busy, busy man, as is his old battlefield companion, Mourie, who, as his recent coaching elevation demonstrates, remains a thinker, always seeking the edge. Frank Oliver, who gave way to Mourie with the Hurricanes but saw it as a chance to grow with the Blues, has had some of the 'rough edges' knocked off him – but not too many. Hobbs is judiciously careful in his answers …

David Kirk's boyish charm but restless energy remains as strong, Shelford still exudes the mana of old and Whetton is now a briskly busy and confident businessman.

And who said the 'modern' captains were different? Justin Marshall and Paul Henderson describe their deep appreciation of the honour bestowed upon them, despite their brief tenures. Sean Fitzpatrick and Randell seem so aware of the special shoes they have most recently been chosen to tread in.

The book does not cover the many fine players who have led the All Blacks in non-test encounters. That distinguished list includes players who toured as vice-captains, such as Mark Nicholls, Charlie Oliver, Ray Dalton (who shared with his son, Andy, the honour of being the only father–son combination to captain the All Blacks), Laurie Haig, Tiny Hill, Des Connor, Kevin Briscoe, Ian MacRae, Sid Going, Bruce Robertson, Mark Shaw, Joe Stanley, Mike Brewer, Murray Mexted, Andy Haden and a good few others.

Unlike the earlier All Black coaches, the All Black captains have always had a high profile. They have more often than not been paid their dues.

The writer has discovered that, like the All Black coaches, there have been remarkably few 'failures' among New Zealand's rugby leaders. And it was a fascinating exercise to learn just how much our illustrious modern captains owe to their predecessors of the 19th century and the evolutionary process that is rugby.

How else would we have arrived at the beginning of 1999 with the All Blacks' test success rate as high as was 71.6 per cent? That is well ahead of its greatest rival, South Africa (65 per cent) or England (50 per cent) or Australia (47.5 per cent).

Until now, the 56 All Blacks who have captained New Zealand in tests have never had their careers and contributions analysed in depth, together with the subject of goal-setting and leadership examined as a theme. For the first time, as a body, these often great leaders are studied in an attempt to understand what drove them to countless international victories and to acknowledge their contribution to our growing pride in the Men in Black.

* The writer was a young reporter on the Christchurch Star in 1973 when he was sent to Lyttelton to interview Bob Duff, the former All Black captain who had just been sacked as All Black coach after the controversial 1972–73 All Black tour of Britain and France, which included the banishment of All Black prop Keith Murdoch. He began working on a book, called *The Power Behind the All Blacks, the Untold Story of the All Black Coaches*, which was published in 1999. *Born to Lead, the Untold Story of the All Black Captains*, was part of that long project and is now the 'sequel'.

# THOSE WHO CAME BEFORE

## *The evolution of the All Blacks and their captains*

NEW ZEALAND did not play its first official test match until 1903. There was no national union until 1892 and no 'test matches' as we know them today until a decade later.

But before that there had been more than three decades of rugby played in the colony and it was inevitable a national team would be formed.

It was the arrival of the first overseas team, the New South Wales side which toured New Zealand in 1882, playing provinces, and losing to Auckland and Otago, which showed some the potential for a national team.

So in 1884 a New Zealand side was chosen to reciprocate the Australians' visit. It won its eight matches in New South Wales comfortably, including three 'tests'. The tour was organised by a Dunedin businessman, Samuel Sleigh, who became the team manager, and William Millton, secretary of the Canterbury union, who was captain of the side and therefore New Zealand's first captain.

Millton, a barrister and outstanding cricketer and rugby player, had captained his province since 1878. He was to die of typhoid, aged 27, three years later.

The team was made up of nominations from the Auckland, Wellington, Canterbury and Otago unions only. It wore a dark blue jersey with a gold fern. The side's good organisation, discipline, unselfishness, modesty in victory and forbearance with umpires' decisions was noted by Australian newspapers.

That 1884 tour was the early climax of the phenomenal growth of rugby in the colony since its introduction in 1870. Rugby had spread like a bushfire. Hundreds of clubs existed within a few years. Combinations of clubs for tours, then unions, had quickly followed. Competition from other Victorian games was extinguished as rugby's popularity enveloped all classes and both European and Maori races.

A combination of Auckland clubs had made the first national tour, in September, 1875. It lost to Dunedin clubs, nine-and-a-half points to a half-point, before 3000 spectators. It lost all its other tour matches, to Wellington, Christchurch, Nelson-Picton and Taranaki clubs.

Three weeks later New Zealand's provincial government system would fall. But the New Zealand provincial rugby system would carry on to become perhaps the finest in the world over the next 120 years.

But after such a promising 'international' start, it would be almost a decade before another New Zealand team was organised, perhaps because the promoters of the 1884 side had been left out of pocket.

New South Wales toured in 1886.

Then in 1888 a British team gave the New Zealand game its first great boost. Andrew Stoddard, an English international cricketer and fine rugby three-quarter, had taken over the captaincy when Robert Seddon was drowned in Australia. Stoddard's team won 13 of 19 matches in New Zealand.

The British did not meet a New Zealand combination. But they sowed the seeds of a new style of game in the colony. And together with what occurred when Thomas Eyton organised the first tour by any rugby team from New Zealand to Britain, the game would never be the same.

This was the New Zealand Native team of 1888–89, whose exploits have taken on a mystical nature, especially the accomplishment of playing 107 matches over 14 months, an average of three games per week.

The 'Natives' – who contained five Europeans, some overseas-born and therefore not 'native' – were a pioneering and inventive team who won 78 games and drew six. Their many fine performances included the win over Ireland and the narrow losses to Wales (0–5) and England (0–7). They were unrecocognisable from the side which had left New Zealand when they returned to beat the finest New Zealand provinces (except Auckland).

The Native team was also to produce two future New Zealand captains, Tom Ellison and Davey Gage. So the Native tour and team were to have a powerful effect on the development of the New Zealand game.

*TOM ELLISON: Was said to plan 'deep, wily schemes'*

## ELLISON, THE FIRST GREAT CAPTAIN

Ellison, the first NZRFU team captain in 1893, was the first of the few truly great men to have guided the development of the game. He may have contributed the most.

Described as 'a magnificent forward' by a contemporary writer, Ellison is credited with inventing the 2–3–2 scrum and its accompanying wing-forward position, but undoubtedly brought many other new features to the New Zealand game after touring with the Natives aged 21. He went on to captain and coach Poneke, Wellington and New Zealand teams and transform the rugby game from what New Zealanders had played pre-1888.

Admitted to the bar in 1901, Ellison successfully proposed, at the first annual meeting of the New Zealand Rugby Football Union in 1893, that New Zealand wear black jersey with silver fern, white knickerbockers and black stockings. Fittingly, he became the first captain to wear the colours later that year on a successful tour of Australia. He wrote perhaps the first coaching book on the New Zealand game, *The Art of Rugby Football*, in 1902, two years before his death at the age of only 36.

Ellison was a visionary. Having endured hardships, with the Natives, beyond the imagination of modern-day footballing tourists, he would write, after a tour to Britain by a New Zealand representative team had been proposed, of the lack of realism in expecting a team and its players to embark on a long tour without adequate out-of-pocket expenses. It would take almost a century before the rugby authorities would fully acquiesce to this line of thinking.

So Ellison's ideas, on this point, came to nought. The All Black Originals of 1905 received three shillings a day in expenses, by 1924 it had gone up slightly, and by 1953–54 Bob Stuart's All Blacks were receiving just 10 shillings a day. Many were the players' grievances that while vast sums of money were brought through the turnstiles on the great tours, the 'entertainers' were paid a starvation rate!

Some history books claim it was the 1905 All Black Originals who introduced specialised scrummaging to the British. The Blackheath RFC, of London, one of the oldest clubs in the world, still claims it was the first club in the world to introduce scrummaging positions to the game, in 1905. But such claims cannot be correct.

In Ellison's book, published three years before that tour, we can still read how 'in the scrum (the Natives) invariably beat the best English packs, not through having better men, but through our more scientific system of packing the scrum, and having specialists in each position, instead of merely fine all-round men; the result being, that our two front-rankers, for instance, simply buried the two Jack-of-all-trades who happened to be pitted against them in the different scrums.' So it is reasonable to assume New Zealand clubs were employing scrum specialists many years before 1905, some perhaps before 1888.

'The England team … should never have won the game against us so easily, but for three early and distinctly erroneous and depressing decisions of the referee, Mr Rowland Hill,' wrote Ellison. Hill, who was 'the most important official [he was the secretary] in the English union … and the father of the team pitted against us' should never have been refereeing the match.

Within two or three years of the Natives' tour, Ellison would devise and then perfect, through his Poneke and Wellington teams, the wing-forward position. He had been frustrated by the offside interferences of players around the scrum. He pulled a man out of the scrum and brought up one of the halves, using them as shields for his halfback. The results were brilliant. This innovation would soon be modified further, with one of the 'shields' becoming the wing-forward, putting the ball into the scrum and becoming a marauder in his own right.

'As the New Zealand game developed from Ellison's invention, it produced the fastest, finest, most exciting rugby that has ever been played,' wrote Terry McLean in *NZ Rugby Legends*. 'Of necessity, the backlines at a scrum were compelled to stand some distance to the rear of their halfbacks because the uncertainty of possession made esssential a steps-and-stairs formation which would compel speed from men racing to take their passes. For about 40 years … the game, because of the backs, initially, had the room to maneouvre, was adventurous, fast-flowing and enterprising.'

Ellison's 1893 All Black team played the wing-forward game on its 10-match Australian tour and carried all before it, bar one of three games against New South Wales.

Charles Marter would write of Ellison that he 'could not only plan out deep, wily schemes, but personally carry them through to triumphant execution.' A man could learn more in a half-hour's talk and exhibition in the gymnasium with Ellison than he would pick up otherwise in years.

The New Zealand union had been founded in 1892. But the 1893 New Zealand team which toured Australia under Ellison had contained no players from Canterbury, Otago or Southland, because these unions had stubbornly remained unaffiliated.

Alf Bayly captained New Zealand to a 6–8 loss to New South Wales at Christchurch in 1894 in the first 'test' ever played in this country. Bayly had been the leading try-scorer on the 1893 New Zealand tour of Australia and later led New Zealand on the 1897 tour there. He would later feature in a rugby tragedy involving his 1897 New Zealand team-mate 'Barney' Armit. In 1899 Armit's neck was broken when he tried to hurdle over Bayly's tackle in the Taranaki–Otago game. Armit died 11 weeks later in Dunedin Hospital.

Otago was admitted to the NZRFU, and Southland readmitted, in 1895. So all unions were now affiliated. But it was still not all to be smooth sailing.

Queensland toured in 1896, losing to Auckland in its first match and then to Wellington, 7–49, the Capital's players scoring 14 tries. The New Zealand selectors announced they regretted the 'unavailability' of the southern star, Jimmy Duncan, when they chose their test team. The Otago union and the NZRFU were in dispute over financial terms for the Queensland–Otago match. The game was cancelled and the tourists played a second match against Canterbury. The Otago union then refused to allow its players to play for the national team. Davey Gage captained New Zealand to a 9–0 win in Wellington.

Duncan, who was to become New Zealand's first national team coach, was in the side which toured Australia in 1897. The team was again captained by Taranaki's versatile Alf Bayly. Again, it took until the third NSW match to make New Zealand the tie-winner.

New South Wales toured in 1901. Played in Wellington, the test produced a record crowd of 8000 and a record gate of £420.

Duncan led the team to Australia in 1903. Brilliant football produced record scores and 63 tries in 10 matches. Large crowds, as many as 35,000, loved the New Zealanders' style.

The 1903 test at Sydney, won 22–3, was New Zealand's first full-scale test, although 13 'inter-colonial' matches had been played against New South Wales between 1884 and 1901, for 10 wins and three losses, while Queensland had been beaten on the seven occasions the teams had met. Australia had played internationals against Britain in 1899.

# JIMMY DUNCAN

## *Pioneer player became 'father' of All Black coaches*

JIMMY DUNCAN should primarily have been remembered for the enormous contribution he made to establishing rugby at the forefront of a young New Zealand nation's psyche and on the international front.

His feats as a master tactician over many seasons with Otago made him an automatic choice for New Zealand. He is also credited with inventing the two five-eighths system of backline alignment. He captained New Zealand in its first test match and was also the first officially appointed coach of a New Zealand test team.

It is sad that while Duncan's memory is particularly revered in the deep south, in the north he is probably better remembered as the coach of the 1905–05 All Black 'Originals' who was usurped by the captain of the side, Auckland's Dave Gallaher, and therefore may have played little part in the success of that ground-breaking team.

Duncan, the player, had begun as a wing-forward but was converted into a back. He later specialised at five-eighth, but could play well anywhere. He was especially well-built for the era, weighing over 13st and being 5ft 9in tall.

By the time he retired, Duncan had played in 50 matches for Otago over 14 seasons – a huge number considering the provincial set-up was just evolving and three matches a season was the average for a union. He captained Otago for nine seasons before making his New Zealand debut on the 1897 tour of Australia.

In 1901, Duncan, then 31, was chosen to captain New Zealand at wing-forward, scoring three tries in the two matches, against Wellington and New South Wales. Duncan scored from the kick-off in the second game.

To capture some idea of Duncan's style, we can go to the book, *Centenary*, by historians of New Zealand rugby, Rod Chester and Neville McMillan: 'Duncan put in a strong run as the New South Welshman held off, waiting for the pass which did not eventuate; and the New Zealand captain ran through to score behind the posts.'

Eye-witnesses of the day reported Duncan was 'a master schemer. From the time he took the field, he never stopped thinking of ways to put off his man, or the whole of the opposing side, by some shrewd move no one could have guessed at.'

He again toured Australia in 1903. This team won all 10 matches including the first official test match between the two countries, 22–3. Scoring 276 points with only 13 against, it was hailed as the 'greatest ever'.

Historians of the era argued the side was better than the 1905 team, especially in the forwards. Jimmy Hunter, one of 15 outstanding players chosen for Terry McLean's book, *New Zealand Rugby Legends*, could not make the side, while Billy Stead, another Legend, couldn't get in the top team on tour.

Billy Wallace scored 85 points at fullback while Opai Asher, the 'Indiarubber Man' from Auckland, dotted down 17 times to set an imposing benchmark for All Blacks of future generations to chase. Duncan McGregor scored 11 tries. The team played before large crowds, including 32,000 in Sydney. The forwards included a great lock in Bernie Fanning (Canterbury) and Gallaher (Auckland).

Duncan's courage was renowned. It sometimes needed to be. The most infamous

*FIRST COACH: Jimmy Duncan became the first official All Black coach in 1904*

rugby match played in New Zealand in the early days was popularly remembered as the 'Butchers' Match', when Wellington beat Otago at Carisbrook, 10–6, in 1897.

The match was the first test of two newly developed styles of play – Otago's with its two five-eighth system and Wellington using its two wing-forwards to develop what was then called the 'wing game'. The over-vigorous tactics of the northerners caused the crowd to go wild. The Wellington wing-forward William McKenzie, nicknamed 'Offside Mac', and the older brother of two All Black coaches to be, had kneed Tommy Wood and closed the Otago man's eye. Other players from both sides were injured.

The then-teenaged Billy Wallace was in the Wellington team and later recalled that Otago's extra five-eighth system had caused him to face overlaps in the first half.

'The first time Jimmy Duncan got the ball in the second half Mac launched himself like a battering ram. He not only skittled him ball and all, but split his scalp as well. Things got a bit lively after that … The crowd took to us as we

left the field. I was the smallest in the team but that didn't stop me getting a crack over the head from a woman's umbrella.

'The crowd, in an ugly mood, shouted 'Dirty butchers, Wellington slaughtermen', this being an allusion to the fact McKenzie and several other players worked for the Gear Meat Company in Petone.'[1]

And Duncan and McKenzie had been All Black team-mates in Australia only two months earlier!

Duncan retired in 1903 at the age of 34. His career as a great player and New Zealand coach ought to be considered in the context that Otago, and its major city of Dunedin, was the country's most prosperous and influential area at the time – and its strongest rugby union. Dunedin, built on the gold rushes of the 1860s, was New Zealand's largest city until the turn of the century, and its most important commercial and financial centre. It is there that many of New Zealand's oldest and largest companies started, and where much old wealth still remains today.

Otago rugby benefitted from that wealth, enterprise and the people who flocked to Dunedin to live and work. Its formative clubs, many of which still prosper today, were innovators who regularly took their teams on tours which benefitted the development of the game nationally. Though the last province to accept the formation of the national union, and only after it had been threatened with 'blacklisting' in 1893, Otago had built an enviable record as Duncan's playing career came to a close.

But fierce provincial rivalries abounded, even then, and Duncan would become a victim before long. He was asked to coach the 1904 New Zealand side which played the touring Great Britain team at Athletic Park, winning 9–3, including two tries from Wellington winger, Duncan McGregor, one of the stars of the 'Originals' tour the following year.

The New Zealand team was announced a week before the arrival of the British, who had completed a 13-match, unbeaten Australian tour, including three tests.

Interviewed before the test Duncan explained why he thought his team would win: 'I have given them my directions. It's man for man all the time, and I have bet Gallaher a new hat that he can't catch Bush [Percy Bush, the uncapped Welshman, who had emerged as a star of the backline on tour]. Bush has never been collared in Australia but he'll get it today. We are going to stick to our own 2–3–2 scrum formation and I think we can win.'

Tremendous interest was aroused by the match, with the governor, the prime minister and most of the ministers of the Crown among the 20,000 crowd. McGregor was carried shoulder high from the ground when spectators invaded the playing area after the final whistle.

So Duncan, 35 in 1904, remains one of the youngest men to be appointed coach of the New Zealand team. Only Vinny Meredith, aged 33 when he took the All Blacks for the first time, to Australia in 1910, was younger.

Amidst controversy, Duncan was appointed to coach the 1905–06 team to tour Britain and France – a team which transformed the game in both hemispheres and became known evermore as the All Blacks. But Duncan was not given rein by senior players to coach the side as he wanted.

Senior players complained that the 26 players chosen were insufficient, especially as only one halfback, Freddie Roberts, was among them. They said that a coach, instead of an extra player, was an expensive and unnecessary luxury. The NZRFU, whose chairman, George Dixon, had been appointed the team manager, relented and Bill Cunningham (Auckland), a burly lock, was added and became one of the major successes of the tour. Duncan was retained as coach.

However, historians are in general agreement that Gallaher, the captain, and Billy Stead (Southland), the vice-captain, quickly informed Duncan they would be running the forwards and backs, respectively.

Correspondence from team members fueled rumours Otago's favourite son was being sorely treated by 'the Auckland members of the side'. A Dunedin newspaper said: 'It was definitely known here on Saturday that the relations between certain sections of the New Zealand football team were very much strained. This can easily be gathered from the contents of a number of letters received by the last mail by friends of the Otago members. The trouble had apparently risen out of the old sore feeling over the appointment of Jimmy Duncan as coach.

'The letters indicate that from the first the Auckland members set themselves up in sharp opposition to Duncan and then to the Otago members in general.

'"He is just nobody", is the way in which one writer sums up the position. It had not been possible to confine the trouble to the question as it affected Duncan; certain other Otago members have been drawn into it, so bitterly that it is rumoured a well-known Otago player gave one of the Aucklanders a good thrashing.'

Morrie Mackenzie, who'd reported on the New Zealand game for many decades, and accumulated a tremendous amount of knowledge from the decades before that, wrote in 1969 that Duncan had been told, gently but firmly, right from the start of the tour, that his services would not be required. He was to relax and enjoy the tour as a first class passenger at the union's expense.

'George Dixon did make some effort to carry out the behest of the NZRFU, but soon gave it up as a bad job. However, Duncan had a wonderful time. He became a sort of P.R.O. for the team, sounding off about this and that for the benefit of all and sundry,' wrote Mackenzie.[2]

However, the great Billy Wallace put a different slant on things. He was complimentary when he wrote about his old Otago team-mate and All Black coach. 'Jimmy put in a lot of hard work behind the scenes,' wrote Wallace. 'Not only has he been a clever player, but he has been able to impart his knowledge to others. He was a keen observer and could quickly pick out faults of the different players. Jimmy's coaching, especially early in the tour, when we were working out our plan of campaign, was of very great value to us and helped to weld us into a very powerful attacking combination. Jimmy put in a lot of time with the injured players and assisted with the baggage. If an early train had to be caught, nobody could dodge Jimmy.'

If there was a serious dispute in the team, it was not apparent to outsiders. After his return home Duncan was quoted as saying the utmost harmony prevailed and the rumour that ill-feeling existed between the players was untrue. But was he then just putting into use his new-found skills at PR?

On the way home from the tour, after Richard (King Dick) Seddon's Government had 'shouted' the team an all-expenses-paid holiday that included friendly games in New York and British Columbia, Duncan played against the All Blacks. He and five All Blacks helped make up a team for an exhibition match at a baseball stadium in Brooklyn. Duncan, a future international referee, refereed the All Blacks' second match against British Columbia, won 65–6.

A saddler by trade, Duncan took up refereeing after the 1905 tour and in 1908 he refereed the first test between New Zealand and the Anglo-Welsh at Carisbrook. He also coached teams at Otago Boys' High School during the 1920s and 1930s, having a great influence on many young players, including Charlie Saxton, whom he immediately recognised as a natural scrum half.

### JIMMY'S STYLE NEVER CRAMPED

Jimmy Duncan, as team photos show, wore a woollen cap on the playing field, especially later in his long career from 1889–1903. It was to hide his baldness.

It is said he had a reputation for using the cap to fool the opposition into thinking he had passed the ball to a team-mate. In an Otago match against Auckland just before the turn of the century, he tricked his opponents into chasing and tackling the man with the cap, rather than the one with the ball.

However, Duncan's baldness did not appear to cramp his style with the ladies. The Llanelli Rugby Club's visitors' book remains witness to a visit by the 1905 All Blacks. As the team left the club, they signed the book. Skipper Dave Gallaher wrote of 'good beer, better girls, good times'. Duncan's comment: 'Also the numbers of young ladies and old widows who are desirous of taking me into partnership, as a sleeping partner only.'

## Jimmy Duncan
## (Otago)

**Captain in one test, one win**
v. Australia, Sydney 1903

**Born:** Dunedin, November 12, 1869.

**Died:** Dunedin, October 19, 1953.

**Represented NZ:** 1897, 1901, 1903 – 10 matches (one test).

**Points for NZ:** 9 – 3 tries.

**First-class record:** Otago 1889–1903 (Kaikorai club); South Island 1897.

**All Black coach:** 1904: NZ 9, Great Britain 3. 1905–06: NZ 12, Scotland 7; NZ 15, Ireland 0; NZ 15, England 0; Wales 3, NZ 0; NZ 38, France 8.

**International referee:** 1908, NZ versus Anglo-Welsh.

**Other:** Served on the Otago RFU management committee 1906–11.

**Occupation:** Saddler.

---

1 *All Blacks in Chains,* J.M. Mackenzie, *Truth,* 1960.
2 *Black, Black, Black,* J.M. Mackenzie, Minerva, 1969.

# BILLY STEAD

## 'Steady' went 42 All Black games without a loss

BILLY STEAD, New Zealand's first captain in a home test match in 1904, vice-captain of the All Black 'Originals' in 1905–06 and captain against the Anglo-Welsh in 1908, played 42 times for New Zealand – and was never in a beaten side.

It was a record that seemed unlikely ever to be beaten, fit to rival that of his All Black team-mate Jimmy Hunter's extraordinary 44 tries on the ground-breaking 1905 tour.*

Stead's four test victories and 100% record as captain of the All Blacks was also a record that would hold for almost half a century. Before Stead's first test as captain he had only one predecessor, Jimmy Duncan, who had captained New Zealand in the first official test ever played by this country – against Australia in Sydney on the 1903 tour.

But it would take until 1951, when Otago's Peter Johnstone did so, for an All Black leader to equal Stead's record.

Through the first half of the 20th century a tradition of stability among the leadership as we know it today, was seldom established, even allowing that tests and test opponents were less frequent. In the last four decades of the 20th century the All Blacks were blessed with a long list of successful, long-term captains. But before that, Cliff Porter, with seven tests, would hold the record for the number of times he led the All Blacks in tests, until the emergence of Wilson Whineray in the late 1950s. Fred Allen had also led New Zealand in six tests in the 1940s. But Porter and Allen had only mixed success.

As a player, and leading contributor to tactics, Stead was a master of his time. A Southland representative who made an outstanding debut with two tries against arch-foe Otago in his debut in 1896, Stead had become a well-rounded footballer by the time he got the national call in 1903. He had played with and against and observed some of the great players of the early years – Tom Ellison, Paddy Keogh, Davey Gage, Barney Armit, 'Offside Mac' McKenzie and Duncan among them.

He played in four backline positions on the 1903 tour of Australia, New Zealand's first full-scale tour, though he did not play in the test, since Duncan was the captain and five-eighth.

Duncan retired and was coach of the All Blacks which met Darkie Bedell-Sivright's British team in 1904. Stead captained New Zealand to a 9–3 win in the only test in Wellington. Public interest in the match, against the 'mother country', was exceptional. The team went into camp in Days Bay for a week and the Premier, RJ (King Dick) Seddon, called Stead by telephone to wish the side good luck.

A first five-eighth on the All Black 'Originals' tour in 1905–06, Stead linked superbly with his halfback, Freddie Roberts, to send their backline away on numerous movements. Their outsides broke scoring records which no other All Black team has come near to equalling. The team scored 243 tries, 205 from the backs!

Team-mates on the tour were to state that Stead's absence from the Welsh test, the only game lost on the tour, was most crucial to the outcome. Reports of the day stated Stead was ill for the game, but writing in Dunedin's *Sports Special*, Stead said: 'When I stood down for 'Simon' Mynott, I was sure I was giving way to a fresher man, one that the Welsh had seen little of, and whose form in the Cheshire match just beforehand had been brilliant. Perhaps that 'Land of My Fathers' from the 40,000 throats had unsettled him, as it did others, but he never rose to the heights he was capable of.'

Stead went on to write that even though Bob Deans had fairly scored his try, the All Blacks had missed opportunities early in the game and … 'on the day we did not deserve to win.'

He played 29 matches on the great tour, second only to Freddie Roberts' 30 games. But it was the pair's unselfish play and grasp of tactics which helped make the tour so successful. He was described by critic R.A. Stone as 'fast … quick to see an opening, his defence was par excellence'. In an obituary in 1959 he was described as 'one of the 'immortals' … a key man in the New Zealand scoring machine, steadiness itself, a good tactical kicker, superb handler and of unruffled temperament.'[1]

At the end of the 1905–06 tour, as the players were looking forward to three weeks' holiday before catching the boat home, Gallaher approached Stead about collaborating in a rugby coaching book. He had been asked by a British publisher, Henry Leach, for a standard work on rugby. The payment was to be £100 (worth about £4500 today). The pair got to work, but quickly found they could make no progress. Gallaher, according to Stead, wanted to give the project up.

Stead, who had a secondary education and some experience in writing, and would later become a perceptive and prolific rugby writer, decided to go on his own. In less than a week, writing longhand, he had completed 80,000 words. *The Complete Rugby Footballer* was an extraordinary achievement, and one which should have revolutionised the British game, had its contents been fully assimilated by the hosts.

Gallaher meanwhile had organised the photographs and the outstanding diagrams of tactical ploys the All Blacks had used against their British counterparts.

In the preface, Gallaher and Stead succinctly point out that they, as authors, were the captain and vice-captain of the All Blacks; that in New Zealand one 'represents' the football played in the North Island and the other of the South Island; and that their specialist knowledge is in the positions of wing forward and five-eighth – 'both positions being to a certain extent new to the players of Great Britain.'

The *Daily Mail* reviewer stated, 'To players of the present, it is indispensible; and in its 300 pages, practically every phase of the game is touched.'

Stead did not play on the 1907 tour of Australia. But he captained the All Blacks in the first and third tests against the 1908 Anglo-Welsh tourists. After the first test win by 32–5 at Carisbrook, where former All Black Jimmy Duncan was the referee, the national selectors

*BILLY STEAD: At home in either inside-back position, halfback Stead (bending for ball) is shown in an early Southland–Otago classic*

*TOUR RECORD: Stead was the five-eighth on the Originals' tour who sent his outsides away on many of their remarkable 205 backline tries – a tour record unlikely ever to be broken. He is shown (at right) with captain Dave Gallaher*

changed the injured Stead and brought in a number of young players. But the match, played in a sea of mud on Athletic Park, and drawn 3–all, was a moral victory for the tourists, who scored the only try. It was also to be the last test in the career of Billy Wallace.

The inclusion of Freddie Roberts, Stead, Jimmy Hunter and Bob Deans in the backline for the third test at Potter's Park, Auckland, gave the All Blacks the back combination that had proved so successful in 1905.

The All Blacks had spent a hard week of training under Gallaher and George Nicholson.

They scored nine tries to win 29–0. This was also the last test for Deans, whose claim to immortality was to evolve over the years from his 'non-try' against the Welsh in 1905. A little over two months later the Canterbury centre, still only 24, was to die from complications after an appendicitis operation.

It was to be Stead's last international playing year. He had played 52 times for Southland, a massive tally considering the very limited fixture lists in provincial rugby of the time.

He was persuaded to lead the NZ Maori team on its 19-match inaugural tour of Australia and New Zealand in 1910. He played in 13 matches.

When the Springboks toured New Zealand for the first time in 1921, Alex McDonald, another 'Original' who also captained the All Blacks on their North American tour in 1913, and Stead, assisted by another 1905 veteran, Nicholson, who was then a national selector, took over the coaching of the All Blacks.

They took the first test in Dunedin comfortably enough, winning 13–5. But South Africa won the second test, 9–5, in Auckland.

There has been historical uncertainty over whether this group actually coached the All Blacks for the third test. Terry McLean, in his 1987 book, *New Zealand Rugby Legends*, in the chapter on Billy Stead, states the trio 'were summarily dumped for the third test, the New Zealand union itself assuming all responsibilities' for the match. Interviewed in June, 1997, by the author, Sir Terry said he was unable to recall where he had gained that information.

Research at the NZRFU headquarters in Wellington by former All Black captain, co-coach and NZRFU councillor Bob Stuart, on behalf of the author, and at the Auckland Research Centre by the author, uncovered evidence to show McDonald and Nicholson were certainly still very much involved in the build-up to the third and final test in Wellington. But Stead was not and the following details may explain why.

Stead, who was part-Maori, had coached the New Zealand Maori team that played the Springboks at Napier 10 days before the third test. In a match in which no quarter was given by either side, the visitors won 9–8. 'To counter the strong Springbok pack, the two Maori hookers put their hard heads together and charged on to the shoulders of two rather than three South Africans. The Springboks did not appreciate this ... The match turned into a general dust-up ...'[2]

However, there was more of a dust-up after the match, when a South African pressman's story was leaked from the telegraph room of the Napier Post Office. The story deplored the racist, anti-white antagonism of the largely white crowd against the all-white South Africans. It was published in the New Zealand press and became an international incident. Questions were asked in Parliament. Four Post Office workers were sacked over the incident, though three were later reinstated. The *NZ Herald*, for instance, had plenty of coverage of the ensuing row over this matter.

The third test was played in atrocious conditions on an Athletic Park covered, to a large part, in water. It ended in a 0–0 draw that meant the first series between the great rugby nations was shared.

Years later, Stead was to write that, 'The strongest feature of the South Africans' play was their lineout play. It was quite illegal. The favourite method was for 'Baby' Michau (17st) and 'Boy' Morkel (16st) to force an opening through the opponents' lineout, drag one of their own comrades (who had possession of the ball) through behind them and then deftly send the ball to one of the giants who had got clear.'[3]

Stead continued to be involved in the game in some capacity, and was a legendary identity in Southland rugby until his death at 81 in 1958.

* 1960s All Black three-quarter Bill Davis (Hawkes Bay) played 53 matches for the All Blacks unbeaten.

## John William Stead

**Captain in four tests, four wins**
v. Great Britain 1904,
Ireland 1905,
Anglo-Welsh (1, 3) 1908

**Born:** Invercargill, September 18, 1877.

**Died:** Bluff, July 21, 1958.

**Position:** Five-eighth.

**Represented NZ:** 1903–06, 08 – 42 matches (7 internationals).

**Points for NZ:** 36 – 12 tries.

**Provincial record:** Southland 1896–1908 (Star club); also South Island 1903, 05; NZ Maoris 1910; Otago-Southland 1904, 05.

**All Black co-coaching record:** 1921: Springbok tour to NZ – NZ 13, South Africa 5; South Africa 9, NZ 5.

**Miscellaneous:** Co-author, with Dave Gallaher, of *The Complete Rugby Footballer* (Methuen, 1906), a 322-page coaching book which the pair wrote, at publisher's request, over three weeks at the end of the 1905–06 All Black tour while still in England. Also a rugby columnist for *Truth* over a number of years.

**Other:** A brother, Norman, played for Southland and NZ Maoris.

**Occupation:** Bootmaker.

---

1 *New Zealand Rugby Almanack*

2 *New Zealand Rugby Legends,* Terry McLean, Moa, 1987.

3 *Southland Times*

# DAVE GALLAHER

## Gallaher set standards that have seldom been equalled

DAVE GALLAHER has aquired a mystique as the leader of the first All Black team to make a major tour overseas and set the standard every All Black side for almost 100 years has since tried to emulate.

Gallaher's tenure as captain was brief – limited to the six months or so the All Black 'Originals' were on tour. He would move on to become a great coach of Auckland and briefly of the All Blacks.

When World War I began Irish-born Gallaher had already served New Zealand in the Boer War. He was now 43 years of age, married with a young daughter. He did not need to serve again. But he was stirred by the news of the deaths of two brothers, Harry and Douglas, each killed serving with the Australian Imperial Force. The Irish restlessness in him practically forced him to enlist.

Gallaher led his men 'over the top' at the height of the Battle of Passchendaele in Belgium and would die of terrible wounds on October 4, 1917. His grave became a shrine that All Blacks and other New Zealanders still visit. The Auckland union, in 1922, commemorated his legacy on a permanent basis with the Gallaher Shield.

The scene was inevitably set, therefore, to make Gallaher the sentimental favourite of all the All Black captains. But just how great a captain was he?

The overwhelming evidence suggests Gallaher's leadership style, honed from time spent in the Boer War, was very effective. He knew how to 'psyche' his team up and on match days would ask each man to spend an hour on his own to 'rest and contemplate the game ahead'. He insisted the team be totally

*LONGTIME WARRIOR: Dave Gallaher pictured in his Boer War uniform*

disciplined and pay attention to detail, both on and off the field – very much a forerunner of the captains who were to follow.

The 1905 'Originals' had a strict team pattern, using code names for moves and

employing extra men into the backline, skip passes, decoys, scissor passes and other ruses. A hooker or wing-forward threw the ball into lineouts. The forwards were adept at close passing, slipping the pass as a player went to ground and supporting the ball-carrier.

It was only the controversial loss to Wales which prevented the 'Originals' from completing a 35-match unbeaten record. Incredibly, the team scored 830 points, including 205 tries, with 39 points against, on the British section of the tour.

A member of that team, Ernest 'General' Booth [who in the 1920s became New Zealand's first 'professional' coach in Southland] was to write that: 'Dave was a man of sterling worth … girded by great self-determination and self-control he was a valuable friend, and could be, I think, a remorseless foe. To us All Blacks his words would often be "Give nothing away: take no chances". As a skipper he was something of a disciplinarian.'

Gallaher's team is immortalised as much for the Bob Deans 'non-try', when it could have saved itself from the tour's only defeat, instead of losing to Wales, 0–3. Deans, the youngest member of the team, was so adamant he had scored he wrote a telegram to the *Daily Mail* stating he'd grounded the ball over the line, but been pulled back by Welsh players. When he died in September, 1908, aged only 24, of complications after an appendicitis operation, a few weeks after playing for the All Blacks against the Anglo-Welsh, he reputedly repeated his claim on his deathbed.

Gallaher was to receive much criticism on the great tour for his play at wing-forward, with frequent complaints he was offside or obstructing play. George Dixon, the All Black manager, who kept a good diary and wrote a book on the tour, and who was a very fair-minded critic, said: 'I have never known a player to be so violently and unjustly attacked as was Gallaher by Welsh papers after the International.'[1]

Gallaher, given the opportunity to defend himself by an English journalist, J.A. Buttery, said the Welsh had 'adopted the wing-forward game in all its nakedness, as they have already modified their back and scrum formation in keeping with ours – perhaps the greatest

*(left) DAVE GALLAHER: Knew how to 'psyche' his Originals team up*

compliment the New Zealanders have received during their tour.'[2]

But his team dazzled its opposition and played before huge crowds. As a leader Gallaher was highly regarded, though not originally a popular choice. On the ship on the way to Britain Gallaher is said to have offered to resign as captain and only a vote among the players saw him happy to continue (although it is said the vote was only 17 to 12 in his favour).

The team's officially appointed coach was Jimmy Duncan, one of the most influential players of the decade to 1903, and the first officially appointed coach of a New Zealand team, against the touring British in 1904. It appears that senior players, especially Gallaher and Stead, quickly consigned Duncan to a minor role.

Gallaher was co-author, with fellow 1905 All Black Billy Stead, of an influential coaching book on rugby, *The Complete Rugby Footballer*, written by the pair near the end of the great tour.

He had not made the All Blacks until the age of 29, when first selected for what would be the unbeaten tour of Australia in 1903. He began the tour as a hooker and ended it as a wing-forward. He played against the 1904 British team.

Gallaher retired immediately after the 1905-06 tour and became a New Zealand selector in 1907. He was in good company, with men like 'Old Vic' Cavanagh, who would invent the ruck and second-phase play and lead many Otago teams to great riches; Vinny Meredith, who would coach the All Blacks in 1910 and 1935; and Jimmy Lynskey, a famous Wellington schoolmaster, among those on the panel up to 1914 and World War I.

In 1908, when the Anglo-Welsh team toured New Zealand, Gallaher coached the All Blacks with his old 'Original' team-mate, George Nicholson. With Billy Stead captaining the side at first five-eighth, outside Freddie Roberts, the All Blacks hammered the visitors 32–5 in the first test at Carisbrook. The selectors decided to blood a number of new players for the second test. But in a sea of slush at Athletic Park the Anglo-Welsh gained a 3–3 draw and were unlucky not to win.

The All Blacks spent a week of hard training under Gallaher and took the field in great shape for the third test at Potter's Park, Auckland.

Roberts and Stead had been recalled, as had Bob Deans. Together with Jimmy Hunter, this quartet had made up one of the successful combinations of the 'Originals' tour. With the great Frank Mitchinson scoring three tries from the wing, the All Blacks won 29–0.

But though he would remain a national selector until 1914, that was to be the last time Gallaher would play a direct role in the All Blacks' preparation. No other tests were played in Auckland until after the war.

From 1905 to 1913 Auckland held the Ranfurly Shield. In those nine seasons it made 23 successful defences. Gallaher was Auckland's sole selector/coach from 1906 to 1916, responsible therefore for most of the preparation during the province's shield tenure. His teams continued their merry way right through to 1912, when age and familiarity inevitably began to catch up with Auckland. Only Wellington and Canterbury had run Auckland close before that season. In 1912 it creaked to a tight win over Taranaki and drew with Otago, 5–5.

The Otago game, incidentally, played at Potter's Park, illustrated the problems rugby was then having with rugby league. About 3000 spectators turned up for the shield challenge, whereas four to five times that number watched the league 'test' between New Zealand and New South Wales at The Domain, Grafton, played at the same time. Historians have speculated that league, which had built a strong following and paid its players, would have become New Zealand's premier rugby code if World War I had not snuffed its progress.

Gallaher's Irish luck with the shield could not hold for ever. In 1913, after a 6–5 cliffhanger against Wellington, his side lost to Taranaki, 14–11.

---

## David Gallaher (Auckland)

**Captain in four tests, three wins and one loss** v. England, Scotland, Wales, France 1905–06

**Born:** Ramelton, County Donegal, Ireland October 30, 1873.

**Died:** Passchendaele, Belgium October 4, 1917.

**Position:** Wing-forward.

**Represented NZ:** 1903–06 – 36 matches (6 internationals).

**Points for NZ:** 14 – 4 tries, 1 conversion.

**Provincial record:** Auckland 1896, 97, 99, 1900, 03–05, 09 (Ponsonby club); also North Island 1903, 05.

**Selector/coach:** Auckland sole selector-coach, 1906–16

**NZ Selector:** 1907–1914.

**NZ Coach:** 1908, with George Nicholson.

**All Black coaching record:** 1908: NZ beat Anglo-Welsh 32–5, drew 3–3, won 29–0.

**Occupation:** A foreman at the Auckland Farmers' Freezing Works until he enlisted in 1916. Died of wounds received in battle at Passchendaele, Belgium and buried in the Nine Elms cemetery, Poperinghe.

**Other:** Immigrated to NZ with his family in 1878, aged 5, when his father took up land at Katikati. Moved to Auckland in 1893 and played junior rugby for the Parnell club before transferring to Ponsonby. Served in the Boer War as a corporal in the 6th Contingent NZ Mounted Rifles 1901, later joining the 10th Contingent with the rank of Squadron Sergeant-Major.

**Miscellaneous:** Co-author, with Billy Stead, of *The Complete Rugby Footballer* (Methuen, 1906). Friends presented the Gallaher Shield to the Auckland RFU in 1922, in his memory, for the inter-club championship. It remains the premier trophy each season.

---

1 *The Triumphant Tour of the New Zealand Footballers,* George Dixon

2 *The Daily Mail*

# JACK SPENCER

## *Spencer held the fort while Originals broke new ground*

IMAGINE BEING chosen to captain your country and then being told the game might be called off because of incessant rain? And then having the test transferred from its venue to a suburban seaside ground?

That is what happened to Jack Spencer when he led New Zealand to its first win over a fully representative touring Australian team in 1905.

Three weeks after the Dave Gallaher-led New Zealand side that would become the All Black 'Originals' departed our shores, Australia opened its seven-match tour of New Zealand. Spencer led the side to a 14–3 win in the only international, played in Dunedin.

But the test, on September 2, did not come without drama. Following continual heavy rain from the Thursday evening, Otago officials considered cancelling the match on the Saturday morning. The Caledonian Ground, then the home of rugby in what was New Zealand's biggest and most thriving city until about 1900, was considered unfit to play on. The match was transferred to Tahuna Park, near St Kilda Beach, where the sandy soil was in surprisingly good order. Three thousand spectators turned out in the inhospitable conditions to watch the teams.

Spencer was by this time a vastly experienced siderow forward. He had first played for Wellington, at that time one of the strongest provinces in the land, in 1898, aged only 17.

He had made his New Zealand debut on the 1903 tour of Australia in the side captained by Jimmy Duncan. But he had been badly affected by a leg injury during that tour and had been unable to win a place in the New Zealand side

*TEST DRAMA: Jack Spencer led New Zealand to victory over Australia*

that met the Great Britain tourists in 1904 or in Gallaher's touring team that was put together throughout the 1905 season.

Jack Spencer was one of four brothers – the others were Walter, George and Bill – who represented Wellington.

George would play on the 1907 All Black tour of Australia with Jack. George, a fullback with a 'slashing' kick, played 49 times for Wellington and five on the tour of Australia.

In 1903, then aged 22 and weighing 13st, Spencer had been chosen in the 22-man New Zealand team to tour Australia. To ensure most team members got a game Spencer was chosen in the Wellington side that decisively beat the national team, 14–5, before it departed. His brother, George, at fullback, also contributed to the victory for Wellington.

But Spencer and his Wellington team-mate, Billy Wallace, had had to leave the field with knee injuries. These were not deemed serious enough to prevent them embarking for Australia. Indeed Wallace made an instant recovery and played in all 11 tour games to become the top points-scorer. But Spencer was not so lucky. The team's ship, the *Moeraki*, departed into the teeth of a southerly gale out of Wellington harbour and during the crossing Spencer fell heavily and badly injured a leg.

He played only two games on the tour – the eighth and ninth matches. But he scored two tries in the 28–0 victory over Queensland, joining illustrious team-mates Opai Asher, Morrie Wood and Wallace on the scorecard. That match was also the first time Dave Gallaher, who would go on to become the much maligned wing-forward of the triumphant 1905 All Black 'Originals', played in that position. He had been chosen in the front row for the tour.

Captained by Jimmy Duncan, the only survivor of the 1897 team, this side had an outstanding tour. It was unbeaten in all games and gained record scores. The team scored 63 tries and delighted the large crowds that came to see the expansive rugby.

George Nicholson, who played on the 'Originals' tour and in other New Zealand teams, would years later say of the 1903 side: 'That's the best team I ever saw or ever played with, and it also had the best five-eighth combination of the lot. Jimmy Duncan at first five-eighth and Morrie Wood at second were the perfect pair.'

On the 1907 tour of Australia, Jack Spencer became the first New Zealand player to come on as a replacement in an international when he took the field for the injured Jack Colman in the first test. Colman, a utility player who was at wing-forward that day, received a nasty cut to the back of the head. New Zealand won the test, in front of 50,000 spectators at the Sydney Cricket Ground, 26–6 and took the series with a 14–5 win in Brisbane. The third test was drawn, 5–5.

There was huge interest in the All Blacks in

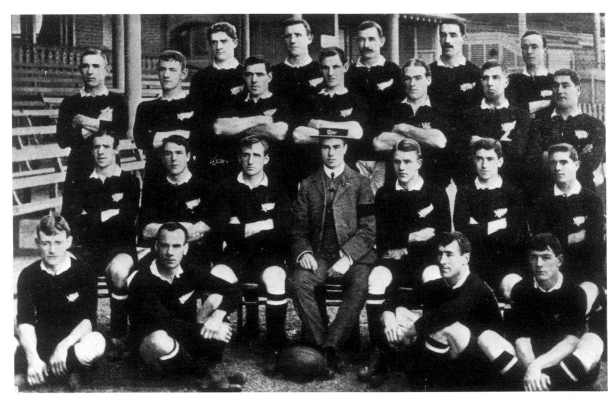

*BROTHERS UNITED: Jack Spencer (left, second-to-top row) toured with his brother George (top row, third from left) in the 1907 All Black team to Australia*

Australia. The first three tour games were played before 122,000 people. Part of the reason was that the game was in strife. Rumours – which would prove accurate – flew that a professional team was soon to be chosen. The All Blacks were made to sign declarations they would remain amateurs before they were chosen. The star of this series for Australia, flying winger 'Dally' Messenger, would join a New Zealand professional team (the 'All Golds') after the third test and go on to become one of Australia's greatest rugby league stars.

But there were slim pickings for the Spencer brothers, who made no further appearances in the internationals. The tourists were badly affected by a 'flu epidemic and injuries. Former All Black George Nicholson was holidaying in Australia, following the tour, and had to be called in midway through the tour. He played in the last four tour matches. The tour captain, Jimmy Hunter, had been so ill from 'flu he had been unable to travel to Brisbane when the team left Sydney.

Both George and Jack would transfer to league and represent New Zealand – George in 1908, 09 and Jack in 1909. But Jack was reinstated to rugby union and coached the Wellington club, Berhampore.

## Jack Clarence Spencer (Wellington)

**Captain in one test, one win**
v. Australia, Dunedin 1905

**Born:** November 27, 1880, Wellington.

**Died:** May 21, 1936, Wellington.

**Position:** Siderow forward.

**Represented NZ:** 1903, 05, 07 – 6 matches (2 tests).

**Points for NZ:** 6 – 2 tries.

**First-class record:** Wellington 1898, 1900–03, 05–07 (Melrose); North Island 1903, 06, 07; Wellington Province 1903, 05; Wellington-Wairarapa-Horowhenua 1905.

**School:** Mt Cook School, Wellington.

**Selector/coach/administrator:** Coached Berhampore club in Wellington.

**Other:** Turned to rugby league in 1908 and represented NZ in 1909. Reinstated to rugby union and coached Berhampore. One of four brothers who represented Wellington. George was on the 1907 All Black tour of Australia with Jack.

**Miscellaneous:** Became first New Zealand player to come on as a replacement in an international when he took the field for the injured Jack Colman in the first test on the 1907 tour of Australia.

**Occupation:** A plumber.

# JAMES HUNTER

## *Slippery Jimmy still holds all-time tour try record*

ONE OF the unsolved mysteries of All Black rugby involves how and why Jimmy Hunter was replaced by Dave Gallaher as captain of the team that would become the All Black 'Originals'.

Hunter became the greatest try-scorer in New Zealand's then-short international history on that tour. He scored 44 tries – a sensational feat that has never been approached in the near-century of New Zealand tours since and is most unlikely ever to be.

Gallaher became the revered leader of an Originals' side that gained immortality by

*SAD ENDING: Successful in sport, Jimmy Hunter would one day turn into 'a pillar of salt'*

scoring 243 tries and winning all but the controversial Welsh test in its 35 matches.

So both men played roles in shocking the British rugby establishment with the force and originality of the New Zealand style that would change the world game forever.

But it was Hunter who seemed destined to lead New Zealand on the big tour, as we shall see. And he would go on to be an undefeated All Black test captain, after being reinstated to the national captaincy in 1907 and 1908.

Gallaher, never a great player in the way so many of his team-mates proved to be, retired after the big tour.

It is therefore fascinating to trace the progression that led to Hunter's replacement by Gallaher in 1905.

Hunter had played in all the backline positions for Taranaki since making his debut in 1898, but had become a seasoned five-eighth. However, it was as a wing he was first chosen for New Zealand, in 1904 against 'Darkie' Bedell-Sivright's British team. But because of an accident at training on the day before the test, Hunter had to be replaced.

The New Zealand selectors wanted him for the big tour though. At the end of 1904 they named 53 players, of whom, they said, the touring side would be chosen. By mid-January of 1905, just before George Dixon was appointed manager, 41 players had signalled their availability. On February 25, 17 players were announced as selections. Hunter was in the group, but Gallaher was not.

Hunter captained the North Island side that beat the South, 26–0, in the main trial, after which the balance of the side was announced.

Hunter was named captain and Freddie Roberts vice-captain of the 19-man team that prepared for the long tour by playing seven matches during July, 1905, three of them in Australia. The team won four, drew two and lost to Wellington in the final game. Gallaher had withdrawn from that tour after being selected.

But the selectors had a change of heart. There had been a power struggle behind the scenes. Besides the team leadership, it also involved the appointed coach, Jimmy Duncan, who would eventually be relegated to a virtual public relations role on the great tour. After the second-to-last game of the preliminary tour, against Canterbury, they announced that Gallaher and Billy Stead would be captain and vice-captain for the British trip. Gallaher then led the team against Wellington in a game lost 3–0. Another Aucklander, lock Bill Cunningham, was added to the team and he too played against Wellington.

It has been documented how the power plays continued when the team sailed to England. At one stage on the journey, Gallaher's right to captain the side was tested by a team ballot – and the result was by no means unanimous! But Hunter seems to have accepted the situation well. While there is evidence of an Auckland-Otago tension in the side, Hunter went about his business with no rancour.

He played in 24 tour matches, including all five tests. But though he scored 44 tries himself from second five-eighths, he gave his outsides – Billy Wallace, Bob Deans, Duncan McGregor and George Smith the most prominent – such quality ball they ran in another 82 tries.

Judging from press reports of the time, 'Hunter must have been a Grant Batty-type player. He was only 5ft 6in tall and under 12st, but had marvellous acceleration. He could spot a gap where others would have thought none existed and had the ability to wriggle past a cluster of opponents. He did not have the blinding pure speed of a sprinter, but over a short distance he could leave anyone in his wake.'

Gallaher and Stead described Hunter's style as 'a peculiar swerve of his own, which came naturally to him and which might best be described as a corkscrew swerve. He travels at no great pace when he is putting it into operation, but it is wonderfully effective.'[1]

British scribe E.H.D. Sewell said he was 'one

*FAMOUS TRIO: Jimmy Hunter (right) shown with Billy Wallace (middle) and Billy Glenn. They had been team-mates on the Originals' tour. Glenn became the first ex-All Black to be elected to Parliament*

of the most sinuous runners I have ever seen. He seemed to glide rather than to run and to go through the opposition as might a snake.' Another wrote of his 'zig-zag, eel-like bursts for the goal-line. His relentless passage through a thick sea of surging opponents is weird, uncanny. He might be covered with soap from the ease with which he eludes the grasp of one strong, fleet man after another.'

'He must have spikes under his jersey. Otherwise, they wouldn't be afraid to touch him,' said an undergraduate watching the Oxford game, where Hunter scored five tries.[2]

Hunter came from a wealthy farming background, as did at least two other 'Original' team members, Bob Deans and Eric Harper. There are stories of how the trio looked after the less financially fortunate members of the team on the long tour on a weekly basis.

Hunter captained the 1907 All Blacks in Australia. The side won two tests and drew a third. Hunter had a quiet tour by his standards, but he and many of the side were affected by a 'flu epidemic which raged through eastern Australia. Australian rugby was also in one of its peaks, with crowds in excess of 50,000 watching the opening game, against New South Wales, and the first test a week later, in Sydney.

In the second NSW game, the tourists were well beaten, 0–14.

Part of the reason for the public interest was that Australian rugby was in a ferment of excitement. A professional team, which became the 'All Golds', was being organised in New Zealand to tour England. Dally Messenger, a winger who would become the sensation of the All Golds' tour, proved a thorn in the side of Hunter's All Blacks. But longterm, the resultant growth of rugby league would mean rugby in Australia would take a back seat for generations to come.

When A.F. Harding's Anglo-Welsh team toured New Zealand in 1908, Hunter played in all three tests, scoring tries in the first and third tests, which the All Blacks won 32–5 and 29–0.

'The public's wish for a sight of the 'Old Buffers' of 1905 – Freddie Roberts at halfback and Billy Stead and Hunter at five-eighth – having been gratified by the decisive victory in the first test, Hunter was the only one retained for the second test.'[3]

He also replaced Stead as the captain. But the game was played in a morass in Wellington and the All Blacks were considered fortunate to escape with a 3–3 draw.

So back came the 'Old Buffers' again, with Deans added to the mix at centre, for the third test in Auckland. Gallaher was by now the All Black coach and trained the side hard all week. In spite of windy conditions, nine tries came the All Blacks' way, with Frank Mitchinson taking three.

It was to be the final test for Hunter, Deans and Stead. Though he was only 24, Deans would die two months later from complications after an operation on his appendix.

Though he lived to 83, Hunter suffered sadness later in life. Three children died either at birth or soon after and one of his two remaining sons, Roberts Deans (named after his team-mate) Hunter, was killed in World War II. He later went totally deaf, a sorry and lonely affliction. He became a man 'who tasted deeply the draughts of triumph and disaster.' A daughter, Dr Alison Hunter, who moved to Wanganui to look after her father in his ailing years, sadly told Terry Mclean, 'My father looked back. He turned into … a pillar of salt.'[4]

When Terry McLean wrote his *New Zealand Rugby Legends* in 1987 he included Hunter as one of the 15 legendary players in the book.

## James Hunter (Taranaki)

**Captain in four tests, two wins and two draws**
v. Australia 1907 (1, 2, 3)
v. Anglo-Welsh 1908 (2)

**Born:** March 6, 1879, Hawera.

**Died:** December 14, 1962, Wanganui.

**Position:** Five-eighth.

**Represented NZ:** 1905–08 – 36 matches (11 tests).

**Points for NZ:** 147 – 49 tries.

**First-class record:** Taranaki 1898, 1900–04, 06–08 (Hawera); North Island 1904–08; Taranaki-Wanganui-Manawatu 1904.

**High school:** Wanganui Collegiate.

**Selector/coach/administrator:** Life member Hawera RFC 1913.

**Occupation:** A farmer in the Fordell area.

1 *The Complete Rugby Footballer*, Billy Stead and Dave Gallaher, Methuen, 1906.

2, 3, 4 *New Zealand Rugby Legends*, Terry McLean, Moa, 1987.

# FREDDIE ROBERTS

## *'Pocket Hercules' often had to live up to his name*

FREDDIE ROBERTS' name had already been cast into the annals of All Black folklore when he captained New Zealand on its 1910 tour of Australia.

Such was Roberts' reputation as a clever and resilient Wellington halfback, the national selectors decided he would be the only halfback chosen for the All Black Originals' tour of Britain and France in 1905–06.

Critics and followers of the sport were naturally concerned. How would New Zealand fare if Roberts lost form or was injured? But the gamble paid off. Roberts played in 30 of the 35 tour matches – more than any other player, including 16 of the first 17 games.

He played in all four home tests, but was rested for the French test, the first international ever played by France. Billy Stead played halfback in the comfortable 38–8 victory.

Stead, who would never play in a losing All Black team in his 42 matches and would later help coach the All Blacks, was one of three five-eighths who partnered Roberts in the home tests. The others were 'Simon' Mynott and Jimmy Hunter.

Together, this group formed a brilliant inside-back combination. From the opening tour game, when they annihilated the reigning English county champion team, Devon, 55–4, the New Zealanders would score a massive 205 tour tries, 80 per cent of them by the backs. Roberts collected 14 tries and 48 points on the tour.

The team lost one controversial match, to Wales. While the debate over the Bob Deans' try (or non-try) has raged for almost a century, it is worthwhile to recall the manager of the Originals, George Dixon, wrote a book called

HARDMAN HALFBACK: *Fred Roberts must rank as perhaps the toughest All Black of all time*

*The Triumphant Tour of the New Zealand Footballers.* He claimed the All Blacks had not deserved to win the test against Wales. The

*ON TARGET: Fred Roberts kicked this penalty against the Anglo-Welsh at Dunedin in 1908*

team's form on the day had been indifferent. The New Zealand backs were off-colour, with the single exception being Roberts.

Welsh writer W.J.T. Collins would write, in *Rugby Recollections*, that Gallaher's team had three superlative players – Billy Wallace, Charlie Seeling and Roberts. 'Think of the powers which go to making of the ideal half: Roberts had them. Great-hearted, class to his fingertips, he was one of the world's great players.'

The Welsh international, Rhys Gabe, in *50 Years of the All Blacks*, wrote 'another great artist I admired was Roberts, the scrumhalf. I never saw him give an indifferent display and he bore his unavoidable buffeting like a stoic.'

Roberts was also a reliable goal-kicker but with Wellington team-mate Wallace in the side, he seldom had cause to call upon that skill. There is a wonderful story about the pair that has been handed down for posterity.

The All Blacks were given an all-expenses-paid holiday back through the United States on their way home, courtesy of R.J. ('King Dick') Seddon's government. When they got to San Fransisco, Roberts fell ill with tonsilitis and Wallace volunteered to stay with him when the team boarded ship for home.

They stayed there for three weeks, but Roberts, confined to bed, did not improve. So the pair visited a Dr Stinson, who said that Roberts' tonsils would have to be removed. The operation was done immediately, without anaesthetic.

While Roberts recuperated, Wallace arranged their passage home on the Ventura. No doubt they were delighted to finally be away – and would have been even more so had they known what was to happen the day after they began their voyage. The horrific San Fransisco earthquake struck, killing hundreds of people. It destroyed the Californian Hotel where the pair had been staying – and it killed Dr Stinson too.

Roberts had made his Wellington debut in

*END OF THE LINE: Freddie Roberts (front row, second from left) led this side against Wellington before departing for an Australian tour in 1910 that would end his great international career. Back row: Vinny Meredith (manager-coach), James Maguire, Bolla Francis, Sam Bligh, David Evans, Alf Budd, Harry Paton, Sandy Paterson, Fred Ivemey, Jim Ryan, Gerald McKellar. Front row: Paddy Burns, Jim Ridland, Ranji Wilson, Frank Mitchinson, Freddie Roberts (captain), Simon Mynott, Jack Stohr, Joe O'Leary, Frank Wilson, Bill Fuller.*

1901 and would represent his province every season through to 1912 (apart from 1905). He eventually set a Wellington record of 58 games, a mark that would be surpassed by 'Ranji' Wilson a few years later.

After the great tour, Roberts continued to be a first-choice selection for New Zealand. In 1907 he played in all eight matches on the All Black tour of Australia led by Jimmy Hunter.

Despite the presence of many of the Originals in this side, the Australians proved stern opposition. The tests were hard-fought, the third being drawn 5–5. New South Wales also won the second tour game, 14–0.

However, in the second test at Brisbane, Roberts often showed he'd lost none of the blindside evasiveness and speed of old. 'Fred Roberts stole away on the blind side of a scrum near the Australian twenty-five. Dally Messenger sensed the danger and came in from the wing to tackle the halfback, leaving Wallace unmarked. Roberts timed his pass well and Wallace had an uninterrupted run to the line.'[1]

The Anglo-Welsh team toured in 1908.

Roberts scored two tries and a penalty in the first test, won 32–5 at Carisbrook, Dunedin, before a record 23,000 spectators. He was injured for the second test at Athletic Park, Wellington, played in dreadful weather in front of only 10,000 people and drawn, 3–3. But he returned for the third and final test at Auckland's Potter's Park, assisting the 29–0, nine-try victory.

In 1910 Roberts, now aged 29, would lead an inexperienced All Black side on its Australian tour. Only seven of the tourists had played for the All Blacks before. They were managed and coached by Vinny Meredith, then an All Black selector who had been a Wellington halfback. He would lead the All Blacks many years later, on the 1935–36 tour of Britain, and later still become Sir Vincent Meredith.

Roberts played in all three tests, all played in Sydney at the end of the tour over a space of eight days. In a series won 2–1 by the All Blacks, the Australians deservedly won the second test, 11–0, after New Zealand's 6–0 first-test win. But a rejuvinated All Black side bounced back to take the third convincingly, 28–13. A key ingredient had been the combination of Roberts and Mynott, who were on their third tour together. Both retired from international football after the tour, Mynott being 34.

Roberts had played 52 times for New Zealand, including 12 tests, and had scored 72 points.

He would continue playing for Wellington for another two years before retirement. Roberts' club, Oriental, after some near-misses, had finally won its first Wellington club title in 1910. He later served Oriental as club captain and on the club committee. He was also a Wellington selector in 1921–22.

Roberts' 1905 tour statistics were 5ft 7in and 12st 4lb.

The *New Zealand Sportsman* of 1949 wrote of Roberts: 'a pocket Hercules' and of 'his rugged physique, speed, uncanny eye for an opening and tremendous capacity to take punishment'.

## Frederick Roberts (Wellington)

**Captain in three tests, two wins and one loss** v. Australia 1910 (1, 2, 3)

**Born:** April 7, 1881, Wellington.

**Died:** July 21, 1956, Wellington.

**Position:** Halfback.

**Represented NZ:** 1905–08, 10 – 52 matches (12 tests).

**Points for NZ:** 72 – 19 tries, 4 conversions, 1 penalty goal, 1 dropped goal.

**First-class record:** Wellington 1901–04, 06–12 (Oriental); North Island 1904, 05, 07, 08, 11; South Island 1902; Wellington Province 1903.

**School:** Thorndon School, Wellington.

**Selector/coach/administrator:** Served Oriental club as club captain and on club committee. Wellington selector 1921–22.

**Other:** Played 58 matches over 11 seasons for Wellington, a huge number in the days when provincial annual programmes were much smaller.

**Miscellaneous:** Replaced Peter Harvey in the South Island team during the 1902 inter-island game though he never played for a South Island provincial team during his career.

**Occupation:** Worked as a clerk for the Wellington Harbour Board.

1 *Centenary – 100 Years of All Black Rugby,* R.H. Chester and N.A.C. McMillan, Moa.

# ALEX McDONALD

## *McDonald led tour that killed North American game*

IT SEEMS a great shame Alex McDonald, whose fabulous rugby career spanned five decades, is remembered primarily for his tragic role in the fate of the 'Forty-Niners'.

There have been some wonderful contributors to All Black rugby in more than a century – men such as Tom Ellison, Jimmy Duncan, the McKenzie brothers, Jack Sullivan and Sir Brian Lochore at their head. But none can compare with the length of time McDonald had as an All Black, selector, administrator and coach. His influence moved through almost 50 years:

- He played in the All Black scrum in each of the four Home Union tests on the 1905 Originals tour, toured Australia with the All Blacks in 1907 and appeared against the touring Anglo-Welsh in 1908.
- After missing the 1910 tour to Australia, he captained the All Blacks in the first test against Australia in 1913 and then captained the team on their ground-breaking tour of North America.
- In 1921 he helped coach the All Blacks for the first time in the tied series against the touring Springboks.
- McDonald served on the Otago union from then until the early 1930s and was an Otago-based New Zealand selector from 1929–32.
- He moved to Wellington, headquarters of the game, and coached Wellington College Old Boys to the club championship in 1933.
- He served on the NZRFU management committee and the council through the 1930s and 1940s and coached the All Blacks on a triumphant, unbeaten Australian tour in 1938, helping the New Zealand rugby psyche recover from the

damage inflicted the previous year by the Springboks.
- He was a New Zealand selector again from 1944–48.
- As coach of Wellington in 1946 McDonald gave the great Kiwis their only defeat on a New Zealand tour after their British tour.
- In 1948 McDonald was appointed to coach the All Blacks for a third tenure – and would bitterly live to regret he'd taken the job.

McDonald led the All Blacks to a 30–5 victory over the touring Wallabies at Athletic Park, Wellington in 1913. The All Blacks were chosen from the 23 players who were about to embark on the tour of North America. A new New Zealand team would win the second test, 25–13, but lose the third, 5–16.

New Zealand had not played international rugby since 1910, so the 1913 side had a new look. Besides McDonald, the captain, only three others had been All Blacks – Frank Mitchinson, Doddie Gray and Jack Stohr.

Mitchinson, the Wellington five-eighth who could play anywhere in the backline, had 11 tests between 1907 and 1913. His 10 tries in those games, including three on his debut, made him the New Zealand record-holder for almost 65 years, until Ian Kirkpatrick's career.

Although All Black teams have customarily stopped off in North America to play one or two games on their way to or from a major tour of Britain and Europe, McDonald's team is unique for the fact it made a full-scale tour there. The All Blacks played 16 matches on the Pacific Coast, all of which were won easily.

The team romped through California and

*BANG-UP BREAKFAST: Alex McDonald (left) with team-mates 'Massa' Johnson, Charlie Seeling and Steve Casey on the Originals' tour*

British Columbia, scoring 610 points while conceding six. In many of the games they had to 'pull the reins in'. American and Canadian pride was hurt and the result was to hurt the game in those parts, rather than to stimulate it.

Of the university teams the All Blacks met, Southern California reverted back from rugby to American football in 1914, followed by California, Nevada and St Mary's in 1915 and Stanford and Santa Clara in 1918.

The Canadians, with British expatriates to call upon, offered sterner opposition to the All Blacks, and their knowledge was better. Their game was already well established and would continue to flourish.

It should be remembered the United States, represented by players from the Californian universities, would win the rugby championship at the Olympic Games of 1920 and 1924, beating France in both finals, 8–0 and 17–3 (though no other major rugby nations were represented).

The question that arises 70 years or so after the tour is why? Why did the All Blacks make such a tour? And why did the game not take off after their missionary expedition?

Rugby had begun to gain a hold in North America when American Football became too dangerous. A statistician claimed that in 1904 there were more deaths from injuries in the game than there had been in the biggest naval engagement of the Spanish-American War of six years earlier! In California, the state governor banned it.

Universities and high schools began to adopt rugby as their game and it became the major football code of the state.

An American Universities rugby team had also toured New Zealand and Australia in 1910. The Americans had come to New Zealand to learn. They spent a week under the tuition of Dave Gallaher, captain of the All Black Originals of 1905, former All Black coach, and in 1910 in the midst of a long tenure as Auckland's sole selector-coach.

The Australians sent a fully-representative team to the Pacific Coast in 1912, and sometimes struggled. Then the California Rugby Union invited New Zealand to tour. In light of what occurred on tour, it would have been better for the future of the game in America if New Zealand had sent a universities or an age-restricted team. Instead, because of the Australians' experience, a fully representative All Black team was sent.

McDonald was described by Terry McLean as 'one of the great gentlemen of New Zealand rugby who never recovered from the mortification of being ignored by the 1949 All Blacks he was appointed to coach through South Africa.'[1]

Much has been written over almost half a century about how and why Alex McDonald won the 1949 All Black coaching job over Vic Cavanagh, the brilliant and proven Otago coach whose team, minus 11 players in South Africa, would successfully defend the Ranfurly Shield while the All Blacks were on tour.

McDonald's appointment – he was on the NZRFU Council at the time – is today thought of as a 'political' one. But it should be remembered that when the triumphant Kiwis of 1946 returned from their tour of the British Isles, France and Germany, and regrouped for a five-match tour of New Zealand, he was still a top coach. The Kiwis' only loss was to Wellington, which played a nine or 10-man game devised by its coach, McDonald.

By the time McDonald toured South Africa he was 66. Fred Allen [see the Allen chapter for more on the tour], captain of the side, said this was the first tragic mistake by the organisers of the tour.

There have been claims through the decades since that at the first training run in South Africa, McDonald was ignored and that Allen called the backs to go with him and the forwards to be coached by vice-captain Ray

Dalton. Later in the tour, McDonald is alleged to have said, as he watched a liner steam out of Cape Town harbour, that he wished he could be on that ship.

But Allen denies any suggestion McDonald was left isolated and ignored by the team at any stage. And Dr Ron Elvidge, who captained the team in the third and fourth tests when Allen became unavailable [and another subject in this book], confirmed to the author in 1997 that any claims McDonald had been ostracised were completely wrong.

Compare the aged McDonald, notwithstanding his record, with the Springboks' Dr Danie Craven, and the difference in the two sides is obvious. Craven was one of the brains behind the great Springbok touring team which whipped the All Blacks in 1937. He was now in his forties. He was a player and coach of enormous depth of vision.

While the scores were usually close, the All Blacks could not kick the goals that mattered. Careers, especially among the inside backs, were destroyed during the tour. There is no doubt a schemer of the calibre of Cavanagh could have altered the way the All Blacks dealt with the problems presented by Hennie Muller, for one.

Meanwhile, McDonald, who had had an extraordinary career of service to New Zealand rugby, took the brunt of criticism for the Forty-Niners' failures. He did not serve on another national selection panel after 1948, but remained on the NZRFU Council until 1950.

## Alexander McDonald (Otago)

**Captain in two tests, two wins**
v. Australia 1913 (1),
v. All America 1913

**Born:** Dunedin, April 23, 1883.

**Died:** Wellington, May 4, 1967.

**Position:** Loose forward.

**Represented NZ:** 1905–08, 13 – 41 matches (8 internationals).

**Points for NZ:** 50 – 16 tries, 1 conversion.

**First-class record:** Otago (34 games) 1904, 06–09, 11–14, 19 (Kaikorai); Otago-Southland 1904; also South Island 1904–07, 13.

**Coaching/Selecting:** Otago coach; NZ selector 1929–32, 1944–48. Shared coaching duties 1921 All Blacks, coached All Blacks in Australia in 1938 and in South Africa in 1949.

**All Black coaching record:** 1921: NZ 13, South Africa 5; South Africa 9, NZ 5; NZ 0, South Africa 0. 1938: NZ 24, Australia 9; NZ 20, Australia 14; NZ 14, Australia 6. 1949: South Africa 15, NZ 11; South Africa 12, NZ 6; South Africa 9, NZ 3; South Africa 11, NZ 8.

**Other:** Served on Otago RFU management committee 1914–16, 20–28; vice-president 1928–32; New Zealand selector 1929–32, 1944–48. Then moved to Wellington, coached Wellington College Old Boys club to championship 1933; NZRFU management committee 1935–36, council 1937–50. Elected life member of NZRFU 1951.

**Occupation:** Brewery worker.

# JOE O'LEARY

## *Joe is only captain from the fullback position*

JOE O'LEARY is the only player to have captained the All Blacks in a test from fullback.

While many other fullbacks have led their countries from the position, the New Zealand style of game and the thinking of the national selectors and coaches has, apart from O'Leary's time in charge in 1913, always precluded a fullback from the job.

But in 1913, after declining selection in the ground-breaking All Black team that toured North America under the coaching/management of George Mason and the captaincy of 1905–06 'Original' and future longtime All Black coach Alex McDonald, O'Leary led New Zealand in the second and third tests against the touring Australian team.

The strength of Australian rugby had been eroded by the growth of rugby league when the second fully representative Australian team made its 1913 tour. Since beating the 1910 All Blacks in one of the three tests of that year, the Australians had undertaken a tour of North America's Pacific Coast in 1912. The side lost five of its 16 matches. So there was some indifference by the New Zealand public to the Wallabies, though they had some outstanding players, including the captain, Larry Dwyer, Hokitika-born Larry Wogan and 'Twit' Tasker.

The All Blacks, without O'Leary and with McDonald as captain, had trounced the Wallabies 30–5 at Athletic Park, Wellington. In the second test at Carisbook, Dunedin, the new New Zealand captain dropped a magnificent goal from inside his own half to give his side the lead early in the game and set it on the way to a fine 25–13 victory. But with the series

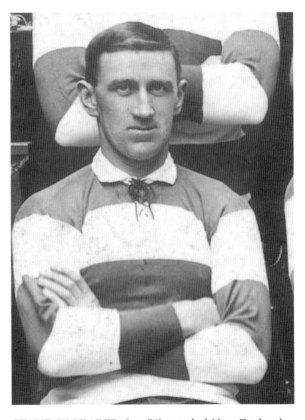

*STAND-IN LEADER: Joe O'Leary led New Zealand while All Blacks toured North America*

decided, the tourists, as so often would happen in later years, would turn the tables on the All Blacks. In the third test at Lancaster Park, Christchurch, though O'Leary played well, Australia emerged a deserved 16–5 winner.

O'Leary had made his debut for the All Blacks in 1910, appearing in the first and third tests at fullback on the tour of Australia. He played in six matches and led the tour points-scoring with 21.

THE UNTOLD STORY OF THE ALL BLACK TEST CAPTAINS

*ON TOP OF HIS GAME: Joe O'Leary (third row, seated, at extreme left) with the powerful Auckland team of 1913, the same year he led the All Blacks*

The All Blacks were coached and managed by Vinny Meredith, a former Wellington halfback who was on the New Zealand selection panel in 1910. He would later become a famous lawyer (Auckland's Crown Prosecutor for 31 years), the Auckland coach of the 1920s who 'discovered' Bert Cooke and the manager-coach of the 1935–36 All Blacks in Britain.

In the crossing from Wellington to Sydney the team had struck the Tasman at its worst and nearly all the players spent the entire voyage in their bunks. According to *Centenary, 100 years of All Black Rugby*, 'one of the exceptions was O'Leary, who turned up for every meal'. Most of the party lost weight, some shedding as much as 10lb.

After a tour which had them beating New South Wales and Queensland twice each, the All Blacks played the three tests in Sydney over the space of only eight days. After a tight 6–0 opening win, an understrength New Zealand team went down 0–11. O'Leary was among the injured not considered for selection. However, a rejuvinated All Black team came back to run riot in the third test to win 28–13.

The 1910 tour had been a rather hurriedly arranged tour which gave only limited training time between games. But it had been successful. O'Leary had won plenty of praise, as did Billy Fuller, Paddy Burns and Frank Mitchinson. But the true stars were the 1905 veterans, inside backs Freddie Roberts and Simon Mynott. Their experience proved invaluable. It was the third All Black tour on which they'd played and they had developed an outstanding combination. They both retired from test football after the tour, Mynott, by then 34, being the oldest back to play for New Zealand right up until the days of Joe Stanley in the 1980s and Frank Bunce in the 1990s.

So by the end of the 1913 series against Australia, after which World War I would curtail O'Leary's All Black career like that of so many other fine players, he would finish with eight matches for New Zealand, including four tests, and 33 points scored. However, he was aged 29.

His consistency was approved by the *Sportsman* journal of the time: 'One will grow old and hoary waiting for O'Leary to play a bad game.'

He could play in most backline positions and often showed his goal-kicking prowess. Goal-kicking was a more difficult task than it is today. The ball was rounder, it had to be held by a team-mate and the ground conditions often meant a far heavier ball and an uncertain run-up. Despite this, O'Leary saved many a match for his teams with his kicking prowess.

O'Leary had first played for Wairarapa in 1900 but was not to gain national notice until he led Wairarapa-Bush against the 1908 Anglo-Welsh team. He then moved to Auckland and would play with the Ponsonby club and for Auckland from 1909 to 1913.

In 1909 he visited Australia with Ponsonby and played in the 'Australasian club championship', as the game was billed, against Newtown in Sydney. Australian reporters described O'Leary as a player with a powerful and well directed line kick who 'completely crumpled' the opposition.

O'Leary returned to Masterton and became a Wairarapa selector in 1922–25 at a time when the province was very strong. In those years it had some titanic Ranfurly Shield battles with its near-neighbour Hawkes Bay. For historical reasons Wairarapa always got the first shield challenge of the season. In O'Leary's time, as the Bay developed into a wonderful combination that included 1924 'Invincibles' George Nepia and Maurice Brownlie and many other players who would wear the All Black jersey, Wairarapa lost 0–6 (1923), 14–30 (1924) and 3–22 (1925).

The Wairarapa team through those years was coached by Ted McKenzie, the longtime New Zealand selector and sometime coach. Hawkes Bay was coached by McKenzie's younger brother Norman, also a longtime New Zealand selector and sometime coach.

After being whipped 14–77 by the Bay in its 1926 challenge, Wairarapa ended the Bay's almost six-year tenure with the famous 15–11 victory in 1927. But the Bay had the right to challenge because of the unions' home-and-away fixture system. A challenge later, in the game that would become known to posterity as the 'Battle of the Solway', the Bay beat an All Black-packed Wairarapa, 21–10. But Wairarapa protested to the NZRFU over an ineligible Bay player and a bitter row between the neighbours ensued. The shield was eventually awarded to Manawhenua, which had beaten Wairarapa in the interim.

A brother, Humphrey, had captained New Zealand Universities in 1908–09 and would later become New Zealand's Chief Justice. Joe O'Leary was a blacksmith.

## Michael Joseph O'Leary (Auckland)

**Captain in two tests, one win and one loss**
v. Australia 1913 (2, 3)

**Born:** September 29, 1883, Masterton.

**Died:** December 12, 1963, Masterton.

**Position:** Fullback and utility back.

**Represented NZ:** 1910, 13 – 8 matches (4 tests).

**Points for NZ:** 33 – 13 conversions, 1 penalty goal, 1 dropped goal.

**First-class record:** Wairarapa 1900, 04–08 (Masterton); Auckland 1909–13 (Ponsonby); North Island 1907–10,12; Wellington Province 1905; Wellington-Wairarapa-Horowhenua 1905; Wairarapa-Bush 1908.

**Selector/coach/administrator:** Wairarapa selector 1922–25.

**Other:** The only player to captain the All Blacks in a test from fullback.

**Miscellaneous:** A brother, Humphrey, captained NZ Universities 1908, 09 and later became Chief Justice.

**Occupation:** Blacksmith.

# DICK ROBERTS

## *Dick's long career brought many rewards*

DICK ROBERTS led the All Blacks on an undefeated tour of Australia during a long career which saw the Taranaki centre achieve many other highlights.

These included a century of points as an All Black in 1913 and 1914, the ground-breaking All Black North American tour, being in only the third provincial team to lift the Ranfurly Shield, touring South Africa with the first side from New Zealand to do so, and battling out a draw with the first Springbok team to tour New Zealand.

Roberts was described as 'not big but strong, a remarkable natural footballer with excellent hands, much speed, a quick sidestep, a deceptive swerve, a fine eye for an opening, a neat way of running his wings into scoring positions, a stout defender and a good goal-kicker.'

He played most often at centre but sometimes appeared at second five-eighth. He usually captained Taranaki, during perhaps its proudest era and at a time when it would develop a host of other All Blacks. His career with Taranaki began in 1909 and ended in 1922.

Roberts' first All Black game came in 1913 when he played the first test against the touring Australian team. His form had been noted in the second tour match, when the Australians just managed to overcome the powerful Taranaki team, 11–9.

Fourteen days earlier Taranaki had won the Ranfurly Shield for the first time. In fact, it had become only the third team to win a shield challenge. Auckland had been awarded the shield (as the best-performed team) in 1902, lost it to Wellington in 1904, won it back in 1905 and had held it through 23 challenges over eight seasons. But on August 16, 1913, at Alexandra Park, Auckland, Taranaki, which

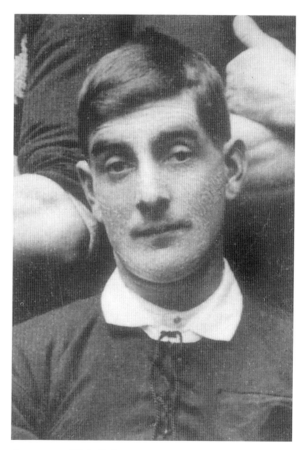

*A younger Dick Roberts*

had been pipped 5–6 in its challenge the season before, lifted the log 14–11.

Roberts was one of the heroes for the challenger, scoring two tries.

Taranaki would hold the shield until its seventh defence, on September 10, 1914, when Wellington would lift it. On the same day Taranaki had repulsed its first challenge against Wanganui at Hawera, Archduke Francis Ferdinand was assassinated in Sarajevo, in the Balkans, thus setting off the events that led to

*MARVELLOUS ERA: Dick Roberts (in front, fourth from left) captained this 1914 All Black team in Australia*

World War I. The successful Wellington challenge therefore would be the last time the shield was played for until August, 1919.

But it was a marvellous era for Taranaki. In this period no fewer than eight of Roberts' team-mates were All Blacks – the big kicking Jack Stohr, Don Cameron, George Loveridge, Jack 'Ginger' Colman, Charlie Brown, Dick Taylor and front rowers Mick Cain and Henry Dewar. Bunny Abbott, the 1905 All Black Original, also made one shield appearance for Taranaki.

Colman had represented New Zealand as far back as 1907–08. He made 49 appearances for Taranaki, at halfback, five-eighth, fullback and wing-forward. Brown would go on to lead the first New Zealand team to tour South Africa – the NZ Army side of 1919. Stohr, a 1910 and 1913 All Black, was reputed to have kicked a penalty between halfway and his own twenty-five with the Army team against Transvaal in 1919.

Later in 1913 Roberts joined the All Black tour of North America with Taranaki team-mates Stohr, Loveridge, Cain and Dewar.

This side was managed and coached by George Mason and captained by the 1905 All Black Original, Alex McDonald. The 1913 team is unique for the fact it made a fullscale tour to North America whereas All Black sides before and since have only stopped off there during major tours of Britain and Europe. Those All Blacks played 16 matches on the Pacific Coast, all of which were won easily.

Roberts scored three tries in the international against All-America, won 51–3.

In 1914 Roberts captained the North Island and then led the New Zealand team in all three tests on the unbeaten 1914 tour of Australia. This team was second only to the 1903 side in points scored in Australia. Roberts was described as 'the complete centre – dashing on attack and fearless on defence'. He scored a try in the second test and two in the third.

On their return from Australia the 1914 All Black team, to a man, volunteered for war service. Those who passed the medical went on to fight on the fields of Gallipoli, France and Palestine. Downing, Black and McNeece were killed in action.

Roberts had played 23 matches for the All Blacks during 1913 and 1914, including five tests. He had scored a century of points for New Zealand, which was still a comparatively rare honour. This tally had included 22 tries.

So, like so many others, Roberts' rugby career was interrupted by World War I. But he served with NZ Rifle Brigade during the war and played for the United Kingdom XV, NZ Services in the King's Cup competition and toured South Africa with the NZ Army team.

This team was led by his Taranaki team-mate, Brown, who would go on to have the rare distinction of playing for the All Blacks both before and after the war. Brown would also become a longtime Taranaki selector-coach and a New Zealand selector in 1944.

Roberts came home to represent Taranaki for three more seasons, until 1922. He captained his province in the famous scoreless draw against the powerful 1921 Springboks, who shared the series with New Zealand and lost only one non-international match, to Canterbury.

Roberts became a farmer on the Waimate Plains and well-known racehorse owner in later life.

## Richard William Roberts
## (Taranaki)

**Captain in three tests, three wins**
v. Australia 1914 (1, 2, 3)

**Born:** January 23, 1889, Manaia.

**Died:** March 8, 1973, Okaiawa.

**Position:** Three-quarter.

**Represented NZ:** 1913, 14 – 23 matches (5 tests).

**Points for NZ:** 102 – 22 tries, 15 conversions, 2 penalty goals.

**First-class record:** Taranaki 1909–11 (Kaponga), 1912–14, 20–22 (Okaiawa), 1915 (Hawera); North Island 1912–14; United Kingdom XV 1918–19; NZ Services 1919.

**Miscellaneous:** Served with NZ Rifle Brigade during World War I and played for the United Kingdom XV, NZ Services in the King's Cup competition and toured South Africa with the NZ Army team.

**Occupation:** A farmer on the Waimate Plains and well-known racehorse owner.

# GEORGE AITKEN

## No beg-pardons when young George got the heave-ho

T HOUGH HE was something of a rugby prodigy, George Aitken would gain a taste of the bitterness that accompanies All Black failure long before he would enjoy the sweetness of long-term victory at international level.

Aitken played for two countries. He is best remembered in Britain as a part of the fabulous Scottish three-quarter line that dominated British rugby in the mid-1920s.

But the reason Aitken had gone to Britain was he had become the first former All Black captain to win a Rhodes Scholarship to study at Oxford University in 1922.

Aitken had captained the All Blacks the year before, when the Springboks toured New Zealand and the two countries began the rivalry that has dominated their national sporting psyches ever since.

The sense of occasion was already powerful. New Zealand and South Africa had both made successful tours to Britain and servicemen had played against one another during World War I and in South Africa when the New Zealand Army team toured there in 1919.

The naming of Aitken as captain came as a surprise. He had not led his province, Wellington. In some quarters, it was felt that Dick Roberts, who had captained New Zealand before World War I, and who was still playing top rugby for Taranaki, should have been the centre and the captain.

Aitken led the All Blacks to a convincing 13–5 victory at Carisbrook, Dunedin in the opening test before 25,000 spectators. After trailing 0–5 at the interval, the All Blacks equalised early in the second spell when a high

GEORGE AITKEN: Joined 'colonial' three-quarter line

kick from Aitken bounced awkwardly for the Springboks' fullback, Gerhard Morkel, and Moke Bellis pounced on the ball to score. Then winger Jack Steel scored one of the great tries when he fielded a crosskick and sprinted half the length of the field to touch down under the posts. Storey added a third try late in the game.

But the All Blacks dropped the second test at Eden Park, Auckland, 5–9, before 40,000 people. In a monumental battle, there was

*GRAND FINALE: George Aitken (extreme right) toured with the British Barbarians of Easter, 1924, while representing Oxford and Scotland*

nothing in it near the end. Locked at 5–5, the Boks' Gerhard Morkel dropped a (4-point) goal in the dying minutes to take the test.

But Aitken, at 23 the youngest All Black captain in history, would be treated harshly by the New Zealand selectors. Among a number of changes, his place would be taken by his Wellington team-mate, Mark Nicholls, while the captaincy went to another Wellingtonian, halfback Teddy Roberts. Nicholls had played at second five-eighth in the first two tests. But the third test, played in mud and pools of water on Athletic Park, Wellington, ended in a scoreless draw. So the series would be shared.

Aitken, who had played first-class rugby for Buller while a 16-year-old schoolboy, would leave New Zealand's playing fields for ever at the end of that season.

He would eventually gain eight caps as a Scotland representative in 1924–29, in the famous all-Oxford University three-quarter line of Johnny Wallace, Phil MacPherson and Ian Smith.

Scotland was the strongest of the home nations in the early 1920s. It had marvellous teams and players, including flashing three-quarters such as Leslie Gracie and Eric Liddell, and stalwart fullback Dan Drysdale.

But the real impact of the Scottish flair came when MacPherson was joined by three 'colonials' – Aitken of New Zealand, Wallace, who was to captain the touring New South Wales 'Waratahs' in 1927–28 and later coached the Wallabies, and the brilliant Melbourne-born winger Smith.

This great Scotland side pulled off the Grand

Slam in 1925 but was surprisingly tripped up by Ireland in the subsequent two seasons.

But ironically for Aitken, who would have had a lot to prove, he did not get the chance to cross swords with the All Blacks when they toured in 1924–25. The Scots refused to play the All Blacks. England, Wales and France had all felt the icy breath of wrathful Scottish boycotts in the past.

The Scots still harboured resentment at the way they'd been outfoxed by the All Black Originals' officials way back in 1905–06, when the Scots declined to give guarantees of £200 a match and instead offered the net gates for the games. The unbeaten (at that stage) All Blacks had attracted huge crowds in Scotland and returned over the border with about £1600, a huge profit. The Scots had also been affronted, after the tour, to learn the All Blacks had been paid three shillings per day per man expenses.

So the Scots declined to be part of the 1908 British tour to New Zealand and would not play the Invincibles, which would have been a superb encounter.

After he graduated from Oxford, Aitken went into business in England. But he returned to New Zealand in 1939 and joined the Department of Industries and Commerce in Wellington.

Aitken stood 5ft 9in and weighed 12st 4lb. He remains one of only four test captains to have led the All Blacks in every match in which they played for New Zealand. The others were Fred Allen, Pat Vincent and Andy Leslie. He is one of only three All Black test captains to have won a Rhodes Scholarship to Oxford University, the others being David Kirk and Chris Laidlaw. He was also the youngest All Black captain in history, until 1929, when Herb Lilburne, aged 21, led the All Blacks.

## George Gothard Aitken (Wellington)

**Captain in two tests, one win and one loss**
v. South Africa 1921 (1, 2)

**Born:** July 2, 1998, Westport.

**Died:** July 8, 1952, Wellington.

**Position:** Centre.

**Represented NZ:** 1921 – 2 matches (2 tests).

**Points for NZ:** Nil.

**First-class record:** Buller 1914, 15 (Westport); Wellington 1917–22 (University); North Island 1921; NZ Trials 1921; NZ Universities 1920, 21; Scotland 1924, 25, 29; Oxford University 1922–24; Barbarians (UK) 1922–25.

**High school:** Westport High.

**Other:** Gained eight caps as Scotland representative 1924, 25, 29, in the famous all-Oxford University three-quarter line which also contained Johnny Wallace, Phil McPherson and Ian Smith.

**Miscellaneous:** Won Wellington and NZ Universities 440yd hurdles titles and runner-up in that event at 1919 NZAAA championships; Rhodes Scholar 1922. One of only four test captains to have led the All Blacks in every match in which they played for New Zealand. The others were Fred Allen, Pat Vincent and Andy Leslie. One of only three All Black test captains to have won a Rhodes Scholarship to Oxford University, the others being David Kirk and Chris Laidlaw.

**Occupation:** In business in England until he returned to New Zealand in 1939 and joined the Department of Industries and Commerce in Wellington.

# TEDDY ROBERTS

## Teddy lived up to expectations of All Black father

TEDDY ROBERTS was a brilliant captain and halfback who led Wellington during perhaps its finest and most creative era.

So it was ironic he should be given the All Black leadership in his final game, in a match that petered to a grim scoreless draw that left New Zealand and South Africa frustrated at the deadlock in their first epic series.

Part of New Zealand's first father-and-son New Zealand representatives, Teddy, a 1913–21 All Black, followed in the footsteps of his father, Harry, who had been a member of New Zealand's first touring side in 1884.

Roberts was described as a halfback who 'was particularly adept at blind-side attacks and was an accurate short-range goal-kicker.' He stood 5ft 6in and weighed 11st 4lb. International rugby photographs of the period often show Roberts, using his brilliant acceleration off the mark, breaking from the All Blacks' 2–3–2 scrum with his forwards ranging up some yards behind in support. He was equally at home at international level as a first five-eighth.

He would use his speed to score 14 tries for the All Blacks, from 26 matches, including five tests. He totalled 112 points for New Zealand, also landing 35 conversions.

Roberts also played a big part in the folklore that developed from the Ranfurly Shield in this period. Wellington had ended Taranaki's seven-match shield era in September, 1914, after Taranaki had become only the third challenger to have lifted the shield. It had beaten Auckland in 1913. Auckland had held the log for eight seasons – since winning it back from Wellington in 1905.

*TEDDY ROBERTS: Played part in Shield folklore*

Roberts had played an inspirational match in that 1914 challenge. But he would come back, after World War I, to captain Wellington during its 1919–20 tenure – the only time in history Wellington has exerted a dominant hold over the shield.

With a change to the shield rules, Wellington was able to take the shield on tour. It had epic battles away from home against New Zealand's finest – such as Canterbury, Auckland, Taranaki

*LIKE FATHER: The first-ever father and son combination to represent New Zealand ... Teddy and father Harry Roberts at the 1946 parliamentary reception for the Kiwis army team*

and Otago. In 1920 it would finally lose the shield to Southland after 11 challenges for the season – a staggering number for the times and more than modern shield defenders commit to.

The Wellington attitude might seem cavalier compared to today's hard-headed approach but it was a glittering chapter in the province's history.

However, Wellington had a wonderful array of talent to assist its philanthropic approach. Its output of All Blacks was huge in this era. More significantly, many of these All Blacks proved to be in the elite of international footballers – players such as Roberts, 'Ranji' Wilson, the Shearer and Tilyard brothers, Umberto Calcinai, and Mark and 'Ginger' Nicholls.

Roberts' All Black career began when he was

chosen for the tour to North America in 1913. However, his appearances were restricted by injury and he played in only five of the 16 matches. He did not play in the only 'test' match of the tour, when the All Blacks beat All-America, 51–3.

There had been no international rugby for the All Blacks since 1910, so the team had a new-look appearance. Only four players – the captain, Alex McDonald, Frank Mitchinson, 'Doddie' Gray and Jack Stohr had played for the All Blacks

The team had lost no time in getting down to hard work. The players had trained hard on board the ship, the *Willochra*, which took them across the Pacific and even trained on the day of their arrival in San Fransisco. 'The following day they went through a solid two hour workout at which Teddy Roberts, who was nursing an injury from the domestic season, was a spectator'.[1]

The All Blacks would romp through their tour, mounting huge scores for 610 points and only six against. In many games they 'pulled back on the throttle'. But the partially-fit Teddy Roberts had a quiet tour by his standards, though he did score six tries.

In 1914 he played in all three tests on the unbeaten tour of Australia. Roberts was originally left out of the selected touring team. He'd been overshadowed by Canterbury's Henry Taylor, a leading player on the North American tour the year before, in the inter-island match. Roberts only came into the side when Clem Green, the Buller halfback, became unavailable. When winger George Loveridge was injured on the tour, Taylor moved out to the wing, scoring three tries from this position in the second test and being second-highest tour points-scorer with 15 tries. But the move enabled Roberts to claim the halfback test berth and have an outstanding tour.

The side was led by Dick Roberts, the Taranaki centre. This team was second only to the 1903 side in points scored in Australia. The sensation of the tour was the South Canterbury flyer, Tommy Lynch, who scored 16 tries and had terrorised the Wallabies the year before. A typical example was a try he scored against Queensland, when he intercepted a pass at halfway and burst upfield, swerving past the home fullback and outpacing the cover-defence to score near the posts.

After the tour the entire All Black team enlisted for service.

But Roberts would become one of a handful of players who would be All Blacks before and after the war. He was selected for the 1920 All Black tour of Australia as a five-eighth and led the points-scoring with 46. Charlie Brown, another pre-war All Black, was the only halfback selected for that tour. However, it was Roberts who played at halfback in two of those 'tests' against New South Wales, as well as at first five-eighth in the other.

Roberts faced stern competition after the war from 'Ginger' Nicholls, the brother of Mark and 'Doc'. All three brothers were All Blacks. 'Ginger' Nicholls had first played for Wellington in 1917 as a 17-year-old and was in

the job again in 1918. Although he did not play for Wellington in 1919, Nicholls was selected in the North Island side with Roberts at first five-eighth and captain.

Nicholls was a controversial choice ahead of Roberts for the first test against the touring Springboks in 1921. But he showed outstanding form and was awarded the gold medal by the NZFRU as the outstanding back of the match.

However, after New Zealand won that test, 13–5, the All Black selectors controversially turned to Roberts to be halfback for the remaining two tests. And after the second-test loss All Black captain George Aitken was dropped and Roberts installed in the job for the third and final test in Wellington. Aitken would later go to Britain as a Rhodes Scholar and gain eight caps as a Scotland representative in 1924–29, in the famous all-Oxford University three-quarter line of Johnny Wallace, Phil McPherson and Ian Smith.

We can gain some insight into the way Roberts and the All Black coaches, Alex McDonald and George Nicholson, prepared the team.

The *New Zealand Herald* of September 14, 1921, reported, in the lead-up to the third test, that 'the All Blacks are doing their training under the public eye at Day's Bay', across the harbour from Wellington city, and that 'the work was proceeding well.'

'At an early hour the men are running up and down the beach to rid themselves of the night's stiffness. Then comes a course of physical drill, after which a plunge into the sea is taken … Then back to the training room for a shower or bath and a massage.

'The hours before dinner [lunch] are spent in football practice, in which scrum work and general combinations receive special attention, with a due regard to tactics, the backs spending time in passing and handling the ball … A rub-down and massage follows.

'The afternoons are devoted mainly to cricket, and other outdoor games, with a good deal of walking exercise. "I have under my charge at present some of the finest specimens of manhood it has ever been my lot to see," said the physical trainer, Dorrie Leslie.

'Mr McDonald is also rendering good service in the coaching work. Mr George Nicholson, famous as a forward in the 1905 touring team, and now one of the New Zealand selectors, joined up yesterday, and will remain with the team, in company with the other selectors, Messrs A.J. Griffiths and Donald Stewart, until the side is chosen on Friday night,' the article concluded.

But after excellent conditions during most of the week's preparation, the weather deteriorated and the test was played in atrocious conditions – much of the playing area was covered in water – and the result was a scoreless draw.

## Edward James Roberts (Wellington)

**Captain in one test, one draw**
v. South Africa 1921 (3)

**Born:** May 10, 1891, Wellington.

**Died:** February 27, 1972, Wellington.

**Position:** Halfback.

**Represented NZ:** 1913, 14, 20, 21 – 26 matches (5 tests).

**Points for NZ:** 112 – 14 tries, 35 conversions.

**First-class record:** Wellington 1910–11 (St James club), 1912–14, 19–21, 23 (Athletic); North Island 1910, 12–14, 19; NZ Trials 1921.

**School:** Brooklyn School, Wellington.

**Other:** Represented Wellington at cricket as a wicketkeeper in the 1910–11 season.

**Miscellaneous:** His father, Harry, was a member of the first New Zealand team, which toured Australia in 1884. His brothers, Harry jnr (1909) and Len (1920), also played for Wellington.

**Occupation:** Worked as a commercial traveller for a baker's supply firm.

1 *Centenary*

# JOCK RICHARDSON

## Jock proved to be the real 'Invincible'

OUT OF sight, out of mind. That is the reason Jock Richardson failed to be recognised as a great player like some of his team-mates.

Richardson was captain of the All Blacks who won all three home union tests on the famous Invincibles' tour of 1924–25.

Cliff Porter was the All Blacks' tour captain but was injured early in the tour and couldn't command a test place after he regained fitness [See Porter chapter for details].

Three test victories, on one tour, may not seem a big deal to the modern rugby follower. But in the first half of the 20th Century, test matches and test opponents were few and far between. In some years the All Blacks played no international rugby.

It should also be remembered that up until the days of Wilson Whineray, who captained the All Blacks 30 times in the 1950s and 1960s, the most tests an All Black captain had been in charge of in the previous six decades was only seven – by Porter.

Richardson, the Invincibles' vice-captain, did a magnificent job in Porter's absence as the side increasingly battled to protect its unbeaten record. He played 28 matches, including all the tests, scoring nine tries and two conversions.

'The trouble was that Cliff got hurt early on the tour and lost his form and fitness,' recalled Richardson years later.

'I felt, and so did Stan Dean, the manager, that Jim Parker was the superior wing forward with Cliff struggling for fitness. We chose Jim for all the tests in Britain and naturally Cliff didn't like it very much. He felt he had become a figurehead captain, which I suppose he had. But he never let on to the rest of the team, how he felt, which was a mark of the man.'

So while there is irony in the fact the

RELUCTANT HERO: Jock Richardson was exiled for the remainder of his life

Invincibles are remembered as Porter's team, when Richardson led them in the most crucial games, there is irony too that, in a team of outstanding forwards, it is Maurice Brownlie, especially after his famous performance against

*NEVER BEATEN: Jock Richardson leads the All Blacks out against Ireland on the tour of 1924–25, followed by Les Cupples, Maurice Brownlie, Jim Parker, Read Masters and 'Son' White. Richardson led the Invincibles in the three home union tests, his only tests as captain*

England after his brother, Cyril, was ordered from the field, who is remembered as 'the greatest' rather than Richardson.

In fact, Richardson's All Black test captaincy record was more extensive than the official statistics show. He had captained the All Blacks in two matches against the touring New South Wales side of 1923. Matches against NSW were not given test match status. But NSW was at that time the de facto Australian team since Queensland had halted playing first-class rugby.

The lack of recognition never concerned Richardson. He had lived in Australia since the early 1930s.

'I never even thought about it,' he said during one of his occasional visits back to his homeland. 'It was an honour to be in such a team as the Invincibles. It was the highlight of my life and I'll bet there are many rugby players who'd gladly have swapped places with me.'[1]

A loose forward in the 2–3–2 scrum of the day, Richardson was a big player for the times. He stood 6ft 1in (1.85m) and weighed 14st 5lb (91.2kg). He was the Otago shot put champion the year before he first led the All Blacks. An

Otago product who had moved to Southland when it had the Ranfurly Shield for the first time, Richardson played a typical robust, southern-style game.

Richardson was described as 'a great forward who was always conspicuous for good work in every game he played. A strong, vigorous rucker, good handler, exceptionally keen in lineouts and always a mighty power with the ball at foot.'[2]

In 1921, only his second season of representative rugby for Otago, Richardson was selected for the All Blacks and proved an outstanding success against the first Springbok team to tour New Zealand. He played in all three tests and would be a first-choice test selection for the rest of his career.

It was on the 1922 tour of New South Wales that Richardson first teamed up with Maurice Brownlie. Richardson played in the three tests, scoring three tries. This devastating form carried over to five other tour matches and he scored nine tries in total to be the team's leading try scorer.

With one lock in the 2–3–2 scrum, the siderow forwards of the day were expected to do their share of the tight work. Brownlie and Richardson were brilliant.

'I always liked playing with Maurice. If I had the ball he was an excellent support player, and if he had it, he could run like a back,' recalled Richardson.[3]

He had first met three of the Brownlie brothers – Cyril, Maurice and Tony – while on service in Palestine in World War I. Tony was killed in action in Turkey. Maurice and Cyril would join him in many of the toughest battles of the 1924–25 tour. A fourth brother, Laurence, played for the All Blacks in 1921 against New South Wales, but did not play with Richardson against the touring Springboks in the same year.

Richardson was hurt at the tail-end of the great tour. He broke a leg during a training session in Canada. The injury would delay his start to the 1925 season in New Zealand and may have hastened his retirement. Richardson – whose given name was Johnstone, not Jock – was to play only one more 'test' – against New South Wales in Auckland in 1925. Only 26, he announced his retirement from international rugby, stating he'd 'had enough.'

It was his interest in cricket that lured him across the Tasman several years later.

'I'd been hearing about this chap Bradman and didn't have anything settled back home, so I thought I'd go to Australia to have a look. When I arrived I got a job with the department of main roads in Sydney. I went back to New Zealand for a while, but decided I liked it better in Australia, so I became a cost accountant for the department and worked for them for years and years,' Richardson said.[4]

## Johnstone 'Jock' Richardson (Southland)

**Captain in three tests, three wins**
v. Ireland, Wales, England 1924–25

**Born:** April 2, 1899, Dunedin.

**Died:** November 28, 1994, Nowra, Australia.

**Position:** Loose forward.

**Represented NZ:** 1921–25 – 42 matches (7 tests).

**Points for NZ:** 58 – 18 tries, 2 conversions.

**First-class record:** Otago 1920–22 (Alhambra); Southland 1923 (Waikiwi), 25, 26 (Pirates); South Island 1921, 22, 24, 25; NZ Trials 1921, 24.

**School:** Normal School, Dunedin.

**Selector/coach/administrator:** Accountant/secretary Southland RFU.

**Other:** Otago shot put champion 1921, 22.

**Miscellaneous:** Moved to Australia in the early 1930s and lived out his long life there.

**Occupation:** After moving to Australia he worked as a clerk in the Public Works Department.

1,3,4 *100 Great Rugby Characters*
2 *All Black Tours,* Syd Nicholls, 1953.

# CLIFF PORTER

## Porter led the way through a fabulous decade

LOOKING BACK, three-quarters of a century after the fact, the achievement of Cliff Porter's 'Invincibles' in becoming the first All Black team to be unbeaten on a tour of Britain and France, remains remarkable. It was to take a half-century for the feat to be, arguably, surpassed.

Porter was New Zealand rugby's most influential leader through the 1920s. Yet, in analysing his career, we find he played only a small on-field role in its finest moments of the decade, did not feature at all on its most challenging tour, and was completely lost to the game once he retired. This was because Porter played in only one of the four home union test matches on the great tour. He missed selection for New Zealand's first tour of South Africa three years later, when his calm direction on the field and care of his men off it was sorely missed.

But time and again, as the golden decade of rugby progressed through into the 1930s, Porter led All Black teams through thick and thin, triumph and calamity. His qualities were such that he came to be revered by his players. His leadership style was consensus-driven. He was only 25 when he captained the 1924 All Blacks. But he already had an invaluable insight into the demands of several positions and so could coach and encourage players and talk tactics.

It was concern for his players that is probably Porter's major legacy to the All Black captaincy and coaching evolution. One of his

*(left) ALL THE SKILLS: Cliff Porter had played as an inside back before changing to wing-forward a year before the great Invincibles' tour*

*PLAYER WELFARE: Cliff Porter led the All Blacks on several overseas tours after the 1924–25 Invincibles tour. His players came to love the captain who always put their welfare before his own interests*

old team-mates from so many of those hard campaigns, George Nepia, was to say of him: 'His first and last thought was for us.'

Porter was never a dictator, even at the end of his career. Merv Corner, the Auckland halfback who became an All Black selector in the early 1950s, recalled coming in for Jimmy

61

Mill in the 1930 series against Great Britain. He was impressed by Porter's invitation to participate. 'He built up my confidence. He was a marvel at getting the best out of each of us.'

When chosen as captain of the 1924 team, Porter had been confronted with a situation that would have daunted even a man of greater age and experience. Ces Badeley was expected to be captain. He led the side on its tour of Australia just before the big tour and captained the side which was convincingly beaten by Auckland on its return. Badeley was still in the seat of honour at the Parliamentary farewell for the big tour, replying to the distringuished tributes to his side. He was still there, at the top table, at the NZRFU farewell the same evening.

Then it was announced that Porter, who'd been outstanding in Australia, would be the captain. It meant he, a comparative tyro, had to lead a side containing at least two former captains and many players far more experienced than him.

When the tour did not begin as well as its predecessor had, Porter took the drastic action of calling the players together and putting the position squarely before them. He told them they must draw up rules of conduct if they wanted to succeed. He said the team must manage itself, since its manager would often be busy with issues at international level. He was well supported by the dominant members of the team. They drew up rules about practices, exemptions, curfews for those playing the next game and other matters. The outlook of the tour changed immediately when the team destroyed the first Welsh club, Swansea. Porter said later that as for practical help with coaching the team, he had got a lot of assistance from the old hands, especially Alf West, who'd been an All Black since 1920.

'We never set out to go through unbeaten,' said Porter many years later. 'We were primarily concerned with avenging the defeat by Wales in 1905. Once it became apparent halfway through the tour, however, that we could get through unbeaten, this became our main desire.

'But I'd never advise any team to try it. It was a terrible burden, knowing we had to win every match. To achieve it, we played our best team every match, midweek and Saturday.' This meant George Nepia, only 19, played in all 30 tour matches, but seven of the team made less than 10 appearances.

'It speaks volumes for the spirit of these men that they continued to train and were as keen as the rest of us for an unbeaten record to be achieved,' said Porter.

But what made the Invincibles such a great team? 'Fitness was probably our greatest attribute, and the fact that each man knew what he had to do.'

Porter was injured early in the great 1924 tour. But the All Blacks became even stronger with his replacement, Jim Parker, in the test team. Porter was not considered for the Irish test, but he had thrown off the injury and was available for the Welsh and English internationals. However, Parker was playing so magnificently the selection committee could not leave him out.

The vice-captain on that tour, Jock Richardson, who captained the 'Invincibles' in their three tests (they did not play Scotland) on the British leg of the tour, spoke years later about the agonising decisions the committee made over the two men.

'It was a terribly hard decision,' said Richardson. 'I don't know what we would have done if Cliff had not got injured. He was a terrific player, but then Jim was something special too.'

'The trouble was that Cliff got hurt early and lost his form and fitness. I felt, and so did Stan Dean, the manager, that Parker was the superior wing-forward with Cliff struggling. We chose Jim for all the tests in Britain and naturally Cliff didn't like it much. He felt he'd become a figurehead captain, which I suppose he had. But he never let on to the rest of the team how he felt, which was a mark of the man.'

Porter accepted the selection committee's decisions without rancour. But he said, years later, he had wanted Parker to play on the wing against England.

'I reckoned England, who wanted to break our run of successes, would play rugged football and that's where I would have been in my element, giving our backs the chance to feed Parker, an unstoppable wing on the day,' said Porter.

'But Jock Richardson didn't see it that way, and rather than cause a rumpus in an entirely happy team, I conceded the point.'

Near the end of the 1924 tour Porter had thrust his name firmly back into the picture with a return to form and replaced Parker for

*CONTROVERSIAL CHOICE: Cliff Porter missed the first three tests of the Invincibles' tour and wasn't happy about it*

the French international. He finished the tour with 17 matches from the 32 played, scoring nine tries.

Porter came to dislike the team manager, Stan Dean, so intensely on tour he vowed and declared he wanted little to do with the man again. Since Dean remained NZRFU chairman for a quarter-century, from 1922–47, seeing off many challenges to his position, Porter was lost to the game once he retired.

In contrast to Porter's opinion, Mark Nicholls was to write how Dean was 'chairman of our selection committee and of all our team talks, to which he contributed as much as the players. He co-ordinated the ideas expounded at the team talks into a set pattern of play (mainly defensive) and we were fortunate to have him at the head of the team.'

Part of the reason for Porter's success as a wing-forward was his experience as a five-eighth and three-quarter in all his early rugby. It was not until 1923, the year before he led the 'Invincibles', that he made the switch to wing-forward. In 1923 he was brought into the All Blacks for the final test against the touring New

South Wales team, which New Zealand won 38–11. He replaced the well-performed Moke Belliss.

After the great tour, Porter was to continue a long All Black career, interrupted only by the strange decision not to choose him for the 1928 tour of South Africa (though he was one of the tour reserves).

He led New Zealand to a 36–10 win over New South Wales at Auckland in 1925 and then took the All Blacks to Australia in 1926. Though the team had 13 of the 'Invincibles', it was affected by illness and injury at the start of the tour. Porter, again assisted by Nicholls with the backs, had to work hard to knock his multi-talented team into winning shape after it had lost to Wellington before departure and then to New South Wales in the opening 'test' of the three-'test' series. The All Blacks then took the other two 'tests', 11–6 and 14–0.

While the All Blacks completed their South African tour in 1928, New South Wales toured New Zealand. Porter led New Zealand to two very narrow victories in the first two 'tests', 15–12 and 16–14, but lost the third in Christchurch, 8–11.

On the 1929 tour of Australia, Porter did not play until the second test and only participated in the final four games of the 10-match tour. The tour was remarkable for several reasons. It was the first time Australia had played in full internationals since 1914. The Wallabies won the series, 3–0, an historic milestone. It was the first time an All Black team had lost all tests in a series.

A number of leading players, including backline kingpins Mark Nicholls, Bert Cooke and Freddy Lucas had been unavailable to tour. A large number of injuries affected the team and at one point, before the final test, Porter left the team and flew from Brisbane to Sydney to arrange treatment for the injured, while the team travelled south by train.

The Wallabies fielded a powerful team, including many stars of the era, such as Alex Ross, Tom Lawton, Syd Malcolm, Eddie Bonis and 'Wild Bill' Cerutti. For the first test, with Porter injured before leaving New Zealand and still not fit, the Auckland three-quarter, Lew Hook, only 10st, was chosen to play in Porter's position. New Zealand lost the opening test 8–9 and could not hold the Wallabies in the second half of the second test in Brisbane. After being tied at 3–3 at the interval, Australia swept to a series win in convincing fashion, 17–9.

Though it gave a much improved performance, in spite of a reorganised backline, New Zealand was pipped 15–13 in the final test. But Porter had a champion's game. 'No-one who saw the match will forget the New Zealand captain's heroic, inspiring effort. He was a rover, on hand in nearly every movement, back on defence as often as he was hurling himself into the attack. His great tackling and his speed in short, sharp bursts were wonderful,' wrote one reporter.

Porter's greatest triumph in the last chapter of his career came when he led the All Blacks to a 3–1 series win over a very competitive Great Britain in 1930. The visitors had pipped the All Blacks 3–6 at Carisbrook in a game played in the most miserable conditions – snow, sleet, rain and wind.

New Zealand took the second test at Lancaster Park, 13–10, with tries shared two each. The British could have won. A New Zealand record 40,000 crowd watched the third test at Eden Park and did not go away disappointed. It was the experience of players such as Porter, Cooke, Lucas and particularly Nicholls, which enabled the All Blacks to win, 15–10. Nicholls was outstanding, as a general, an opportunist and as a tactical and goal kicker. As they had done in all three tests, the New Zealand forwards took a firm grip on the game in the second half and were this time well rewarded.

But the British had been in the game throughout and could never be discounted. So in Porter's home town, Wellington, the crowds again turned out in huge numbers for the fourth test – almost 40,000 of them. This time the All Blacks made it a no-contest, scoring six tries to one, with Porter and Cooke claiming two tries each, winning 22–8. It was said to be Porter's finest match. It was also a brilliant way to go out for a number of All Blacks stars of the previous decade. The series ended the test careers of Nepia, Cooke, Lucas, Nicholls, Stewart, Finlayson, Mill, Irvine and Porter.

Porter was by then a towering personality of the game and looked capable of beginning an administrative or selection/coaching career at national level. But, according to the veteran rugby journalist, Morrie Mackenzie, 'the Hierarchy had no place in their calculations for outstanding personalities or outspoken types who wouldn't toe the party line, even if they came from Wellington.'

In 1932 'they refused him a hearing at the annual meeting ... Worse still, when the election of the management committee came up, the Hierarchy ganged up on Cliff, who was beaten by one vote for a seat on the committee. I never asked Cliff about this, but I can only assume that after these rebuffs he washed his hands forever of rugby administration, as did other great figures before and since, rather than submit meekly to victimisation and intrigue.'[1]

## Clifford Glen Porter (Wellington)

**Captain in seven tests, four wins and three losses**
v. France 1925,
v. Australia 1929 (2, 3),
v. British Isles 1930 (1, 2, 3, 4)

**Born:** Edinburgh, Scotland, May 5, 1899.

**Died:** Wellington, November 12, 1976.

**Position:** Wing-forward.

**Represented NZ:** 1923–26, 28–30 – 41 matches (7 internationals).

**Points for NZ:** 48 – 16 tries.

**Provincial record:** Wellington 1917, 18 (Wellington College OB), 1923, 25–30 (Athletic) and Horowhenua 1921, 22 (Hui Mai); North Island 1924–26, 28, 29; Wellington-Manawatu 1923; Wellington-Manawatu-Horowhenua 1925.

**Occupation:** Partner in paper bag-manufacturing business in Hutt Valley.

1 *Black, Black, Black*

# MAURICE BROWNLIE

## *Early contender as All Black of the century*

MAURICE BROWNLIE may well have been the finest All Black forward ever to lace up boots. When the great Colin Meads was awarded 'the All Black player of the century' by popular vote organised by the *New Zealand Rugby World* magazine in 1999, Meads himself pointed out there were not too many people who had witnessed Brownlie's extraordinary feats around to argue his case.

Deciding objectively between the two champions is impossible. There is no doubt they bestrode the international and provincial stages of their eras like colossuses.

Brownlie had played a record 61 times for the All Blacks when he retired – a record that would hold until broken by Kevin Skinner 28 years later. He also scored 21 tries in the black jersey.

He was one of three brothers who played for the All Blacks. The youngest, Laurence, was the first to win national honours, in 1921, but a knee injury forced him to retire. Cyril, the oldest, at 6ft 3in and 15st, was a huge forward for the era. He played 90 first class matches over a nine-year career and toured Britain and France in 1924 and South Africa in 1928 with the All Blacks. Cyril became the first player to be ordered off in an international, against England.

Maurice and Cyril Brownlie went off to war as young men, being posted to the 2nd Mounted Rifles. They fought in Palestine and took part in the long chase of the Turks to Damascus. The brothers came home to farming at the family farm at Puketitiri, near Hastings, and to rugby.

It was the selection of Laurence, to play for the All Blacks against New South Wales in 1921, which was the spur for Maurice and Cyril. Their father, James, urged them to get fit and try to emulate their little brother.

Maurice played in the Hawkes Bay-Poverty Bay team which held the 1921 Springboks to 8–14. Within a year he was an All Black, touring Australia, where his robust style had the critics in raptures. From this point he would go on to become one of New Zealand's greatest forwards – talked about for many decades with the same reverence as was Meads 30 and 40 years later.

He was a loose forward whose greatest attributes were courage and legendary strength – perhaps setting the mould for tight-loose players like Meads and others after him. He was 6ft tall and little more than 14st, but played, as the saying goes, well above that weight. Work on the farm had made Maurice and Cyril tremendously strong. Stories abound, in the same vein as those about the Meads brothers, of Brownlie carrying sheep under each arm, dragging the family car out of a river and hefting 70lb bales of hay high onto the stook all summer's day.

We are indebted to Norman McKenzie, the great rugby coach, selector and administrator, who became Maurice Brownlie's mentor, for the most intimate pen portrait of the player. In his book, *On With the Game,* completed by Arthur Carman after McKenzie's death in 1960, he said Brownlie was 'the greatest man I have ever seen as a siderow forward: great because he was great in every aspect of forward play.'

'He could handle the ball like a back, he could take the ball in a lineout and burst clear, he could stimulate movements, and, greatest of all, he had the ability to lead his forwards out of a tight corner, yard by yard, along the touchline.'

'For sheer tenacity I have seen no-one to equal Maurice Brownlie. His outstanding qualities were strength and resolution. He was in every respect a remarkable man and one of the finest specimens of manhood I have ever seen.

'He always took the field physically fit, and I don't know that he did a great deal of training – that is, training as we regard it today. He

*THREE BROTHERS: Laurence (right) was the first of the three Brownlie brothers to gain All Black honours, followed by Cyril (left) and Maurice (centre)*

constantly invigorated his friends with his offensive spirit. He was a hard, but never a tough player, and though he was often a marked man and set upon, he never complained, but got on with his game.'

McKenzie, who was to become an All Black coach and a national selector for many years, was, remarkably, the Hawkes Bay coach from 1916 to 1946. With Maurice Brownlie as his captain, he was to guide Hawkes Bay through its most famous Ranfurly Shield era, when it repulsed 24 challenges between 1922–27, and nurture great players such as George Nepia, Bull Irvine, Jimmy Mill, Lui Paewai, Jack Ormond, the Brownlie brothers and Bert Cooke (who moved there from Auckland).

At the end of the shield era Brownlie was to gain a little notoriety when he and fellow 'Invincible' Quentin Donald were ordered off in the infamous Battle of Solway, the controversial shield match between Wairarapa, the new holder, and Hawkes Bay, in 1927. The referee was Norman McKenzie's brother, Bert, while the opposing coach was another brother, Ted.

There have been few players able or willing to turn on the sheer consistency of performance throughout such a long career as Brownlie. His determination was the key to his ability to focus on a team's task in match after match. On the 'Invincibles' tour, for instance, he played in 25 matches and scored 11 tries. In the Hawkes Bay shield era he played in 19 games and scored 10 tries.

The 'Invincible' tour in 1924–25 was possibly the high point of Brownlie's career. In the company of other great forwards such as Cliff Porter, Jock Richardson, Jim Parker, Bull Irvine and his brother Cyril, Maurice stood out as exceptional.

Observers rated the England test, after his brother had been ordered off the field – unfairly, as Maurice and the other All Blacks felt – as his finest performance. He played like a man possessed and helped inspire New Zealand to a 17–11 victory.

The try Brownlie scored that day was

described by Wavell Wakefield, captain of England that day: 'I could see him going straight down the touchline, though it seemed impossible for him to score. Somehow he went on, giving me the impression of a moving tree-trunk, so solid did he appear to be and so little effect did various attempted tackles have on him. He crashed through without swerving to right or left and went over for one of the most surprising tries I have ever seen.'[1]

So he had already forged a reputation as perhaps the greatest forward New Zealand had produced when he was given the task of leading the All Blacks on their first tour of South Africa. Never one to sidestep a challenge Brownlie knew little about the problems – both with the geographical nature of South Africa and the nature of the men who would oppose his team – that would beset him.

Depending on the source of information, the 1928 tour was said to be a playing and diplomatic disaster – or a happy trip where much was learned and the honours shared equally. Certainly, to win two of the four tests and tie the rubber, was a feat that put Brownlie's team above its successors, the humiliated 1949 team and the 1960, 1970 and 1976 touring sides.

But it took time for respect to grow for Brownlie's team's effort, as each succeeding attempt failed. In 1928, New Zealand rugby enthusiasts had thought they had a team to match the 'Invincibles' of four years earlier and so were bitterly disappointed when the All Blacks suffered five losses and a draw on the gruelling tour. The critics had a field day.

Setbacks included the withdrawal, after the team was chosen, of Bert Cooke, on business grounds, and the ineligibility of Maori players, including George Nepia. A freakish midfield back, Cooke would become the first New Zealand player to score 100 tries in first class rugby. He would finish his 131-game career with 119 tries, a remarkable strike rate considering he was often very heavily marked. The 1928 All Blacks scored only three tries in this series, against the Boks' five. Cooke's ingenuity was clearly missed.

'If we'd had Nepia and Cooke, we wouldn't have lost a match,' Brownlie was to state, somewhat wishfully, after the tour.

The vice-captain of the team, Mark Nicholls, as famous as Brownlie in his heyday, wrote a

CHAMPION INDEED: Maurice Brownlie was an indomitable player who played 'well above his weight', as the saying goes

book on the tour and made many perceptive observations on South African rugby in general and the tour in particular. Nicholls pinpointed the All Blacks' scrum weaknesses as the major obstacle that was never truly overcome on tour. After experimenting, with some promise, with the 3–4–1 scrum being used so devastatingly by all their South African opponents, the All Blacks reverted, because 'it was not congenial to the forwards', back to their old methods after the loss to Transvaal in the fourth game.[2]

Nicholls never alluded anywhere to the fact he played in only the last of the four tests, although a member of the tour selection panel. This anomaly has fascinated rugby historians since that tour. Nicholls, whose brilliance had helped the All Blacks to victory many times in past years, kicked the team to victory in that test and the question will always be asked if he could have done the same in one or more of the others?

According to Terry McLean, who wrote a

chapter on Maurice Brownlie in his book, *New Zealand Rugby Legends*, the 1928 tour brought up many issues about Brownlie:

'His own form, which a leading South African critic considered indifferent until the last three weeks; his hostility to the newspapermen, not forgetting the two New Zealanders, Graham Beamish and Syd Nicholls, a brother of Mark's, who were with the team throughout; his having to put up with a manager who was so unthinking that at a formal dinner in Pretoria he casually remarked: 'You know the last time I was in this town was when we were fighting you blokes in the Boer War'; incompetence in the backline, magnified by the loss of Kilby; an anti-Mark Nicholls clique in the selection committee, two members of which, Neil McGregor and Ron Stewart, harboured grudges from the '24 tour; and, not least, Brownlie's qualities of captaincy.'

But Brownlie's leadership and example was not found wanting at the end of the tour. In the lead-up to the fourth and deciding test, after losing to Western Province, Brownlie again ordered a week of complete rest. On the morning after the Province match Brownlie assembled the team. 'These are my orders for the week, gentlemen,' he said. 'They are few, and simple. Each of you will go for a walk of about an hour. You will go to bed at a reasonable hour. For the rest, you will do what you like – with this proviso: Under no circumstances whatever is anyone of you so much as to touch a rugby ball until we play the Springboks in the last test.'[3]

Against predictions, New Zealand scored a magnificent 13–5 victory in this test. The All Black forward pack dominated the game, and Mark Nicholls, playing at second five-eighth, kicked two penalties and a dropped goal. It was the first time South Africa had been beaten on Newlands for 37 years.

In almost providing the blueprint for the motto proclaimed by later All Black touring captains like Whineray, Lochore, Kirkpatrick, Leslie, Mourie, Shelford and Fitzpatrick, Nicholls was to write that 'the game will always live as an example of what determination and confidence can achieve with the biggest odds facing a team.'

Perhaps the last word should be left to Brownlie: 'Our improved form was due to the week's rest. We had become tired and jaded, because of all the travelling, to which we are not accustomed. So we did very little training and brightened up as the week progressed, with the result we were able to put all our energy into the game.

'In all our matches we have found South Africans most worthy foemen, and we shall carry with us most pleasant recollections of the many hard matches we have enjoyed.'

Brownlie retired from big football after the tour, although he did play for Hawkes Bay against Great Britain in 1930. He played 119 first class games.

## Maurice John Brownlie (Hawkes Bay)

**Captain in four tests, two wins and two losses**
v. South Africa 1928 (1, 2, 3, 4)

**Born:** Wanganui, August 10, 1897.

**Died:** Gisborne, January 21, 1957.

**Position:** Loose forward.

**Represented NZ:** 1922–26, 28 –61 matches (8 internationals).

**Points for NZ:** 63 – 21 tries.

**First-class career:** Hawkes Bay 1921–27, 29, 30 (Hastings club); North Island 1922–25, 27; Hawkes Bay-Poverty Bay 1921; Hawkes Bay-Poverty Bay-East Coast 1923.

**High school:** Sacred Heart College (Auckland) and St Pat's Wellington, First XV 1912, 13.

**All Black player-coaching record:** 1928: South Africa 17, NZ 0; NZ 7, South Africa 6; South Africa 11, NZ 6; NZ 13, South Africa 5.

**Miscellaneous:** Brownlie was also a noted boxer. He was beaten in the 1921 NZ amateur championships heavyweight final by Brian McCleary, who was to join him in the 1924–25 All Black 'Invincibles'.

**Occupation:** Farmer.

1 *Rugger*, W.W. Wakefield.
2 *With the All Blacks in Springbokland 1928*, Mark Nicholls.
3 *Legends*, Terry McLean.

# HERB LILBURNE

## Herb was the youngest ever All Black captain

HERB LILBURNE was only 21 and in his second year with the All Blacks when asked to captain the side. He remains the youngest ever All Black captain.

He would go on to play for the All Blacks for many years and be one of the few players to truly bridge the eras between the passing of the beloved 2–3–2 scrum and the advent of the modern scrum, with its connotations of suppressed attacking backplay.

Another claim to exclusivity was Lilburne's versatility. He began his test career as a first five-eighth, moved out a place for other tests and ended as a test fullback. He would play 40 matches for the All Blacks, including 10 tests. He was still only 26 when, disappointed at missing the great 1935 All Black tour to Britain, he switched to rugby league. He was by then the only current All Black left from the 1920s.

But his only time as the New Zealand captain must have been a knock in confidence for the brilliant young player. He had already amassed a lot of experience. He had first played senior rugby for the Albion club in Christchurch as a 16-year-old and had been introduced into the Canterbury team at 18 in 1926. The next year he was in the side which won the Ranfurly Shield for Canterbury for the first time in its proud history. In 1928 he was part of the historic first All Black tour to South Africa, playing in two of the tests in the tied series.

But he led the All Blacks on to the Sydney Cricket Gound on July 6, 1929 only because of an unusual set of circumstances.

Cliff Porter, the veteran All Black captain famed for his leadership of the 1924 All Black 'Invincibles', had been injured before leaving New Zealand for the Australian tour. He did not play until the second test. The vice-captain, Lilburne's Canterbury team-mate and fellow 1928 All Black tourist, Bill Dalley, had been injured in the second tour game and would not play again on the tour.

Lilburne had his Canterbury team-mates, Charlie Oliver and Sid Carleton, outside him in the backline, but the test would be lost, 8–9. There were extenuating circumstances. This was the first fully representative Australian team since 1914. There were some famous players in the Wallaby team, including the vastly experienced Tom Lawton, who would mark Lilburne and lead Australia. Others were Syd Malcolm, one of the finest halfbacks in the world, and forwards such as 'Wild Bill' Cerutti and Eddie Bonis.

Lilburne's team lacked experience. Unavailable to tour had been Mark Nicholls, Bert Cooke and Fred Lucas, for instance. It was a debut test for a number of players. The famous George Nepia took his place at fullback that day. However, he would suffer a back injury in the match and take no further part in an injury-plagued tour.

The 1929 All Blacks set an unenviable record by becoming the first New Zealand team ever to lose all tests in a series.

A well-built player of 5ft 8in and 12st, with all the running and kicking skills, Lilburne had started his rise to the All Blacks in 1927. Canterbury's North Island tour that year was to include a challenge for the shield with Hawkes Bay. Canterbury had never won the shield, in spite of 10 challenges made since 1904. So there was much disappointment when the Bay,

*PRODIGY UNLEASHED: Herb Lilburne, who had 'all the skills', was 20 when he toured South Africa and had first played senior rugby at only 16*

It won the match, 17–6. But more importantly for players such as Lilburne, it proved a lucky break for the Canterbury players. 'With the shield goes publicity, and it was not surprising that the Canterbury union nominated a good proportion of the team to take part in the extensive trials for South Africa,' explained Jim Burrows, a future All Black coach who would join Lilburne on the tour to South Africa.

Lilburne was one of the stars of the 1927 inter-island match played in superb conditions at Athletic Park, Wellington. It brought a 31–30 win to the South in what is regarded as one of the greatest of the now discontinued inter-island series. Final trials were held a few days later.

Lilburne's province did not hold the shield for long. And interestingly, his transfer to Wellington in 1931, where he stayed through to the end of his rugby career in 1935, meant he missed Canterbury's first long shield tenure from 1931 to 1934 and again in 1935, when the shield began its remarkable 16-year stay in the south of New Zealand. However, he became part of a star-studded Wellington backline.

On the tour of South Africa Lilburne played in 14 of the 22 matches, including the third test at first five-eighth and the fourth at fullback. He played in all three tests on the ill-fated 1929 tour and finished as the leading points scorer with 40 points from eight games.

The competition for places was hot when Great Britain toured in 1930. Lilburne played the first test at first five-eighth, with Bert Cooke and Fred Lucas outside him. But Great Britain upset the All Blacks, 3–6. So he gave way to Mark Nicholls. Nicholls was moved to second five-eighth to allow Archie Strang to play the pivot in the third test. Lilburne regained a place, at second five-eighth, when Nicholls was unavailable for the fourth test.

The brilliant six tries-to-one victory by the All Blacks signalled the end of a fabulous era of attacking rugby. That season marked the end of the road as All Blacks for greats such as Nepia, Lucas, Cooke, Nicholls, Jimmy Mill, 'Bull' Irvine, Ron Stewart, Porter and 'Bunny' Finlayson.

But for Lilburne, still only 22, it was an invitation to greener fields. He moved from Christchurch to Wellington and would become a kingpin in a Wellington backline that

which had held the shield since 1922 and still looked invincible, lost to Wairarapa. But the shield then moved from Wairarapa to Manawhenua.

So Canterbury's match at Palmerston North became a challenge. Canterbury fielded 12 who had worn or were about to wear the silver fern. The team was Harris, Robilliard, Carleton, Steele, Lilburne, MacGregor, Dalley, Scrimshaw, Jackson, White, Godfrey, Pickering, Alley, Clarke and Burrows.

included future All Blacks such as Frank Kilby, 'Rusty' Page, Nelson Ball, 'Bunk' Pollock, Jack Griffiths and 'Joey' Sadler.

Kilby recalled Lilburne as 'a sound footballer in any position and definitely a match-winner. He could adapt himself to any circumstance and few players could size up as quickly as he could the correct tactics necessary to win a game. Often those tactics meant keeping a game tight and spoiling it as a spectacle, but the means suited the end from his point of view.'

In 1931 Lilburne played at second five-eighth in the only test against Australia at Eden Park. The All Blacks were a little fortunate that Ron Bush was able to win the game with his goal-kicking.

There was another tour to Australia in 1932. Lilburne was at fullback for the first test, lost 17–22. It was his only international in that series, which the All Blacks won 2–1. There was no international rugby in 1933. But in 1934 Kilby again took the All Blacks to Australia and Lilburne was on his third tour there.

He appeared at fullback for the second test. The team had a strong Wellington influence, with Kilby at halfback, Page at first five-eighths, Griffiths at second five-eighths and Lilburne at fullback. All four would captain New Zealand in tests. The match, following Australia's resounding 25–11 victory in the first test, was drawn 3–3 to give Australia the series and the Bledisloe Cup. Lilburne had had a chance to retain the trophy late in the game, but his penalty attempt grazed an upright.

So Lilburne's memories of Australian opponents were of very tough, worthy adversaries. The ledger against them was not weighted his way. Still only 26, he was a leading contender for the 1935–36 tour of Britain under manager-coach Vinny Meredith.

The very first edition of the *New Zealand Rugby Almanack* had chosen Lilburne as one of its five players of the year for 1934. 'He is probably the soundest inside back in New Zealand – and his versatility makes him always a valuable man for a tour,' it said. 'This year he should be at the top of his form and he will no doubt make the All Black side for the tour of the British Isles. New Zealand will not have to look far for a captain of her tourists, for Lilburne is one highly capable of leading, and has been vice-captain in two teams.'

But the uncapped Mike Gilbert got the tour as the only fullback and played well in all the tests. Lilburne's vast experience and versatility were sorely missed in a team captained by his old Canterbury team-mate, Jack Manchester.

Among his 100 first-class matches were 20 for Canterbury, 22 for Wellington, two for the South Island, three for the North and 40 for New Zealand.

Lilburne switched to rugby league after missing selection for the great tour and represented New Zealand against Australia in 1935. He moved to Dunedin after World War II, was reinstated to rugby union and coached the Zingari-Richmond club.

## Herbert Theodore Lilburne

**Captain in one test, one loss**
v. Australia 1929

**Born:** March 16, 1908, Burnham.

**Died:** July 12, 1976, Dunedin.

**Position:** Five-eighth and fullback.

**Represented NZ:** 1928–32, 34 – 40 matches (10 tests).

**Points for NZ:** 65 – 6 tries, 12 conversions, 5 penalty goals, 2 dropped goals.

**First-class record:** Canterbury 1926, 27, 29, 30 (Albion); Wellington 1931–35 (Hutt); South Island 1927, 29; North Island 1931–33; NZ Trials 1927, 29, 30, 34, 35.

**Selector/coach/administrator:** Coached Zingari-Richmond club in Dunedin after World War II.

**Other:** Switched to rugby league after missing selection for the 1935–36 All Black tour of Britain and represented New Zealand against Australia in 1935. Reinstated to rugby union after World War II.

**Miscellaneous:** At 21 years and 112 days remains the youngest ever All Black test captain.

**Occupation:** Worked at the Railways, later became a fruiterer.

# ARCHIE STRANG

## *Brilliant five-eighth quit game at peak of his powers*

ARCHIE STRANG was a meteorite of All Black football. Regarded by All Black team-mates as 'a wonderful player to have inside you' Strang accomplished much in his short career, including successfully captaining New Zealand. But he quit the game at the peak of his powers at the age of only 24.

Strang is probably best remembered for his match-winning dropped goal in the second test of the inaugural All Black tour of South Africa in 1928. His effort 10 minutes from fulltime allowed New Zealand to tie the series at one-all when the All Blacks held on to win the test, 7–6.

He had played in the first and second tests as a second five-eighth but was dropped for the third and fourth tests. This was his first experience of the All Blacks. It must have been a huge learning curve for the 21-year-old. Apart for the 1919 New Zealand Army side, no New Zealand rugby team had toured South Africa. But the outstanding record of the Springboks at home and away was well respected. The chairman of selectors, Ted McKenzie, considered the material in the team was better than that of the 1924 side that became the 'Invincibles'.

But no place could be found for Cliff Porter, longtime All Black captain and the side was captained and coached by Maurice Brownlie.

Strang's efforts in the second test won huge acclaim. He was described as 'kicking the winning dropped goal from an accute angle' and 'was outstanding in the backline, snapping up opportunities and exercising ingenuity at all stages.'[1]

Strang's ability to play halfback helped the

*FULL REGALIA: The All Blacks trained in uniform when Herb Lilburne and Archie Strang were integral parts of the side*

1928 All Blacks when Frank Kilby was injured. Strang played five games there. He played 14 of the 22 tour games.

He was not available for the 1929 All Black tour to Australia. Strang was recalled to the All Blacks for the third and fourth tests against the touring Great Britain in 1930, playing in his favoured first five-eighth position. Unusually, the tour consisted of only five matches – a

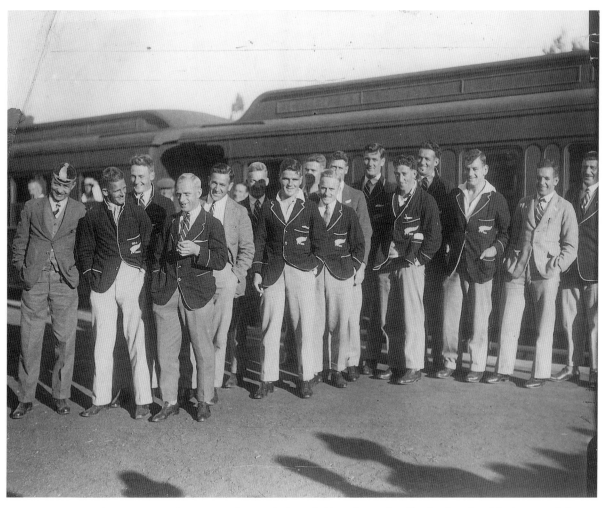

*ONCOURSE SUBSTITUTE: Archie Strang (seventh from left) and Frank Kilby (at his shoulder) enjoyed their first tour when the All Blacks visited South Africa in 1928. When Kilby was badly injured in the 10th tour game, Strang deputised at halfback for the rest of the tour.*

warm-up game against North Otago and four internationals. But New Zealand struggled at first, losing the opening test at Carisbrook, Dunedin 3–6 and scraping home 13–10 at Lancaster Park, Christchurch.

In the third test on a soft Eden Park, Auckland, Strang was to play an unwitting role in an unusual but well executed try in the first half after the Lions had led early. At a scrum on the British 25 Nicholls changed places with Strang, waving left winger Freddy Lucas out wider. From the successful hook, the ball came quickly to Nicholls who punted accurately for Lucas. The flying winger gathered the ball well and eluded his opposite, Morley, and then Bassett, to score under the posts. Strang converted to tie the scores at 5–5 at the interval. But it was Nicholls who had a great game,

orchestrating the play almost at will and helping the All Blacks to a 15–10 victory.

A fortnight later and Strang would play a part in one of the finest victories the All Blacks had produced in a home series. A local-record 40,000 crowd turned up at Athletic Park, Wellington to watch the six-tries-to-one demolition evolve in the final 30 minutes. Cliff Porter and Bert Cooke celebrated by scoring a brace of tries each while Strang kicked two conversions.

Porter, who had led New Zealand teams on many occasions since he captained the 1924 'Invincibles', would retire after the 1930 series. It was also the end of All Black careers for other greats, including George Nepia, Freddy Lucas, Bert Cooke, Nicholls, Freddy Mill, 'Bull' Irvine and 'Bunny' Finlayson.

So Strang was appointed All Black captain to

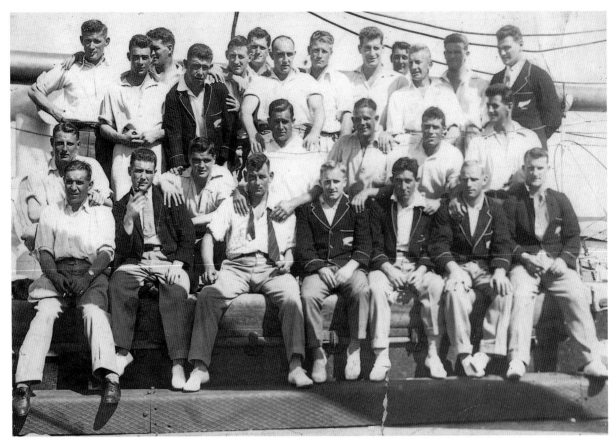

*TRIPLE TREAT: Three future All Black test captains feature in this informal photo taken on the 1928 tour of South Africa. They are Archie Strang (front, third from left), Frank Kilby (front, fifth from left) and Herb Lilburne (front, far right).*

meet the touring Wallabies of 1931. There was only one test, played at Auckland and won 20–13.

The Wallabies were the first fully representative team from Australia since 1913 to tour New Zealand. The revival of the game in Queensland and Victoria had resulted in Australia fielding a winning team for three tests against the touring All Blacks of 1929 as well as one test against the 1930 Lions.

The Wallabies included players such as Alex Ross, Malcolm Blair, Cyril Towers, Syd Malcolm and Bruce Judd, all of whom were veterans of the 1927–28 Waratahs tour of Britain and France. However, by the time of the test, the seventh of 10 tour games, the visitors had won only one match.

There were eight newcomers to the All Blacks – 'Rusty' Page, Ron Bush, 'Kelly' Ball, Frank Solomon, Ted Jessep, George Purdue, Don Max and Tom Metcalfe. Surprise ommissions were Cooke and Nicholls, who had played in the

inter-island game the month before. Hugh McLean and John Hore, who had had fine matches against the Lions the season before, were also considered most unlucky. But the side was expected to win easily.

Instead, it struggled. Only the superb goal-kicking of Ron Bush saved the All Blacks from defeat. The Wallabies' backs enjoyed the fine conditions and outscored New Zealand three tries to two.

Strang retired after that test, aged only 24. His career had been of the meteoric variety – quality rather than quantity. But these were the worst of the Depression years and Strang was unable to obtain leave from his employer to play regularly after 1931.

He had first come to notice as an outstanding schoolboy player, representing Southland Boys' High School's 1st XV in 1929 before the family moved to Timaru and young Strang had three seasons in the Timaru Boys' High 1st XV of 1922–24.

He had come under the wing of the renowned and dual-Boys' High-High School Old Boys' coach, the 1913–14 All Black, E.A. 'Cocky' Cockroft, who had also been influential in the rise of the 1924 Invincible, Ron Stewart, and other eventual All Blacks in Jack Manchester, Clinton Stringfellow and Dave Lindsay (who toured South Africa with Strang in 1928).

Strang had captained South Canterbury on a West Coast tour in his first year out of school.

During his career Strang was equally at home at halfback or either of the five-eighth positions. He was a master tactician. An All Black team-mate said Strang 'was wonderful to have inside you because you always knew he would deliver a perfect pass at the right time and was very much an authority on what was good or bad ball.'

After retirement he coached the Timaru HSOB club and was selector-coach for the Tauranga sub-union and also for army teams during World War II. He worked as a stockbuyer in Timaru but moved to Tauranga in the 1930s, remaining there for more than 50 years.

## William Archibald Strang (South Canterbury)

**Captain in one test, one win**
v. Australia 1931 (1)

**Born:** October 18, 1906, Invercargill.

**Died:** February 11, 1989, Tauranga.

**Position:** Five-eighth and halfback.

**Represented NZ:** 1928, 30, 31; – 17 matches (5 tests).

**Points for NZ:** 44 – 5 tries, 11 conversions, 1 penalty goal, 1 dropped goal.

**First-class record:** South Canterbury 1925–27, 31 (Timaru HSOB), 1929, 30 (Temuka); South Island 1927, 29, 31; NZ Trials 1927, 30.

**High school:** Southland BHS, 1st XV 1921, Timaru BHS 1st XV 22–24.

**Selector/coach/administrator:** Coached Timaru HSOB club and was selector-coach for the Tauranga sub-union and also for army teams during World War II.

**Miscellaneous:** His brother, Jack, represented South Canterbury and the South Island 1935.

**Occupation:** Was a farmer and later a stock buyer.

1 *Centenary*

# FRANK KILBY

## *Kilby was too frank for the martinet*

FRANK KILBY captained the All Blacks on two tours to Australia in the early 1930s and had a long, successful career as a pugnacious and durable halfback.

But his chance to lead the All Blacks on their most important tour of the era – the 1935 tour of Britain – may have been doomed by back-room rugby politics.

So there was some justice when he was able to manage the All Blacks on one of their most successful jaunts through the Home Unions and France many decades later.

Kilby was the dominant captain in New Zealand rugby in the early 1930s, although opinions of the day were divided as to whether Kilby or the Aucklander, Merv Corner, was the better halfback.

Kilby led the All Blacks to Australia in 1932. But both were chosen for the 1934 tour to Australia, with Kilby again captain. But Corner got the nod for the big 1935 tour to Britain, which Kilby missed.

Kilby was considered unlucky not to be chosen to tour Britain in 1935. Critics expected him to be the captain. But the leadership was given to the Canterbury loose forward, Jack Manchester, who, because his province was captained by the 1929–32 All Black hooker, 'Beau' Cottrell, had little captaincy experience. The team fared worst of the three All Black sides to make that tour to that stage.

Manager-coach of the 1935 All Blacks was Vinny (later Sir Vincent) Meredith, a forceful and self-opinionated character, who insisted the players address him as 'Mr Meredith', for instance.

Critics such as the well-informed Terry McLean, whose brother Hugh was an All Black on the 1935 tour, have surmised that once Meredith got the manager's job, there was no room for another forthright character such as Kilby.

Meredith 'had acquired, during years of selecting and coaching club and provincial teams, an autocratic belief in the divinity of his selections,' McLean told the author in 1997. 'Kilby had one disqualification. He knew his own mind. Since no assistant manager or coach was appointed, this quality was sufficient to make him unacceptable to Meredith.'

Manchester was an honest, hard-working player whose mind was too frank and open to compete with Meredith's subtle shifts and manoeuvres, according to McLean.

But Kilby would gain delayed satisfaction 30 years later. In 1963–64 he was a part of the outstanding trio who led the All Blacks on their triumphant tour of Britain and France. As the manager, Kilby worked in tandem with coach Neil McPhail and captain Wilson Whineray. The side played consistently well over the long, 36-match tour and was prevented from achieving the Grand Slam only by a scoreless draw with Scotland.

Kilby's first class career from 1925 to 1936 saw him play for four unions – Southland, Wellington, Wanganui and Taranaki – as well as both South and North Islands. But it was while with Wellington he gained most of his honours.

His career had taken off when he played for Southland in 1925 as a 19-year-old and for the South Island the next year. He moved to Wellington in 1927 and was chosen for the North Island.

It was from that game that Kilby was chosen to tour South Africa in Maurice Brownlie's All Blacks in 1928, a team whose sharing of the series was to remain New Zealand's best effort in that country for more than 60 years. A broken ankle restricted him to only five matches on the

*BORN LEADER: Frank Kilby cleverly led the All Blacks on tours to Australia in 1932 and 1934 but surprisingly missed the big tour to Britain*

*FIRM GRASP: Frank Kilby and Australian skipper Tom Lawton make acquaintance before the first test of the 1932 series*

tour, but Kilby learned much that would carry him through his later career as a captain.

He was only 5ft 6in tall and about 11st, but was described as 'showing up brilliantly, especially when playing behind heavy forwards. In defence he had a wonderful sense of anticipation'.

He captained the 1932 and 1934 All Black teams to Australia. The All Blacks won the 1932 series, but in 1934, after the Wallabies had toured South Africa in 1933, the Wallabies gained a win and a draw in the two test matches.

The 1932 tour came at a time of vast change at the top of New Zealand rugby. The end of New Zealand's greatest era to that time, the 1920s, had come to a grinding halt when there was a mass exodus from All Blacks who had served the side for much of the decade. The 3–1 victory over the British team in 1930 signalled the end for George Nepia, Fred Lucas, Bert Cooke, Mark Nicholls, Jimmy Mill, Cliff Porter,

'Bunny' Finlayson, Ron Stewart and 'Bull' Irvine.

Australian rugby was strong. The Wallabies had whitewashed the All Blacks 3–0 on the 1929 tour of Australia. In the 1930s their rugby was even better and they included true Wallaby greats in Alec Ross, Tommy Lawton and 'Wild Bill' Cerutti in the sides which opposed Kilby's young tourists.

When the All Blacks lost the first test in 1932, it was the first time they had packed a 3–4–1 scrum. The side included Manchester for the first time.

Kilby's leadership, together with that of coach Billy Wallace, enabled the All Blacks to make an impressive recovery from the early reversal, the 17–22 loss to Australia in Sydney. They trounced Australia 21–3 at Brisbane, forcing their selectors to panic. The most dramatic move was the dropping of the captain, Lawton. The All Blacks made certain of taking home the impressive Bledisloe Cup – presented by the then-governor general of New Zealand for play between the two countries – by winning, 21–13.

On that tour, Kilby had several Wellington team-mates in the test backline. 'Rusty' Page played outside Kilby in all three tests while 'Bunk' Pollock at second five-eighth, Nelson Ball on the wing and Herb Lilburne at fullback also played in the series at some stage.

New Zealand did not take part in any international rugby in 1933 but made the tour of Australia in 1934. Kilby was again appointed captain and Page, who played the two tests, was the vice-captain.

But the All Blacks found Australia's test team much stronger than they had two years earlier. The Wallabies had toured South Africa the year before. They had lost 10 of their 23 matches but had performed very creditably in the tests. Australia had lost the five-test rubber to the Springboks, 2–3. But the significant result of the South African tour was it raised Australian standards at the top level. On the 1934 tour the All Blacks lost the first test 11–25 and drew the second, 3–3.

Page led the All Blacks in the first test when Kilby could not play because of a knee injury suffered in the first New South Wales game. Corner played in Kilby's place at halfback.

A bank manager, Kilby served rugby well as an administrator. Included among his many roles were his being on the NZRFU management committee 1955–74.

## Francis David Kilby

**Captain in four test, two wins, a loss and a draw**
v. Australia 1932 (1, 2, 3)
v. Australia 1934 (2)

**Born:** April 24, 1906, Invercargill.

**Died:** September 3, 1985, Wellington.

**Position:** Halfback.

**Represented NZ:** 1928, 32, 34; – 18 matches (4 tests).

**Points for NZ:** 10 – 2 tries, 1 dropped goal.

**First-class record:** Southland 1925, 26, (Star), Wellington 1927, 30–36 (Wellington club); Wanganui 1929 (Pirates); South Island 1926; North Island 1927, 31–33, 35; NZ Trials 1927, 30, 35..

**High school:** Southland BHS, 1st XV 1921, 22.

**Selector/coach/administrator:** Wairarapa RFU management committee 1944, 45; Auckland selector 1951, 52; NZRFU executive 1955–74; manager NZ Maori team to Australia 1958 and 1963–64 All Blacks to Britain and France; elected life member of NZRFU 1976.

**Miscellaneous:** Represented Southland at cricket.

**Occupation:** Bank manager.

# JAMES 'RUSTY' PAGE

## Leadership should have come easily for 'Rusty'

LEADERSHIP SHOULD have come easily to 'Rusty' Page. He had spent his late teens training as an officer at one of the world's great military colleges and would go on to become one of New Zealand's most decorated leaders in World War II. Yet he lost the only test he was called upon to lead the All Blacks.

An outstanding schoolboy footballer, Page had played for Southland Boys' High School's first XV for four years, 1923–26. However, on leaving school he travelled to England to attend the Royal Military College at Sandhurst for the next four years.

While overseas he played for the London Scottish club and was a reserve for the Scottish international team.

He returned to New Zealand in 1930 and began playing for Wellington. At that time Wellington could call on a host of topline five-eighths such as Lance Johnson, Mark Nicholls, Bert Cooke and Brian Killeen.

The following season he was called into the All Blacks to meet the Wallabies at Auckland in the only test of the tour. Page replaced the injured Charlie Oliver. He usually played at first five-eighth but made his maiden international appearance at centre. Oliver had been forced to withdraw the day before the match and Page was rushed to Auckland on the overnight express to arrive on the morning of the match.

It was the first fully representative Australian team to tour since 1913. They had won only one of their six games so the test was expected to be one-sided. However, as so often happens in transTasman encounters, the game proved otherwise and it was only the excellent goal-

*LEADER OF MEN: Rusty Page didn't have much luck as the All Black captain but proved a fine wartime leader and would retire as an army brigadier*

kicking of fullback Ron Bush which kept the All Blacks ahead. The score was 20–13.

In 1932 Page played for Wellington in the

warm-up match for the All Black tour to Australia. Wellington won the game, 36–23. When one of the touring party, George Hart, was injured and forced to withdraw, Page took his place. So he had won his first two All Black selections when others had withdrawn.

Page was chosen in his usual position for the three tests of that tour. He played outside his Wellington team-mate, Frank Kilby, in a side captained by Kilby and coached by the great Billy Wallace.

New Zealand did not take part in any international rugby in 1933 but made a tour of Australia in 1934. Kilby was again appointed captain and Page, who played the two tests, was the vice-captain.

The All Blacks found Australian rugby much stronger than they had two years earlier. The Wallabies had toured South Africa the year before. They had lost 10 of their 23 matches but had performed very creditably in the tests. In fact, Australia had only lost the five-test rubber to the Springboks 2–3.

But more importantly it raised Australian standards at the top level. On the 1934 tour the All Blacks lost the first test 11–25 and drew the second, 3–3.

Page led the All Blacks in the first test when Kilby could not play because of a knee injury suffered in the first New South Wales game. Merv Corner played in Kilby's place at halfback.

With Page at first five-eighth, the All Blacks played Oliver outside him, with a three-quarter line of George Bullock-Douglas, 'Pat' Caughey and George Hart and Arthur Collins at fullback. Hugh McLean was at No 8, with Don Max and Jack Manchester the other loose forwards. Arthur 'Bubs' Knight and Rod McKenzie locked the scrum and Bill Hadley, the hooker, was propped by Artie Lambourn and Jack Hore.

Chosen for the great 1935–36 tour of Britain under the leadership of captain Manchester and manager-coach Vinny Meredith, Page had a wretched tour.

He had taken the team for training on board the *Rangitiki*, this drill increasing with intensity every few days, and was in top physical shape himself when the All Blacks trained at Newton Abbot, the Devonshire town that had also been the starting headquarters for the 1905 and 1924 New Zealand teams.

But a serious knee injury against Midland Counties in the second game of the tour

restricted him to only one more tour appearance. He had to rest the knee until the twenty-first game of the 30-game tour. This was against North of Scotland. He took the field with the knee heavily bandaged and looked to come through the game fairly well. However, he had so aggravated the injury he never played again.

Charlie Oliver, who with Eric Tindill wrote a tour book, said that he was 'convinced that had Page not suffered injury we would have been a far stronger attacking team closer to the scrum.

'He was sadly missed as no other first five-eighth in the side was so quick off the mark and his equal at finding openings.'

He retired having played 18 times for New Zealand, including six tests. His statistics were 5ft 7in and 11st 2lb.

Page had a distinguished military career. He was a lieutenant colonel at the age of 33, commanding officer of the 2nd NZEF 26th Battalion, won the DSO in 1942 and retired from the New Zealand Army with the rank of brigadier in 1963.

## James Russell Page (Wellington)

**Captain in one test, one loss**
v. Australia 1934 (1)

**Born:** May 10, 1908, Dunedin.

**Died:** May 22, 1985, Auckland.

**Position:** First five-eighth or centre.

**Represented NZ:** 1931, 32, 34, 35.

**Points for NZ:** 9 – 3 tries.

**First-class record:** Wellington 1930–34 (Wellington club); North Island 1933; NZ Trials 1934, 35.

**High school:** Southland BHS, 1st XV 1923–26.

**Selector/coach/administrator:** Wellington club president 1963–67, Wellington RFU executive 1947–49 and NZRFU executive 1953–54.

**Miscellaneous:** Honoured with CBE 1954.

**Occupation:** After long peacetime and wartime military career he retired as brigadier in 1963.

# JACK MANCHESTER

## *Manchester's team was on a 'mission impossible'*

JACK MANCHESTER'S reputation as captain has suffered through history because he led an All Black team that was inevitably compared with its two great predecessors.

Manchester captained the All Blacks on their great tour of Britain and Canada in 1935–36, following in the big footsteps of the 1905 All Black 'Originals' and the 1924 'Invincibles'.

When the evidence is examined minutely, it is not hard to see that Manchester's task, because of rising British playing standards and the shape of the tour itinerary, was almost impossible.

There is also a theory, examined below, that the team's management was at fault.

The 1935 All Blacks' results and success rate must be looked at in context with the times. Tours to Britain are commonplace nowadays, but then there had not been a similar tour for 11 years. The public's expectations were high.

British rugby was much stronger and better organised than it had been when the All Blacks made their earlier tours. It had taken two, even three decades for English rugby to recover from the disastrous split of its northern clubs to play Northern Union (later rugby league) in 1895. Most of the best players had been in the north and playing numbers did not climb back until the 1930s. The 1935 team encountered stronger and better organised opposition than had the 1905 and 1924 teams.

A probable influence on the results was that the 1935 All Blacks had played 19 matches in the lead-up to their four tests – far too many. Then they played four tests within nine matches.

They beat Scotland and Ireland handsomely

*LONG LEAD-UP: Jack Manchester's side had too many matches before its first test*

enough, but were then pipped by Wales, 12–13. Welsh wing Geoffrey Rees-Jones was able to

*UP AGAINST IT: Jack Manchester leads Mahoney, McLean, King, Reid and Lambourn out for the Irish test on the 1935–36 tour. Manchester's side met opposition far stronger than its predecessors, the Originals and the Invincibles*

control an awkward bounce over the All Blacks' goal-line to score the decisive try with only six minutes remaining.

The 0–13 England debacle followed. This was the game in which the Russian Prince Obolensky scored two brilliant tries for England. And it is the game that controversial All Black selections may have played a decisive role.

The All Blacks' only other loss was to Swansea, 3–11, in their fifth match. Swansea fielded a pair of brilliant, teenaged inside backs, Haydn Tanner and Willie Davies. In one of the more memorable quotes to filter down through All Black history, Manchester was reported to have said after the Swansea game: 'Write what

you want, but just don't tell New Zealand we were beaten by a couple of schoolboys.'

The All Blacks also drew with Ulster.

Another major problem throughout the tour was the team's scrummaging. The IRB had made the three-fronted scrum compulsory four years earlier. New Zealand's domestic game had been slow, indeed reluctant, to adapt. At international level the All Black forwards, nurtured on the 2–3–2 scrum, could hardly cope.

Another controversial view was that management was the prime cause of Manchester's team's undoing. According to Terry McLean, Vinny Meredith, the coach-manager, 'had acquired, during years of selecting and coaching club and provincial teams, an autocratic belief in the divinity of his selections.'

McLean contended that Frank Kilby, the Wellington and All Black captain during the early 1930s, should have been the captain of the 1935–36 All Blacks. McLean had learned a lot about the tour from his brother, Hugh, who was a member of the team and who died in 1990.

'Kilby had one disqualification. He knew his own mind. Since no assistant manager or coach was appointed, this quality was sufficient to make him unacceptable to Meredith.'[1]

Manchester was an honest, hard-working player whose mind was too frank and open to compete with Meredith's subtle shifts and manoeuvres, according to McLean.

There is little doubt Meredith's autocratic methods when he took the 1935–36 All Blacks to Britain would not have been tolerated by later generations of New Zealand players.

His selections, dropping key players from the final test match of the tour, almost certainly contributed to the biggest loss the All Blacks have ever suffered in Britain.

In 1997 a team member, Jack Griffiths, then aged 85, told the author the All Blacks had seldom had the benefit of Meredith's expertise as a coach.

'He was so involved with official matters that the team did not often benefit from his knowledge at training sessions,' said Griffiths, who would go on to captain the All Blacks and be on the NZRFU executive and council.

'Tactics were left to discussions by team members plus the experience of Jack Manchester, as the captain, and Charlie Oliver, the vice-captain.'

Griffiths denied all knowledge of a 'curfew incident' – that he and other key players had been dropped after missing a New Year's Eve curfew at Porthcawl – and said the decisions were entirely on the basis of form.

But Meredith was a stickler for formality, the All Blacks' attendance at after-match functions and many other formal dinners and occasions being high on his list of obligations. He attended every function himself and expected the majority of the players to do so, although he did operate a roster system whereby a few of the team were excused each function.

But Meredith's insistence the All Blacks wear dinner jackets at formal functions caused derision, both among some of the team and especially in New Zealand. 'New Zealand was still climbing out of the Great Depression. Egalitarianism was all. Dinner suits were snooty,' said McLean. Meredith also insisted the All Blacks call him 'Mr Meredith' at all times.

Standing 6ft 1in and weighing 14st 3lb, Manchester was described as 'a great lineout forward, a tireless worker in the rucks and very fast in the loose.' He also was renowned for an uncanny sense of anticipation.

His 1935 team-mates, Eric Tindill and Oliver said Manchester had had a 'very difficult task. In New Zealand he had always been an outstanding loose forward, but he had to change his style of play by becoming a scummaging forward. He led his forwards well toward the end of the tour, but lacked the necessary experience to be a great leader.'[2]

He had first been selected for the All Blacks for the tour to Australia in 1932. He had made his debut as a replacement in the tour warm-up game against Wellington, in which he scored a try.

A lot of emphasis was placed on this tour to regain the ascendency the All Blacks had almost always had over the Wallabies. The rather fortuitous win over the touring Australians in the only test of their 1931 tour had done little to assuage the bitter memories of the unprecedented 3–0 series loss in 1929.

It was also a period a great transition for the All Blacks. Gone were all the stars of the 1920s such as the Brownlie brothers, Mark Nicholls, Fred Lucas and Bert Cooke, while George Nepia was unavailable. Billy Wallace coached the team.

Manchester played in all three tests on the tour. The All Blacks came back from a first-test defeat to win the second and third tests. They steadily developed into a fine team, setting a points-scoring record by playing attractive football. The memory of the 1929 debacle was well and truly erased, with Manchester one of the fledgling All Blacks to enhance his reputation considerably.

He was an automatic choice for the next All Black tour, again to Australia, in 1934. He appeared in both internationals. However, this team found Australian rugby much stronger than two years earlier. The reason was that the Wallabies had toured South Africa in 1933 while there had been no international rugby for

New Zealand that year. The All Blacks lost the first test and drew the second in the two-test series.

The same selectors who chose the 1934 team were retained to choose the side for the big tour. They discarded 11 of the 25 players from 1934. Manchester was chosen to lead the 1935–36 All Blacks. He captained the All Blacks in 20 of their 30 tour games, including all four tests. This made him the first All Black captain to play in all tests on a tour of Britain.

Manchester returned to captain Canterbury in 1936 and was selected for the first test against the touring Wallabies. But he had to withdraw because of business reasons. He retired after that season.

Manchester had earlier played a part in the Ranfurly Shield's journey in the 1930s. The shield's movement reflected much of New Zealand society's instability and uncertainty of those years. Southland, Wellington, Canterbury (twice), Hawkes Bay and Auckland all had turns with the shield. But only Canterbury, which held it from 1931 to 1934, when it had 16 straight successes, showed any great long-term success.

These were the years of the great economic depression, times were indescribably hard and in the struggle for daily bread rugby wasn't able to loom large in the lives of many young family men.

Manchester was in the Canterbury team that lifted the shield from Wellington in 1931 under the captaincy of All Black Charlie Oliver. He had picked up more leadership tips when 'Beau' Cottrell, an All Black front rower, captained the side that fended off six challenges in 1932. Canterbury had a skilful side, including backs such as George Hart, Oliver and Gordon Innes, and a well-drilled forward pack. Its coach was the former All Black, Jim Burrows, who would go on to become All Black coach against the mighty 1937 Springboks and then a leading military leader in wartime and peacetime.

The Canterbury team continued its splended shield run through 1933, after which Burrows retired as coach. But in the first challenge of 1934, Hawkes Bay – still under the guidance of Norman McKenzie, who had coached it through its magnificent tenure of the 1920s – gained an emphatic 9–0 victory and the shield for the second time.

But years later Lancaster Park patrons still fondly shared the memory of Manchester leaping to seize the ball in a lineout moments after the start of a shield game, turning and flinging it straight to his centre, Oliver, to give Canterbury a shock try.

Manchester finished with 102 first-class games – 59 for Canterbury, three for the South Island, four New Zealand trials and 36 games for New Zealand.

He settled in Dunedin after World War II and coached the University club from 1947 to 1952.

## John Eaton Manchester (Canterbury)

**Captain in four tests, two wins and two losses**
v. Scotland, Ireland, Wales, England 1935–36

**Born:** January 29, 1908 at Waimate.

**Died:** September 6, 1983 at Dunedin.

**Position:** Side-row forward.

**Represented NZ:** 1932, 34–36 – 36 matches (9 tests).

**Points for NZ:** 23 – 7 tries, 1 conversion.

**First-class record:** Canterbury 1928–34, 36 (Christchurch); South Island 1931–33; NZ Trials 1930, 34, 35.

**High school:** Timaru Boys' High School 1st XV 1924–26.

**Selector/coach/administrator:** Coached Otago University 1947–52; Christchurch club life member.

**Occupation:** Dunedin manager of stock firm NMA Ltd.

1 *Legends*

2 *The Tour of the Third All Blacks,* Charlie Oliver and Eric Tindill, Sporting Publications, 1936.

# JACK GRIFFITHS

## *Griffiths was a little man with a big heart*

JACK GRIFFITHS captained the All Blacks in one of their most stylish victories to recover the Bledisloe Cup from their great rival of the late 1920s and early 1930s, Australia.

Griffiths had gained a reputation as 'the little man with a big heart' when he toured Britain with Jack Manchester's All Blacks in 1935–36. It was a difficult tour, against vastly improved sides compared to the teams the 'Originals' and the 'Invincibles' had met.

But the versatile Griffiths repeatedly saved the All Blacks with his big defence. Team-mate Charlie Oliver wrote of him as 'a godsend to us especially on defence. Without him we would have been hopelessly in trouble on many occasions.'[1]

Standing 5ft 8 in and weighing just over 10st, he was renowned for his tackling. 'My opponents at second five-eighth were usually a stone or two heavier than me, but I never had a problem with that,' Griffiths, aged 87, told the author in 1999.

Griffiths was also fortunate his family were deeply involved in rugby and proved a major influence in his formative years. His father, A. J. Griffiths, had played for Wellington in 1904–05 and was an All Black selector in 1920–23. His uncles, Jim (1913–20) and Fred Tilyard (1923) were All Blacks. More importantly, both were five-eighths.

'We used to have lunch with Fred every Saturday when I was a boy,' recalled Griffiths. 'There were plenty of tips about rugby.'

So it was the reputation earned on the great tour that led to him being appointed captain of the All Black team that met the touring Wallabies in 1936. After the All Blacks struggled to an 11–6 win at Wellington, Griffiths' was moved from first to second five-eighth for the Dunedin test, with Otago's Colin Gillies coming into the pivot position and 'Brushy' Mitchell reinstated to centre.

With Australia ahead 13–11 at halftime, Griffiths led the All Blacks to one of their greatest victories, 38–13. The All Blacks scored nine tries. Mitchell, Jack Rankin, George Hart and Tori Reid all scored twice while the flying Otago winger, Jim Watt, got the other.

It had taken Griffiths until his fourth representative season to gain an All Black trial. But he impressed enough to gain a place on the 1934 tour of Australia. He played in the second test at second five-eighth outside his Wellington team-mates, Frank Kilby at halfback and 'Rusty' Page at first five-eighths. Kilby and Page were the tour captain and vice-captain respectively.

The tour proved tough. Australian rugby was strong. It had beaten the touring All Blacks three tests to nil in the series of 1929 while New Zealand had clawed back some pride with a 2–1 win in 1932. With Kilby injured, the All Blacks, still fielding a very experienced team, were trounced 11–25 in the first test. This was the heaviest defeat by an Australian side over New Zealand. In 1893 New South Wales had beaten New Zealand 3–25. It would take the Wallabies nearly 30 years – until 1964 and their 20–5 victory – to gain a bigger win.

The All Blacks only managed to salvage a draw from the second test because of some excellent work by Griffiths. He had raced through the Australian forwards early in the second half before transferring the ball to hooker Jack Hore when his progress was halted. Hore scored to even the score at 3–3, the final score. So the Bledisloe Cup passed to Australia, though it would be the last time for many years.

Griffiths therefore went on the great tour of Britain in 1935–36 as the second-string first five-eighth to Page. But Page injured a knee so

*EXALTED COMPANY: Jack Griffiths (with ball) is captain of this NZEF wartime team. Immediately behind him is Tom Morrison, his 1938 All Black team-mate and future All Black coach and NZRFU chairman. Seated, extreme right, is Jim Burrows, 1928 All Black and All Black coach against the Springboks in 1937.*

badly early in the tour he made only one more appearance and retired from rugby after the tour. Overall, Giffiths played 16 tour matches, 10 at first five-eighth, five at second five-eighth and one at centre.

He was not chosen for the final international, against England, when Eric Tindill took his place. The actions of the tour manager, Vinny Meredith, especially his selections, dropping key players from that final test, have come under scrutiny from critics over the years. It has been said Meredith almost certainly contributed to the biggest loss the All Blacks had ever suffered in Britain.

McLean claimed that Meredith had put a ban on three key players for disciplinary reasons. Interviewed in 1997 by the author, and recently knighted for services to journalism, Sir Terry said the main source of information for his viewpoint was his brother, Hugh McLean, an

All Black who was on the 1935 tour and who died in 1990.

According to the McLeans, the All Blacks had retired to Porthcawl to prepare for the England test on January 4. The Porthcawlians put on a bang-up New Year's party. Meredith had laid down a curfew of midnight for the team to be back at their hotel and he stayed up to see it was strictly observed. Though, it is said, other team members returned even later, Meredith caught halfback Joey Sadler, winger George Hart and Griffiths – who had all played in the previous three tests – returning late.

However, the rugby historians, Chester and McMillan, attributed the trio's absence from Twickenham solely to a loss of form.[2]

The tour book by Oliver and Tindill also strongly supports this. It makes no mention of any incident like the one McLean described. That might not be surprising, since the authors would not have wanted to 'rock the boat' as concerns their own All Black futures, and were clearly at odds with the opinions of other team members in summing up Meredith's strengths and weaknesses.

Griffiths denied all knowledge of the 'curfew incident' and said he had been dropped entirely on the basis of form.

In spite of his 1936 triumphs, and a strong game in a beaten Wellington side the week before the first test, Griffiths was unable to break into the All Black team that lost the series 1–2 to the touring Springboks in 1937. The seven national selectors stuck with Otago's Dave Trevathen and Canterbury's Jack Hooper as the five-eighths throughout the series.

Griffiths had captained Wellington in the 0–29 loss, but 'was noticeable for his consistently good defence and well-judged kicks. Had it not been for the captain's solid tackling, the home team would have been beaten by a much wider margin.'[3]

But he made a comeback the following year when the All Blacks toured Australia. Though he was not a first-choice in a classy backline that contained Trevor Berghan and Jack Sullivan as the five-eighths and Brushy Mitchell at centre, Griffiths came back, at second five-eighth, for the third test when Mitchell was hurt and Sullivan moved to centre. The All Blacks won the series, 3–0.

A bank manager often on transfer, Griffiths gave plenty of time back to rugby after his serious playing days were over. He served as Poverty Bay selector in 1939. After World War II he served on the Manawatu and Wanganui management committees and on the NZRFU Council from 1961–65 and the Executive Committee from 1965–72.

While in North Africa, he captained the 19th Infantry Battalion to win the Freyberg Cup in 1940 and the 2nd NZEF team to beat Combined Services in 1940.

He had a distinguished war career, rising to the rank of major and winning the MC and being mentioned in despatches. He served as ADC to General Freyberg.

Griffiths was retired and living with his wife, Jean, in Paraparaumu, in 1999.

## Jack Lester Griffiths (Wellington)

**Captain in two tests, two wins**
v. Australia 1936 (1, 2)

**Born:** April 9, 1912, Wellington.

**Position:** Five-eighth or centre.

**Represented NZ:** 1934–36, 38 – 30 matches (7 tests).

**Points for NZ:** 50 – 3 tries, 14 conversions.

**First-class record:** Wellington 1931–38 (Poneke); North Island 1934, 36; NZ Trials 1934, 35, 37.

**High school:** Wellington College, 1st XV 1928.

**Selector/coach/administrator:** Poverty Bay selector 1939; Manawatu and Wanganui management committees; NZRFU Council 1961–65; NZRFU executive committee 1965–72.

**Other:** Distinguished war career, rising from a private to the rank of major, winning the MC and being mentioned in despatches; served as ADC to General Freyberg.

**Miscellaneous:** Between 1929 and 1954 the All Blacks had 16 test captains of which only Griffiths and Johnny Smith were North Island-born. While in North Africa, captained the 19th Infantry Battalion to win the Freyberg Cup 1940 and the 2nd NZEF team to beat Combined Services 1940. Played Hawke Cup cricket for Wanganui 1950–53. His father, A.J. Griffiths, represented Wellington 1904, 05 and was an All Black selector 1920–23. His uncles, Jim (1913, 20) and Fred Tilyard (1923) were All Blacks.

**Occupation:** Bank manager.

1 *The Tour of the Third All Blacks*
2 *Centenary*
3 *The Visitors,* Chester and McMillan, Moa, 1990.

# RON KING

## *Boks blotted the King's fine record*

RON KING was the captain of the All Blacks when they were humiliated by the 1937 Springboks. But it should be remembered Philip Nel's South African team remains perhaps the finest international side ever to tour New Zealand – a team with the power, the skills, the speed and the rugby brains to put even the 1971 British Lions in the shade.

King was one of New Zealand's outstanding forwards during the 1930s. He had been an All Black since 1934.

But the decision of the New Zealand selectors to appoint him as captain for such a major series has been called into question by historians. The question of whether South Africa or New Zealand was fit to call itself the 'world champion' had still not been decided. The 1921 series in New Zealand had been tied and so had the 1928 series in South Africa.

King's appointment 'seems a staggering decision in hindsight. It's true that injuries forced the selectors' hands a little, but even so, to name a captain as quiet and introspective a personality as the West Coaster was surely not the best option.'[1]

All Black team-mates remembered him as a shy fellow who, when he could be enticed out of his shell, would amuse them with tales of his gold-mining fortunes on the West Coast. 'To a stranger he could seem gruff, but those who knew him said he was a pleasant chap, concerned with making sure he didn't let down the team.'

The new skipper led by example, giving a tigerish display in each of the tests – as he was to do in all his All Black appearances. But the Springboks went from strength to strength, aided by shrewd selections and the clever strategy of their leaders, Philip Nel and Danie Craven.

King had the former All Black hooker and

*MISSION IMPOSSIBLE: Ron King had perhaps the hardest task in the history of the All Black captains*

successful Canterbury Ranfurly Shield coach, Jim Burrows, as the All Black coach. After the All Blacks won the first test at Athletic Park, 13–7, Burrows was joined by Billy Wallace, who had coached the All Blacks earlier in the decade. He was made assistant manager and coach of the backs, all of whom were uncapped before the first test.

The move enabled Burrows to concentrate on moulding the forwards, but it was to no avail. The Springboks improved as their tour moved on. They won the second test 13–6 at Lancaster Park. At Eden Park in the third test, the big Bok pack humbled the All Blacks in a one-sided display, allowing Craven to give one of his greatest displays in serving a fleetfooted backline. South Africa scored five tries to nil to win 17–6 to rightly claim the fictitious world crown.

As Burrows recalled in his 1974 autobiography, *Pathway Among Men*, of series between the two countries, 'They were the best team to visit New Zealand. For their all-round good football they deserved all the praise showered on them. They left us with a message that rang loud and clear throughout the land – you cannot score points in rugby unless you gain possession of the ball.

'We knew what we were up against in the scrums, but we didn't have the Springbok technique, nor did we have any front row men the size of the Springboks. We played the best front row available, and they were all excellent forwards, but they were much smaller than their opponents.'

'Brushy' Mitchell, the Southland winger, would probably have captained the first-test team, but was injured after having to play in three trial games after a brilliant display in the inter-island match – the necessity for which was known only to the national selectors. Another captaincy prospect, halfback Joey Sadler, was also out injured and never played again.

New Zealand was unstinting in its praise for the South Africans, whom it called the greatest team ever to leave New Zealand. The All Blacks had been beaten by a superior and very great side, it was agreed.

In analysing the difference between the two countries it was to be found that New Zealand's forward play was too loose, its knowledge of the 3–4–1 scrum still too sketchy and it did not have the players big enough to handle the Bok scrummagers.

As Artie Lambourn, the Wellington hooker who played in all three tests, recalled of the Springbok pack years later: 'It was different to any the All Blacks of that era had played against. It was a scrummaging machine, very difficult to scrum against. Firstly, they were all

*ON WITH THE GAME: Ron King became a New Zealand selector in 1957–60*

big men, and strong. Secondly, they all had absolute concentration. We had never come up against such big props before. We just didn't have any props that big.'

King had begun his career a decade earlier. He played for West Coast as a wing in 1928, while still at Hokitika District High. But over the next few seasons he was unable to hold a place in the rep team. He played twice in 1929 and once in 1931.

King stood 1.88m (6ft 2in) and weighed 88.9kg (14st). So he switched to the forwards in 1931. His strong build and speed proved an instant success. He played in the Coast's full seven-match programme in 1932 and in six matches the following winter.

He first won All Black honours on the 1934 tour of Australia under the captaincy of Frank Kilby. He had turned in a fine game in the South Island trial in Oamaru and repeated that form in the North-South game at Auckland.

The second test of that tour began an unbroken sequence of 13 test appearances for King right up until the outbreak of World War II.

After the tour of Britain in 1935–36, the tour book by Charlie Oliver and Eric Tindill, King's team-mates, described him as 'the best of our forwards for general play. Always fit, he proved an excellent lock and excelled in every department of the game. We could not have done without him.'

King played 25 of the 30 tour matches, more than any other forward. Only the fullback, 'Mike' Gilbert, played more with a total of 27. King and Gilbert, coincidentally, were the last West Coast players to represent the All Blacks.

Winston McCarthy said King was 'a magnificent specimen – big, fast and tough'.

King had had to leave the field with a shoulder injury in the test against England. But with no replacements allowed, he returned to the field a few minutes later and, though clearly struggling, helped prevent the Englishmen from running up more points than their eventual record 13–0 victory.

He formed an outstanding partnership with Tori Reid. They would lock the All Black scrum in every test on the tour, against Australia in 1936 and in the three tests against the Springboks the following year. The pair returned from the tour with reputations as powerhouse forwards who asked no favours and gave few in return.

King played in the tests against the touring Australians in 1936 and then was honoured with the captaincy in 1937. He toured Australia with the All Blacks in 1938 in a team captained by 'Brushy' Mitchell.

King would have been a certainty for the 1940 tour of South Africa. The team was selected by Norm McKenzie, the only sole selector in the history of All Black rugby. But McKenzie, also an All Black coach and coach of the fabulous Hawkes Bay team of the 1920s, declined ever to make public the side he had chosen.

The big, mobile West Coaster played 42 matches for the All Blacks, including 13 tests, between 1934–38.

He continued to play for the West Coast through World War II until 1945 – a span of 18 seasons. When his speed diminished he still showed his strength with bullocking runs and remained a fine tackler. He had played 70 games for the Coast, often in losing sides, yet he usually managed to stand out.

Without a break from the game, King took up coaching the West Coast in 1946 and continued an unbroken run through to 1952. He later became a South Island selector and then a New Zealand selector from 1957–60.

## Ronald Russell King (West Coast)

**Captain in three tests, one win and two losses**
v. South Africa 1937 (1, 2, 3)

**Born:** August 19, 1909 at Waiuta.

**Died:** January 10, 1988 at Greymouth.

**Position:** Lock.

**Represented NZ:** 1934–38 – 42 matches (13 tests).

**Points for NZ:** 21 – 7 tries.

**First-class record:** West Coast 1928–39 (Hokitika Excelsior), 1940–45 (Cobden); South Island 1934, 36–39; NZ Trials 1934, 35, 37; West Coast-Buller 1937.

**High school:** Hokitika District High School 1st XV 1924–28.

**Selector/coach/administrator:** Selector-coach West Coast 1946–52, 64, 66; South Island selector 1952–60; NZ selector 1957–60.

**Other:** King, with fellow 1935–36 team-mate, fullback 'Mike' Gilbert, were the last of West Coast's seven All Blacks.

**Miscellaneous:** A brother, A. King, played for West Coast.

**Occupation:** A gold miner when he first became an All Black, King later became the proprietor of King's Hotel, Greymouth for many years.

# BRUSHY MITCHELL

## Brushy's All Black cap made up for woes of the father

**B**RUSHY MITCHELL'S leadership on the unbeaten tour of Australia in 1938 capped off a great career. It also helped New Zealand restore some of the national pride so battered by the unprecedented anihilation of the All Blacks by the Springboks the previous year, an experience that for Mitchell had also been the nadir of his time in the game.

The son of a fine player who had been chosen for an All Black tour but who never played for them, Mitchell was renowned as a splendid wing or centre with strength, speed, deception and determination. The doyen of New Zealand rugby scribes, Sir Terry McLean, included Mitchell among the 15 All Blacks he called his *New Zealand Rugby Legends* in 1987.[1]

'Many a time I have seen him emerge triumphant with the ball when as many as six or seven of the opposition have confronted him,' said Eric Tindill, a 1935–36 All Black team-mate. 'He possessed a deceptive swerve, dummied well and had a good body wiggle.'[2]

Educated at Waihopai and St George Schools and Southland Boys' High School, Mitchell played in the first XV in 1928–29. He made his representative debut in 1932.

In 1934, in the inter-island fixture at Dunedin, Mitchell took his first big step up to stardom, landing two tries in the South's six-try, 27–20 victory. With the big tour approaching, a learned authority such as Norman McKenzie, the famous Hawkes Bay coach and future All Black coach, could write in the *New Zealand Free Lance*: 'Mitchell is a big fellow, difficult to upset, fairly pacy, young and just the one to improve on such a tour.'

On the 1935–36 All Black tour of Britain

*NO SOFTIE: A strong and deceptive wing or centre, Brushy Mitchell helped revive New Zealand spirits after the hammering the touring Springboks had handed out*

under manager-coach Vinny Meredith, Mitchell

was said to be the most improved player in the team. After 22 matches and 12 tries, including all the internationals, he emerged as 'a rugged, fiery, steely three-quarter' who had played seven times at centre and 15 times as wing. 'He was a typical Jack Steel type,' said team-mate Charlie Oliver. 'Right from his first game, Mitchell played really outstanding football,' added Tindill.

Mitchell was available for only one of the two tests against Australia in 1936. Playing at centre in the Carisbrook test, he scored two of the All Blacks' nine tries. Australia, which had lost the first test by only 11–6, was crushed 38–13.

Mitchell was at the peak of his powers at the start of what all New Zealand hoped would be a momentous 1937 season against the touring Springboks. He aided the South Island to a superb victory over the North, 30–21, five tries to two. But the intense All Black trials that followed during the next week took a terrible toll when Mitchell suffered a knee cartilage injury, was unfit to play for several weeks and was therefore unavailable for the first two tests.

With Jim Burrows now coach of the All Blacks, they won the first test at Wellington, 13–7. Two brilliant tries by centre Jack Sullivan meant the All Blacks were sniffing a series victory when they led the second test in Christchurch, 6–nil, at halftime. But Philip Nel's men battled back strongly to take the match, 13–6, and set up the great expectations for the final test in Auckland.

The New Zealand selectors were desperate for Mitchell to be available for the decider. They pulled him up from Dunedin to play in Auckland before the test. He scored a try for an Auckland XV against Combined Services and looked to have regained his old form. But his still heavily bandaged knee did cause the selectors to worry.

'We talked it over for a long time, several times,' said Burrows years later. 'We wanted to play him, yet we were cautious. Would 'Brushy' stand up to what was certain to be a rugged, demanding, physical contest? Believe it or not, in those days, there was no provision for the selectors to use, or consult, medical advisers. We had to go on what we saw of Mitchell in the preceding week.

'Well, we all know what happened. Within minutes of the kickoff, 'Brushy' became a

passenger. We were reduced to 14 men. The All Blacks had no chance. It was our mistake, the selection panel. All I can say is we acted for the best.'[3]

Mitchell had to move from centre to wing but could not run at full speed. He could not get near to the Springboks' speedy Dai Williams on several occasions. The South Africans played brilliantly that day, scoring a five-tries-to-none 17–6 victory which in the latter stages had the All Black forwards down to a dejected walk.

But Mitchell, the captain, and Alex McDonald, the coach, formed an outstanding combination on the 1938 All Black tour of Australia. McDonald, an All Black of the 1905–06 Originals' tour and captain of the All Blacks on their 1913 North American tour, had co-coached the All Blacks against the touring Springboks in 1921 and would go on to coach the ill-fated 1949 All Blacks as a 66-year-old.

But his 1938 team was unbeaten in nine matches in Australia. The Wallabies were strong at this time. In 1937 New South Wales had beaten the Springboks, on their way to New Zealand, and the Wallabies had lost the tests by fairly slim margins, 5–9 and 17–26.

New Zealand fielded perhaps one of its best backlines in history, with Charlie Saxton and Trevor Berghan in the halves, Jack Sullivan and Mitchell in midfield, Tommy Morrison and Bill Phillips on the wings and Jack Taylor at fullback in the first two tests. Johnny Dick and Jack Griffiths came into the third test team.

'In the last 50 years, no All Black backline has been superior. It might rank with the line of the '24 'Invincibles' though none would dare compare it with the number one lineup of 1905,' wrote McLean in his *Legends*.

Mitchell was right back to his best. Australian writers said he was the finest international three-quarter to have toured since World War I. It must have made him feel good, especially after his tribulations the year before at both national and provincial levels.

Mitchell had become the victim of the fanaticism the Ranfurly Shield engenders in 1937. He played for Southland from 1932–34, 1936 and 1937 and would transfer to Otago in 1938 and 1939. These provinces dominated New Zealand rugby like no others, excepting perhaps Auckland in the 1960s and 1980s–1990s and Hawkes Bay in the 1920s. From 1935 to 1950 no one except Otago or

*NURTURE COLLEGE: Southland Boys' High was a great nursery for All Blacks in the first half of the 20th century. Brushy Mitchell (right), Frank Kilby (left) and Billy Stead were three All Black captains who learned their rugby trade there*

Southland held the shield, a remarkable 16-year span which of course included World War II. The rivalry between the two, particularly in the 1930s, was exceptional. The 'local derbies' were unsurpassed in the history of the trophy.

'Great expeditions by train and car went from one city to the other, according to the shield's ownership of the time, and the two provinces were totally committed to the last man, woman and child,' wrote McLean in *Legends*.

In 1937, Mitchell had been hurt in the All Black trials. Southland challenged Otago for the shield on July 31, several weeks before the test series was to begin. The NZRFU instructed Southland not to play Mitchell but he yielded to pressure. Twenty minutes into the game Mitchell made his first big move and a try seemed inevitable. But faced with one defender, he felt his hamstring give out and limped from the field. Mitchell's replacement, Artie Wesney, would score eight of the points Southland totalled to claim the shield, 12–7.

The Southland team members were treated as triumphant heroes on their return to Invercargill but Mitchell's reception was different. A rumour spread that he had tried to 'sell' the game to Otago. When he took his turn to lift the shield aloft at the railway station, the crowd broke into a deafening boo.

'The hell with that,' Mitchell whispered to a team-mate, handing over the shield. Unobtrusively, he drifted to the back of the throng, exited out the rear of the carriage and bemusedly walked home. It was said Invercargill's small boys mercilessly taunted him for days, saying he 'tried to sell the shield.'

He would never play for a Southland team again. But he played for Otago when it lost the shield to Southland in 1938 and when it failed in its 1939 challenge against his old team.

He had been injured near the end of the Australian tour and had not played the third test. Meanwhile, Otago regained the shield in the first challenge of 1938, 7–6, only to lose it back to Southland after six defences, 10–5. Southland would repulse Otago's 1939 challenge, 23–4, and would not lose the shield until the first challenge (Otago won 17–11) of 1947.

But it was with great relief he had returned to his country a hero once more after leading his country in the 1938 tour of Australia, though more worldly-wise about the fickle nature of the fans.

Mitchell went off to the war in the desert. In 1950 he was running a family pub at Washdyke, near Timaru. He coached the South Canterbury team in 1950 and 1951. On September 16, 1950 South Canterbury won the Ranfurly Shield from Wairarapa at Masterton. However, North Auckland lifted the shield at the first challenge on September 30.

Mitchell had married his wife, Pixie, in 1945. She had been married to Cyril Pepper, also an All Black and team-mate of Mitchell's on the 1935–36 tour. Mitchell had been godfather to their daughter, Betsey. Pepper, who had been awarded the Military Cross for bravery at the Battle of Sidi Rezegh, was terribly wounded in a later battle and was invalided home. He died on May 31, 1943.

Mitchell's father, Alf, played rugby for Otago 1908–10 and Southland 1911–12. He was chosen for the 1910 All Blacks to tour Australia but was unable to travel. According to Terry McLean the reason was that Alf Mitchell had been ordered off in the club game a week or so before the All Blacks' departure.[4]

## Neville Alfred 'Brushy' Mitchell (Otago)

**Captain two tests, two wins**
v. Australia 1938 (1, 2)

**Born:** Invercargill, November 22, 1913.

**Died:** Auckland, May 21, 1981.

**Position:** Threequarter.

**Represented NZ:** 1935–38 – 32 matches (8 tests).

**Points for NZ:** 60 – 20 tries.

**First-class record:** Southland 1932–34, 36, 37 (Old Boys); Otago 1938, 39 (Alhambra); South Island 1934, 37, 38; NZ Trials 1934, 35, 37.

**High school:** Southland BHS, 1st XV 1928, 29.

**Selector/coach/administrator:** South Canterbury selector 1950–51.

**Miscellaneous:** Represented Southland at cricket. His father, Alf, was selected for the 1910 All Blacks' tour of Australia but did not travel. An uncle, Jack, also represented Otago.

**Occupation:** A hotel manager, later became a bookseller and then a wholesale liquor merchant in Auckland.

1, 3, 4 *Legends*
2 *The Tour of the Third All Blacks*

# ROD McKENZIE

## Rod helped lift New Zealand from depths of despair

A FTER A long All Black career Rod McKenzie was accorded the honour of captaining the team in a match that would prove the last test for the entire side.

McKenzie was the hardest-worked player in the 1938 All Blacks who toured Australia in 1938 under the leadership of coach Alex McDonald and captain 'Brushy' Mitchell. This was a team which would quickly wipe away the memories of the previous year, breaking scoring records on an unbeaten tour.

Standards were high, as well, because most of the side had their sights on the upcoming 1940 tour of South Africa, but were soon to find themselves embroiled in a much more serious campaign. None of this team would ever play for the All Blacks again.

The team was compared favourably with the 1937 Springboks, who had been closely held by Australia in the tests.

McKenzie played in all but one of the tour games, at siderow or lock, and emerged as one of the outstanding tourist forwards with King, Harold Milliken and Les George. The classy All Black backline included Charlie Saxton, Trevor Berghan, Jack Sullivan, Tom Morrison and Mitchell.

A strained leg kept Mitchell out of the third test and McKenzie was accorded the honour of leading the All Blacks in a test. The match was convincingly won, 14–6.

So, ironically, McKenzie, an honest toiler with few pretensions to greatness, had led an outstanding All Black team in which a number of players would exhibit leadership skills of the highest ranking in the years to come. These included Saxton, who would captain the Kiwis

*WE WUZ ROBBED: Like so many others, Rod McKenzie was robbed of much of his test career by the war*

army team and manage the great 1967 All Blacks in Britain and France, and Sullivan and Morrison, who would both go on to become

*ON THE DOUBLE: Rod McKenzie (shown front row, sixth from left) became a 'double' international when he represented Scotland against England in a wartime international*

coach of the All Blacks and chairman of the NZRFU.

McKenzie had played for five years for the All Blacks by 1938. The Manawatu player had gained his first All Black jersey in 1934 when he toured Australia in the side captained by Frank Kilby, who had led the All Blacks on a highly successful tour there only two years earlier. But this time the All Blacks found the Australians much improved for they had toured South Africa in 1933, winning two of the five tests. The Wallabies had stars such as captain and fullback Alex Ross, centre Cyril Towers and halfback Syd Malcolm, while in the pack were former All Black Ted Jessep at prop, hooker Eddie Bonis and second rower 'Weary' Dunlop.

This tour was to provide vital preparation for the All Blacks' tour of Britain in 1935, but disappointingly, only 14 team members were able to win selection. However, among the other first-time All Blacks in 1934 were McKenzie,

Bill Hadley, Ron King, Artie Lambourn and Jack Griffiths – all of whom would develop splendidly and serve New Zealand well in the coming years.

McKenzie had played in the first 1934 test as a 6ft, 15st lock. The All Blacks made a fine start to this game in Sydney, watched by 40,000 spectators, and led 11–6 at halftime. But that was the end of the scoring for them as the Wallabies surged back to add another 19 points and take the game, 25–11. The second test was drawn, 3–3, but McKenzie had been playing on the side of the scrum for the tourists by then and King and Don Max locked the test scrum.

He was chosen for the 1935–36 All Black team which toured Britain under the captaincy of another flank forward, Jack Manchester. This side struck British rugby at its strongest. It had at long last recovered from successive catastrophies such as the schism which led to rugby league (when the number of North

*HOT ROD: Rod McKenzie was at his rampaging best on the 1938 tour of Australia*

England clubs was decimated), World War I (which claimed many international players among the casualties) and the Depression (which decimated Welsh rugby in particular).

Managed by the controversial and autocratic Vinny Meredith, the team had to play 19 matches before the first of its four internationals. It beat Scotland and Ireland, but may have been stale by the time it was pipped by Wales, 12–13, and beaten by England, 0–13, still the largest margin scored against an All Black team in Britain.

McKenzie played 15 tour games, including the Scottish international, where he played on the side of the scrum. He emerged as the highest scorer among the touring forwards with a tally of five tries and a goal from a mark.

In the Scottish test, he helped the All Blacks to an 18–8 victory in which Pat Caughey scored three tries from wing. Fellow forwards Manchester, Jack Hore and Hadley played outstandingly well.

McKenzie was described by Charlie Oliver, who was the vice-captain and wrote a book with another team member, Eric Tindill, on the tour, as 'a fine loose forward … Always in the picture and played harder football than anyone.'

He was regarded by team-mates as a great humourist and practical joker. Known as 'Big Mac' back home, McKenzie gained another nickname, 'Squire', on that tour. The social side brought the team into frequent contact with Britain's landed upper classes. Not to be outdone in the acreage 'Who's Who' stakes, he invested himself with a considerable but imaginary estate back home in New Zealand. He told an English baron he 'farmed on Lambton Quay.'

Mike Gilbert, the fullback on that tour, recalled how McKenzie, who worked for the Post Office, sometimes received telegrams, usually about quite mundane subjects. 'But Rod would smite his brow, look absolutely devastated and proclaim to the Brits, 'Another earthquake in New Zealand. That's 5000 of my sheep lost.''

McKenzie had also made somewhat different financial arrangements to his fellow tour team members. It is believed he gave his money to Mr Meredith to look after. He could then 'touch him up' whenever he needed funds. Others had their funds with a New Zealand bank which was not always accessible. 'So McKenzie lent a few bob to guys who were short. He told me, with some satisfaction, that he, a humble Palmerston North postman, had helped out team-mate Pat Caughey (later Sir Harcourt Caughey, of the wealthy Caughey family of Smith & Caughey department store fame) when Caughey was short of the readies,' said Bob Luxford, the curator of the New Zealand Rugby Museum, Palmerston North.

In 1936 the Wallabies toured New Zealand and McKenzie made the first test side, which struggled for the win, 11–6, at Athletic Park. Ron Ward took McKenzie's place for the second test, in which the All Blacks eventually romped to an outstanding nine-try, 38–13 victory at Carisbrook.

With former All Blacks Jim Burrows and Billy Wallace as coaches, the All Blacks faced the might of the touring Springboks in 1937. The size of the South African pack clearly troubled the New Zealand selectors. Otago's Alan Parkhill, at No 8, and McKenzie and Canterbury's outstanding but lighter Jack Rankin were the preferred loose trio. But Ward took Rankin's place for the first test when Rankin fell ill. Rankin was dropped for Ward for the deciding test.

But the All Blacks were clearly outclassed in the front row, as well as other areas of the game, as the series unfolded. Tied at one-all, the third test at Eden Park attracted a record 58,000 people but the great Springboks had reduced the All Black pack to a 'shambling rabble' by the end after calling for scrums rather than lineouts (as the rules allowed) and scoring a five-tries-to-nil 17–6 victory. However, McKenzie had done well in the lineouts. So he was a certainty to be retained the following year, when the Australian tour provided New Zealand the chance to assuage the bitter 1937 memories.

Danie Craven, the Springbok halfback on the 1937 tour who became the South African coach and longtime South African chairman and IRB delegate, selected McKenzie as first-choice flanker in his 'world' team in one of his many books, *Springboks Down the Years*.

'Hard-working in the scrum, deadly round the scrum and always wherever the ball touched the ground, this hard and strong loose forward would be a credit to the side,' wrote Craven.

McKenzie would have been a certainty to tour South Africa in 1940 had World War II not intervened. Though in his mid-30s, McKenzie still enjoyed top-level rugby near the end of the war while based in Britain. He played for New Zealand Services in 1944 and 1945, Combined Dominions in 1945 and twice for Scotland in service internationals in 1945.

He played his last first-class game in 1945 before returning home. His career had spanned 16 years and at the time only five players had exceeded his tally of 129 first-class matches. He had scored 38 tries, 21 for Manawatu, which was a record.

McKenzie later coached the Kia Toa senior club side and was also president of the Manawatu RFU.

McKenzie died in Palmerston North in March 2000, aged 90. He had been living in Ranfurly Home, Auckland.

## Roderick McCulloch McKenzie (Manawatu)

**All Black captain in one test, one win**
v. Australia 1938, third test

**Born:** September 16, 1909, Rakaia.

**Died:** March 2000, Palmerston North.

**Position:** Siderow and lock.

**Represented NZ:** 1934–38 – 35 matches (9 tests).

**Points for NZ:** 36 points – 11 tries, 1 goal from a mark.

**First-class record:** Manawhenua 1930–32 (Kia Toa), Manawatu 1933–39 (Kia Toa); North Island 1933, 34, 37–39; NZ Trials 1934, 35, 37, 49; NZ Services 1944, 45; Scottish Services 1945.

**Miscellaneous:** Played two international for Scottish Services in 1945. His brother, Jack, also represented Manawatu.

**Occupation:** Was a mailroom supervisor with the Post Office.

# FRED ALLEN

## *Shattered Fred heaved boots into the ocean*

FRED ALLEN became New Zealand's most successful coach when he guided the All Blacks to 14 victories out of 14 in the late 1960s. He had earlier captained the All Blacks in every one of the 21 matches he played for New Zealand. But if Allen's seems like the perfect rugby career, he would be the first to stress it wasn't.

Rugby is usually a character builder and Allen's career showed it was. After captaining Canterbury as a 19-year-old 'prodigy' in 1939, he went off to World War II like many another young player. He served in the Solomon Islands and Egypt as a lieutenant, was wounded twice, and discovered the self-discipline that would later carry him to footballing and business success.

Allen would emerge as a more brilliant but mature five-eighth. After the triumphant tour with the Kiwis, Allen became the All Blacks' first post-war captain. His team beat the touring Wallabies in both tests in 1946 and the following year he led the All Blacks on an outstanding tour of Australia.

Allen was a beautifully balanced five-eighth. Weighing 12st 6lb and standing 5ft 10in tall, he was one of the best post-war players, equally at home at first or second five-eighth. The great commentator, Winston McCarthy, wrote: 'Allen was one of the finest five-eighths of all times … one of the greatest of side-steppers off either foot. He could make them, big or small, but always at pace. He was an immaculate player, neat in all he did. There can be no doubt that in blindside play there was never his equal.'[1]

But his great run against Australia would be the end of Allen's golden times. The 1949 tour of South Africa would provide bitter disappointment. The series was lost 4–0. Injury robbed Allen of his form, he did not play in the final two tests and he took the All Blacks' whitewash heavily and personally.

*AGONY AND ECSTACY: Fred Allen would one day become the unbeaten coach during one of the greatest All Black eras. But he ended his playing career in utter despair*

He would return to New Zealand a shattered man. 'I never thought too much about rugby for the next few years,' Allen told the author in 1997.

But Allen's disillusionment with rugby did not last forever. After a few years he got into club coaching and in 1957 became Auckland's coach. In 1959 his team lifted the Ranfurly

Shield and began a record-breaking run that made Allen famous. His All Black coaching career followed on from the mid-1960s.

Looking back to 1949, Allen will never forget that year. The All Blacks actually lost all six tests played – four against South Africa, but also two at home to Australia while Allen's team was away.

There were a number of factors which contributed to the losses in South Africa. Choosing the team after trials in 1948; not having any international matches in 1948; the choice of the All Black coach; the 27-day journey by boat; the immense distances travelled by train between games; the 'No Maoris' policy of the time, which prevented fine players such as Johnny Smith, Ben Couch and Vince Bevan from possible selection; the refereeing; the poor goal-kicking form of Bob Scott, who goaled only two penalities in the series; All Black shortcomings at halfback; the devastating influence of Springbok No 8 Hennie Muller; the unerring boot of Springbok Okey Geffin; the brilliant scheming of Danie Craven ....

The All Blacks were clearly up against it before they began and it would have taken a miracle for any captain to have beaten those odds. That the All Blacks would take almost another half century to win a full-blown series in South Africa would come as no surprise to Allen.

He strongly rejected any suggestion that Alex McDonald, the 66-year-old coach of the team, who had been a 1905 All Black 'Original', captained the All Blacks on their 1913 tour of North America, and coached or co-coached the All Blacks against the Springboks in 1921, and again in Australia in 1938, was cynically rejected by the team as being too old.

'Alex was a lovely old man. But it was hard enough for young people to be up on the high veldt and he was sick a lot of the time,' said Allen.

'I only played the first two tests. I started to take over the training because old Alex was crook. Something had to be done. Some of the other players didn't like the fact I wasn't playing. But I felt I couldn't do any more by playing, so when it came to picking the third test, I said: "Start with me – I'm out"', said Allen, who was one of the team selectors.

'Then I basically took over the test team training, with Alex taking the dirt trackers when he could. It was a hard tour.'

'I'm not making excuses for it. I'm quite proud of that side. But we had 27 days on the

boat on the way over. What could you do on the boat? It wasn't the Queen Mary. We jogged around the deck with the Indian Ocean rolling a bit and people twisting ankles. And then you retire to the bars and everything's going on.

'Once we got there, about four of the fellas were three stone overweight. They'd eaten too much. At Hermanus, for a week before our first game, we were fêted and wined and dined by high society. Danie Craven really sewed us up.

'We travelled by train and at one stage spent 10 out of 13 days travelling and playing two games. It got so that at night we used to get off the train while it was filling up with water and coal and work out in the dark. Just for good measure we had a train smash in Rhodesia – head-on about one o'clock in the morning. Our big lock Charlie Willocks buggered his shoulder and several of us were thrown out of our bunks. One rail employee was killed.'

The All Blacks had their line crossed only eight times in 24 games on tour. There was little in it. Allen still firmly believes if the team had had Vic Cavanagh as coach it would have at least squared the rubber. 'He was the greatest coach never to coach the All Blacks, no doubt about it,' said Allen.

Why then was Allen, the captain, so proud of that team?

'When we boarded the boat for home, I asked our manager Jim Parker and Alex to let me talk to the team in private, because I'd like to straighten out a few things. The team was a bit hot with Alex and Jim, who were pretty good guys really. I'd already retired. I'd kicked my boots into the Indian Ocean.

'I just said: "It's all over and in a thousand years' time the score is still going to be 4–0." I said: "All the complaining, and bleating and blaming of management and referees, which I believe you're thinking of doing, just let's cut it". For about 15 years it never came out. Although the tour's results almost broke my heart, the attitude of the team afterwards made me very proud.'

Among those who felt Allen should have remained the on-field commander was team-mate Johnny Simpson, who would later forge a fabulous coaching partnership with Allen at provincial level.

'Fred, unfortunately, blamed himself for our problems. But none of them were of his making,' said Simpson. 'That was the nature of the man –

POST-WAR LEADER: Fred Allen led the first All Black team after World War II. This side thrashed Australia 31–8 at Carisbrook, Dunedin, in the first test of 1946. Back row: Manahi Paewai (reserve), Johnny Smith, Jack McRae, Ron Elvidge, Jack Finlay, Bob Scott, Morrie Goddard, Jimmy Haig. Middle row: Fred Lucas (selector), Stan Dean (NZRFU chairman), Has Catley, Charlie Willocks, Wally Argus, Morrie McHugh, John Dunn, Harold Strang (selector), Alex McDonald (selector). Front row: Pat Rhind, Ken Elliott, Fred Allen (captain), Roy White, Harry Frazer, Tom Budd.

he was so conscientious. But our players couldn't vary the tactics, which was needed to counter the menace of Hennie Muller in the loose.'

There is another indicator to the collective memory of Allen's team – it has never held a reunion. Team member Peter Henderson told Denis Edwards in a 1999 NZ Rugby Monthly interview that he 'suspects some of the bigger names saw it as an embarrassing failure, wanted it buried and have refused to revive its memory'. Henderson said he had tried unsuccessfully to organise a get-together in 1981. In 1999, only 16 players survived.

It is impossible to objectively compare the All Black coaches of the different eras, just as it is impossible to compare the All Blacks themselves. However, Fred the Needle's unbeaten run through the late 1960s established a record which has never been matched by any other All Black coach, before or since. Allen coached the All Blacks through 1966–68, his teams cutting a swathe through the best the

rugby world had to offer – with the notable exception of South Africa (though he'd assisted Neil McPhail to beat the 1965 Springboks in New Zealand). Then he quit.

Those 14 test victories have only been approached by the magnificent run of Alex Wyllie. Had Allen continued through 1969 – when the Ivan Vodanovich-coached All Blacks destroyed the Five Nations champion Welsh team – and taken the team to South Africa in 1970, could he have achieved the elusive series win? Like Wyllie – whose era of dominance came when South Africa had not quite emerged from the political wilderness – Allen never locked horns with New Zealand's great rival.

Allen still wishes he had taken the All Blacks on safari. 'I do regret it very much, because that was my intention in 1967. We were supposed to tour South Africa, but went instead to the UK and France when the tour was cancelled,' said Allen. 'That was a bloody good side, still rated one of the best since the war. They rate that

*UNHAPPY LEADER: Fred Allen had little luck in the test series in 1949 but managed to score this try (v. Natal) on the tour*

team, the 1951–52 Springboks, the 1984 Wallabies and strangely the 1946 Kiwis. That's the general consensus of the good writers.

'I would love to have done the South African tour and I would have loved to have stayed on as All Black coach. But I sensed behind the scenes that people weren't fully supportive of me. Perhaps there was a bit of jealousy about the unbeaten record? I wasn't going to give them the opportunity to dump me, so I packed it in.

'I know a few of them who toured in 1970 – Kirky, Meads, Lochore, Fergie McCormick –

said if I'd been there they would have won the series. You never know.'

Allen will not speak ill of the dead. But the author has learned from other parties that Allen's coaching job may well have been in jeopardy. Chairman of the NZRFU then was the late Tom Morrison, himself a former All Black coach. The man who replaced Allen as coach was the late Ivan Vodanovich, who was to become an NZRFU councillor. Morrison and Vodanovich were business partners. There was criticism made by councillors of Allen's handling of certain All Blacks, and their tactics, during the 1968 Australian tour. A coup was a possibility, though the dumping of an unbeaten All Black coach would have caused a furore.

Allen's early coaching triumphs were with Auckland between 1957 and 1963, in partnership with Simpson in the early period. This included a then-record tenure of the Ranfurly Shield for 25 matches (1960–63). In 1964 he became an All Black selector, under the convenorship of then-All Black coach, Neil McPhail. Allen helped McPhail plan the defeat of the 1965 Springboks in New Zealand.

The following year began the most successful era any All Black coach has undertaken. The 1966 British Lions became Allen's first victims, white-washed 4–0, the All Blacks scoring 79 points to 32 against. Only the second test at Wellington produced a reasonably close score, 16–12.

That year also signalled one of many outstanding decisions which were to lift Allen from the pack as an international coach. He chose Brian Lochore to replace the long-serving Wilson Whineray as captain. Outsiders would have ranked Kel Tremain, Ken Gray, Colin Meads or Chris Laidlaw ahead of Lochore in the favouritism stakes.

The 1968 season, which was to become Allen's last with the All Blacks, provided series wins over Australia (away) and France (at home). But the All Blacks did not put away their opposition with the same precision as of old. There was the famous penalty-try test at Brisbane, won 19–18, when Australian referee Kevin Crowe 'saved' the All Blacks (and Allen's unbeaten record) with a penalty try in the dying moments of the game. However, injuries to key players, such as Lochore, Gray and Tremain, had affected the performances.

Allen is one of only four test captains to have led the All Blacks in every match in which they played for New Zealand. The others were George Aitken, Pat Vincent and Andy Leslie.

Allen has led a busy life since he wound down his women's clothing company and retired to Whangaparaoa. In 1995 he travelled to the World Cup, the 100th test between New Zealand and Australia, and to Europe with the Kiwis' reunion party. In 1996 he followed the All Blacks in South Africa.

At 80 he looks fit and strong. He still does his own lawns, digs in the garden and tries 'to do what he has always done.'

## Frederick Richard Allen (Auckland)

**Captain in six tests, four wins and two losses**
v. Australia 1946 (1, 2),
v. Australia 1947 (1, 2),
v. South Africa 1949 (1, 2)

**Born:** Oamaru, February 9, 1920

**Position:** Five-eighth.

**Represented NZ:** 1946, 47, 49 – 21 matches (6 internationals).

**Points for NZ:** 21 – 7 tries.

**Provincial record:** Canterbury 1939–41 (Linwood club); Marlborough 1944 (RNZAF); Waikato 1944 (Army); Auckland 1946–48 (Grammar).

**Other matches:** 2nd NZEF 1945, 46 (Kiwis) in Britain and NZ; Barbarian (UK) 1946.

**Selector/coach:** Auckland 1957–63, incl 25-match tenure Ranfurly Shield.

**NZ selector:** 1964–68.

**NZ coach:** 1966: Beat Lions 20–3, 16–12, 19–6, 24–11. 1967: Beat Australia 29–9; beat England 23–11, beat Wales 13–6; beat France 21–5, beat Scotland 14–3. 1968: beat Australia 27–11, 19–18; beat France 12–9, 9–3, 19–12.

**Other activities:** Co-author, with Terry McLean, of a rugby coaching book, *Fred Allen on Rugby* (Cassell, 1970).

**Occupation:** Retired; was women's dress manufacturer.

1 *Haka! The All Black Story,* Winston McCarthy, Pelham Books, 1968.

# RON ELVIDGE

## *Ron was often just what the doctor ordered*

ALL BLACK legend is replete with tales of heroics and matches won in final moments by something special from a player inspired by the occasion. But few anecdotes come more special than the courage shown by Ron Elvidge when his country called in 1949 and 1950 for him to lead the All Blacks at a time of direst need.

The Otago man had long been renowned as a player with a rare skill level and ruggedness to play the ideal game at top level demanded by the rules of the day.

Elvidge was an integral part of the Otago teams under Vic Cavanagh junior which dominated New Zealand rugby after World War II. He was already famous, especially in the south, where his feats in Ranfurly Shield matches had given him 'a god-like status'.

The *Otago Daily Times* at the time described him thus: 'When he walks down the street he turns more heads than Bing Crosby would.'

Playing at second five-eighth or centre, Elvidge used his strong build (5ft 11 in, 13st) and extreme fitness to fill a vital cog in the second-phase game plan Cavanagh employed to revolutionise rugby. He ran hard, possessed an extraordinary fend and a tactical nous which allowed him to be used as a 'target' by the great Otago forwards to run on to and set up rucks. He also used these skills to exploit openings and score or create many tries. He was the forerunner of many excellent All Black midfield backs who have been used to set up second-phase attack.

The commentator and author, Winston McCarthy, wrote: 'He used to play in the Otago way. Once into the 25 area he would run, he would go down, he'd get out of it, he'd be back in position. He'd have another go on the right side, and he'd end up scoring perhaps after the

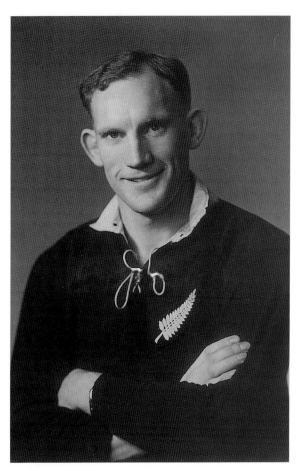

*LION HEART: Ron Elvidge would prove indomitable in adversity in the 1949 and 1950 series*

third or fourth ruck. He was a good player with a well thought-out approach.'[1]

Elvidge is best known as the captain who courageously returned to the field in the third test against the British Lions in 1950, after serious injury, and dived through the tackle of fullback Billy Cleaver to score and help the All Blacks to victory.

But his All Black career and his time leading

*CAPTAIN COURAGEOUS: The All Blacks were already a player down when Elvidge was led from the field near halftime with chest cartilage and facial injuries. He would return to score a dramatic try that helped save the third test against the 1950 Lions but would still be on the injured list for the fourth test*

Otago made him a considerably more influential player than during that one great moment that made him famous.

Elvidge played 19 times for the All Blacks during 1946–50, including nine tests, in a career interrupted and shortened by study commitments. He was unavailable for the 1947 All Black tour of Australia, for instance.

During a period when All Black rugby would face the most testing time in its history, he captained New Zealand in five tests at the end of his career, for two wins, two losses and a draw.

Elvidge played in all the tests in South Africa in 1949. When tour captain Fred Allen declared himself unavailable for selection for the 3rd and 4th tests because of a shoulder injury, Elvidge took over the captaincy. He

moved from his favoured centre position to second five-eighth to fill the role.

Elvidge did not hesitate to accept the challenge, even though the All Blacks were already 2–0 down in the series. But in order to appreciate Elvidge's position, we need to examine the dilemma the team had found itself in. The All Black inside backs were hammered mercilessly throughout the 1949 series, with Springbok No 8 Hennie Muller the main destroyer of any hopes New Zealand held for attacking rugby.

The New Zealanders had never experienced the tactic adopted by all the South African No 8s encountered on tour, who stood out beyond their lineout, opposite the first and even the second five-eighths. They did not corner-flag but ran aggressively at the opposition backline when it had the ball from a lineout. Their activities were devastating. Five-eighths often received the ball at the same time as these big, powerful No 8s arrived.

The rules of the day allowed for this to happen. There was no compulsion to be part of the lineout, as there is today. And players getting 'offside' as we understand it today, were given leeway to retire rather than be penalised. The same applied to players leaving the scrum, ruck or maul early. The laws also said that only a member of the team playing the ball could be offside. So the No 8, for instance, could start his charge at the opposing five-eighth at the moment the ball left the hand of the winger of the (opposing) side throwing the ball into the lineout.

So Elvidge was 'on a hiding to nothing' in accepting the new responsibilities. But he never shrank from the task and indeed scored a try in the fourth test. The Boks completed their whitewash however, 9–3 and 11–8.

But the Forty-Niners were not a weak team. Only eight tries were scored against them in 24 matches and 18 sides failed to score tries against them. But the refereeing left a lot to be desired and the All Blacks were not allowed to play their rucking game. To be fair, Bob Scott's goal-kicking was also woeful.

Of the big hits that Muller put on the All Blacks, Elvidge shrugged it off. 'I was used to it. When you're young and fit you can take it. It was a bit like they're doing in Super 12 and test football nowadays – only there's a lot more now and they're a lot harder. I wouldn't like to be hit by some of those.'

During the tour of South Africa, Elvidge was

the honorary team doctor. He got unexpected duty when the train the side was travelling on as it returned from Rhodesia to Pretoria was involved in a head-on crash. None of the team was badly hurt, but a railways employee trapped in the engine cab later died. 'I gave him an injection to relieve the pain but his chest had been crushed,' recalled Elvidge, who attended to many of the other injured.

Elvidge retained the All Black leadership the following year, when the British Lions toured. It was Elvidge who saved the game for New Zealand when he beat three men and scored in the corner in the dying minutes of the first test to earn a 9–all draw.

The All Blacks took the next two with narrow wins, but Elvidge was unable to regain fitness for the last test because of the injuries sustained in the third – chest cartilage and stitches to the head above the eye. With the series already won, the All Blacks scrambled home, 11–8, under Otago team-mate Peter Johnstone's captaincy.

Of the third test, Elvidge recalled the All Blacks were in deep trouble after he was heavily tackled late in the first half. They had already lost the great prop, Johnny Simpson, with a knee injury serious enough to end his career. Elvidge went off for treatment but with his team down to 13 men (no replacements were allowed in international rugby), he knew he had to get back on the field somehow.

He returned just after halftime. 'I just went out there as a sort of rover. I really didn't think I could do much for the team. In fact, I could have got in Bob Scott's way and hindered the team. But I happened to be in the right place at the right time. It just so happened I was there when the ball was passed to me and I knew I could make it,' Elvidge told the author in 1999.

The impact of the image of the pain-wracked hero on the New Zealand psyche was powerful. He had levelled the score at 3–3 and the All Blacks would go on to a narrow victory. The effect on the populace of his sacrifice was reinforced when Elvidge could not take his place in the fourth test played 28 days later.

Elvidge retired after the Lions' series. He said he would have liked to have played several more years, but had to think of his career.

'Work came first always,' explained Elvidge. 'Rugby was very much an amateur game.

'For years it had been a bit of a struggle fitting studies in with big rugby. It got so bad one season, I can remember going to my father and explaining that with all the club and Ranfurly Shield commitments, there was only one day a week to study properly. He said, 'Opportunity knocks but once. Take it with both hands and treasure these times.' So I put some of my exams back to the following year. How many fathers would have thought like that, I wonder?'

Stories abound among old All Blacks of the legendary stinginess of the NZRFU in those amateur days. But Elvidge can happily recall he was able to persuade the union to provide one big concession.

'I insisted that if they wanted me for big matches and trials, they had to fly me to and from the fixtures, rather than spend two or three days extra travelling by train or bus, when I would have missed even more lectures or exams,' he said.

Elvidge's father, John, and his sister, Betty, were his greatest supporters and harshest critics. His father managed J Rattray & Sons in Dunedin and would always slip away from work (usually followed by most of the other staff in descending rank) to watch Ron and Otago in midweek shield fixtures at Carisbrook.

His father was part of the supporters' party which followed the All Blacks in South Africa in 1949. When team manager Jim Parker found all the official duties too much to handle, John Elvidge assisted him and was made an honorary member of the team and awarded a team blazer.

'I'll always remember Dad seeing the team at Hermanus (where the All Blacks prepared for their first tour game after weeks on the boat travelling to South Africa) and stating, 'You all look like a pod of stranded porpoises' in reference to the fact we'd put on weight, some a lot more than others,' added Elvidge.

So Elvidge had achieved much since making his debut for Otago in 1942 at 19 years of age. The following year he made the first of five appearances for the South Island. When Otago lifted the Ranfurly Shield from neighbouring archrival Southland in 1947, Elvidge, now Otago's captain, scored two tries after solo runs. He led the team throughout its famous shield tenure until the end of 1948. He and 10 other Otago players then toured South Africa with the All Blacks, while their replacements valiantly defended the shield. It was finally lost in 1950, but without Cavanagh or Elvidge at the helm.

Elvidge acknowledged there was a form of hero-worship in those heady days in Dunedin in the 1940s. 'It didn't worry me unduly or give me a swelled head. But it's a reciprocal sort of thing. I did my best for Otago rugby and the Otago rugby public were absolute enthusiasts.

'With the crowd behind you, the team grew six inches and it made a world of difference. You gained a sort of innate feeling that there were more than 15 players on your side.'

Elvidge had been a fine allround sportsman. At John McGlashan College, Dunedin, besides being a top student, he played for the First XV and First XI for four years (1937–40), was the athletics champion for three years and school champion in swimming, fives and boxing.

Elvidge went to England in 1950 to complete post-graduate studies in obstetrics and gynaecology at hospitals in London, Oxford and Shrewsbury. There were no openings in his field in Dunedin, where he would have preferred to resettle. So when he returned to New Zealand in 1956 he became involved in private practice in Auckland. Later he was a visiting consultant at National Women's Hospital and St Helen's Hospital.

Elvidge's busy career precluded any great coaching or administrative activity. He coached Eden (Auckland) with Morrie Moslen for one season but found the lack of time to put into the team a major frustration. However, he served on the medical panel at Eden Park for many years and happily recalled that was a fine way to stay in touch with the game he's always loved.

He and wife Dawn have three children and seven grandchildren and are retired and living on Herald Island, Auckland. His office and garage are filled with rugby memorabilia.

## Ronald Rutherford Elvidge (Otago)

**Captain in five tests, two wins, two losses and a draw**
v. South Africa 1949 (3, 4)
v. British Isles 1950 (1, 2, 3)

**Born:** March 2, 1923, Timaru.

**Position:** Second five-eighth and centre three-quarter

**Represented NZ:** 1946, 49, 50 – 19 matches (9 tests).

**Points for NZ:** 15 points – 5 tries.

**First-class record:** Otago 1942–48 (University), 1950 (Union); South Island 1943, 45–48; NZ Trials 1948–50; NZ Universities 1945, 46.

**Miscellaneous:** Elvidge's father, John, who had played for Otago, was made an honorary member of the touring 1949 All Blacks and awarded an All Black blazer for completing official duties on behalf of the team. A nephew, Dennis Elvidge, played for NZ Universities.

**Occupation:** Retired; was obstetrician and gynaecologist.

*1 Haka, the All Blacks' Story*

# JOHNNY SMITH

## *Johnny Smith created 'some sort of record'*

JOHNNY SMITH showed his sense of humour after captaining the All Blacks in the two losing 1949 tests against the touring Wallabies.

Smith led the second New Zealand team of that winter to be unsuccessful. At the same time, the first All Black team was battling to a 4–0 series loss in South Africa – a tour that Smith, a Maori, was barred from because of the republic's racial policies.

It was the worst season in All Black history and the double-challenge test programme has never been repeated by the NZRFU.

But to mask his disappointment at the home losses, Smith quipped how he thought he'd 'created some sort of record. We lost both tests, making me the only captain in New Zealand history to lose every game he captained.'

Smith's historical knowledge was not as good as his footballing skills, since two other All Black captains had also had the doubtful pleasure of losing the only matches they led the All Blacks. Herb Lilburne (1929) and Rusty Page (1934), also both against Australia, had captained in one test only. To this day the trio remain the sole All Black captains to share this sad legacy – the 'unbeatable' record.

Smith was picked in 1952 but was injured. He never regained his place in the All Blacks, though he was to go very close to making the tour of Britain and France in 1953–54. Ironically, that team was led by Bob Stuart, who had been Smith's vice-captain in 1949 and who had also been in the All Black wilderness ever since.

Smith's career had blossomed when he was talent-spotted by the selectors of the Kiwis army team for the tour of Britain and Europe in 1945–46. After joining the army Smith had made his first-class debut in New Zealand for

*SETTING 'EM UP: Johnny Smith is about to score this one for himself on the Kiwis' triumphant 1946 tour of Britain and Europe but more often Smith was servicing the team's four top-class wingers*

the 12th Brigade Group team in 1942 at the age of 20 and played the first of his inter-island matches the following year. He scored a memorable try for the North, chased the length of the field.

That try was described by commentator and author Winston McCarthy: 'He grabbed the ball on his own 25 ... and started to race up the sideline. Now Johnny was never particularly fast, but he was fast enough, and chasing him was Johnny Dick, who had played for New Zealand, and was playing on the right wing for the South Island. He was much faster than Johnny Smith. Smith kept tearing up the

*AMBLING GENIUS: Johnny Smith is about to clear from this situation on the Kiwis' tour but more often than not he ran the ball - with remarkable results*

paddock, almost in the centre, and then I saw the greatest piece of rugby strategy ever. He realised that Dick was faster than he was and kept cocking his eye over his shoulder like a wall-eyed horse. Just as Dick was ready to dive at him Smith would move a little to the left while he was still running. Then he crowned everything for me to make it perfect because he knew that he was going to be overtaken. As he got up ... to the 25, he sensed Dick was going to have a despairing dive at him and he almost stopped dead – he almost stopped and Dick overdived, hitting him in about the back, and Smith just stepped out of the tackle, ran on and dotted the ball down. It really was a remarkable try.'[1]

He must have been a scourge for the South Islanders. His name features in many tries and try-scoring movements in the seven inter-island matches he played.

In the 1947 North-South match, another Smith effort was remarkable.

'Jack Kelly was fullback for South that day and Smith must have seen him coming in for the tackle a few yards short of the line. So he swung infield towards Kelly, reached out and grabbed him by the shoulder, swung right again as he pulled Kelly off balance, and dived across the line for one of the best manoeuvred tries I have seen.'[2]

Smith had served in Italy with the 21st Battalion. Then, under the expert gaze of Kiwi captain and pre-war All Black halfback Charlie Saxton, Smith was one of the many stars of the 1946 Kiwis. No team member played in more than Smith's 28 tour games. He would relish the open, running rugby that was the Kiwis' philosophy. But more importantly, he would lay the foundation for his later reputation as 'the perfect centre' – the one who wingers dreamed of playing outside.

Smith scored six tries on the tour, but it was his service to the wingers that really showed in statistics. Jim Sherratt scored 24 tries, Wally Argus 12, Eric Boggs 15, Bill Meates eight. They all acknowledged Smith as the master of setting them up for the run to the line.

Winston McCarthy wrote: 'Johnny remains among the unforgettable players, a player who

*JOY UNBOUNDED: Unlike many rugby teams, the Kiwis army side didn't have much trouble smiling for the camera. They loved to play. Johnny Smith is seated at right, next to Fred Allen*

had everything, plus an ice-cold brain while on the field. So great a player was he that he could make a mediocre wing look the tops …

'He was just as liable to go right into a tackle before releasing the ball to his winger as pass it to him while 10 yards away from an opponent. Big in the thighs he could break a tackle by an imperceptible lengthening of stride. He had a terrific fend, a two-footed sidestep and an educated boot.'[3]

Bob Scott, the great fullback of the 1940s and 1950s, and Kiwi team-mate, summed up Smith by comparing him with Bert Cooke. 'Cooke's lightning speed from the mark, his talent for being exactly in the right place at the right time, made him the perfect foil for Mark Nicholls.

'Smith was less flamboyant, less speedy, but in art, cunning and breakaway he perhaps combined the effective skills of Nicholls and Cooke. Certainly, I have never tired of watching him at work, so patient, so careful, so thoughtful and so singularly successful.'[4]

'I say without reservation that I was in mortal fear of Smith every time I played against him,' added Scott.

But for reasons that included injury, lack of form and plain bad luck, Smith was never really able to emulate his Kiwis' brilliance with the All Blacks. His test record of playing only four tests – one in 1946, one in 1947 and the two of 1949 – doesn't seem especially outstanding.

However, it is the opinions of contemporary opponents and team-mates in particular that must be recalled when judging Smith. Mark Nicholls, the All Black midfield great of the 1920s, an All Black selector in 1936–37 and a North Island selector in 1948, said Smith was the equal at least of Bert Cooke, Nicholls' 1924 Invincibles team-mate.

After the Kiwis returned from their European triumphs, Smith had injured an ankle playing for North Auckland against the touring Wallabies. He struggled in the first test against the Australians and had to withdraw from the second test.

On the tour of Australia in 1947 injuries again restricted his appearances. He played in only the second test in the series.

However, that was it. There was no international programme in 1948, though Smith did captain the NZ Maoris to Fiji that year. Smith, like other leading players such as Vince Bevan and Ben Couch, was excluded from consideration for the tour to South Africa, where critics would later claim he was desperately missed.

He would continue to play for North Auckland until 1954, for the North Island each season from 1946–50 and 1953, and for the NZ Maoris in 1951 and 1952.

Smith captained North Auckland through the early 1950s and led it to victory in a Ranfurly Shield challenge over South Canterbury in 1950. In the third challenge of 1951 Smith's team would lose the shield to Waikato, 3–6, with 17-year-old Don Clarke kicking two penalties for Waikato and Smith a penalty for the holder.

Peter Jones was one of many contemporaries who paid tribute to Smith for his understanding of the game and the way he built spirit into the North Aucklanders.

A natural sportsman who had been a New Zealand junior tennis champion, competitive swimmer and would become a good cricketer and a five-handicap golfer, Smith was an easy-going personality who was not considered the most dedicated of formal trainers. He stood 5ft 9in (1.75m) and weighed 12st 10lb (80.7kg) at his prime but tended to put on weight and was heavier as his career wound down.

Smith's brother, Peter, joined him in the 1947 All Blacks. Peter died suddenly, aged 29, in 1954. Their father, Len, played for North Island Country 1912.

Smith was in ill health later in his life and when he died in 1974, aged 52, he was blind.

## John Burns Smith (North Auckland)

**Captain in two tests, two losses**
v. Australia 1949 (1, 2)

**Born:** September 25, 1922, Kaikohe.

**Died:** December 3, 1974, Auckland.

**Position:** Centre and second five-eighth.

**Represented NZ:** 1946, 47, 49 – 9 matches (4 tests).

**Points for NZ:** 9 – 2 tries, 1 dropped goal.

**First-class record:** North Auckland 1946–54 (Kaikohe); North Island 1943, 46–50, 53; NZ Trials 1947, 50, 53; NZ Maoris 1948, 51, 52; 2nd NZEF 1945, 46.

**High school:** Kaikohe District High School, 1st XV 1935–37.

**Selector/coach/administrator:** North Auckland selector 1956.

**Other:** His father, Len, played for North Island Country 1912 and his brother, Peter, joined him in the 1947 All Blacks. Peter died suddenly, aged 29, in 1954.

**Miscellaneous:** First recipient of the Tom French Cup in 1949 as the Maori player of the year. Between 1929 and 1954 the All Blacks had 16 test captains of whom only Jack Griffiths and Johnny Smith were North Island-born. NZ junior doubles tennis champion, with Alan Burns, in 1939.

**Occupation:** A baker.

1 *Rugby in My Time,* Winston McCarthy, Reeds, 1958.

2, 3 *Haka! The All Blacks Story*

4 *Bob Scott on Rugby,* Bob Scott and Terry McLean, Nicholas Kaye Ltd, 1955.

# PETER JOHNSTONE

## *Loose forward was an unbeaten All Black captain*

PETER JOHNSTONE achieved an unbeaten record as captain of the All Blacks, leading the team in four tests during 1950 and 1951 for four victories.

In its day, Johnstone's tenure was exceptional. In the last four decades of the 20th century the All Blacks were blessed with a long list of successful, long-term captains. But in Johnstone's time, exactly midway through the century, there had been no tradition of long-term leadership. Cliff Porter, with seven tests, would hold the record until the emergence of Wilson Whineray in the late 1950s. Fred Allen had led New Zealand in six tests.

But Porter and Allen had only mixed success. Remarkably, Billy Stead, with four victories in four tests back in 1904–08, was the only other All Black captain to compare with Johnstone's unblemished record.

A versatile Otago loose forward who weighed 13st 7lb and stood 6ft tall, Johnstone represented New Zealand from 1949–51, in 26 matches and nine internationals.

However, it was Johnstone's leadership qualities on the tour of Australia in 1951 that deserves special mention. With the internationally inexperienced Len Clode appointed assistant manager/coach of the All Blacks, Johnstone took on extra responsibility in terms of game leadership, team tactics, training and preparation. The team had a spectacularly successful unbeaten tour.

Johnstone had first got the captain's job when Ron Elvidge, who had led the All Blacks in the final two tests in South Africa the year before and in the opening three tests of the 1950 series against the British Lions, had to cry off from the final test. Elvidge, the hero of the third test when he returned to the field after suffering head and chest cartilage injuries and scored a try which helped his team to a narrow 6–3 victory, was still unfit.

Johnstone could not understand why people were calling out congratulations as he cycled to his carpentry job in Mosgiel. On reaching work he found out why. His boss told him he had been named on the radio news as the All Black captain for the series finale in Auckland.[1]

The fourth test was regarded as by far the best of the series and one of the finest internationals seen at Eden Park. New Zealand led 8–3 at halftime but in the last quarter came sensational incidents that featured the international-class sprinters fielded by both sides. The Lions' fullback, Lewis Jones, only 19 and a replacement midway through the tour, ran from his own goal-line, drew Bob Scott and lobbed the ball inside, over covering Peter Henderson's head, to the Olympic sprinter, Ken Jones, on halfway. The Welshman scored under the bar with chasing All Blacks in his wake. The visitors went close to scoring twice in the dying minutes, when Henderson, a Commonwealth Games sprinter, brought off a magnificent tackle and saved a certain try when he cut down the Lions' centre, Bleddyn Williams, with a clear run to the line. The All Blacks survived to win 11–8.

Johnstone took over the captaincy at a vital time in New Zealand rugby. Most of his team retired from international football after the 1950 series. Henderson, Roy Roper, George Beatty, Elvidge, Vince Bevan, Pat Crowley, Lester Harvey, Arthur Hughes, Jack McNab, Johnny

*NEW CHALLENGES: Peter Johnstone took over the captaincy as the All Blacks struggled against the touring Lions. Most of his team then retired and Johnstone successfully led the fledgling replacements through Australia*

Simpson, 'Brownie' Cherrington and Graham Mexted never played another test. Bevan, Cherrington and Mexted toured with future All Black sides, while Bob Scott, who also announced his retirement, would come back to play in the tour of 1953–54.

The winning of the series against the Lions

had done much to raise the prestige of the All Blacks from the ashes of the previous year. In 1949 New Zealand had lost all six tests – four in South Africa and two when Australia toured New Zealand at the same time and uplifted the Bledisloe Cup.

It was also a time for rebuilding, with the

VERSATILE LEADER: Flanker Peter Johnstone moved to the wing during the third test against the British Lions at Wellington's Athletic Park in 1950, after captain and second five-eighth Ron Elvidge had been badly injured. Johnstone took over the captaincy for the fourth test when Elvidge was unable to play

*OLD MASTERS: Peter Johnstone (third from left) pictured with Laurie Haig (fourth from left) and the great Otago coach, Vic Cavanagh jnr (fifth from left) at an Otago gathering*

1953–54 tour to Britain and France coming into the focus of the national selectors. Many of the older players from the post-war era retired at this point. More than half the test players of 1950 were unavailable to tour Australia in 1951. Most of the 15 new All Blacks were backs.

Johnstone then captained the side in Australia. His coach, Clode, had never coached a provincial team or been a national selector. He had captained his club team, Invercargill (Blues), to a championship, coached the senior team and been a Southland selector when it defended the Ranfurly Shield against Otago in the mid-1940s. But he was living in Wellington at the time and had been on the NZRFU executive committee since 1949, representing his old province of Southland.

In 1999, aged 90 and the oldest former NZRFU executive member, Clode recalled to the author how he had got the job.

'Of the three New Zealand selectors that year – Merv Corner, Arthur Marslin and Tom Morrison, the convenor – none were available

to take the team to Australia,' he said. 'I was coaching at the Onslow club with Tom Morrison one day and he said, 'Why don't you apply for the job?' So I did and I was appointed.'

Although he knew Johnstone and a number of the other Otago players in the team, such as Ray Bell, Norm Wilson, Laurie Haig and Kevin Skinner, and the Southlanders, Bill McCaw and Eddie Robinson, Clode was introduced to some of the team on assembly.

But that did not make much difference. The 1951 team rates with the best. It maintained an unbeaten record, scored a record number of points for a New Zealand team in Australia, and regained the Bledisloe Cup.

The veteran of the team was Lachie Grant, who had toured Australia with the 1947 All Blacks. Three other forwards, Johnstone, Skinner and Norm Wilson, had, like Grant, toured South Africa. Those wearing the All Black jersey for the first time were Cockerill, Bell, Ercerg, Jarden, Lynch, Wightman,

Fitzpatrick, Len Wilson, Reid, Steele, Burke, Duff, Hammond, McCaw and Robinson.

The star of the 1951 team was Ron Jarden. He 'was a sensation in every match he played' and ended the tour with 88 points, 45 of which came from 15 tries. Jarden, who was already in Australia when the All Blacks arrived, playing for NZ Universities and 'wearing a beaten track to Australian goal-lines', was regarded as the finest winger to have toured that country since World War II by the Australians.[1]

'Peter Johnstone, with all his experience, was a great help in running the team. After the side aquitted itself well in the first test, and being a believer in never changing a winning team if all played to their ability, I then stuck to the same players, where possible, for the remaining two tests,' said Clode.

Johnstone captained the team to wins in all three tests. The All Blacks had to play Auckland just six hours after returning to Auckland on their Sunderland flying boat. They had had a busy time shopping and celebrating in Sydney for two days after the third test in Brisbane and had flown into the Waitemata Harbour just before 8am on the day of the match. Twenty-five thousand people turned up at Eden Park for the game, one the All Blacks would have preferred not to play. It was a dull game, won 9–3 by New Zealand.

Johnstone, who had played a leading part in the tactics and preparation of the touring All Blacks, and Hec Wilson both retired at the end of the 1951 season, while Tommy Lynch accepted a league offer in England. A number of young players were never called on to wear the All Black jersey after this tour. Of this team only seven players – Jarden, Fitzpatrick, Haig, Tanner, McCaw, Skinner and White – would go on to tour in 1953–54.

It is remarkable nowadays to note how the southern provinces, Otago, Southland and Canterbury, had a virtual stranglehold on the Ranfurly Shield for two decades, from 1931 to 1950. Otago and Southland shared the shield exclusively for 15 of those years, from 1936 to 1950.

Johnstone played his part for Otago during its most famous shield era under Vic Cavanagh jnr from 1946 to 1949, though he was one of 11 Otago players away with the 1949 All Blacks in South Africa when Cavanagh's depleted team successfully defended the log from allcomers.

So he was part of a fabulous 'talent factory' that churned out dozens of exceptional players through the 1940s. The Otago players who made the 1949 trek, for instance, were Elvidge, Jim Kearney, Bill Meates and Ian Botting in the backs and Skinner, Norm Wilson, Ray Dalton, McNab, Johnstone, Charlie Willocks and Lester Harvey in the forwards. Future All Black captains to develop in this period included Elvidge, Johnstone and Skinner.

Johnstone played in 12 of the 24 matches on the tour of South Africa, including the 2nd and 4th tests.

He later became an Otago selector 1959–61 and president of the Otago union. He was the Taieri club's senior coach, selector, committeeman, president and life member. The club ground is named in his honour.

## Peter Johnstone (Otago)

**Captain in four tests, four wins**
v. British Isles 1950 (4)
v. Australia 1951 (1, 2, 3)

**Born:** August 9, 1922, Mosgiel.

**Died:** October 18, 1997, Wanaka.

**Position:** Flanker and No 8.

**Represented NZ:** 1949–51 – 26 matches (9 tests).

**Points for NZ:** 12 – 4 tries.

**First-class record:** Ashburton County 1943 (Canterbury Cavalry); Otago 1946–48, 50, 51 (Taieri); South Island 1948, 51; NZ Trials 1948, 50, 51.

**High school:** Mosgiel District High School

**Selector/coach/administrator:** Otago selector 1959–61 and president Otago RFU. Senior club coach, selector, committee member, president and life member of the Taieri club.

**Miscellaneous:** Taieri club ground is named in his honour. His brother, Jim, represented Wellington 1955–57.

**Occupation:** A bridge-building contractor.

1 Chris Tobin, *Otago Daily Times,* June 18, 1992.

# KEVIN SKINNER

## Black-tie dinners weren't for this All Black captain

SOME OF the finest All Black captains of modern times, such as Wilson Whineray, Andy Dalton and Sean Fitzpatrick, have been front rowers. So it seems a little strange that when Kevin Skinner captained New Zealand in the early 1950s he became the first front-row player to do so.

Skinner led the All Blacks in the shared two-test 1952 series against Australia and was being groomed to captain the side on the great tour of Britain and France in 1953–54. He had become an integral part of the All Blacks' game since coming into the team as a 21-year-old on the tour of South Africa in 1949.

But Skinner never felt the front row was the ideal place to lead the All Blacks under the rules of the day. And he was even less enamoured with the idea he'd have to front all the black-tie dinners the All Blacks traditionally faced on tours to the UK.

'I could see what was intended for me,' Skinner told the author in 1999. 'It didn't appeal at all – all that "Lords, ladies and gentlemen" stuff wasn't for me, no thank you!

'I had spoken to Jack Manchester [the 1935 British tour captain] and guys like that about it. I just let it be known quietly to Arthur Marslin [the All Black selector who would coach the team on the 1953–54 tour] that I didn't want to do the job. He said, "That's OK".

'They chose Bob Stuart as captain. It suited him and he did a great job. I did lead the team a few times in the midweek games. Maybe things could have been different if I'd had another year to prepare? But I'm quite happy with the way it turned out.'

Skinner went on to have another

*BIG OCCASION: Prop forward Kevin Skinner would break the All Black match record with 63 games by 1956. But in his provincial debut, for Otago when it beat Southland to lift the Ranfurly Shield in 1947, Skinner, aged 19, had played his first game ever in the front row*

outstanding tour in 1953–54. He played in 27 tour matches, including all five tests. He

*SHARING HONOURS: Kevin Skinner captained this All Black team in the shared 1952 series against Australia. But he found the front row was not ideal for leading the side*

announced his retirement at the end of the 1954 New Zealand season. He had played in 18 consecutive tests and his 61 matches for the All Blacks had equalled the record held by Maurice Brownlie.

But after playing some club rugby in Dunedin in 1955 he moved to Waiuku, south of Auckland. He made a comeback and played for Counties the next season. When the Springboks toured and the desperate All Black selectors came calling, Skinner felt he wasn't fit enough. He turned down their request that he make himself available for the second test. But with

the series locked at 1–1 and the unprecedented nationalistic fervour that abounded, Skinner agreed to join the team for the third test at Christchurch.

Skinner's captain in 1956 was Bob Duff, who would later coach the All Blacks. Duff remains adamant that Skinner, a former New Zealand heavyweight boxing champion, was not chosen for pugilistic skills above those skills which were to take him to a record-breaking 63 appearances by the end of the series.

The veteran Springbok props, Jaap Bekker and Jan Koch, had proved powerful opponents earlier in the series. Koch had dominated All Black loosehead props Mark Irwin (retired with damaged ribs, first test) and his replacement, Frank McAtamney (dropped to the reserves after the second test).

Skinner was brought in to partner Ian Clarke. He swapped sides with Clarke at halftime, causing years of speculation and debate that he had been chosen primarily to deal to the Bok giants, one after the other. There were certainly some fisticuffs, first as Skinner marked Koch and later with Bekker. The outbreaks led to referee Bill Fright calling aside the captains, Duff and Basie Viviers.

The media legend goes that Skinner had a vendetta to settle with the Boks, especially Koch, whom he had marked in two tests way back in the humiliating 4–0 whitewash of the 1949 All Blacks. But Duff rubbishes that theory, as well as that there was any other sinister motive for the swap.

'Kevin did get into a few skirmishes, especially early on with Koch. But that was normal practice in those days. The players would sort themselves out on their own. There was none of the incidents where all the other players ran into the melee, as has become common over the last few decades,' explained Duff.

'The exchange of Kevin and Ian Clarke was simply because Ian had a very sore cauliflower ear. He asked me at the interval whether they could change positions and I said I was happy for them to swap.'

So Skinner contributed to the victories of the third and fourth tests that swung the mythical world crown New Zealand's way for the first time. He also completed his career with 63 games for New Zealand, a new All Black record, as well as becoming, with Don Clarke and others, the special heroes of the epic series. He then retired for good.

But his pugilistic reputation needs some revision. Skinner had won the New Zealand amateur boxing championship in 1947 – a decade earlier. But he never boxed after the age of 19 – because of rugby commitments. And in all those 61 games for the All Blacks previously he'd never gained a reputation for anything more than being a hard but fair opponent.

Skinner told the author in 1999 it was boxing that had helped him learn how to attain high levels of stamina and hardness later in his career. He had begun boxing as a 13-year-old and

rubbed shoulders through the years with Archie Leckie, Boz Murphy, Morrie McHugh, Phil Dunn and Don Mullett. 'Yes, I enjoyed boxing and the gyms. It was a different, and for me, an easier way to get fit than how most footballers did in those days.'

South African journalist Max Price's tour book, *Springboks at Bay*, probably contributed to the legend when he wrote that at the third test dinner 'there were several bruised and patched faces to be seen, and very jocularly Jaap Bekker remarked to Skinner that he hoped to see him in action at the Olympic Games in Melbourne later in the year.' Bekker's brother, Daan, represented South Africa in boxing at those Olympics, where he won a bronze medal, and went one better four years later in Rome, when he won a silver.

Skinner's rise to All Black fame had begun at St Kevin's College, Oamaru at the end of World War II. He was plucked out of the First XV, at the age of only 16, to play in the 1944 Otago Town versus Country senior match. Within three years he was part of Vic Cavanagh's fabulous Otago team. His representative debut came against Southland in Invercargill in 1947, a match Otago won, 17–11, to take the Ranfurly Shield. The shield then was almost a permanent fixture in the south. Southland and Otago between them held it from 1935 to 1950.

That game was also his first experience in the front row. He would quickly develop into a strapping 6ft, 15st 4lb tighthead (or loosehead) prop with all the skills. Eleven of Cavanagh's Otago team got into the 1949 All Blacks.

The All Black front row of Johnny Simpson, Has Catley and Skinner was called 'the best I played against' by famous Springbok Hennie Muller.[1]

Skinner was a huge success, even though the All Blacks were whitewashed. He revelled on the rock-hard grounds, which suited his supreme fitness. But the series result was disappointing for the youngster. 'In a way I never got that out of my system and helping us beat them at home in 1956 was a way of squaring my account with them,' he said.

This early reversal seemed to act as a spur for Skinner. The next year, 1950, he proved a nemesis for the touring British Lions, contributing directly to their defeat on four occasions. In 1951, on the tour to Australia, he scored three tries – the only tries he scored as an All Black. So it was a mark of this ability that he

*EARLY LESSONS: Kevin Skinner never forgot the lessons learned from the great Otago coach, Vic Cavanagh jnr (at left) in his early career*

was appointed captain for the 1952 series, with the tour as the longterm objective.

Skinner's side was rocked when the Wallabies won the first test at Lancaster Park, Christchurch, 14–9, after the All Blacks had led 6–5 at the interval. The tourists outscored New Zealand three tries to one. But after numerous team changes, the All Blacks came back well in the second test at Athletic Park, Wellington, to win 15–8. An unusual feature was a 'try' scored by Ron Jarden on the blindside which was disallowed by referee, Mr J. Frood, after he had been knocked to the ground in the play leading up to the try and was unsighted.

Winston McCarthy said 'Skinner's main claims to fame were his great work at No 2 in the lineout, where his strength and experience were of outstanding value, and his remarkable ability to stop rushes. His value as a tighthead prop is unexcelled.'[2]

Fred Allen, who captained the 1949 team,

told the author in 1999 that Skinner 'was a wonderful player. He combined tremendous strength with mobility. But he was also a fine front-of-the-lineout jumper, was fearless at stopping rushes and was a rock when it came to taking the ball from kick-offs.'

And despite the legend, Skinner wasn't always prepared to act as the traditional hardman of All Black packs. He recalled an amusing incident on the 1953–54 tour. 'We took the field against Llanelli and, in no time, Keith Bagley (an All Black lock) came to me. "I may need some help," he said. "I'm marking the light heavyweight champion of Wales."

'"That's your affair, Keith," I said. "I'm marking the heavyweight champion"'

His sense of humour has never left him either. He recalled the train crash that involved the All Black team on one of their long journies on the 1949 tour of South Africa. 'It was bad. At least one carriage flew up and over the engine. I was lucky. I was in a wall bunk. But Charlie Willocks hurt a shoulder and Ron Elvidge [Skinner's Otago team-mate, who was a doctor] treated many injured, one of whom died from a crushed chest.

'It was 2am. I recall Des Christian waking up next to me. 'We must have hit an elephant,' he said, and promptly went back to sleep.'

In 1960 Skinner moved to Auckland, mainly so one of his daughters, Sue, who is deaf, could attend a school for the deaf. He took over a supermarket business and later a coffee bar in Henderson. He and his wife, Laurie, nowadays live in retirement in the area.

## Kevin Lawrence Skinner (Otago)

**Captain in two tests, one win and one loss** v. Australia 1952 (1, 2)

**Born:** November 24, 1927, Dunedin.

**Position:** Loosehead or tighthead prop.

**Represented NZ:** 1949–54, 56 – 63 matches (20 tests).

**Points for NZ:** 9 – 3 tries.

**First-class record:** Otago 1947, 48, 50–54 (Pirates); Counties 1956 (Waiuku); South Island 1948, 50–53; NZ Trials 1948, 50–53; Bay of Plenty-Thames Valley-Counties 1956.

**High School:** St Kevin's College, Oamaru, 1st XV 1943, 44.

**Other:** Played Town-Country match in the Otago annual trial while still a school pupil. His 61 games as All Black had equalled the record of Maurice Brownlie when he retired in 1954. His two tests of 1956 created a new record of 63 games.

**Miscellaneous:** Won the Otago heavyweight amateur boxing championship in 1946 and the New Zealand title in 1947. He was the first front row player to captain the All Blacks in a test match.

**Occupation:** Retired, but was a farm worker in Waiuku and later a grocer and coffee bar proprietor in Henderson, Auckland.

1 *Tot Seins to Test Rugby,* Hennie Muller, Howard Timmins, 1953.

2 *Round the World with the All Blacks,* Winston McCarthy, Sporting Publications, 1954.

# BOB STUART

## *Stuart revived the art of great captaincy*

BOB STUART is said to have 'personally revived great captaincy in New Zealand rugby.'

In his tour book, *Bob Stuart's All Blacks*, Terry McLean wrote that Stuart 'personally revived great captaincy in New Zealand rugby ... no finer leader of forwards could have been imagined, and if his captaincy tended to emphasise caution at the expense of adventure, the general effect was such that tribute to his ability as a field-captain of the old-fashioned kind could be made with utter sincerity.'

In *Round the World with the All Blacks*, 1953–54, Winston McCarthy wrote that 'Stuart will go down as one of the finest captains of our generation. Ill for a month ... Stuart came back to lead his team to a near victory against Wales just a week after rising from his bed. He played in 17 out of the next 18 games, an amazing feat. A great leader, an amusing and witty after-dinner speaker, a fine, tough forward, Bob Stuart's name will always be revered in the British Isles.'

Stuart therefore had at last proven to the world what a master tactician he was, after previously having briefly been an All Black in 1949. But he had turned 33 on the great tour and would now retire. He would exert considerable influence in New Zealand rugby circles from that time on. He was already one of the country's 'most passionate theorists' and quickly became a coach. He was co-opted as the All Black forward coach by the national panel led by Tom Morrison to defeat the 1956 Springboks and selected and coached Canterbury in 1958–59, a highlight being the defeat of the British Lions, 20–14, in 1959.

His All Black co-coaching appointment, though highly successful, also represented the last time any coach has been officially co-

BOB STUART: Was said to 'have revived great captaincy'

opted to guide or help guide the All Blacks. The coach has always come from the selection panel during the past 40 years, whereas, previously, there were a number of cases of co-opted coaches, both in partnership or in a sole capacity.

But when the possibility of the national limelight beckoned again, Stuart, an agricultural economist, went to Rome to represent New Zealand at the United Nations

Food and Cultural Organisation and in other trade talks for many months.

He would return, more than a decade later, to serve the game as an administrator at the highest levels for more than 20 years. Stuart served on the NZRFU executive 1974–89, and was the NZRFU delegate on the International Rugby Board 1977–89. Later he was the IRB honorary development officer, 1990–96. He had an especially close association with the development and organisation of the World Rugby Cup in 1987, 1991 and to a lesser extent 1995.

But with regard to Stuart's return to the All Blacks in 1953–54, and elevation to the leadership, after so long away and at the end of a long career, we need to look to others.

Kevin Skinner had led the All Blacks in a split series with Australia in 1952. Only 24 and already with a wealth of experience behind him, Skinner was being groomed for a longer-term tenure. But Skinner was never at ease with the captaincy. He told the author in 1999 that he had felt the front row was not the ideal position to lead from and also found speech-making nerve-wracking.

With the emphasis the British placed on formality and black-tie dinners, Skinner began to dread the thought of captaining the All Blacks as the tour loomed. So he was a relieved man when Stuart got the job.

According to Stuart, other factors apart from personal ambition kept him playing when he could easily have retired to concentrate on his career. One was that his younger brother, Kevin, the Canterbury fullback, was well in the running for a tour place – though eventually missing out to Bob Scott and Jack Kelly, as a utility back.

Stuart said he was 'brought down to earth very quickly' at the start of the 1953–54 All Black tour by the opposition's tendency to 'kill the ball' at breakdowns and the toleration by referees of offside play.

'I thought we would encounter teams that would play a style not unlike the 1950 Lions in New Zealand, a brilliant team. In fact, it was the opposite. We had difficulty creating platforms to get clean ball and it was very difficult to develop back play.

'We had some excellent backs and two sets of forwards that consistently won 60 or 70 per cent of possession. But you couldn't open it up when you had opposition offside in your backline.'

A great controversy arose back in New Zealand during the tour when veteran first five-eighth Laurie Haig was preferred for most of the big matches over the brilliant running Guy Bowers.

'Guy was young and had tremendous potential. We didn't want to put him under enormous pressure and sacrifice him in the short-term when he looked an All Black prospect for many years to come. Haig was mature, he could take the hidings. We got to the crazy situation where, after defeating England, where Haig played outstandingly, the critics wanted him dropped for the Scotland test. Against pressure, I insisted that Haig play. It was a freezing day at Murrayfield and he played magnificently.

'Guy played outstandingly against Ireland, but it was an easier game, even though we played most of the game with 14 players. It was probably a mistake to put him in against France (lost 0–3). That was a very tough match for him – and all of us. It wasn't a matter of being conservative in our selections. It was a matter of being pragmatic.'

The team also lost the Welsh test, 8–13. Stuart said the 36-match grand tour was arduous and that no All Black team had attempted to repeat an itinerary containing five internationals, over a five-month period, since.

As an All Black, Stuart's only matches before the 1953–54 tour had been when he had played as No. 8 and flanker in two tests against the 1949 Wallabies. He recalled how he had been vice-captain and the legendary Johnny Smith captain of that team, which lost its two tests at home to a strong Australian team while the All Blacks were also in the process of losing 4–0 to South Africa. Smith had been left at home because he was Maori.

'Norm McKenzie was in charge in '49. He just gave me general instructions to take the forwards and work in with Johnny Smith and get some sort of teamwork developed,' said Stuart. 'I didn't know John very well, so it was a strange situation. I hadn't had the Canterbury team at that stage at all, so it was just thrown on me.'

The national selectors were not to call on Stuart again for four years, but it was during that time he got his grounding in captaincy and tactics. Otago had drubbed Canterbury 31–0 in its 1948 Ranfurly Shield challenge, but with its next opportunity, in 1950, Canterbury was to win 8–0. However, it was not without a lot of behind-the-scenes drama.

Stuart wanted to employ tactics that would counter Otago's famous second-phase game perfected by Vic Cavanagh jnr. Stuart contended that the way to counter Otago was not to get sucked into its rucks if you had arrived at the breakdown second, and, if you were first, then to continue the drive onwards and maintain momentum. 'Why get in and support them and hold them up?'

However, Stuart's theories were not accepted by the Canterbury management. 'I was supposed to have been captain that year, but I forfeited the leadership because of my opposition to Canterbury's tactics.

'So we staged a "revolution". I guess it was one of the first players' "revolutions" in New Zealand. Anyway, we received a very fair hearing and won our case. To the credit of our coaches, Jack Rankin and George Mortlock, there was agreement to disagree.

'Jack and George, in the ensuing weeks, added the polish and enthusiasm. The shield was won and, in retrospect, this was the catalyst for a great red-and-black resurgence.'

The shield went onto a merry-go-round from this point, until a Bob Stuart-led Canterbury team whipped Wellington in 1953, 24–3, to begin one of the great shield eras, lasting until 1956 (though Stuart had retired after the 1953–54 All Black tour).

Casting his memory back to the 1956 tour by the Springboks, Stuart said that the entire prestige of New Zealand rugby was seemingly at stake for everyone closely involved in planning the defeat of the tourists.

'I worked closely with Tom Morrison, Jack Sullivan and Arthur Marslin (his assistant manager on the 1953–54 All Black tour).

'I think they had changed the tactics after the 1953–54 tour and the forward play had become loose. They thought perhaps I could restore cohesion and drive again, a component of our forward skills that no team in the world could match.

'Tom Morrison approached me first in Christchurch and we had three or four discussions. From my point of view, whatever status I had was at stake too. To a degree, I was dependent on team selections for which I had no responsibility. But their heads were on the block too. They were going to risk everything on a co-opted coach.'

'I'd have my say in the selections, but the final decisions were made in the other room, or another city. Maybe I didn't agree with every decision, but that was natural and part of the deal. Players' form was erratic early in the season, but by the time of the third test I couldn't fault the chosen teams.'

Though designated as the forward coach only, Stuart's plans depended very much on the entire 15 ensuring that the tactics were successful.

His appointment was handled discretely and the media did not appreciate his input. There was also some irony in Stuart's situation at the time, because in the Springbok camp there was leadership controversy of a different kind, but also kept 'under wraps' from the public until after the tour. The Springboks' assistant manager and designated coach of the team, Dan de Villiers, quickly had a falling out with manager Dr Danie Craven. The players preferred Craven to coach the team and at one stage de Villiers threatened to go home. De Villiers, a lawyer, was said by the players to be a political 'minder' from the Broederbond, the secret society which helped maintain power in Afrikaner hands during all the years of apartheid.

The captaincy of the Springboks was also tinged in controversy. The veteran lock, Salty du Rand, was to have been the tour captain, but had a fight with Jan Pickard, another tourist, after a trial game just before the tour. They had been the rival captains in the trial. Pickard's nose was broken during the fight. The Springbok leadership then went to fullback Basie Viviers, who was not a test certainty, and according to Craven, was not an original team selection. It was a compromise decision and many of the players did not fully accept Viviers.

But it had not all been plain sailing for Stuart in the series either. In a 1997 interview with the author Stuart revealed there had been a move to oust him after the second test loss. 'Unbeknown to me at the time, there was a special meeting called. My understanding is that Tom Pearce (the Auckland administrator) wanted Johnny Simpson (the former All Black, also of Auckland) in my place. To his credit, Tom

Morrison held out for the status quo,' said Stuart. Independent research by the author backed up Stuart's revelation.

Stuart was 35 in 1956. Of all the All Black coaches, only Vinny Meredith, aged 33 when he took the All Blacks for the first time, to Australia in 1910; Jimmy Duncan, 35 when he became the first-ever officially appointed New Zealand coach in 1904; and Morrison, 36 when first appointed All Black selection convenor and coach in 1950, can compare for youth.

So a question to be asked of Stuart is why he did not seek to continue, on a more formal basis, his career as an All Black selector and coach? Stuart said he was offered a position on the South Island panel the year after the Springboks. 'I then asked Neil McPhail (the Canterbury coach) if he was interested. He said he was, so I didn't stand,' recalled Stuart.

McPhail would go on to be a national selector and coach the All Blacks most successfully in the 1960s. Stuart instead took on the Canterbury coaching job, his major achievement being the win over the 1959 Lions. Other priorities would then prevent his own climb. His work as an agricultural economist and the responsibility of a young family were two.

## Robert Charles Stuart (Canterbury)

**Captain in five tests, three wins and two losses**
v. Wales, Ireland, Scotland, England, France 1953–54

**Born:** Dunedin, October 28, 1920.

**Position:** Loose forward.

**Represented NZ:** 1949, 53, 54 – 27 matches (7 internationals).

**Provincial record:** Manawatu 1941 (St Patrick's Old Boys) and Canterbury 1946–53 (University club), captain from 1951; South Island 1948, 49.

**High school:** St Kevin's College, Oamaru.

**Selector/coach:** Canterbury selector/coach 1958, 59.

**All Black co-coaching record:** 1956: New Zealand beat South Africa 10–6, lost to South Africa 3–8, beat South Africa 17–10, beat South Africa 11–5.

**Service to rugby:** Served on NZRFU executive 1974–1989; NZRFU delegate IRFB 1977–1989; IRFB honorary development officer 1990–1996; close association with development and organisation of the World Rugby Cup.

**Other:** A younger brother, Kevin, was an All Black fullback in 1955 and represented Canterbury 1949–56, while another brother, John, played for Canterbury in 1957.

**Miscellaneous:** Served in the Royal Navy in England during World War II, in the Atlantic and Burma; Honoured with OBE in 1974 for services to agriculture and rugby.

**Occupation:** Retired; was an agricultural economist with the Department of Agriculture and the NZ Dairy Board; executive director of the Agrigcultural Production Council; first director of the Vocational Training Council.

# IAN CLARKE

## *Wishbone never replaced backbone for Ian Clarke*

NAME THE player who led the All Blacks in a winning series not long after he had begun his international career and then was deposed as captain? He would never play another test in the position he filled as captain. Yet this 'ironman' would go on to play tests for almost another decade.

It sounds like a tricky quiz question and of course the reader can guess that Ian Clarke was the player concerned. But looking back into the history of the All Blacks, there would be few with a career history to match Ian James Clarke.

Clarke was a largely unsung hero of All Black rugby from 1953 through until 1964 – a period when the All Blacks steadily built their game into the most consistently successful in the world. It was his brother, the incomparable Don, who took the kudos, breaking record after record with his prodigious boot, at the same time sometimes saving the All Blacks from ignominious defeat.

Ian Clarke had played 83 matches for the All Blacks, including 24 tests, when he retired in 1964. He also held the record for the most first-class matches by a New Zealander. His great durability had taken him through 253 such games, still a huge number even by today's standards.

Standing 1.78m (5ft 10) and weighing 95kg (15st), Clarke was not a big forward. But besides his speed, he had good ball skills, was a strong scrummager and an excellent tackler. He was described by Terry McLean as 'especially gifted in having a most unusual degree of speed ... astonishing durability and inexhaustible energy built upon consistent physical fitness.'

He used this fitness to round off his game, becoming noted for his blocking work in the lineouts, an ability to charge down kicks around lineouts and rucks and his enthusiasm for putting pressure on the opposition by following up kicks of team-mates.'

'I've never met a man who trained harder; his amount of running was amazing,' said All Black team-mate Peter Jones. 'It was remarkable how he so seldom struck injuries and that he always played a good game. You'd never see him looking tired or lazy and you'd never find him in a sour or gloomy mood.'[1]

This last trait made Clarke the ideal tourist – a valuable characteristic for the long tours the All Blacks undertook in those days.

'An amusing man: at the parties, he could take off, to perfection, even to the falsetto at the end, the Inkspots in 'The Best Things in Life are Free', or sing a Spike Jones gobbledegook like a professional,' said McLean.[2]

Clarke was Taranaki born and bred. He went to Hawera Technical College before the family moved to the Waikato. The Clarkes joined the local Kereone club in 1947. Ian played for Waikato Juniors in 1949 and made the Kereone senior side the following year.

Dick Everest, who would build a fabulous Waikato team out of what had previously been a ragtag, country union, brought Ian and Don Clarke into the Waikato team in 1951. Ian would play all 13 matches that season, including the 6–3 win over North Auckland to lift the Ranfurly Shield when Don, then only 17, kicked the two penalties that won the game.

While Don would succumb to a knee injury that would delay for several years his rise to become the greatest matchwinner the All

*IN THE FAMILY: In 1961 the five Clarke brothers – Doug, Brian, Graeme, Ian and Don – played for Waikato against Thames Valley. It was an unusual feat*

Blacks had ever known, Ian became an integral part of the Waikato team. During the next two seasons, the shield would be lost to Auckland, regained a fortnight later and then finally handed over to Wellington.

Ian Clarke gained North Island representation in 1953, the first of seven inter-island matches for him. It was also a stepping stone for his selection in the All Blacks for the long tour to Britain and France. He made his test debut against Wales but was displaced by 'Snow' White for the other internationals. But he played 17 tour games, including two at No 8.

So, after just one test, Clarke was elevated to the captaincy for the series against the touring Wallabies in 1955. He played No 8. The series was won 2–1, the third test at Eden Park being lost 3–8.

However, it was very much an experimental year for the selectors. Clarke would lose the leadership role for the Springboks. He would also go back to the front row. But he held his place throughout the momentous series.

Clarke had also helped set the seal on the tour when he helped Waikato down the tourists in the opening match. 'It was one of those rare games where everything went exactly as we planned it,' said Clarke.[3]

Ian and Don became the first set of brothers to appear together in a test for New Zealand since Maurice and Cyril Brownlie played against France in 1925 when they strode out onto Lancaster Park, Christchurch, for the third test.

They would go on to help New Zealand in many series at home and away over the next seven years. Ian would play his last test in 1963 against the touring England team and Don on the 1964 tour v Australia. Ian was superseded by bigger, younger rivals but Don gave way to a

*FITNESS FREAK: Ian Clarke's fitness was legendary. Here, against NSW, with hooker Dennis Young on his shoulder, he scurries to recover lost possession*

knee injury at the beginning of 1965. Don's kicking feats are likely to remain a part of All Black folklore for long into the new millennium.

The Springboks of 1956 presented New Zealand with its first opportunity to beat the 'world champions' since the humiliations of 1949. All Black selector and coach Tom Morrison had written a form letter to over 800 players in the summer of 1955–56 – every first-class player from the previous season – asking them to get fit for the challenge.

This is what Don Clarke wrote of that summer:

'The Clarke family slaved at rugby for hours a day, seven days a week. We built weight-lifting gear with great chunks of firewood on the ends of heavy piping. Ian packed down against fence posts to build up his shoulders and strength for the rugged scrumming we knew lay ahead. My elder brother, Doug, fielded behind the goalposts during the thousands of shots at goal which soared off my boots.

'Slogging distance running around and around that home paddock in the dusk after milking more than 100 cows. Sweating, straining, seeking. And wondering if it was all worthwhile. It was, and for many reasons.'[4]

In 1957 Ian Clarke toured Australia with the All Blacks under the coaching of his Waikato coach, Everest. He played in two tests on the record-breaking tour. He appeared in both tests when the Wallabies came to New Zealand in 1958.

When the British Lions toured in 1959 Clarke played in the two opening tests but gave way to the heavier Mark Irwin for the third and fourth tests. The All Blacks toured South Africa in 1960 under coach Jack Sullivan, and Irwin and Nev MacEwan, normally a lock, were tried in Clarke's position in the first and third tests in an effort to counter the Springboks' power. Clarke got the second and fourth tests in a series lost 1–2.

Clarke was still in the tighthead position when France toured in 1961, Australia in 1962 and England in 1963. He also toured Australia in 1962 and completed his All Black days without a test on the big 1963–64 tour. Clarke had also led the All Blacks in tour games in England and Australia.

But it was his dropped goal from a mark against the All Blacks in the last game of the British section of the tour which stood out. Clarke had been chosen in the Barbarians side. He claimed a fair catch 35yds from the All Blacks' line and kicked the first points of the game. In fact, they were the only points for the home side as the All Blacks ran riot, scoring eight tries (with six conversions by brother Don) in the 36–3 demolition.

Back in 1961 against France, the Clarke brothers had been one of three sets of brothers on the field. The others were Colin and Stan Meads and the Frenchmen, Andre and Guy Boniface.

Clarke's final test, against England at Lancaster Park in 1963, allowed both he and brother Don to break 'Tiny' White's test appearance record.

When Clarke gained selection for his second tour to Britain, 10 years apart, he accomplished something that had never been done before. British tours, with those to South Africa, were the 'plum' tours for any All Black, but were many years apart for the first three-quarters of the 20th Century.

'I enjoyed playing and while I enjoyed it I just kept playing. The thrill and honour of being an All Black never diminished,' Clarke said.[5]

The Clarkes must rank as among the most remarkable families in New Zealand rugby history. The five brothers played for Waikato during the 1950s and 1960s. In one game in 1961, all five – Doug, Brian, Graeme, Ian and Don – played for the province against Thames Valley.

It was a feat to match the famous McKenzie brothers of the Wairarapa and the McMinn brothers of Manawatu. The five McKenzies played for Wairarapa in the earlier days. Ted and Norm, became All Black selectors and coaches, and a third, William ('Offside Mac') McKenzie, was an All Black captain. Five McMinn brothers played for Manawatu, with Archie and Paddy becoming All Blacks. The McKenzies and McMinns thus reached a pinnacle that could be compared with Ian and Don Clarke's All Black exploits.

Ian Clarke reached first-class level as referee, handling many provincial games.

He was elected junior vice-president of the NZRFU in 1991 and so became the first All Black test captain to become NZRFU president in 1993.

## Ian James Clarke (Waikato)

**Captain in three tests, two wins and one loss**
v. Australia 1955 (1, 2, 3)

**Born:** March 5, 1931, at Kaponga.

**Died:** June 29, 1997, at Morrinsville.

**Position:** Prop and No 8.

**Represented NZ:** 1953–64 – 83 matches (24 tests).

**Points for NZ:** 16 – 4 tries, 2 conversions.

**First-class record:** Waikato 1951–59, 61–63 (Kereone); North Island 1953–57, 59, 61; NZ Trials 1953–63; New Zealand XV 1954–56; Barbarians (UK) 1964.

**High school:** Hawera Technical College.

**Selector/coach/administrator:** Elected junior vice-president of the NZRFU in 1991, became the first All Black test captain to become NZRFU president in 1993.

**Miscellaneous:** Reached first-class level as referee, handling many provincial games. One of five brothers who played for Waikato during the 1950s and 1960s. In one game in 1961, all five brothers – Doug, Brian, Graeme, Ian and Don – played for the province against Thames Valley.

**Occupation:** A dairy farmer in the Morrinsville area, he became a meat buyer with AFFCO in the 1980s and farmed a small block part-time.

*(left) WELL-ROUNDED: The durable Ian Clarke held the record for the most first-class matches – 253 such games was a huge number for his era. He also had skills unusual for a prop forward of the time*

1, 3, 5 *100 Great Rugby Characters*
2 *Willie Away*, Terry McLean, Reeds, 1964.
4 *The Boot, Don Clarke's Story*, Don Clarke and Pat Booth, Reed, 1966.

# PAT VINCENT

## Bok tamer could not produce three in a row

PAT VINCENT was one of only four test captains to lead the All Blacks in every match in which they played for New Zealand.

The others were George Aitken, Fred Allen and Andy Leslie and, interestingly, all four had All Black careers which foundered on the rock that was New Zealand's nemesis for so many years, South Africa.

Aitken was a young Wellington centre who was dropped after the touring Springboks squared the series, 1–1, in 1921, the first time the two rugby giants had met. He went on to round out his career in the brilliant Scotland three-quarter line of the 1920s.

Allen never played serious rugby again after leading the All Blacks on the disastrous tour of South Africa in 1949. Leslie, after leading New Zealand back on a successful path in the mid-1970s, could not quite swing the series in South Africa in 1976.

Vincent's role in the most memorable series ever to have been played by the All Blacks is often under-estimated. He was a veteran Canterbury halfback who had first played for the province in 1945. In that time he had built up an outstanding record of leadership, culminating in Canterbury's long tenure as Ranfurly Shield holder from 1953 through to 1956. Critics have written that Vincent, aged 30, was probably past his best by 1956.

But the selectors were looking for leadership and Vincent certainly played his part in the early stages of the 1956 series. He led the All

*(left) SWEET AND SOUR: Pat Vincent led the All Blacks to victory in the first test of the 'gargantuan' 1956 series. But the Springboks, remarkably, had never lost two tests in a row since 1896. He would pay dearly*

Blacks to a deserved 10–6 victory in the first test in Dunedin. A week later he captained Canterbury to another of its wins over Springbok teams.

But the All Black selectors made five changes to their team for the second test at Wellington, disregarding the old adage that 'you never change a winning team.' Vincent came under severe criticism after this match for his tactical approach and for his own play, which at times came under severe pressure from the Springbok loose forwards.

But the Springboks, remarkably, had never lost two tests in a row since 1896. When they battled to an 8–3 victory in the heavy, cold conditions, Vincent was one of the victims as Tom Morrison and his fellow selectors made seven changes for the third test.

'Ponty' Reid, the tiny Waikato halfback with the reputation of tightly harnessing his forwards' efforts, was brought in. He had played a test in 1952. Robin Archer, Ron Hemi, Peter Jones and 'Tiny' Hill were added. But the most significant replacements were Don Clarke, who would begin a decade-long All Black career that would influence test outcomes as never before, and Kevin Skinner.

Bob Stuart was the co-opted All Black forward coach of that series, brought in to get the forward momentum back into the team. Stuart, aged only 33, had led the All Blacks on the great tour of Britain and France only three years earlier. He had also captained many Canterbury sides with Vincent in the team.

'I played no part in the selections, though Tom Morrison, Jack Sullivan and Arthur Marslin listened to my views,' Stuart told the author in 1997. 'Some of the players' form was erratic right through the many trials. Don Clarke did not play well. Peter Jones was overweight

133

*CHANGING TIMES: Pat Vincent and Bob Duff – captain and vice-captain of the All Blacks. Duff had played all his rugby – for school, province and country – under Vincent's leadership. Until now …*

and out of condition. Skinner was nowhere to be seen early in the season.'

'So there were players who should have had form, but didn't have at the start. The selectors got the blame for not picking them, but you couldn't,' Stuart said. 'In a sense, with a four-test series and a win in the first one, the second test became expendable.

'Pat hadn't had a good second test. The All Blacks had frittered away their chances with the wind in the first half, making too many mistakes. They needed someone who would drive the bigger, more powerful forwards now in the side. To some extent Pat was a victim because he had not had the strongest of teams to lead early in the series.'

But no one in New Zealand could argue with the selections and the tactics after the third test, won 17–10 at Christchurch. The result turned the series around and the side was able to go on at Auckland and complete the series win, 11–5.

So Vincent's All Black career was over – three weeks after it had begun. Ironically, his Canterbury team-mate, Bob Duff, would be elevated to the All Black captaincy and lead the team to success. Duff, who had come into the Canterbury team in the same game as Vincent, against Ashburton County in 1945, had played his entire career, right back to Christchurch Boys' High First XV school days, under Vincent's leadership.

But Vincent had enjoyed a long and fruitful time with Canterbury. He became the first player from the province to play 100 games.

Canterbury's great run with the Ranfurly Shield was led by Jack Rankin through to 1955 and then by Neil McPhail and Jack Morton. Canterbury had some memorable moments with the shield – and some narrow escapes. When his team, down 0–9 against Otago in 1954, just scraped home with a last-minute 9–all draw from a Derek Mayo try, Vincent would drolly say at the after-match function: 'We can't leave our run any later than that.'

Lindsay Knight, in his great book, *Shield Fever*, wrote that 'in spite of his impressive deeds in provincial rugby there was far from universal acclaim for Vincent's talents' and he 'was constantly overlooked for higher honours. His detractors said that while he may have been a tactical maestro he lacked the necesssary qualities for the highest level because of a lack of speed.'

Vincent was a rugged halfback, standing 5ft 9in and weighing 12st 5lb. He delivered a quick pass and had a fine break from the scrum.

He became a Canterbury selector-coach in 1959–62 before moving to the United States in 1967. He coached teams in California and managed the California Grizzlies on their tour of New Zealand in 1972.

## Patrick Bernard Vincent (Canterbury)

**Captain in two tests, a win and a loss**
v. South Africa 1956 (1, 2)

**Born:** January 6, 1926, Wataroa.

**Died:** April 10, 1983, Pittsburgh.

**Position:** Halfback.

**Represented NZ:** 1956 – 2 matches (2 tests).

**Points for NZ:** Nil.

**First-class record:** Canterbury 1945 (Training college), 46, 48–56 (Christchurch HSOB); South Island and NZ Trials 1951, 53, 56.

**High school:** Christchurch BHS, 1st XV 1943.

**Selector/coach/administrator:** Selector/coach Canterbury 1959–62; president Christchurch Secondary Schools' RFU 1966, 67; coached St Mary's College (California) and the Californian Grizzlies to British Columbia 1971; managed the Grizzles on their New Zealand tour in 1972; president of North California RFU 1973–76; governor of the United States RFU 1975–77.

**Other:** One of only four test captains to have led the All Blacks in every match in which they played for New Zealand. The others were George Aitken, Fred Allen and Andy Leslie.

**Miscellaneous:** Became first player to reach 100 games for Canterbury. Brothers Bill (Canterbury 1931, 32 and West Coast 1935, 36) and Bob (West Coast 1939) also played representative rugby.

**Occupation:** Was a master at Christchurch Boys' High 1947–67; then in real estate in San Fransisco before being an administrator of St Mary's College.

# BOB DUFF

## *When the winner takes all*

ONE OF the many ironies of Bob Duff's long rugby career came when he replaced Pat Vincent as All Black captain for the third and fourth tests against the Springboks in 1956.

He had been vice-captain when Vincent led the All Blacks to a first test win and second test loss in the series, after which Vincent and others were axed for a new-look side which included Don Clarke, Kevin Skinner, 'Tiny' Hill, 'Ponty' Reid and Peter Jones.

But Duff had played under Vincent's leadership for many, many years. They had first played together in the Christchurch Boys' High School First XV in 1943. They made their debut for Canterbury in the same game, against Ashburton County, in 1945. The pair later helped spearhead the great Canterbury team which held the Ranfurly Shield from 1953 to 1956 and produced many All Blacks.

Vincent would be dumped after leading two teams, the All Blacks in the first test, and Canterbury a week later, to victory over the mighty Springboks. He was believed to be the first person to accomplish this feat, within this timeframe.

But sentiment counted for little in this momentous series. Every All Black, especially Duff, knew the remaining tests had to be won for the glory of New Zealand, which had never beaten the Springboks in a series at home or away since the two world giants first clashed in 1921. That Duff led his All Blacks to two great victories puts him on a special pedestal among All Black captains.

*(left) SELF BELIEF: New Zealand had never beaten the Springboks in a series. But with Bob Duff as captain, and after vital selection changes, the 1956 All Blacks became an irresistible force that changed the face of international rugby for ever*

Ever since that fateful afternoon on August 18, 1956 when he led the All Blacks out from under a Lancaster Park stand to face the mighty Boks with a certain Kevin Lawrence Skinner jogging behind him, Duff has faced controversy in dealing with Skinner's reputation for 'stoush'.

But South African journalist Max Price's tour book, *Springboks at Bay*, summed up the Springbok attitude to the All Black approach to beating the Boks for the first time:

'We had been aware long before of the great forward strength of New Zealand teams, but when it hit the Springboks full blast at Waikato with fierce rucks flattening out roads to the Springbok defence line, we sat back almost stunned.

'This was something entirely new. However tough it was thought the forward play of New Zealand would be, none, not the Springboks, nor the selectors, press and public of South Africa, were prepared for forward play of this hard-hitting commando-like character.'

Morrie Mackenzie, in his 1960 book, *All Blacks in Chains*, asked how good was Bob Duff's side, so swiftly elevated from years of mediocrity to the slippery heights of world supremacy?

'The two best previous sides of our modern era were the 1924 All Blacks and Philip Nel's 1937 Springboks. I do not think that either could have beaten Bob Duff's All Blacks, certainly not in the third and fourth tests.

'Such tremendous physical strength and controlled power as the 1956 All Blacks possessed up front, plus the goal-kicking fullback of the majestic range, under pressure, of Don Clarke, will swamp and crush to death the most brilliant footballers who ever lived.

'What a collection of human tanks were

these. Skinner, Hemi and Ian Clarke in the front row; two sons of Anak, Duff and White, locking the pack in a grip of iron; with Hill behind them driving it relentlessly forward; while the superheavyweight sprinter Jones and the ghostlike Clark alternately angled their pushing power or sped like guided missiles to their targets in midfield.

'Here (alas, for one test series only) was gathered together the finest set of forwards I have ever seen.' It was high praise indeed from a journalist who had observed generations of international rugby players.

Duff told the author in January 2000 that an abiding memory was the intensity of that series.

'The win over the Springboks certainly gave us immense satisfaction but I believe we will always have lasting memories, probably more grim than pleasant, of the demanding expectations of the news media, the general public and the NZRFU,' he said.

The unprecedented preparations, master-minded by the chairman of selectors and head coach, Tom Morrison, were fully documented for the first time in the book, *The Power Behind the All Blacks*, by the author. Morrison's private papers were released by his family.

'Tom Morrison told me some time later he had never known of such a demanding build-up for a test series and expressed the hope no players in the future would be subject to the pressures and tensions of those matches,' Duff said.

Duff's All Black playing career spanned 1951–56, all of it spent in the mighty All Black engine room, locking the scrum with the legendary 'Tiny' White. Duff played in all of the three tests when the All Blacks toured Australia in 1951, clean-sweeping the series. Two tests followed when the Wallabies toured New Zealand in 1952.

A new accountancy practice meant he was unavailable for the decade's most important tour, the 1953–54 trip to Britain and France, the All Black team captained by Bob Stuart, his Canterbury captain, the man who would assist the national selectors in plotting the downfall of the Springboks. Duff made a comeback in 1955 against the touring Australians, after being unavailable for the opening test through injury.

Duff fondly recalls his long partnership locking All Black scrums with White, whose All Black career spanned 1949-56. 'Tiny was

one of the great players and that comes through when you see his name is always mentioned in these 'All Black Greats' selections every few years,' said Duff.

'He was a superb physical specimen, very athletic, fast, had plenty of skills and possessed a genuine spring to his jump. I guess I was lucky to play alongside him,' said Duff, before reconsidering that he had other skills that complemented White's. 'We were both over 6ft 3in and 16st. That might sound puny compared to some of the big locks of 6ft 7in and 18st today, but in the 1950s that was big.'

Duff may long be remembered for another chapter in All Black rugby's folklore. This one, as infamous as the first was famous, was that he was coach of the touring 1972–73 All Blacks from which Keith Murdoch was banished.

For some, the 1972 tour – and Bob Duff – are remembered only for the Keith Murdoch incident, the actions of the so-called 'Mafia' within the All Black ranks, and the loss to the Barbarians in a splendid running match which the British have dined out on and employed as a 'coaching manual' ever since.

But that's not how Duff and the team remember it. Grant Batty described it as 'the happiest tour I ever went on'. Bryan Williams recalled the build-up to the great victory over Wales as 'the best build-up to any test in which I played.' Alex Wyllie, who would return to Britain as coach of the All Blacks nearly 20 years later, said that the 1972–73 team carried an unjust reputation. The team could have faltered with the expulsion of Murdoch after the first of its five tests. Instead, in adversity and under pressure, it grew stronger.

'Bob Duff was vital to us. He got on well with all the players, and he was well respected. He had such a young team, probably one of the youngest the All Blacks had ever had on tour,' said Wyllie.

Sid Going was another who felt Duff had unfairly taken the blame for problems on the tour. Going stated how Duff had cleverly played to the young team's strengths. 'He wanted the forwards to dominate and the backs to keep play close and eliminate mistakes. He restored tightness to the forwards that had been lost in South Africa and against the Lions.'

Though he received little credit for the achievement, Duff's brief era as coach of the All Blacks was to lay the foundations for a brilliant decade through the 1970s. How else can one explain the fact that so many of the brilliant youngsters he took to Britain and France in 1972 became the backbone of the All Blacks, season after season?

His All Black team should have become the first All Blacks to win the Grand Slam. They beat Wales, Scotland and England and then suffered the ignominy, after dominating throughout, of a 10–10 draw when Ireland scored in the final moments.

'The team did not carry out the plan I had asked of them,' said Duff of the Irish test, when interviewed in 1997. 'We were superior and should have won it.'

It is also notable Duff's team's achievements came between the two great Lions tours of 1971 (beating the All Blacks in New Zealand) and 1974 (beating the Springboks in South Africa). British rugby was at its strongest level in history, before or since.

The Grand Slam was therefore left for Jack Gleeson's 1978 All Blacks to achieve.

Duff lost the coaching berth to JJ Stewart for the England test in 1973 and was dropped from the panel at the end of that season. He told the author he would be less than honest to state it didn't disappoint him.

The All Blacks returned to Britain in 1974 under Stewart and new captain Andy Leslie. The team did well and it seemed a bold new era. But the team that beat Wales in 1974 contained 11 players from Duff's side: Karam, Batty, Williams, Robertson, Hurst, Going, Kirkpatrick, Macdonald, Whiting, Lambert and Norton. It was a new-look team with old-look players!

Duff, who became deputy mayor of Lyttelton, near Christchurch, now lives in retirement in Christchurch with his wife Neroli. They both play bridge and golf.

## Robert Hamilton Duff (Canterbury)

**Captain in two tests, two wins**
v. South Africa 1956 (3, 4)

**Born:** Lyttelton, August 5, 1925.

**Position:** Lock forward.

**Represented NZ:** 1951, 52, 55, 56 – 18 matches (11 internationals).

**Provincial record:** Canterbury 1945–53, 55–57; South Island 1951–53, 55–57.

**High school:** Christchurch Boys' High School, First XV 1942–43

**Selector/coach:** Canterbury 1963–66, South Island 1967–72.

**NZ selector:** 1971–73.

**NZ coaching record:** 1972–73: beat Australia 29–6, 30–17; 38–3; beat Wales 19–6, beat Scotland 14–9, beat England 9–0, drew with Ireland 10–10, lost to France 6–13.

**Other:** Life member, NZ Trotting Club; former chairman, Addington Raceway; former board member, NZ Racing Industry Board (formerly the NZ Racing Authority).

**Occupation:** Accountant.

# ALAN 'PONTY' REID

## All Blacks' little Napoleon took back step to no one

ONE OF the smallest players ever to wear the All Black jersey, 'Ponty' Reid stood only 5ft 3 in and weighed under 9st 7lb. But he was an outstanding tactical halfback who was a master at whipping the behemoth forwards who usually packed down before him for Waikato and the All Blacks into formidable combinations.

But Reid's size was misleading. He was a strong, wiry man. At New Plymouth Boys' High, where he played four years in the First XV, he had also been a fine gymnast.

He used his suppleness, quick reflexes and strong wrists on the rugby field, as many a giant forward who underestimated his nippiness could testify. He had a quick, long pass, a handy repertoire of kicks and could make the quick dashes around the scrum or ruck to link with his loose forwards as required.

Reid was an integral part of a Waikato team which had made the rest of New Zealand sit up and pay attention. From the early 1950s its brilliant coach, Dick Everest, honed a hard, basic style of winning rugby from his country players. Waikato had strong players in key positions. Reid the ring master was complemented by dedicated and skilful stars such as hookers Has Catley and Ron Hemi, and forwards Ian Clarke, George Nola, Hugh McLaren and Jim Graham, with a young Don Clarke a rock at the back.

When the New Zealand selectors decided to bring Reid and Clarke into the test team that was battling the touring Springboks for the mythical world crown in 1956, they were an instant success. When they teamed Reid as captain with Everest as coach the following year, the fireworks really crackled.

Reid had first toured with the All Blacks to Australia in 1951. But he did not make his test debut until the first test of the series against the touring Wallabies in 1952.

It was a four-year wait for Reid to regain his test jersey. But the delay may have been worth it when he was part of a rejuvinated All Black team that fought back from a 1–1 series to beat the Springboks in the third and fourth tests of 1956. Reid replaced the All Black captain, Canterbury's Pat Vincent. It was the first time New Zealand had ever beaten South Africa in a series.

Reid's promotion was due in large part to the way he had led his Waikato team to its great 14–10 victory over the Springboks in their first tour game. Reid and his players gave most of the credit to the wily Everest.

The way Waikato confronted the huge Springboks from the opening whistle impressed the critics from both countries. A South African journalist was later to write that the tourists never quite recovered from the greeting.

'As an old soldier too, Everest knew the importance of surprise,' wrote veteran Kiwi journalist, Morrie McKenzie of the game. 'I never seemed to get around to check on the story that 10 minutes before the Waikato match against the Springboks, he had his men out on the practice area behind the stand, and put them through their drill at top speed.

'If it isn't true, it ought to be, because right

*PLENTY OF ROOM: Ponty Reid works the 'box kick' as team-mates (from left) Bill Clark, Tiny White, Ian Clarke and Ron Hemi block the Springboks in the third test, 1956, at Christchurch*

from the opening whistle, the Waikato pack tore in like a pack of fiends, hit the first man who took the ball, with such an ungodly wallop that they cleaved the Springbok defences asunder like a hard-hit wedge in splitting a log.

'Before the bemused world champions could gather their startled wits, Ponty Reid had worked the blindside as no other half in New Zealand could do since Jimmy Mill, and Malcolm McDonald, the Waikato wing, was over for the first try of the tour.'[1]

As the Waikato effort flagged, the Springboks fought back to 14–10 with two converted tries.

Continued Mackenzie: 'And then when the Waikato forwards looked completely done, little Ponty Reid rallied them in the most emotional incident of a memorable game.

'Astonished observers gasped as a 9st halfback, a pigmy among Springbok giants, came charging through a gap at the head of a dribbling rush, flanked by Ian Clarke and the equally lion-hearted Jim Graham. There was no holding men who could call on such reserves of will, when their physical powers were almost exhausted. Waikato with their 14 men saw it out. They not only won, but they struck a moral blow for New Zealand, which was both the beginning and the end of the 1956 Springbok tour.'

In the third test against the Springboks at Lancaster Park, Christchurch, Reid had been provided plenty of freedom in which to work, with a muscular forward pack that included Kevin Skinner for the first time in the series, plus 'Tiny' Hill and Peter Jones. In the first half particularly, he kept the game close either by kicking into touch or over the line of forwards into no-man's land.

His opposite, Tommy Gentles, on the other hand, was constantly troubled by forwards booting through, and the little South African scrum-half had to face a withering assault, particularly from the giant forward, Jones.

Meanwhile, Don Clarke was kicking some huge goals, which helped the All Blacks to a 17–11 victory and the impetus that was not relented in the fourth test at Eden Park. The All Blacks won 11–5 to take a series over their archrivals for the first time in 35 years.

Reid was appointed captain of the All Blacks for their triumphant 1957 tour of Australia. That side is still rated one of the finest international teams to visit Australia. It set all sorts of records, including a total of 463 points in 13 official matches. Don Clarke, with 163 points, eclipsed Ron Jarden's mark for a New Zealand player in Australia. Russell Watt, the

*SIZE DOESN'T COUNT: Tiny Ponty Reid is pictured front row, second from right. The team is the combined Waikato-King Country-Thames Valley which played the British Lions in 1950.*

speedy Southland three-quarter, with 17 tries, at last equalled the mark of the 1903 team's Opai Asher. There were other records too.

Reid led his side to victory in both tests, 25–11 and 22–9. In the opening test, he nursed through two forwards who were making their tests debuts. Wilson Whineray and Colin Meads would go on to forge wonderful records and make the All Blacks virtually unbeatable over many years.

Reid led an unchanged side in the second test and, as in the first test, his players scored four tries to one. Meads, deputising on the wing, scored the first of seven tries throughout his 15-year international career. Don Clarke kicked a 45-yard goal from a mark, with his brother, Ian, holding the ball. It was the first such goal since Mark Nicholls had landed one against the Lions at Lancaster Park, Christchurch, in 1930.

Whineray, who would take over from Reid as

the All Black captain the next year, remembers the style of Reid and Everest as very consultative.

'We would go back to the team's hotel after a game and before attending the official function that evening. There Dick and Ponty would go over the game with us. They were completely constructive, which was a great help to young players like myself.'

This tour proved to be Reid's swansong for he retired from first-class rugby after one game for Waikato the following season.

He had made his debut for Waikato in 1950, the season Everest began building the first of so many superb Waikato sides in subsequent decades. Reid, McLaren, Nola and Graham would all make strong impacts on Waikato's fortunes in the seasons ahead. Waikato also had the remarkable Catley, a great All Black hooker who had made his representative debut at 19 in 1935 and would play his final game for Waikato

20 years later. In 1951 the Clarke brothers, Ian and Don, would come into the team.

The tiny halfback replaced the much more robust Bill Conrad, who had been one of the All Blacks whose careers were destroyed on the ill-fated 1949 tour of South Africa. Conrad was the antithesis of Reid, weighing almost 13st but was too slow a passer for the international game. He retired after one game for Waikato in 1950.

Reid was virtually unknown to his fellow Waikato players in that first winter. He had just arrived from Auckland Teachers' College to teach in Raglan. Recalled Gordon Brunskill, who played as first five-eighth for Waikato at the time: 'I first saw him at a training run and I looked at him with amazement. I thought to myself, "Who's this little jockey they've got hold of now."' But playing outside him Brunskill soon learned the worth of the little man.[2]

Waikato, with Reid manipulating the play, won the Ranfurly Shield from North Auckland, 6–3, in 1951, the teenaged Don Clarke kicking two penalties. It would lose the shield the next season to Auckland, 9–0, but win it back 6–3 some 14 days later and hold it through until Wellington lifted the log on August 1, 1953. Though the shield had gone, Waikato remained very much a power through subsequent seasons.

After he retired from representative football, Reid continued to play for the Kereone club until 1961.

He then coached the senior side in 1963–64 and was a Waikato selector in 1966–69.

## Alan Robin Reid (Waikato)

**Captain in two tests, two wins** v. Australia 1957 (1, 2)

**Born:** April 12, 1929, Te Kuiti.

**Died:** November 16, 1994, Morrinsville.

**Position:** Halfback.

**Represented NZ:** 1951, 52, 56, 57 – 17 matches (5 tests).

**Points for NZ:** 6 – 2 tries.

**First-class record:** Waikato 1950 (Raglan), 1951–57 (Frankton), 1958 (Kereone); North Island 1950–52, 56, 57; NZ Trials 1951, 53, 56, 57; NZ XV 1952; Waikato-King Country-Thames Valley 1950.

**High school:** New Plymouth BHS 1st XV 1944–47.

**Selector/coach/administrator:** Coached Kereone club 1963–64 and Waikato selector 1966–69.

**Occupation:** A schoolteacher 1950–58, then a mercer in Morrinsville.

1 *All Blacks in Chains*
2 *Shield Fever*

# WILSON WHINERAY

## Whineray may be popular choice as 'greatest' captain

REMEMBERED FOR his leadership qualities above all else, Wilson Whineray still ranks as perhaps the finest All Black captain of all time.

It is impossible to objectively compare Whineray with the All Blacks' many other outstanding leaders, such as Brian Lochore, Graham Mourie, Andy Dalton and Sean Fitzpatrick. He had a longer tenure than that group as captain and a greater success rate. But he also led a superbly strong team and played under different rules.

Whineray was also the first of the truly great long-term All Black captains. Before Whineray, during almost eight decades of New Zealand representative rugby teams, Cliff Porter, the famous captain of the 1924 Invincibles and the dominant leader through to 1930, was the skipper with the most tests. But his total was only seven.

Whineray became the All Blacks' third-youngest captain in 1958, at the age of 23. Only George Aitken in 1921 and Herb Lilburne in 1929 were younger. Whineray had played in two tests in Australia the year before. He was to lead New Zealand through until 1965, apart from 1964, when he took a year off to complete university studies.

His record was 30 tests as captain, with only five defeats. Overall, he had played 77 matches for the All Blacks, 68 as captain.

Whineray's only series loss was to the Springboks in South Africa in 1960. South Africa won two tests, New Zealand one, and one was drawn. But there was controversy over the fourth test, lost 3–8, after a try by All Black Frank McMullen was disallowed.

Whineray had scored two tries in his first test as captain, against Australia in 1958, but they were to be the only tries the loosehead prop forward would score in his long test career.

Whineray's men won that series 2–1, and others against the British Lions in 1959, France in 1961, Australia in 1962 (home and away series), England in 1963 and South Africa in 1965.

Perhaps the highlight of Whineray's career was the 1963–64 tour of Britain and France. Rugby writer Terry McLean wrote that Whineray was mature beyond his years and a firm but calm leader who commanded unqualified admiration. 'I would unhesitatingly acclaim him as New Zealand's greatest captain,' said McLean.

The tour was a great success, although the Grand Slam was denied the All Blacks by the draw with Scotland.

But he became the first All Black captain to win a test at Cardiff Arms Park. And in the finale to the tour, when his side beat the Barbarians, 36–3, he scored the final try, with a stylish and well-timed dummy clearing the way to the posts. 'I think I was always a loose forward at heart,' recalled Whineray in 1999, with more than a hint of sincerity.

But he was sometimes criticised for being too conservative in his approach. In *Mud in Your Eye*, former team-mate Chris Laidlaw claimed the reason All Black backs throughout the 1960s, with the possible exception of 1967, never appeared to be up to much, was the demands placed upon them by forward captains, particularly Whineray.

'Rightly in terms of results, and wrongly in

terms of the evolution of New Zealand back play, Whineray, and of course the coaches of the day, dictated that most of the well-won posession, rather than being fed to the backs to exploit, was first made available for forward moves.'

'But Whineray knew how to win matches, and understood very well that he had been uncommonly lucky to have emerged at a time when the finest imaginable group of forwards seemed to appear from everywhere. With companions such as Tremain, Meads, Graham, Clarke, Young and MacEwan, he could hardly go wrong. He didn't.'

But this view should be tempered with a study of the rules of the day. Whineray was a product of the 1950s, when gargantuan forward battles were the norm. The true potential of the momentous 1963 rule changes had also not been realised.

But Laidlaw also had praise. 'All sorts of qualifications of the word 'great' were applied to Whineray's All Blacks. Several times the team fought back from seemingly impossible situations, as much as 11–0 on two occasions, and at the end of every match were in top gear.'[1]

Interviewed by the author in 1999 Whineray said his onfield captaincy style had not been consultative.

'There is not time for that. To change the run of the game, when things are not going well, sounds easy, but in fact is not,' said Whineray.

'The pace of a test match can be terrific – just a blur for the young player having his first test, for instance. You don't get many chances to communicate. My method was to say to the players, 'Just do what I ask – I'll take responsibility afterwards if the result doesn't turn out well.''

Whineray told the author it hadn't been difficult, on the few occasions when the All Blacks were well down on the scoreboard, for him to decide to change tack. 'The captain has to make an instant decision to uplift the tempo or pull a move out of the hat.

'But the hardest part is deciding how to handle a narrow lead. Do you try to preserve that lead – by working the blindside or dropping a forward out into the backs – or increase the attacking tempo? There's a degree of risk whatever you decide.'

Unanimity was the key to tactical success, Whineray said. 'Remember Lucien Mias and the 1958 French team which became the first to beat the Springboks in South Africa. If 15 players do the 'wrong' thing, they can still succeed.'

The 1960 series was notable for the stupendous front row battles. Whineray marked the very powerful Piet du Toit, who had toured New Zealand as a 19-year-old with the 1956 Springboks. By 1960 he had matured into a ferocious scrummager who liked nothing better than to wreak havoc with the front rows. He would become even more devastating in Britain the following year, when players in the Oxford and Cambridge games walked off the field, disgusted by his tactics.

'It is all illegal today,' recalled Whineray. 'In fact, it was illegal then too. The collapsing of the scrums wasn't the problem, for me, that the media made out. The All Blacks' tighthead count over the entire series was something like 16–4 in our favour. Sometimes I used to go down in the front row, just so we could reset the scrum and get the ball in quickly, before Piet could re-start his capers.'

Recalling his career in 1999, Whineray described the 1960 series loss as a lowpoint. But the result 'went right down to the wire in the fourth test, when Frank McMullen clearly scored a try that should not have been disallowed.'

In fact, Whineray completed a very successful career against the Springboks. In eight tests, he won four. He was also in winning teams for Canterbury and NZ Universities (1956) and Auckland (1965) against South Africa.

The high of a long career was the tour to Britain and France under coach Neil McPhail, who must rival Fred Allen, among several outstanding candidates, for the 'title' of greatest All Black coach. 'It was a very professional team on the field and a very happy one off it,' recalled Whineray. 'It set in place the careers of a lot of players who would play for the All Blacks for some years to come.'

Whineray had first played senior rugby for the Waikaia club in Southland as a 16-year-old in 1952. While on a government rural cadet

*(left) WILING AWAY: Wilson Whineray croons a high note, as Dennis Young writes home and Bill Davis strums the ukulele on another railway station in Britain*

*NO DUMMY: Wilson Whineray was not a big prop, having converted from a halfback in the Auckland Grammar First XV into a No 8. But he was agile enough, as this tackle on a Welsh opponent on the 1963–1964 tour shows.*

scholarship he played for Wairarapa as an 18-year-old in 1953 and had played for another four unions – Mid-Canterbury, Manawatu, Canterbury and Waikato – before settling back in Auckland in 1959 for the remainder of his career.

He had played in seven Canterbury Ranfurly Shield defences, beaten the 1956 Springboks with Canterbury and NZ Universities, toured overseas with NZ Colts, NZ under-23 and All Black teams, and was captain of New Zealand by then.

He captained Auckland to lift the shield from Southland in 1959, playing in his beloved No 8 position. But Bob Graham became the Auckland captain while Whineray was in South Africa in 1960 and held the job during a long and successful period under coach Fred Allen. Whineray was always happy to play under Graham, seeing good sense in the continuity of Auckland's leadership by doing so.

The record-breaking shield era ended in 1963 when Wellington lifted it. Taranaki took the log at the first challenge and held it until Auckland regained it in 1965. Whineray's last of 240 first class matches was in 1966, when Auckland lost the shield to Waikato.

After attending Harvard Business School in 1967–69, Whineray eventually became managing director of Carter Holt Harvey. After a long career in the corporate business world he still has a number of directorships.

Reflecting on his tenure as All Black captain, Whineray said he had slowly come to the realisation of the glorious era he had played in. 'When you're younger you take it all for granted,' he said. 'But it was a huge privilege to be involved with and against some of the best players in the world, and to travel to faraway places and be with your team-mates.'

Whineray pondered at the change in international rugby from amateur to professional – 'the circumstances that drive players on into their thirties nowadays involves money.'

Whineray coached club rugby in Auckland and Wellington after he retired and retains a keen interest.

Whineray was knighted for services to sport in 1998. He and his wife, Elizabeth, live in Remuera, Auckland. They have three children.

---

# Sir Wilson James Whineray (Waikato and Auckland)

**Captain in 30 tests, wins, five losses and three draws**
v. Australia 1958 (1, 2, 3)
v. British Isles 1959 (1, 2, 3, 4)
v. South Africa 1960 (1, 2, 3, 4)
v. France 1961 (1, 2, 3)
v. Australia 1962 (1, 2 in Australia and 1, 2, 3 in NZ)
v. England 1963 (1, 2)
v. Ireland, Wales, Scotland, England, France 1963–64,
v. South Africa 1965 (1, 2, 3, 4)

**Born:** July 10, 1935.

**Position:** Prop.

**Represented NZ:** 1957–65 – 77 matches (32 tests).

**Points for NZ:** 24 – 7 tries, 1 dropped goal.

**First-class record:** Wairarapa 1953 (Martinborough club); Mid-Canterbury 1954 (Rakaia); Manawatu 1955 (University); Canterbury 1956–57 (Lincoln College); Waikato 1958 (City); Auckland 1959–63, 65, 66 (Grammar); South Island 1957; North Island 1958, 59, 61–63, 65; NZ Trials 1957–63, 65; NZ Under-23 1958; NZ Colts 1955; NZ Universities 1956, 57.

**High school:** Auckland Grammar First XV 1950, 51.

**Selector/coach/administrator:** Coach Grammar 1970–73, including one Gallaher Shield title, and Onslow club 1974.

**Miscellaneous:** NZ Universities boxing champion; awarded OBE 1961 and knighted in 1998. Former chairman of the Hillary Commission and life member of the NZ Sports Foundation. Honorary colonel of the 1st NZ SAS.

**Occupation:** Was deputy managing director of Carter Holt Harvey; now chairman of Carter Holt Harvey and the National Bank and a director of Auckland International Airport, Comalco New Zealand, Wilson & Horton, and Nestle Australia.

---

1 *Mud in Your Eye,* Chris Laidlaw, Reeds, 1973.

# JOHN GRAHAM

## *Caretaker Graham kept great All Black record intact*

THE ALL Blacks of the 1960s built the finest record in New Zealand rugby's great history. In the years between 1960 and 1970 they did not lose a series. The two long-term captains of that era were Wilson Whineray and Brian Lochore. But in 1964, Whineray took a year off big rugby, passing the reins to his longtime compatriot, John Graham, who led the side to a 2–1 series win over Australia.

But there was irony in the fact that Graham, after an outstanding All Black career, would lead the All Blacks to defeat in his final match for New Zealand.

It was a loss which, while Graham felt it keenly, his All Black team-mates considered unjust for such a fine servant of the black jersey and a player who had maintained such high standards throughout his career.

A team-mate that day, the incomparable Colin Meads, who would suffer even worse ignominy at the end of his career when he captained New Zealand in the losing 1971 series against the Lions, said: 'The one great miscarriage of justice in the Australians' 20–5 victory in the third test of 1964 was that it occurred when New Zealand was under the captaincy of Graham. He, least of all, deserved that.'

'Deputising' for Whineray – who had led New Zealand continuously since 1958 and

*(left) HIGHLY RATED: John Graham – here, in the headgear, recovering possession from broken play against England in the first test of 1963 – was rated as the finest captain a prominent team-mate ever played under*

would come back to help defeat the touring Springboks in 1965 – Graham had already led the All Blacks to a win in the series, New Zealand taking the first two tests, 14–9 and 18–3.

Graham had contributed so much to one of New Zealand's finest eras in a long career of 22 tests since 1958. Playing under All Black coaches Jack Sullivan and Neil McPhail, the All Blacks had seldom tasted defeat in those eras. Apart from the close-fought 1960 series in South Africa, the All Blacks would not lose a series between 1949 and 1970.

But that Australian defeat hurt Graham's pride. 'The enormity of it is what shattered us. There were no excuses,' he said. He would not play for the All Blacks again, although he was a reserve throughout the 1965 series.

Graham had by this time played 53 matches for the All Blacks, against the world's strongest nations. He had also led Canterbury and the South Island from 1961 to 1965. The inter-island victories of 1962 and 1963 are among his favourite memories to this day. His team was always the underdog, but with much planning and 'psyching up' of his team-mates he was able to pull off great victories.

'The North Island were so strong they always had All Blacks in their reserves. But they were on a hiding to nothing – because they were always expected to win. For the South Islanders, it was a way to play your way into the All Blacks,' explained Graham.

'Tactically, we never passed it, we put the boot to it often and prayed for rain. Both teams used to stay in the same hotel in those days. They played cards to wile away the hours. But

I would tell our guys not to play with them. We would mooch around, concentrate on the job at hand and then grab the chance to do something special. It drove the North Islanders crazy!'

Chris Laidlaw, another subject for this book, told the author that Graham rated as the finest captain he ever played under, including Whineray. 'His tactical brain, especially playing in a position where he could see everything happening, was awsome,' said Laidlaw. It should be remembered that Graham's brother, Bob, captained Auckland over Whineray.

Graham might never have become more than a good club player had not his New Plymouth Boys' High First XV coach of 1950–52, John 'JJ' Stewart, who would later become the All Black coach, written a letter to him. Graham was then a first five-eighth and the letter stated: 'You are bloody slow as a back but you'll be very fast as a forward.'

'I was heartbroken,' Graham revealed to the author in 1999. 'I kept the letter for many years. But I quickly accepted that 'JJ' was right and from that point worked as hard as I could to learn the loose forward's game.' He recalled he was not the only future All Black of that era to make a similar drastic positional change. 'In my first big interschool game, against Auckland Grammar, Wilson Whineray was the halfback for Grammar and scored the winning try!'

From that point Graham was a No 8 or flanker. He was reasonably small (13st 2lb and 5ft 11in) in an era when national selectors were usually obsessed with size. But he had attributes such as speed, intelligence, mental hardness and a high skill level that allowed him to outplay bigger rivals. He was a deadly tackler and a specialist at setting up the ruck from the tackled ball.

After high school, Graham moved to Auckland and joined the University club. He played 20 times for Auckland between 1955 and 1957, including meeting the 1956 Springboks.

'I had only played five or six games for Auckland when we met the Boks. It was a brutal game. 'Snow' White and Jaap Bekker started hoeing into each other at the very first scrum. I wondered what the hell was going to happen,' recalled Graham. Though South Africa finished with only 13 men, it won the dour match, 6–3.

Graham moved to Canterbury in 1958. The attraction was his future wife, Shiela. But his rugby was to blossom also. He made his All Black debut at No 8 that year against Australia and scored a sensational try. Graham broke from a lineout, kicked over the fullback's head, regained the ball on the full and scored.

But after playing the second test he was dropped. A knee cartilage operation put him out of contention for the touring British Lions in 1959, allowing his future great rival, 'Red' Conway, to establish himself in the team.

But Graham had recovered to be part of Canterbury's victory over the Lions that year and described the preparation by coach Bob Stuart (who had been an All Black captain, and a co-opted All Black forward coach in 1956) as 'unbelievable'.

'Bob was a hard man. He told 'Tiny' Hill that if the Lions started obstructing in the lineouts, he was to stop the game and tell the referee (Mr C.F. Robson) that 'there will be a bloodbath unless you do something about this'. 'Tiny' did exactly that and the referee began to penalise the Lions,' recalled Graham.

Graham would regain an All Black place on the tour of South Africa in 1960. He played in the second and third tests, as a flanker. The second test, at Cape Town, won 11–3, is his favourite test because it epitomised what every rugby-playing New Zealander hoped to achieve – beat South Africa on their turf.

South African journalist A.C. Parker would write of Graham: 'He developed into one of the cleverest and quickest loose forwards in the side and the Springboks made no secret of their relief at his omission from the fourth test.'[1]

But from this point Graham would begin a run of 18 consecutive tests – against the hapless French in 1961, Australia in 1962 (home and away) and 1964, England in 1963, and on the great tour of the British Isles in 1963–64.

These triumphs included some memorable incidents. In the second test against France at Wellington's Athletic Park in 1961, he was sent back to be a second fullback to help Don Clarke as the All Blacks battled into the gale-force wind in the first half. In the third test of that series, at Lancaster Park, Christchurch, one of the finest tries of the era was scored when the All Blacks ran the ball from their 25 and Graham completed the movement unopposed. On the 1962 tour of Australia Graham captained the All Blacks to a world record 103–0 win over

*CLOSE TIMES: John Graham unloads to Ray Moreton, as Neil Wolfe watches in the background. It's 1962 at Athletic Park, Wellington, in the drawn test against the Wallabies. Graham would switch to open-side flanker for the next test, won 3–0*

Northern New South Wales. And later that year he led Canterbury to a 5–3 victory over Australia.

But he saved some of his finest play for the long tour of Britain. He played 20 tour matches, including all the internationals, mostly on the side of the scrum. The All Blacks were undefeated in the tests, though they drew the Scotland game. They lost only one tour game. But they managed to beat Ireland by only 6–5 and would have lost had not Graham, late in the game, saved the day with an inspired piece of cover-defending. The All Blacks had lost the ball over their line and two Irishmen pounced. But Graham came from nowhere to beat them to the ball and touch down.

Terry McLean described Graham's captaincy thus: 'He was a man of strong opinions who goaded and scourged his men in demands for new life and greater vigour. 'The ball! The ball!'

he used to bellow whenever there was a melee.'

Graham's brothers were outstanding footballers, both considered very unlucky not to become All Blacks. Older brother Jim was a prop (1950–57) in the first great Waikato team, coached by Dick Everest, which held the Ranfurly Shield twice. Jim played for the North Island four times and in New Zealand trials.

Younger brother Bob played for Auckland in 1958–65. He was No 8 and captain during Auckland's record-breaking shield tenure under coach Fred Allen, including the famous 1960 Canterbury challenge (which included John) when Waka Nathan's final-minute try helped save the shield.

In comparison, John never managed to be in a shield-winning side. In 1964 Bob and John captained the North and South Island teams – the first time brothers had done so – and Bob's team won 12–9.

'It was a pity they didn't get a black jersey,' John Graham told the author in 1999. 'Both were good enough. If they got there, they would have stayed in the All Blacks. I was a bit lucky in the position I played, where there was perhaps less depth than at prop, for instance.'

Although his educational career prevented him from taking a large long-term role in rugby after his playing retirement, Graham helped two Auckland coaches, Eric Boggs, (1974–76) and Graham Henry (1991–93) as their assistant/forward coach. Auckland lifted the shield from Wellington in 1974. Henry's teams were also hugely successful.

In 1964, the year he was All Black captain, and 1965, his final year, Graham was instrumental in guiding the fledgling efforts of a future All Black loose forward and All Black coach, Alex Wyllie. 'John passed on plenty of knowledge in my first year in the Canterbury team,' Wyllie would later state. Longtime All Black Andy Haden also praised Graham's coaching skills and ethos, saying it had had a strong impact on his personal development as a player and person.

However, Graham looks back on an All Black career and says simply that 'Whineray's team set the highest of standards, both as players and as people. It was a privilege and indeed a great responsibility to be involved with them.'

An honours graduate in history, Graham would go on to become a famous headmaster of a famous New Zealand institution, Auckland Grammar, for 21 years. He remains one of New Zealand's most highly regarded educationalists and in 1994 was awarded the CBE for services to education. In 1996 he founded the privately-funded, 450-pupil Senior College in Auckland with Dawn Jones.

Nowadays he lives in Parnell, Auckland, with Shiela. They have three grown-up children.

But life is hardly quiet. Interviewed in September 1999 for this book Graham had just completed three years as manager of the New Zealand cricket team, which included New Zealand's second series win on a tour of England. He was also chairman of the Owens Group of companies, on the University of Auckland council (in September, 1999 he became chancellor of the university), a director of Renaissance (a public company), chairman of the Auckland University Bookshop (a private company), chairman of the trustees of the Educational Scholarship Trust, chairman of Parenting with Confidence, a trustee of Project K (Graeme Dingle's project for dysfunctional youngsters), on the board of trustees for Southern Cross School (formerly Nga Tapuwai College), trustee of the Woolf Fisher Trust and president of The Rugby Foundation.

Graham was on the special six-man NZRFU panel which chose the new All Black coaches at the end of 1999.

## David John Graham (Canterbury)

**Captain in three tests, two wins and a loss** v. Australia 1964 (1, 2, 3)

**Born:** January 1, 1935.

**Position:** Flanker and No 8.

**Represented NZ:** 1958, 1960–64 – 53 matches (22 tests).

**Points for NZ:** 33 – 11 tries.

**First-class record:** Auckland 1955–57 (University); Canterbury 1958–65 (Christchurch HSOB); South Island 1958, 61–65; NZ Trials 1958, 60–63, 65; NZ Universities 1957.

**Selector/coach/administrator:** Auckland assistant coach 1974–76 (under Eric Boggs) and 1991–93 (under Graham Henry); president Auckland RFU 1996–1997.

**Miscellaneous:** Awarded CBE in 1994 for services to education; manager NZ cricket team 1997–99, which included a series win in England; former radio rugby commentator.

**Occupation:** School principal Auckland Grammar, 1973–93; Company chairman and director.

1 *The All Blacks Juggernaut in South Africa*, A.C. Parker.

# Brian Lochore

## Lochore was a man for all seasons

I N 1971, then in semi-retirement, Brian Lochore was surprisingly recalled by the All Black selectors to lock the scrum with Colin Meads in the third test against the Lions, after an injury to Peter Whiting. Lochore and the selectors were criticised for the decision after the game, which the All Blacks lost.

But for Lochore there was no other choice but to oblige when Bob Duff, a selector, called him.

'We have an emergency. Peter Whiting is not able to play. Colin Meads and Ian Kirkpatrick are doubtful starters. We need a lock, but if neither Colin nor Ian can play we also need someone who can captain the team. You are the only player who can do the job. Will you play?' pleaded Duff.

Years later Lochore recalled in his book, called simply *Lochore*, that 'the general charge was that I did myself a disservice (in playing).'

But that was the least of Lochore's considerations.

'How could I possibly have lived with myself knowing I had been approached to help New Zealand in an emergency and turned my back? Of all the challenges I took up in my life as a player this was probably the greatest. I do not regret confronting it. I regret bitterly only that I was not better prepared for it.'

That then signified the mark of this great man, who was knighted for services to sport in 1999.

Lochore had ended his playing career in 1970 with a brilliant record as captain of the All Blacks. In 18 tests he led New Zealand to 15 wins and three losses. That represented a success rate of 83.33%. He has often been compared with his predecessor as captain of the All Blacks, Wilson Whineray. His winning percentage was 81.66% but was made up from 30 tests played for 22 wins, five losses and three draws.

*INSPIRATION: Brian Lochore would become a shock choice as All Black captain when Wilson Whineray retired. But he would prove an inspired choice by coach Fred Allen*

So Whineray's career was much longer and to be fair, probably contributed to Lochore's success, since the foundations of the stable Fred Allen era of the mid-to-late 1960s were laid

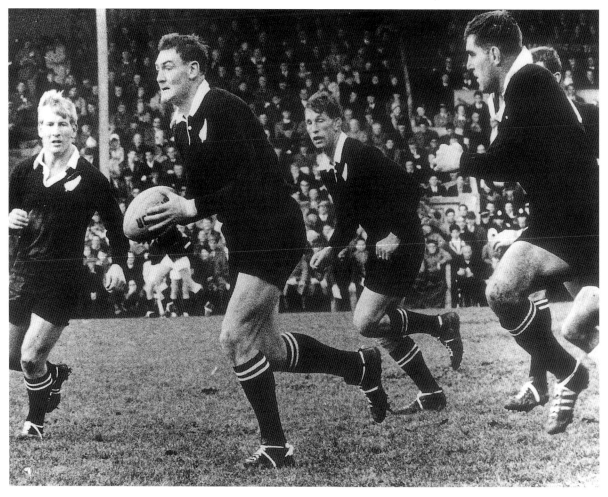

*ON THE BREAK: Brian Lochore, back after injury, leads by example in the victory over the touring French at Athletic Park, Wellington in 1968. Chris Laidlaw, Kel Tremain and Colin Meads are in support. Lochore had broken a thumb on the Australian tour some weeks earlier*

from the selections and policies from 1960 onwards.

Lochore had made his debut for Wairarapa as an 18-year-old flanker in 1959. By the 1963 season he was an All Black reserve against the touring England team and later that year was chosen in Whineray's 1963–64 side which toured Britain and France with resounding success under coach Neil McPhail. He played in two internationals on that tour – the English and Scottish tests.

After John Graham had led the All Blacks against Australia in 1964, when Whineray took a season off, Whineray returned to complete his career with a 3–1 series win over the 1965 Springboks. Lochore had missed the three Australian tests, but played in all four against South Africa.

But from 1966 until 1970 Lochore captained the All Blacks to many triumphs. His ascendency to the captaincy, which coincided with the change of All Black coach from McPhail to Allen, caused controversy. More senior players like Meads, Ken Gray, Kel Tremain or even Chris Laidlaw were seen as the more likely contenders.

Allen told the author in 1997 he was never in doubt about raising Lochore to the captaincy. 'It was my decision to make and it was the one least expected by my fellow selectors, Des Christian and Les George. I could not go past Lochore.

'It was the integrity and the quiet dignity of the man. Whineray had it. The army had taught me about the qualities of leadership and Brian had what I always looked for – strength of character, the capacity to provide discipline by example. He had a resilience. He would have been a leader of men in any field.'

Allen's faith in Lochore was soon rewarded. A 4–0 whitewash of the Lions in 1966 was followed by a resounding win over the Wallabies in the test to celebrate the New Zealand union's 75th jubilee in 1967.

The unbeaten tour of Britain and France at the end of 1967 was probably the peak of Lochore's time as captain, especially on tours away, as it turned out. Led by Allen and manager Charlie Saxton and with 10 new All Blacks, the team had genuine depth, talent and experience. Twelve of the side had toured with Whineray in 1963–64.

The leading New Zealand critic of the time, Terry McLean, in his tour book, *All Black Magic*, rated Lochore with Meads and McCormick as the team's most important players. Lochore was certainly rated among the finest of the All Black captains during that tour and some thought he might even exceed his predecessor, Whineray, reckoned McLean. It was high praise indeed.

A broken thumb in the first test in Australia in 1968 ruled Lochore out of rugby until the second and third tests against the touring Frenchmen. The All Blacks won the two Australian tests, scraping home 19–18 in the second at Ballymore in the most controversial circumstances. Referee Kevin Crowe awarded the All Blacks a penalty try with two minutes to play after it seemed the Wallabies would deservedly end their opponents' great winning sequence of 33 matches, including 11 internationals, since 1965. Although the All Blacks were to win the French series of 1968, 3–0, it was evenly contested and, apart from Sid Going's superb tries in the third test, often lack-lustre. Lochore returned from injury for the second French test.

The team that undertook Wales' first tour to New Zealand in 1969 was the Five Nations' champion and so big things were expected of it. But it was outclassed by Lochore's men, losing 0–19 at Lancaster Park and 12–33 at Eden Park. The Welsh series also represented a changing of the guard in that Allen had quit as All Black coach and selection convenor, citing unnecessary interference from the NZRFU.

He had been replaced by Ivan Vodanovich, and while the 'mean machine' ticked along just

as before against the Welsh, it was to stutter and splutter in South Africa a year later. In spite of being undefeated outside the tests and racking up many huge scores, the All Blacks lost the series, 1–3. The losses were to be the only international defeats suffered by Lochore as captain of the All Blacks. Coach Vodanovich was to take much of the blame for the failure from a disappointed New Zealand rugby public.

Lochore too moved into coaching. In 1982 he guided Wairarapa-Bush into NPC. He was to recall that in 1982 people in high rugby positions were already thinking about the projected 1985 tour to South Africa. They saw him as an ideal coach with the experience to win a series there for the first time, after he had served his 'apprenticeship' on the panel. So he joined coach and convenor Bryce Rope and 'Tiny' Hill in what was a happy relationship.

New Zealand rugby was still struggling to recover from the woes of the 1981 Springbok tour of New Zealand. But when Lochore won the All Blacks' coaching job in 1985 and began planning for the South African tour, 70 or so top players were also looking to crown their careers with a victorious tour. Before that Lochore had to win matches against Australia and England. But the tour was to be scuppered by legal action, when it was claimed it was against the NZRFU's constitution to promote and foster rugby. An Argentinian tour was organised for end-of-season, with Jock Hobbs taking over as captain for the unavailable Andy Dalton.

In 1986 Lochore had a one-test tour by France, a three-test tour by Australia and a tour to France to prepare for, as well as lay plans to try to win the inaugural World Cup allocated to New Zealand and Australia in 1987. But the drive to beat South Africa was to prove as disruptive for Lochore's plans in 1986 as it had been the previous year. It was to become the year of the Cavaliers and, consequently, also the year of the Baby Blacks!

The Cavaliers, beaten in the 'test series' by the Boks, had returned to New Zealand by the time the French had arrived. But the NZRFU, angry at the tour and the duplicity of the South Africa union about it, declared the Cavalier players ineligible for the first two tests of the year..

Colin Meads, who had been 'reprimanded' by his national union for being the Cavaliers' manager, then re-joined Lochore and Hill to select an almost entirely new All Black team to meet the French. Apart from David Kirk and John Kirwan, who had declined to join the Cavaliers, the side was raw.

It is part of the game's folklore that Lochore was able to calm his young charges down in their build-up to the test on Lancaster Park to prepare a game plan that would beat the French. It was another David and Goliath story. But the fairytale came to an end a week later when the Wallabies scraped to a one-point win, 13–12, in Wellington. A changed side won the second test but lost the third.

Lochore took the team to France later that year for a successful tour – until they struck a fired-up French team in the second test in Nantes. 'The All Blacks were shattered by that loss in Nantes,' Lochore said. But it was the best thing to happen in terms of the World Cup in 1987. 'Remember Nantes' became the rallying cry which enabled Lochore to get his players focused on the task ahead and remind them they could take no-one, on any given day, lightly.

Joined by Alex Wyllie and John Hart as selectors, the trio instantly recognised how they wanted to play to win the World Cup in 1987. The All Blacks seemed to peak anew with each stage of the arduous series of cup matches. It was to be New Zealand's year. No team came near to seriously challenging the All Blacks, even France in the final.

The achievement of 1987 becomes richer with each passing year, particularly as the feat has not been repeated. A comparison with soccer's World Cup – Brazil's 1950s ascendency has proved incredibly difficult for it to emulate – is an appropriate way to show why New Zealand cannot guarantee future successes as rugby's world grows.

Lochore retired after the 1987 Bledisloe Cup win, although there were several overseas and home assignments. But in 1995 he was back into the fray once again. He joined Laurie Mains' World Cup efforts as the campaign manager. He assisted through the training camps and with the All Blacks when they slipped quietly into South Africa, not among the odds-on favourites to win the World Cup. Another outstanding campaign, its onfield fireworks more brilliant even than in 1987, did everything but bring the cup home.

Regarding the way 18 All Blacks were laid low by food poisoning on the eve of the final, Lochore doesn't subscribe to all or any of the theories such as British bookmakers. 'I have no idea whether it was a mistake or an accident or whatever,' he told the author. 'All I know is it happened.'

## Sir Brian James Lochore (Wairarapa)

**Captain in 18 tests, 15 wins and three losses**
v. British Isles 1966 (1, 2, 3, 4
v. Australia 1967 (1),
v. England, Wales, France, Scotland 1967,
v. Australia 1968 (1)
v. France 1968 (2, 3)
v. Wales 1968 (1, 2)
v. South Africa 1970 (1, 2, 3, 4)

**Born:** Masterton, September 3, 1940.

**Position:** Back row and lock forward.

**Represented NZ:** 1963–7 – 68 matches (24 internationals).

**Points for NZ:** 21 – 7 tries.

**First-class record:** Wairarapa 1959–70. (Masterton club) and Wairarapa-Bush 1959, 65, 66, 71; North Island 1964–69.

**High school:** Wairarapa College First XV 1956.

**Selector/coach:** Masterton club 1966, 67, 75–78; Wairarapa-Bush 1980–82.

**NZ Selector:** 1983–86.

**NZ coaching record:** 1985: beat England 18–15, beat England 42–15, beat Australia 10–9; beat Argentina 33–20, drew with Argentina 21–21. 1986: beat France 18–9; lost to Australia 12–13, beat Australia 13–12, lost to Australia 9–22; beat France 19–7, lost to France 3–16. 1987: World Cup Pool matches: beat Italy 70–6, beat Fiji 74–13, beat Argentina 46–15. Quarter-final: beat Scotland 30–3. Semi-final: beat Wales 49–6. Final: beat France 29–9. Beat Australia 30–16.

**Other:** Coached overseas teams in IRB centenary 1986; Honoured with OBE; knighted in 1999.

**Occupation:** Farmer at Hastwell near Eketahuna.

# CHRIS LAIDLAW

## *Connor's revenge was thwarted by that penalty try*

CHRIS LAIDLAW once authored a stimulating rugby book called *Mud in Your Eye*, in which, among some overdue criticism of New Zealand rugby, he gently pointed the finger at the leadership of his first All Black captain, Wilson Whineray, for 'safety-first rugby.'

'Whineray knew how to win matches,' wrote Laidlaw. But most of the possession from the superb forward pack was used for forward moves, rather than being fed to the backs to exploit. Laidlaw remembered Whineray rarely issued tactical instructions to the backs and would sometimes bark at them if they made a mistake, so that, 'faced with this attitude any sense of daring was well and truly nipped in the bud.'

It was ironic then that given his only opportunity to lead the All Blacks in a test match, Laidlaw, hoping to release his backline talents frequently, came within a moment of losing the chance of glorious victory.

The occasion was the second test of the 1968 tour of Australia in Brisbane. Tour captain Brian Lochore had been injured in the first test in Sydney, when the All Blacks had demolished the Wallabies with a six-try, 27–11 scoreline. Other leading test captaincy candidates Kel Tremain and Ken Gray were also injured.

Australia's new coach was Des Connor, who five years earlier had been one of Laidlaw's rivals for the All Black halfback position. Connor had been one of the world's leading halfbacks in representing and captaining Australia from 1957–59 but then moved to Auckland. He played for the All Blacks from 1961–64 but had been a surprise omission from

*NEARLY SOLD SHORT: Chris Laidlaw struck the mischievous short-lineout tactics of his former rival, now coach Des Connor, in his only test as All Black captain – and almost came unstuck*

the team that toured Britain and France in 1963–64. Instead, Kevin Briscoe and 19-year-old Laidlaw got the two positions. Connor returned to Australia two years later and became a national selector and then coach.

'Des was a cunning bugger,' recalled Laidlaw to the author in 1999. 'He used short lineouts for the first time in a test match anywhere. His idea was to disrupt the All Blacks and it worked a treat.

'Our game plan was to spin it and keep spinning it. Des knew we had the better backs and came up with this as a way of stopping us. We really didn't have a 'Plan B' and our forwards spent the whole game trying to work out where they should be – in the lineout or out of it.'

The referee, Kevin Crowe, dealt harshly with these errant All Black players and with time ebbing out the Wallabies were ahead. Then the All Black backs, who'd had a quiet day, decided to try to save the game. Bill Davis headed for a gap and punted ahead. But his opposite number, Bobby Honan, bowled him over with a late tackle as the centre tried to pursue his kick into the in-goal area. At the same time Alan Cardy obstructed the winger, Grahame Thorne, from following up.

Mr Crowe awarded a penalty try for the Honan infingement and Fergie McCormick kicked the easy conversion to allow Laidlaw, with the final score at 19–18, to maintain his unbeaten record as All Black test skipper.

All Black coach Fred Allen said the Australian tactical approach was a tragedy for rugby. Laidlaw, with youthful bravado, spluttered how the game was 'never in doubt' to incredulous Australian journalists. Whineray would have enjoyed the irony.

'Des Connor managed to have a laugh about it too. But I felt justice had been done because we were the only team trying to play football,' said Laidlaw.

But rugby's foibles also turned against Laidlaw on at least one occasion. He almost had a moment of glory at the expense of the All Blacks. While in the diplomatic service in Fiji he coached the Fiji team that met New Zealand in Suva in 1974. The All Blacks were playing their final game of a tour that had been unbeaten in Australia under the new leadership of coach JJ Stewart and captain Andy Leslie. They had to come from behind to pip Fiji 14–13.

Laidlaw, who came under the tutelage of All Black halfback and 1946 Kiwi captain Charlie Saxton while at school, as well as Bert Dowling, has been called New Zealand's finest passing halfback. His powerful build allowed him to throw long, accurate passes that gave his first five-eighths the proverbial armchair ride out of the reach of marauding loose forwards. He also possessed a clever reverse pass and a fine tactical kick behind the scrum or lineout, was a courageous defender and an excellent captain who led many provincial and university teams to victories.

Early in his career he faced competition from Briscoe and Connor while much later there was Sid Going. But Laidlaw was replaced by Going, on form, only once in their rivalry – for the test against France on the 1967 tour.

Accolades for Laidlaw's skills included those from Colin Meads: 'There was so much to this chap's football – he could kick well, could break in a scuttling, low-slung way. He named Ken Catchpole as the greatest of his time. But I have never seen a halfback who could fire out such a stream of immaculate passes as from a pre-set gun.'[1]

Terry McLean, of the 1967 tour, wrote that in the game against Scottish Districts, after he'd been dropped for Going for the French test, Laidlaw gave 'the finest display of passing I had ever seen from an All Black halfback, or from any international since Danie Craven bombarded Tony Harris with one magnificent pass after another while the Springboks were demolishing the All Blacks in 1937'.[2]

Laidlaw was a rugby prodigy. After three seasons in the King's High (Dunedin) First XV he had all the skills. At 18 he was solidly-built, being 1.75m (5ft 9in) and 76.2kg (12st). In 1962 he made the Otago team and came to major notice in the South Island's last-minute upset win over the North at Lancaster Park. The *Rugby Almanack* named him one of New Zealand's five promising players.

It was also the year he first partnered Earle Kirton. Their combination would flourish at club, provincial, university and All Black levels. In nine tests together between 1967 and 1970 they experienced defeat on one occasion.

Laidlaw had followed his first season with another series of top games in 1963. He was in the Otago team that beat England, had another win for the South Island and starred for NZ Universities.

He was the youngest member of the Neil McPhail-Whineray-led All Black team that had such a fine tour of Britain and France in 1963–64. He played the French test and the grand finale to the tour, the 36–3 victory over the Barbarians.

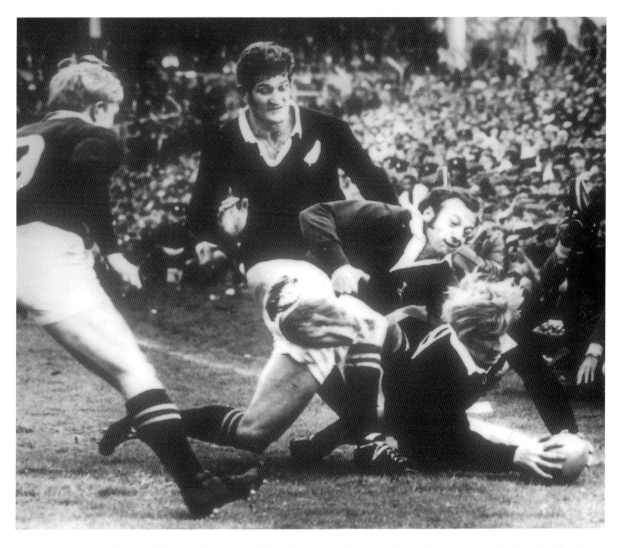

*WINNING WAY: Chris Laidlaw makes sure of this fine try in the second test in 1970, won by the All Blacks 9–8. Alan Sutherland is in support*

'It was a great occasion,' said Laidlaw. 'The match had everything. The All Blacks ran everything we could, deciding to take the risks we had not been accustomed to taking in the other tour matches.'

Laidlaw's career did not run entirely smoothly from this point. He was replaced by Connor for the second and third tests against the touring Wallabies in 1964.

But from the next season, when he played in all four tests against the touring Springboks – the series being won 3–1 – Laidlaw was a first-choice selection until the end of his career.

However, Laidlaw became a casualty against the Boks – not for the only time in his career either. He was concussed while playing for NZ Universities but insisted on returning to the

field and dropping a goal as the students were down to 12 players (with no replacements allowed) at one stage. He then collapsed and was led off the field for the last time in the game.

Laidlaw gained an unusual record of five wins over the 1966 British Lions – four in the whitewash of the test series and the other with Otago. Touring had become a busy occupation for him. In 1967 he toured the Far East with NZ Universities and then went on the unbeaten Fred Allen-Brian Lochore-led tour of Britain and France.

The following year he played in the series against France at home – though a broken thumb kept him out of the third test – after touring Australia.

Laidlaw is one of only three All Black test captains to have won a Rhodes Scholarship to Oxford University, the others being David Kirk and George Aitken. He took up the scholarship at the end of 1968 and captained Oxford to a 6–3 win over the touring Springboks in 1969. 'It was in front of 5000 spectators and about 7000 police,' he recalled later about the troubled tour.

He returned to New Zealand in 1970 and made the tour to South Africa. He was heavily concussed in the infamous double-tackle involving Frik du Preez's fist in the first half of the first test but was not replaced by Sid Going until the second half. In the second test he scored a try that helped the All Blacks win 9–8 and tie the series. After a quiet game in the 3–14 third-test loss Laidlaw missed the final test because of an appendix operation. He returned to Oxford after the tour.

He had played 57 matches for the All Blacks, including 20 tests, between 1963 and 1970. He finished his playing career in France when he continued study at the University of Lyon. Sports writers for *L'Equipe* newspaper voted him player of the year in France in 1971.

He joined the diplomatic service in 1974 and served in Fiji, Paris, London, Wellington and Harare. He then became New Zealand's race relations conciliator and later a member of Parliament for Wellington Central for one term. Today he is a writer, local body politician and columnist/commentator.

He lives in Wellington with his wife Helen Kedgley. They have two children.

## Christopher Robert Laidlaw (Canterbury)

**Captain in one test, one win**
v. Australia 1968 (2)

**Born:** November 16, 1943.

**Position:** Halfback.

**Represented NZ:** 1963–68, 70 – 57 matches (20 tests).

**Points for NZ:** 48 points – 11 tries, 5 dropped goals.

**First-class record:** Otago 1962–67 (University) and Canterbury 1968 (Shirley); South Island 1962–66, 68; NZ Trials 1963, 65–68, 70; NZ Colts 1964; NZ Universities 1962–67; Oxford University 1968–70; Lyon University (France) 1971–72.

**High school:** King's High School (Dunedin), 1st XV 1959–61.

**Selector/coach/administrator:** Coached Fiji to a 13–14 loss to the All Blacks in Suva in 1974; now a director Hurricanes Super 12 franchise.

**Miscellaneous:** One of only three All Black test captains to have won a Rhodes Scholarship to Oxford University, the others being David Kirk and George Aitken. Author of the rugby book *Mud in Your Eye* (Reed, 1973) and *Rights of Passage*, about New Zealand's identity in 1999; also contributor to several other books about New Zealand.

**Other:** Earned placings at the NZ junior swimming championships; represented Otago at age grade water polo and basketball; Otago junior surfing champion.

**Occupation:** Joined Diplomatic Service in 1974 and served in Fiji, Paris and London, before becoming foreign affairs adviser to Prime Minister David Lange in 1984; NZ's first ambassador to Africa (1986–89); Race Relations Conciliator (1989–92), member of Parliament for Wellington Central (1992–93); chief executive World Wildlife Fund (1994–98); member of Wellington Regional Council (1998); syndicated columnist on rugby and international affairs.

1 *100 Great Rugby Characters*

2 *All Black Magic, the Triumphant Tour of the 1967 All Blacks,* Terry McLean, Reed, 1968.

# KEL TREMAIN

## 'Freak' qualities gave Tremain the All Black forward scoring record

WHEN KEL Tremain strode out on to Lancaster Park to lead New Zealand to a tight 12–9 victory over France in the first test of 1968, little did he know the curtain was starting to fall on his great All Black career.

'Bunny' Tremain had bestrode the international test arena for a decade as an integral part of an indominatable All Black pack. The All Blacks had not lost a series since 1960. His nine tries in tests was the highest recorded by an All Black forward and was only one fewer than Frank Mitchinson's New Zealand record that had stood for 55 years!

But the third test against the Frenchmen was to prove the final international for Tremain. He had played in 38 tests since 1959, a figure only exceeded by Colin Meads, who had played a record-breaking 47 by this match.

Tremain had gained the honour of leading his country when Brian Lochore – who had broken a thumb in the first test on the tour of Australia a month earlier – was unavailable. But Lochore was restored to lead the All Blacks to a 3–0 series win. Thus Tremain had become the first All Black captain from Hawkes Bay since the great Maurice Brownlie in 1928.

But the signs had been out for a year or so that Tremain's time at the top would be tested. The youthful Ian Kirkpatrick had replaced him for the French test on the tour of Britain and France in 1967. When Tom Lister and Kirkpatrick were named as the flankers by coach Ivan Vodanovich for the first test against the touring Welsh in 1969, Tremain knew it was time to bow out. He had played played 86 times for the All Blacks, scoring 36 tries.

*UNCANNY HABITS: Kel Tremain was a lock's size, ran like a loose forward and had rare anticipation*

He would continue leading his beloved Hawkes Bay, even after it lost the Ranfurly Shield to Canterbury in the final challenge of 1969.

Accolades for Tremain were many. Colin

*SETTLED COMBINATION: Kel 'Bunny' Tremain bears down on a hapless Lion in the first test of the 1966 series. Stan Meads, Bruce McLeod and Brian Lochore at right. The All Blacks made only one change (a winger in the 4th test) in the series, won 4–0*

Meads, in his autobiography, wrote that 'Kel's try-scoring feats are a chapter in New Zealand rugby. But he was so much more. He had the strength and the size to provide the impetus for one of the All Blacks' most effective tactics. He was an effective lineout player, a man gifted with sharpness of reflex and a natural anticipation. Within 10 yards of the opposition line with the ball in hand he was the hardest man in world rugby to contain.'

Another All Black team-mate, Fergie McCormick, said: 'Kel was built like a lock, could drive like a tight forward, run like a loose forward and his anticipation when the try was on was matchless.'[1]

His former coach, Allen, would say: 'We in

New Zealand have been fortunate in possessing the finest lineout-driving forward in the world in Kel Tremain. I am quite sure he was one of the most potent figures in the fine packs that New Zealand fielded in his time.'[2]

Early in his career, Tremain followed a similar, itinerant path to that of his All Black captain, Wilson Whineray, representing Southland (1957) as a 19-year-old, Manawatu (1958), Canterbury (1959 and 1961) and Auckland (1960) before settling down with Hawkes Bay from 1962–70. Like Whineray, he studied at Lincoln on a government farming rural cadetship. He became a farm appraiser and stock agent, though later he established a successful real estate and travel agency in Napier.

*NO BUNNY: Kel Tremain was at his punishing best when the All Blacks whitewashed the touring Lions of 1966*

Standing 6ft 2in (1.88m) and weighing 15st at the start of his career, Tremain was a formidable 16st at his peak. Tremain had played his early representative rugby as a lock but it was as a flanker that he made his mark. He was still a lock when he toured Japan and Hong Kong with the New Zealand Under-23 side that included 14 present and future All Blacks.

But his meteoric rise began in 1959 when Canterbury coach, the former All Black captain and co-opted 1956 All Black forward coach Bob

Stuart, told Tremain, 'If you want to be a lock don't bother coming back to another training session.'[3]

Tremain heeded the advice and was part of Canterbury's victory over the British Lions, where he scored two tries. The game came a week after Don Clarke had kicked New Zealand to an unimpressive 18–17 win over the Lions in the first test.

He was chosen for the second test and quickly established himself in the All Black team. Apart from injury and a controversial dropping, with other leading players, for a test in 1962 when coach Neil McPhail gave the team a shakeup, and a test on the 1967 British tour under Fred Allen, he would be an integral part of the All Blacks' loose forward combination for a decade.

Tremain toured South Africa in 1960, playing in all four tests. He returned to New Zealand to play for Auckland that year, being a part of its famous 19–18 midweek shield victory over Canterbury. He scored a try but was knocked out by a punch from his 1959 All Black and Canterbury team-mate, Tiny Hill, and was not on the field when Waka Nathan scored the shield-saving, final-minute try.

He returned to Canterbury in 1961 but the highlight of his season was the bizarre second test against France, played in a gale at Wellington's Athletic Park. As France led 3–0 with 15 minutes remaining, Tremain scored a freak try when he literally took the ball off Claude Lacaze's boot as the fullback tried to clear, and fell over the line. Don Clarke succeeded with the conversion by kicking parallel with the 25 line and drifting the ball between the posts. The final score was 5–3.

Triumph followed triumph during the ensuing years. Playing in all five tests on the 1963–64 tour of Britain and France, he almost helped the All Blacks to their first-ever Grand Slam when he was brought down a yard short of the Scotland line. That game was drawn, 0–0.

He was probably at the peak of his powers at this stage. In the four tests against the touring Springboks in 1965 Tremain scored three tries and was at the van of a magnificent, unchanged forward pack. Three tries came in the inter-island game that year and he gained another nine tries and a goal from a mark for Hawkes Bay. The All Blacks steamrolled the hapless Lions in 1966, 4–0. In 1967 Tremain made his second tour to Britain and France, in yet another outstanding side.

His international career would end abruptly the following year, but Tremain was by then in the midst of leading Hawkes Bay's second great Ranfurly Shield era. He had captained the Bay in its successful challenge over Waikato in 1966 and rebuffed seven challenges in 1967. The Bay would hold the shield through 1968 and on to the last challenge of 1969. Tremain would have one more season for the Bay before retiring.

He always rated his time as the Magpies'

captain among his best: 'We were playing in an area where you knew everybody. The whole population were a part of the shield team,' he said.[4]

Tremain died at the age of 54. His contribution to New Zealand rugby had continued when he became chairman of the Hawkes Bay union from 1985 to 1990. A major achievement was to introduce the Hawkes Bay-wide club competition. He was voted on to the NZRFU Council in 1990, but died in office. He died in Napier on May 2, 1992 after becoming ill while managing the New Zealand team at the Hong Kong Sevens tournament in April of that year.

## Kelvin Robin Tremain (Hawkes Bay)

**Captain in one test, one win**
v. France 1968 (1)

**Born:** February 21, 1938, Auckland.

**Died:** May 2, 1992, Napier.

**Position:** Loose forward.

**Represented NZ:** 1959–68 – 86 matches (38 tests).

**Points for NZ:** 108 – 36 tries.

**First-class record:** Southland 1957 (Riversdale); Manawatu 1958 (University); Canterbury 1959, 61 (Lincoln College); Auckland 1960 (Grammar); Hawkes Bay 1962–70 (Napier HSOB); South Island 1959, 61; North Island 1962–68; NZ Trials 1958–63, 65–69; NZ Under-23 1958; NZ Universities 1958, 59, 61.

**High school:** Auckland Grammar, 1st XV 1954, 55.

**Selector/coach/administrator:** Chairman Hawkes Bay RFU 1985–90; NZRFU Council 1990–92 (died in office).

**Miscellaneous:** A son, Simon, was a flanker for Otago (1988, 89), Wellington (1990–92) and Hawkes Bay (1993) and for NZ Universities.

**Occupation:** Initially a farm appraiser, then a stock agent, he owned a real estate and travel agency company in Napier.

1, 2, 3, 4 *100 Great Rugby Characters*

# COLIN MEADS

## *'Player of the century' couldn't tame the Brits*

COLIN MEADS was 35, had played for the All Blacks for 14 years and, though still the finest lock in New Zealand, was past his best when called upon to captain the team against the 1971 British Lions.

The series loss was a sad ending to the career of the 'greatest' All Black in history. But it was a challenge he would never have turned down.

Meads had long before become a legend in New Zealand and world rugby in the same way that Maurice Brownlie, the great siderow forward of the 1920s, had been in his heyday. There were few more exciting sights than Meads, ball in one giant hand, bearing down on the hapless opposition.

By the end of his 15-year All Black career between 1957 and 1971 Meads had set a record of 55 tests played, 47 as lock, five on the side of the scrum and two at No 8.

He stood 1.93m (6ft 4in) and his weight was about 102kg (16st). Renowned for his fitness, strength, mobility and aggression, Meads honed these attributes on his King Country sheep farm, where the steep hill country gave him the perfect fitness arena on a daily basis.

The legends included that he trained with a sheep under each arm. He certainly played with a broken arm, encased in a protector, on the 1970 tour of South Africa. Remarkably, when Meads fell sick from the food poisoning that ravaged the All Blacks on the eve of the World Cup final in Johannesburg, South Africa in 1995 – where he was manager of the team – it was said to be the first day of his adult life he'd ever spent sick in bed.

And when Meads had broken his back in a motor accident in late 1971 the nation was shocked. Yet his 'ironman' reputation was intact when he made a comeback to rugby the following year and played for his club, Waitete, until 1975. The legend lived on.

But let us look at a few accolades:

Noel Holmes in 1960, after Meads had just completed his first major tour: 'New Zealand's best forward. After Don Clarke, New Zealand's best player. Thrived on hard work. Determined, conscientious, willing. Outstanding in every department. One out of the box.'[1]

Terry McLean, after the 1967 tour of Britain and France: 'He was sustained by devotion, absolute, untrammelled devotion ... He hauled people out of bed at 6am ... to go running ... and however fit they were, they couldn't keep up with him. He trained concentratedly, relentlessly.'[2]

Fergie McCormick described Meads as 'a terrible man with the silver fern on. He regarded the jersey as pure gold. He could do so many things so much better than anyone else in a match that he stood alone as the greatest player I have ever seen.'[3]

Fred Allen, one of five All Black coaches who were delighted to have Meads in their sides, said he was the ideal tourist. 'His consistency developed from his willingness to train. Yet it could never be said of Colin while he was on tour that he made training such a fetish that he was incapable of enjoying himself. Those weekend enjoyment sessions of his became a famous part of New Zealand rugby – but once he'd had his fun he resumed training as keenly as ever.'

'In mythical All Black teams of all time, Meads would always be chosen.'[4]

*SIZE XXXOS: Colin Meads and Willie John McBride are about to swap jerseys after the British Lions had won a series in New Zealand for the first time*

'He was an inspiration to play with,' said Chris Laidlaw. 'He was not the sort of personality who gravitated naturally toward captaincy but he was the best ally every All Black captain he played with could ever wish for. The very fact of his presence generated visible apprehension in any opposition team. Some of that apprehension was based on the knowledge that Meads was an utterly ruthless operator on the field. He grew accustomed to hurting opposing players and he was well aware of the pervasive power of this physical intimidation.'[5]

It should not surprise the reader to learn that today, three decades after Meads' retirement, there is a flourishing Colin Meads Fan Club. It meets every June 3, his birthday. 'Members wear the No 5 jersey, as Meads did, quote from their 'bible' [Meads' 1974 alltime best-selling biography by Alex Veysey], drink from a 5oz glass and often telephone Meads. The club has

branches from Dunedin to Wales. Sometimes Meads, who takes these things in the spirit intended, turns up to share a beer and a yarn with those celebrating. Many club members were not born when Meads retired. Such is his enduring fame in New Zealand, and further afield.'[6]

Meads' place in the All Blacks was seldom threatened. But there were a few occasions. He missed the first test of the 1959 series when the selectors had preferred 'Tiny' Hill and Nev MacEwan. In 1962 the All Black coach Neil McPhail shook up the established All Blacks when he dropped Meads for his brother, Stan, as well as Kel Tremain, Ian Clarke and Dennis Young for the second test against Australia.

But from this point Meads played 31 consecutive tests, the sequence broken only when he suffered a broken arm before the opening test of the 1970 series in South Africa.

During his career he confronted a passing

parade of great locks such as Willie John McBride, Bryn Thomas, Brian Price and Delme Thomas (Lions), Frik du Preez, Johaan Claassen and 'Tiny' Naude (South Africa), Benoit Dauga (France) and Dick and John Thornett (Australia). He had not been bested by any of them.

When it is recalled that Meads still somehow managed to stand head and shoulders above such great team-mates as Wilson Whineray, Ken Gray, Kel Tremain, Brian Lochore, Ian Kirkpatrick, and Meads' brother, Stan, only then can the reader gain some sense of the 'supernatural' powers that seemed to drive Meads.

But Meads' career was soured by several incidents. On the 1967 tour, in the test against Scotland, he was ordered off by referee Kevin Kelleher. He had aimed a flykick as Scotland's flyhalf David Chisholm stooped to pick up the ball in loose play. The decision was considered 'borderline' but it besmirched his reputation. He thus became only the second international player of any country to be ordered off in a test – the first being another All Black, Cyril Brownlie, in 1925. Interestingly, Meads and Kelleher traded Christmas cards for many years afterward.

Meads was also vilified in Australia in 1968 when he pulled Wallaby halfback Ken Catchpole from a ruck, causing a groin injury that ended Catchpole's international career. In 1966 he punched British Lion David Watkins and in 1969 he broke Welsh hooker Jeff Young's jaw. Meads therefore was not an 'angel'. But those were the days when retaliation was acceptable and common.

Meads was of course sometimes on the receiving end too. The French did him over in the 1967 test in Paris and he completed the game with bandages protecting a gaping head wound. In 1970, after outstanding form in the early tour matches in South Africa, Meads broke an arm when kicked by Eastern Transvaal's Skip Henderson. He missed the first two tests but came back protected by an armguard to play in the third and fourth tests.

In 1986, Meads, then a New Zealand selector, was briefly reprimanded by the NZRFU after accompanying the rebel Cavaliers on their tour of South Africa, as coach of the side. He was soon after dumped as a selector but battled back to become an NZRFU councillor in the mid-1990s and manager of the All Blacks at the 1995 World Cup.

Meads had toured Australia and Ceylon (Sri Lanka) with the 1955 New Zealand Colts in his first year of provincial rugby.

He made his All Black debut on the tour to Australia in 1957. His first cap came as a flanker in the first test, but by the second test had had moved into lock – a position he was to call his own for the next 15 years!

In the second test of the 1957 series, Meads scored the first of seven tries he would score in his test career, while deputising for Frank McMullen on the wing.

Meads played all three tests against the touring Wallabies in 1958 and, after missing the first test against the 1959 Lions, was brought back for the rest of the series.

His overseas tours included the 1960 and 1970 tours in South Africa, Australia in 1962 and 1968, and the British Isles and France in 1963–64 and 1967.

He played in home series against France in 1961 and 1968, Australia in 1962, 1964 and 1967, England in 1963, South Africa in 1965, the British Lions in 1959, 1966 and 1971, and Wales in 1969.

Of the 1971 series against the Lions, Meads was to state that his coach, Ivan Vodanovich, had 'unfairly taken the blame for everything' that went wrong in the series, as well as the 1970 tour of South Africa. Meads said it had been easier for an All Black coach and captain in the 1960s.

'Then we had at least six of the pack who were provincial captains and who were always thinking positively,' said Meads when the author, working on the *Dominion*, interviewed him upon his retirement in 1972.

Meads' greatest disappointment during those 15 years was that he had failed to lead his team to victory over the Lions.

'They were the first Lions team to have a coach, Carwyn James. He was a great thinker and instilled in them the faith that they could beat us,' he said.

'They were a great side, but we had the beatings of them, specially in the first test in Dunedin. It was hard for so many inexperienced players to go straight into their first tests.'

Meads' All Black career included 133 matches, still a record. It surpasses the tallies of Sean Fitzpatrick (128), Andy Haden (117), Ian Kirkpatrick (113) and Bryan Williams (113).

But his 55-test record has long been surpassed, by players who played many more tests per season than in his day. Sean Fitzpatrick (92), Ian Jones (79), John Kirwan (63), Gary Whetton (58) and Zinzan Brooke (58) all overtook Meads' mark in the 1990s.

He finished his career with 361 first-class matches (including 139 for King Country), which remains a record. Only Fergie McCormick, with 310 games between 1958 and 1978, of the Meads era, approached it, while of the modern players, not even Sean Fitzpatrick (347), Andy Haden (327) and Richard Loe (321) were able to overtake the mark.

A few years after his retirement, the fact the King Country union turned down his nomination for life membership was received with incredulity by observers. 'They were afraid I might give up after I got the award,' Meads joked to the author in 1999.

But undeterred, he went on to serve the union as president and coach, as well as become a national councillor, selector and All Black manager. He has been on the King Country union 'all the way through' and eventually won his life membership. He also serves on the Rugby Foundation and was part of the NZRFU group that reviewed procedures before the new All Black coaches, Wayne Smith and Tony Gilbert, were appointed in 1999.

Of the new professional era and the World Cup disappointments, Meads said 'there is a place for the corporate culture – provided it's not making too many demands on the All Blacks that might affect their performances.'

Meads is also a strong believer in the future of rugby as a world game. 'Give it 20 years. Handled properly, in places like North America and Europe, rugby could be bigger than soccer and the Olympics.'

## Colin Earl Meads
## (King Country)

**Captain in four tests, one win, two losses and a draw**
v. British Isles 1971 (1, 2, 3, 4)

**Born:** June 3, 1936, Cambridge.

**Position:** Lock.

**Represented NZ:** 1957–71 – 133 matches (55 tests).

**Points for NZ:** 86 – 28 tries, 1 conversion.

**First-class record:** King Country 1955–72 (Waitete), North Island 1956–59, 62 ,63, 65–69; NZ Trials 1956–61, 63, 65–71; NZ XV 1958, 68; NZ Colts 1955; NZ Under-23 1958; Wanganui-King Country 1956, 65, 66, 71; King Country-Counties 1959.

**High school:** Te Kuiti HS, 1st XV 1950.

**Selector/coach/administrator:** Coached King Country; North Island selector 1982–85; New Zealand selector 1986; chairman King Country RFU 1987–94,-management committee 1977–2000; NZRFU Council 1992–96; manager All Blacks 1994–95.

**Miscellaneous:** Meads' brother, Stan, made his All Black debut against the touring French side in 1961, but it was not until 1964 that the brothers regularly locked the All Black scrum. They teamed up in 11 tests in total. A biography, *Colin Meads All Black* (Collins, 1974), written by Alex Veysey, sold a record 57,000 copies. Honoured with MBE 1971. A son, Glyn, captained King Country and was an All Black trialist, while a daughter, Rhonda, played for the Silver Ferns, the New Zealand netball team.

**Other:** Nickname is 'Pinetree'.

**Occupation:** Farmer near Te Kuiti.

1 *Trek Out of Trouble,* Noel Holmes, Whitcombe and Tombs, 1960.

2 *All Black Magic,* Terry McLean, Reed, 1968.

3 *Fergie,* Alex Veysey, Whitcoulls, 1976.

4 *The Encyclopaedia of World Rugby,* Keith Quinn, Shoal Bay Press, 1991.

5 *NZ Rugby World,* December, 1999.

6 *A Century of Rugby Greats,* Keith Quinn, Celebrity Books, 1999.

# IAN KIRKPATRICK

## Prince of loose forwards 'born to the purple'

IF EVER there was an All Black 'born to the purple' it was Ian Kirkpatrick. This prince among loose forwards played for the All Blacks for 11 years, in 113 matches, including 39 tests.

Standing 1.90m tall and weighing 101kg, Kirkpatrick had great pace and strength and was devastating with ball in hand. He would score 114 tries in his first-class career. His skills enabled him to adapt equally well from heavy conditions in New Zealand, Britain and sometimes Australia, to the hard, fast fields of the veldt. He was to score a record 16 tries in 39 tests, and 50 in all matches for New Zealand.

His try against the 1971 Lions, when he ran half the length of the field in a solo effort, was one of the great tries.

John Reason, no great friend of New Zealand rugby, described the try, which sealed the second test for the All Blacks, in his tour book, *The Mighty Lions*.

Near Lancaster Park's halfway line on the Embankment side Kirkpatrick broke 'clear of the two Lions at the back of the ruck and then his own phenomenal strength took over. He broke away from Gareth Edwards and stormed on past JPR Williams and although Barry John caught him, he did not get into the back of Kirkpatrick's knees with his tackle and he slid to the ground off the flying heels in front of him.

'Kirkpatrick then had 25 yards to run to the corner and with Bruce Hunter running in such a support position that David Duckham and JPR Williams could not get at him, he hurled himself over the line for a try.

'There are few more magnificent sights in rugby football than Ian Kirkpatrick going forward with the ball in his hands. When he scored that try, he had been playing 70 minutes of the most gruelling football on a stamina-sapping paddock, and yet he still had the power and the pace to run through three tackles and sprint 50 yards to score. He was applauded all the way back to the halfway line.'

Yet it is probable he would have happily forfeited some of those appearances, and memories, just to have the opportunity to 'grow' into the captaincy which had been thrust on him – and then taken away – at a particularly difficult time in the All Blacks' history.

Kirkpatrick first played for the All Blacks on the unbeaten Fred Allen–Brian Lochore-led tour of 1967. He displaced Kel Tremain for the French test.

The next year he began a record run of 38 consecutive tests with three tries against Australia in the first test. The three-try tally had not been achieved by an All Black since 1935. He had gone on at No 8 as a replacement for captain Brian Lochore in the 22nd minute of the game.

Kirkpatrick's star continued to rise for the remainder of Lochore's tenure. He was a key part of the pack that demolished the touring Welsh in 1969 and the team that toured South Africa.

But then came a time of change and turmoil in All Black rugby. After the series loss in 1970 and to the British Lions of 1971, and the retirements of Lochore and Colin Meads, Kirkpatrick became captain.

Late in 1971, Meads had been injured in a car accident, and declared himself unavailable for 1972. So 'Kirky' got the job. He would lead the All Blacks on an internal tour and then against Australia for three easy wins in 1972 and on the tour of Britain and France in 1972–73 under coach Bob Duff, and against England in 1973 when JJ Stewart took over as the coach.

Kirkpatrick's 1972–73 team should have become the first All Blacks to win the Grand Slam. They beat Wales, Scotland and England

*THRASHING TIME: Ian Kirkpatrick would get his All Black captaincy off to a bright start against the 'Woeful Wallabies' of 1972. But things would get soon get harder for the young farmer*

and then suffered the ignominy, after dominating throughout, of a 10–10 draw when Ireland scored in the final moments.

'The team did not carry out the plan I had asked of them,' said coach Duff of the Irish test, when interviewed by the author in 1997. 'We were superior and should have won it.'

The banishing of Keith Murdoch from the team is the abiding bad memory of 1972–73 tour, though there were other side issues.

Kirkpatrick will never forget the Murdoch incident. It came after Murdoch had been one of the All Black heroes, scoring New Zealand's only try, in the 19–16 win over Wales. Murdoch punched a Welsh security guard in the team's Cardiff hotel, the Angel, during the celebrations on the night of the test.

It was Duff who finally persuaded Murdoch

*(left) ESTEEMED COMPANY: The International XV's Ian Kirkpatrick wants the ball during the English centenary celebration match*

to go to his room, which he shared with Lin Colling, an old friend from his days with Otago. The next day Duff and Kirkpatrick, and later Sid Going, spent a lot of time with team manager Ernie Todd, trying to ensure that Murdoch got a 'fair hearing'.

They all went to bed believing Murdoch was not going home and he was actually chosen for the next game. But unbeknown to them, the British put pressure on Jack Sullivan, then chairman of the NZRFU, back in New Zealand. Sullivan made the final decision and ordered Todd to send Murdoch home.

Kirkpatrick said of the Murdoch incident that he would have led a player rebellion, to reinstate his player, if he had had some advance notice that Murdoch was being sent home. 'It's one of my few regrets in rugby,' he said.

He recalled the first few weeks after the Murdoch banishment as the toughest he ever faced as captain. 'You couldn't expect the players to quickly put aside what had

*ON THE CHARGE: Ian Kirkpatrick has Bill Bush on his shoulder in the second test against the British Lions at Lancaster Park, Christchurch in 1977. But the Lions would win 13–9 to tie the series*

happened,' he said. 'I was not surprised when we lost at Moseley. They weren't a very good side and we could have won.'

Fellow All Blacks were to say Kirkpatrick was a fine captain who led by example and particularly looked after the youngsters in the side. But there were charges that he was not well enough supported by the older players in the team.

Grant Batty described it as 'the happiest tour I ever went on'. Bryan Williams recalled the build-up to the great victory over Wales as 'the best build-up to any test in which I played.' Alex Wyllie, who would return to Britain as coach of the All Blacks nearly 20 years later, said the 1972–73 team carried an unjust reputation. The team could have faltered with the expulsion of Murdoch after the first of its five tests. Instead, in adversity and under pressure, it grew stronger.

'Bob Duff was vital to us and so was Kirky. They had such a young team, probably one of the youngest the All Blacks had ever had on tour,' said Wyllie.[1]

It is notable that Kirkpatrick's team's achievements came between the two great Lions tours of 1971 (beating the All Blacks in New Zealand) and 1974 (beating the Springboks in South Africa). British rugby was at its strongest level in history, before or since. Kirkpatrick's tyros faced defensive-minded teams with shallow backlines and they often played in bleak, cold and wet conditions. They still scored 103 tries in 34 matches, averaging more than three tries per game.

The Grand Slam was left for Jack Gleeson's 1978 All Blacks to achieve. The All Blacks also returned to Britain in 1974 under Stewart and new captain Andy Leslie. The team did well and it seemed a bold new era. But the team that beat Wales in 1974 contained 11 players from the side that Duff and Kirkpatrick had led: Karam, Batty, Williams, Robertson, Hurst, Going, Kirkpatrick, Macdonald, Peter Whiting,

Lambert and Norton. It was a new-look team with old-look players.

However, the 1973 domestic season turned into a shocker for Kirkpatrick and his players. After the projected Springbok tour was cancelled, a hastily arranged internal tour and a visit by England replaced it. The All Blacks lost to the New Zealand Juniors and then to England.

'Frankly, the players had had a gutsful of rugby after four months in Britain and France, and then playing teams like the Juniors and the President's XV,' said Kirkpatrick. 'It was hard to get stirred up for that programme. Travelling on the same bus as the Juniors is no way to get motivated to beat them.'

So the axe fell on many players and on the captain. Coach JJ Stewart told the author in 1997 that he had felt Kirkpatrick wasn't enjoying the role of captain. He replaced him with the veteran Leslie in 1974. But Kirkpatrick retained his place in the All Blacks and became Leslie's faithful lieutenant, and an even better player.

The much respected Tane Norton, who at 35 became the oldest All Black captain after not playing a test until he was 29, and then playing under three captains, reckons Kirkpatrick should have been allowed to grow into the job.

'I reckon they should have kept Kirky as the All Black captain. He'd have turned out one of the greatest – if they'd given him the chance,' Norton explained.

But when interviewed by the author in 1999, Kirkpatrick said losing the captaincy hadn't worried him. 'Never,' was his succinct answer.

Dropping him as an All Black at the end of 1977 was a different matter. With Norton retiring, the selectors elevated Mourie to the captaincy. If they thought Kirkpatrick's presence on the French tour might somehow undermine Mourie's authority, they must have had short memories after the way Kirkpatrick had supported his two successors as captain.

'I wanted to go to France all right. But the selectors only took three siderowers [Lawrie Knight, Kevin Eveleigh and Mourie]. I guess they thought I wasn't up to it any more. They beat me to my decision to retire by a month or so.'

His dropping from the All Blacks, coming after the heroics of the narrow series win over the 1977 British Lions, was to cause a public outcry.

An amiable and modest character, Kirkpatrick picked up honours and records throughout his career. He captained both South and North Islands, helped win the Ranfurly Shield from Hawkes Bay with Canterbury in 1969, and created records for tries for the All Blacks.

Kirkpatrick was awarded the MBE in 1980. He was manager of the rebel Cavaliers team which toured South Africa in 1986, the year after the official All Black team had been prevented, by court action, from touring the republic.

## Ian Andrew Kirkpatrick (Poverty Bay)

**Captain in nine tests, six wins, two losses and a draw**
  v. Australia 1972 (1, 2, 3)
  v. Wales, Scotland, England, Ireland, France 1972–73
  v. England 1973 (1)

**Born:** May 24, 1946, Gisborne.

**Position:** Flanker.

**Represented NZ:** 1967–77 – 113 matches (39 tests).

**Points for NZ:** 180 – 50 tries.

**First-class record:** Poverty Bay 1966, 70–79 (Ngatapa); Canterbury 1967–69 (Rangiora); South Island 1968, 69; North Island 1971–75; NZ Trials 1967–76; NZ Under-23 1967; Poverty Bay-East Coast 1966, 71, 72, 77, 78.

**High school:** King's College, First XV 1962–64.

**Selector/coach/administrator:** Coached Ngatapa club in late 1970s-early 1980s.

**Miscellaneous:** Is the only player in history to captain both the North and South Islands; awarded MBE 1980; his biography, *Kirky* (Rugby Press, 1979) was written by Lindsay Knight; his brothers, David, John and Colin also represented Poverty Bay, with David also playing for Hawkes Bay and having an All Black trial.

**Occupation:** Farmer.

2 *The Power Behind the All Blacks*

*NEVER TOO LATE: Andy Leslie was in his 11th season for Wellington when asked to captain a new-look All Black team in 1974. He would lift the All Blacks back to near the top of the international ladder*

# ANDY LESLIE

## 'Oh captain, my captain'

UNLIKE MOST other great All Black captains, Andy Leslie did not 'grow' into the job while observing the leadership style of his predecessor at first hand.

The remarkable aspect of Leslie's successful tenure as All Black captain in 1974–76 was that he had long thought the chance to wear the black jersey had passed him by when chosen to lead New Zealand for the first time.

Leslie had played for his province, Wellington, for 10 years, including 96 consecutive appearances, before he was to get the call from the All Black selectors.

He was appointed captain of the All Blacks to tour Australia in 1974, ahead of the established captain, Ian Kirkpatrick, who also toured.

Under coach JJ Stewart, Leslie was to lead the All Blacks out of the wilderness many believed they had wandered into with the unsuccessful 1970 tour of South Africa, the 1971 series loss to the British Lions, the 1972–73 tour of Britain and France which included Keith Murdoch's banishment from the tour, and the loss to England in coach Stewart's first test at the helm in 1973.

The book, *The Power Behind the All Blacks, the Untold Story of the All Black Coaches*, states that one of the great accomplishments of Stewart as coach was he took a large group of provincial 'also-rans' and quickly converted them into a team that climbed back to the top of the international ladder.

'In harness with his captain, Andy Leslie, Stewart's All Black teams gained a reputation for harmony, sociability and attractive rugby and helped restore the All Black image at home and abroad. Stewart's impact as New Zealand coach set the standards and the modus operandi for his immediate successors and therefore went far beyond the simple win–loss record.'

Sixty percent of the All Black team that toured Australia in 1974 were new. 'It was no criticism of anyone at all. There is certainly a myth that I was instructed by the New Zealand union to leave certain players out of the team. I never had a word of instruction or advice from anybody,' said Stewart.[1]

Another myth that arose from the Stewart era was that he handpicked Leslie to lead the reformation of All Black rugby. Not so, according to the coach.

'People have said Leslie was selected to be captain, but that isn't true. He was selected in the team and then we started to look for the captain,' Stewart told the author.

'I didn't know Andy Leslie. I'd met him at one or two after-match functions when I coached Taranaki and Wanganui. To illustrate how well I knew him, I recall thinking I was talking to Andy Leslie at one such function and calling him by that name, only to be told I was actually talking to Dennis Waller. They both looked a bit the same to me.

'I know, in retrospect, that the decision we made, which may have been a gamble, was very, very successful. Andy didn't have much opportunity to lead his country in New Zealand. So he's probably not regarded with the same mana as he is overseas. In the British Isles, South Africa and Australia, Andy Leslie is King.'[2]

The hardest part for Leslie was taking over from Kirkpatrick. 'Kirky' was one of the first to congratulate Leslie after the announcement and became probably Leslie's most able and faithful supporter over the next several seasons. Kirkpatrick's mother sent Leslie one of his first congratulatory telegrams.

But Leslie's appointment was not well received at first by others and he recalls on the

*IRISH EYES NOT SMILING: Andy Leslie led the All Blacks back to near the top of the international ladder on the tour of Britain in 1974*

night of the selection, whether they were celebrating or drowning their sorrows, players giving him a hard time.

'I can remember players being upset and with split loyalties. Grant Batty and Joe Karam, who had toured with Kirky and were also in the Wellington team, were very upset for him. There was another group of All Blacks, including Grizz Wyllie, who'd just been dropped and were also upset. There was a wee bit of a standoff, such as "just who is this guy Leslie?"' Leslie told the author in 1999.

In retrospect, Leslie believes the ousting of Kirkpatrick as captain was probably not required in order to regain the All Blacks' prestige. His view is that Kirkpatrick's senior players of 1972–73 had not supported him strongly enough. There was therefore some irony in the fact that Kirkpatrick was always Leslie's most loyal lieutenant.

Leslie found Stewart a marvellous All Black

coach. 'It was amazing how much we were on the same wavelength in our attitude to the game. He could have been the All Black coach 10 years beforehand. I think our group were lucky to have him when we did.

'We were labelled "Dad's Army" at first. But with hard work he certainly turned us into a very competitive team. There were few stars and we struggled for size at times, particularly in South Africa,' Leslie told the author in 1999. 'It all came back to that pride in the black jersey – not just for the guy who had played in it before you but for the ones who had worn it through the previous 100 years or so.'

Leslie's team was unbeaten in Australia and in Ireland, Wales and England in 1974. No modern-day team had ever been set the formidable assignment of playing the equivalent of three tests in eight days. Having beaten Ireland and Wales, the All Blacks confronted the Barbarians – in fact, the 1974

British Lions team which had, a couple of months earlier, completed a rout of South Africa – and fought a 13–13 draw.

'We had to play through the "hate" thing between New Zealand and Wales, a bit media-fanned I must say, that had developed since the Angel Hotel incident 2 years earlier. Then the Barbarians decided our team wasn't going to get out of the British Isles undefeated. So we were into it at the deep end,' said Stewart.

Leslie said, in retrospect, the reputations of the 1972–73 All Blacks as the 'Unsmiling Giants' and his side as the 'Smiling All Blacks' was 'all a bit dramatic and media-inflated.' But he admitted the team had had 'an open-door policy' of inclusion for everybody involved, including the media. 'There was no hierarchy – we all got on well. I recall Hamish Macdonald saying at the end of the tour how he wished we could just keep on touring and playing.'

Sid Going, reinstated for that tour, would recall that Leslie had done a magnificent job. 'He used Kirky and the others of us to support him, which was the right thing to do. He fulfilled his captain's role well, even though he was probably fortunate to be in the test lineup for that final week, with a taller guy like Lawrie Knight on the sideline.'

'For all that, Andy played those final three games outstandingly well, as well as I've ever seen him go.'

Then Leslie led New Zealand to home victories over Scotland and Ireland. One of the most famous games was the masterful display in the 24–0 win over Scotland on the waterlogged Eden Park in 1975. Leslie recalled that, unbeknown to the All Blacks, the Scots had wanted to call the game off and play the next day.

The 1976 tour of South Africa, begun so optimistically, was almost inevitably to follow a similar pattern to some of its predecessors. The series was lost 1–3, the chance of tying the rubber hanging in the balance until the final whistle of the fourth test, lost 14–15.

In the fourth test, for instance, late in the game and with the score 12–11 to the home team, South African referee Gert Bezuidenhout was called upon to make a decision that clearly called for a penalty try. All Black Bruce Robertson chipped into the in-goal area, a try for the taking, only to be taken out of the play by Springbok fullback Ian Robertson. Instead of six points, and the likely winning of the game, the referee

*BROTHERS GRIM: Andy Leslie's 1974 team was called the 'smiling All Blacks' but Andy is not so happy in this shot*

awarded a penalty, which yielded three points.

He believes the referee could easily have awarded a second penalty try in the fourth test, again involving Bruce Robertson and deliberate obstruction.

So the tour ended on a sour note. There had been some selection blunders and the goal-kickers, as with previous tours, could not match the Springboks. But this team had played itself to a standstill and failed to share the series by the tiniest margin possible.

It was to prove the end of the All Black road for both Leslie and Stewart. Leslie had played in 14 of the 24 tour matches, including all four tests. Overall, he had played and captained the All Blacks 34 times, including 10 tests. He played for Wellington from 1964–77.

The 1976 *Rugby Annual* stated Leslie was 'one of the finest ambassadors New Zealand has ever sent overseas ... a man of exceptional patience and understanding, traits which helped account for the All Blacks' several sensational comebacks … his own No 8 play scaled great heights, his leadership was inspiring, sportsmanship always came first in his book.'

Having struggled to reach All Black status, Leslie always maintained a down-to-earth approach to his status in the game. 'We got $3 a day expenses or whatever and sometimes had to buy our own beer on tour, whereas today's players are paid hundreds of thousands of dollars. But I wouldn't have had it any other way.

'I can recall being at an All Black mayoral reception in Melbourne on the 1974 tour. A lady asked me "what does that feather on your blazer mean?" It put things in perspective and showed me how New Zealand and rugby is like a big fish in a small pond.'

Leslie was a proud father when his sons, Martin, a former Wellington loose forward, and John, a former Otago captain, were part of the Scottish team which won the Five-Nations championship in 1999 and played in the 1999 World Cup. He had coached John in the Wellington Colts and Martin in the Wellington representative side, but says he never pushed the pair.

'It was difficult enough them living in the shadow of a father who'd been an All Black captain. I was so delighted they made it onto the world stage. Instead of "John (or Martin), the son of Andy Leslie", it's now "Andy, the father of Scottish international John Leslie."'

Martin toured New Zealand with Scotland this year, while John was recovering from troublesome ankle injury.

Leslie is one of only four test captains to have led the All Blacks in every match in which they played for New Zealand. The others were George Aitken, Fred Allen and Pat Vincent.

Leslie was a fine allround sportsman. He also represented New Zealand at softball (1966 world championships) and water polo (colts level) and was an NZ trialist at indoor basketball. His father was a New Zealand soccer representative, having been a professional player for Scottish club Hibernian before migrating to New Zealand.

# Andrew Roy Leslie (Wellington)

**Captain in 10 tests, six wins, three losses and a draw**
v. Australia 1974 (1, 2, 3)
v. Ireland 1974 (1)
v. Scotland 1975 (1)
v. Ireland 1976 (1)
v. South Africa 1976 (1, 2, 3, 4)

**Born:** November 10, 1944, Lower Hutt.

**Position:** No 8.

**Represented NZ:** 1974–76 – 34 matches (10 tests).

**Points for NZ:** 28 – 7 tries.

**First-class record:** Wellington 1964–77 (Petone); North Island 1977; NZ Trials 1970–72, 74–76.

**Selector/coach/administrator:** Coached Wellington 1990–92, finishing 6th, 5th and 6th in NPC; coached Garryowen club, Ireland 1993–94, finishing 1st and 2nd in the All-Ireland League.

**Other:** One of only four test captains to have led the All Blacks in every match in which they played for New Zealand. The others were George Aitken, Fred Allen and Pat Vincent.

**Miscellaneous:** Also represented New Zealand at softball (1966 world championships) and water polo (colts level) and was an NZ trialist at indoor basketball. His father represented New Zealand at soccer, having been a professional player for Scottish club Hibernian before immigrating to New Zealand. Two sons, Martin and John, former Wellington and Otago representatives respectively, were part of the Scottish team which won the Five-Nations championship in 1999 and played in the 1999 World Cup.

**Occupation:** Former sports shop proprietor, Petone.

1,2 *The Power Behind the All Blacks*

# TANE NORTON

## *Tane showed Lions what a grand caretaker skipper he was*

Tane Norton capped off a remarkable All Black career when he led the All Blacks to a hard-fought 3–1 series win over the British Lions in 1977.

Norton had become the oldest All Black ever to be offered the captaincy when new All Black coach Jack Gleeson sought a replacement for the much respected but now retired Andy Leslie.

So Norton was able to add another notch to a career that had been unusual for many reasons.

He had played under three All Black captains – Colin Meads in 1971, Ian Kirkpatrick in 1972–73 and Leslie in 1974–76. Besides the variations in leadership styles he would glean from this trio, and put into effective practice, Norton would also wryly observe the vagaries of an international footballer's career.

Kirkpatrick, for instance, had been born to the purple – if ever a young All Black could be said to have been so. Ascending to the All Black elite level at a tender age in 1967 under the tutelage of Fred Allen, 'Kirky' would lead the All Blacks to Britain and France in 1972–73. But after a loss to England at home in 1973 he was relieved of the captaincy.

Kirkpatrick had followed Colin Meads, captain in the losing 1971 series against Lions after a magnificent career stretching back 15 years. And Kirkpatrick would bow to Leslie.

Now it was Norton's turn. But he told the author he didn't enjoy the responsibility when he was made captain for the series against the Lions.

*AGEING WELL: Tane Norton was the oldest All Black captain in history when he won the 1977 series over Phil Bennett's Lions*

'I reckon they should have kept Kirky as the All Black captain. He'd have turned out one of the greatest – if they'd given him the chance,' Norton explained.

*HARD LESSONS: Tane Norton would one day lead the All Blacks to a series win over the Lions. But in this photo he is having his first test, at Carisbrook, Dunedin, six years earlier. The All Blacks lost the game and the series. His captain, Colin Meads, having his last series, watches on*

'I can recall Colin Meads saying after the 1971 series against the Lions that to be captain in one series was the toughest task of all. If Meads had led the 1970 tour in South Africa, 1971 could have had a different outcome for him. In a home series, you're worried about even making the next test.

'The selectors should have said, before a tour, 'we also want you for the home series next year'. If they'd said that to Lochore in 1970 and Leslie in 1976, it would have provided some continuity of leadership for major series against the Lions.

'Throwing Andy Dalton into it in 1981 against the Springboks was another example. They should have sounded Graham Mourie out much earlier about his availability to play the South Africans.

'It makes it very difficult because taking on the captaincy is a huge responsibility.'

Norton remembers the final few minutes of the series against the Lions best. Lawrie Knight had put the All Blacks ahead, 10–9, and 3–1 up in the series if they could hold on.

'Then Willie Duggan drove for our try-line

from a 5m scrum and must have missed a try by inches,' said Norton. 'The final moments seemed to tick away so slowly.'

The All Blacks had earlier earned the derision of some critics for putting down three three-man scrums (which are nowadays outlawed) when they were under enormous pressure from the Lions.

'John McEldowney, our prop, had also taken a pounding and went off with a neck injury,' Norton told the author.

'Before his substitute, Billy Bush, could be cleared to come on, we called the first of those three-man scrums. I was not prepared to have to put Lawrie Knight into the front row.'

Norton added that the All Blacks had almost scored a try from one such scrum. 'The Lions didn't have a clue what we were up to and had still packed eight men.'

By then aged 35, Norton had a physiotherapist put the displaced vertebra in his neck (the injury had come in the test) back into place and retired. He had been 28 when he played his first game for the All Blacks and yet had gone on to play 61 games for the team. He had played 82 matches for Canterbury and had led the NZ Maoris for several years, being awarded the Tom French Cup as the outstanding Maori player in 1973 and 1974.

Norton was described as being 'always the ideal player for a coach – consistent and clear-thinking. He was a good all-round forward – not a specialist hooker of the ball as were players like Has Catley, and not a rampant forward like Sean Fitzpatrick, but a player of his times nonetheless, and one who made a sizeable contribution to many spheres of rugby.'[1]

His statistics were 1.83m (6ft) tall and weighing 87.2kg (13st 10lb).

Norton told the author that today's game is vastly different from his era. 'I doubt that I'd be able to foot it with these fellows of today. But the requirements for the hooking role were different in the 1970s.'

Norton played through an era when the hooker's role was changing. The Lions of 1971, Norton's first year in the All Blacks, packed a tremendously strong scrum. But Norton quickly demonstrated his resilience and adaptability. His subsequent All Black coaches, Bob Duff, JJ Stewart and Gleeson all worked tremendously

hard on scrummaging, with Norton taking a leadership role.

So, from an 18-year-old playing his first representative game for Mid-Canterbury in 1961, through to 1977, Norton had been part of a major evolutionary development of the scrum. In the 1950s and 1960s hookers swung loosely off their props and aggressively chased tightheads. They therefore did not push too vigorously, if at all.

But through the 1970s, as scrums were 'powered up' in a development led by the Argentinians and the British, the entire eight forwards were expected to contribute to the push. Scrums were much, much lower and Norton would say he could recall hooking the ball with his forehead on the odd occasion in the British Isles.

Despite the All Blacks' progress, it was also harder at times to match the scrum cohesion achieved by touring teams able to practise longer and more frequently. Hookers were also expected to throw the ball into lineouts by the end of Norton's long career.

'From a New Zealand perspective, it was the British who introduced the power scrummaging to us in the 1970s,' Norton told the author in 1999. 'They were able to exert enormous pressure on our front row in 1977, for instance, and the All Blacks just weren't used to it, even though we had countered their scrums on our tours of 1972–73 and 1974.'

Norton had played three games for Mid-Canterbury in 1961, at the age of 18. One of those games was against Canterbury, when he hooked against Dennis Young, the current All Black hooker.

'I psyched myself up for about three weeks for my clash with Dennis. I convinced myself I was going to hold my own with him. But things didn't work out that way. At one scrum, when our halfback was about to put the ball in, Dennis said to his halfback, Frank Whitta, "Do you want this one?" Whitta said "Sure" – and to my complete dismay, he got it.'

But Norton's career as a bank officer took him to small towns such as Oamaru, Kaikoura and Temuka and he was unable to gain recognition from representative selectors.

So in 1967 he moved to Christchurch and joined the Linwood club, the club of famous All Black fullback Fergie McCormick, among other topline players. Thus began his rise

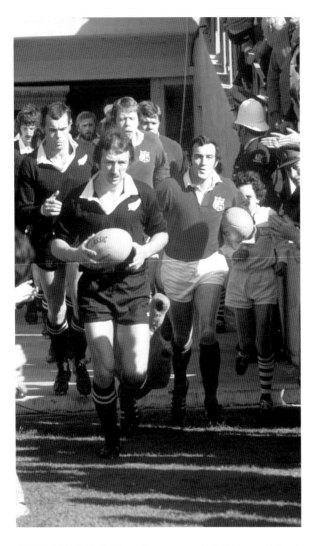

*LION-HEARTED: Tane Norton and Phil Bennett lead their teams into battle in the 1977 series*

through Canterbury B (1968), Canterbury A and the NZ Maoris.

Norton played in all Canterbury's big Ranfurly Shield defences of 1970. Canterbury had five players away in South Africa with the All Blacks, but still managed to defend the shield on seven occasions.

'It was a great year,' recalled Norton. 'We were not expected to retain the shield, but thanks to some astute coaching from Jim Stewart Canterbury still turned on some wonderful rugby.'

'There were huge crowds and it was marvellous to be a part of. I can look back now and attest that any player who has not had the good fortune to be part of that has missed a great rugby experience.'

Then, following the inevitable retirements after the 1970 South African tour, Norton earned a place in the final All Black trial of 1971, opposing the established Ron Urlich, who had played 'understudy' to the now retired Bruce McLeod in South Africa.

Norton reckoned trial rugby was very tough in his day. He recalled being in the thick of a 1970 trial scrum in Christchurch when Keith Murdoch opposed Alister Hopkinson. They would both make the 1970 All Black side to tour South Africa. But in the trial the scrum was shuddering as the two props fought for dominance. Then Hopkinson threatened Murdoch, 'Stop that, or I'll hit you.' Murdoch replied: 'You're too frightened to hit me, Hoppy.'

Norton was in the Canterbury front row that opposed the British Lions in 1971 in a torrid affair that resulted in the two Lions' props, Sandy Carmichael (broken cheekbone) and Ray McLoughlin (a broken thumb), going home injured.

Instead of choosing Urlich, the selectors went for Norton in 1971. He played in all four tests against the Lions. Although the All Blacks lost the series, Norton was to become a permanent fixture as hooker. He went on to build a fine record of 27 consecutive test appearances, including the successful captaincy tenure.

In 1972–73 he toured with the young team captained by Kirkpatrick and coached by Duff. It missed the Grand Slam only when the Irish managed a last-minute draw. Interviewed by the author in 1999 Norton said he had only one career regret and that was that he had not stood up for Murdoch when he was expelled from the team for hitting a Welsh security guard on the night after the win over Wales.

'Everyone got into our manager, Ernie Todd, for not being strong enough. But we must all take some blame because we didn't take a stand at the time.'

Norton survived the 1974 clean-out by new coach Stewart after the All Blacks' one-off loss to England in 1973. He was part of Stewart's superb resurgence with the tours to Australia (1974), Ireland, Wales and England (1974) and to South Africa (1976) and the home wins over Scotland (1975) and Ireland (1976).

Norton recalled the South African tour as one of the toughest assignments for front rows. The All Blacks had to overplay Billy

Bush and Kent Lambert when Kerry Tanner and Brad Johnstone were injured. The Springboks were especially allowed to cause havoc in the third test. Johan Strauss unsettled tour replacement Perry Harris, who had come in for Bush, who had been forced to play nine games in succession and finally got a foot injury.

'The Boks mucked us around all right, helped by the referee,' recalled Norton, who won the tighthead battle in the series overall, as he usually did. 'After we formed up, they would deliberately crab sideways. They wouldn't meet us head-on, instead coming in side-on and unsettling Perry all the time.

'But between the third and fourth test, thanks to Kent and Peter Whiting, we devised a way to combat Strauss.'

The following year came Norton's elevation to the captaincy.

Norton has maintained a close interest with the game. He has been on the Linwood club's committee; was coach of the Shirley BHS First XV for several years and is on the players' committee of the NZRFU.

Norton was on the special six-man NZRFU panel which helped choose the new All Black coaches at the end of 1999.

Norton is married to Jacky and the couple have four sons and two grandchildren. The sons all followed their father into rugby and the Linwood club. Andrew played and coaches at the club; John plays there; Richard now plays in Japan; and Chris now plays in the UK and Italy.

Formerly a bank officer, Norton has been a market gardener for the past 22 years.

## Rangitane Will Norton (Canterbury)

**Captain in four tests, three wins and one loss**
v. British Isles 1977 (1, 2, 3, 4)

**Born:** Waikari, March 30, 1942.

**Position:** Hooker.

**Represented NZ:** 1971–77 – 61 matches (27 tests).

**Points for NZ:** 4 – 1 try.

**First-class record:** Mid-Canterbury 1961 (Methven); Canterbury 1969–77 (Linwood); South Island 1971–75; NZ Trials 1970–72, 74–77; NZ Maoris 1969–75, 77.

**High school:** Methven District High.

**Selector/coach/administrator:** Linwood RFC president; coach Shirley BHS First XV; Canterbury RFU vice-president; on the Rugby Foundation; on players' committee of NZRFU and was part of the special six-man NZRFU panel which helped choose the new All Black coaches at the end of 1999.

**Other:** Four sons all followed their father into rugby and the Linwood club. Andrew played and coaches at the club; John plays there; Richard now plays in Japan; and Chris now plays in the UK and Italy.

**Miscellaneous:** Norton's 197 first-class games included three for a World invitation XV in South Africa in 1977. He became the oldest All Black captain (35 years, 136 days) in 1977, pipping Colin Meads (35 years, 72 days), the 1971 captain. Andy Dalton (35 years, 216 days) would have been older, but was unable to take the field, because of injury, in the 1987 World Cup.

**Occupation:** Bank officer; then an insurance representative; market gardener for past 22 years.

*HEARTLAND WAITS: Graham Mourie leads out Taranaki and Kevin Eveleigh leads Manawatu. One of the great provincial battles of the 1970s is about to begin, with two of the finest open-side flankers in the game*

# GRAHAM MOURIE

## *Have the All Blacks had a better tactician?*

IF THERE was a way the rugby gods could objectively select the finest All Black tactical captain of all time, Graham Mourie just might rate as their first choice.

Mourie did not play in or win as many tests as great captains such as Sir Wilson Whineray or Sean Fitzpatrick. But the stand-out feature of his tenure was the way he devised brilliant and often original tactics to drive his All Black teams, some of which were limited in talent, to often close-run victories.

He captained the All Blacks 58 times in the 61 matches he played as a flanker between 1976 and 1982 and was only on the losing side six times.

Mourie played under three All Black coaches – and their success levels speak much for Mourie's wonderful ability as a leader. Jack Gleeson had a 92.3% success rate in all games, Eric Watson 82.9% and Peter Burke 77.8%. It was noticeable that when Mourie was unavailable for some tours or series, the All Blacks' success rate sometimes dropped.

Mourie seemed to save his best for Europe. He played 11 of his 21 tests in Britain and France. His great triumphs included the 1977 second test victory over France, the first All Black Grand Slam tour of Britain in 1978 and the trouncing of Wales in its centenary match of 1980.

Bryan Williams, the great All Black wing who played under six All Black captains, said Mourie was the ideal captain. He would analyse the opposition to find their weaknesses and was a master tactician and organiser on the field.

Mourie told the author he saw the captaincy as just a part of being an All Black. 'I didn't really have much experience of the team while not leading it. But I was just glad to be there and if the captaincy was part of that, then I was happy to do it,' he said.

Some of Mourie's All Black teams struggled, but he had a priceless ability to change tactics midgame or raise the team's performance with a tactical or encouraging word to individuals.

'An all-important point was that if you lost a game, it was essential to come back the following game and win it well if possible, after working out an alternative plan,' said Mourie.

Following the extreme stablity of the 1960s, the All Blacks went through a transitional stage in the 1970s. There were more regular changes of personnel, coaches sometimes struggled and the results reflected the difficulties.

'When I was playing the team was not as settled as it would become in the 1980s, when it had developed a stronger core,' said Mourie. 'As the captain, I suppose I didn't know any other way. A settled team certainly made it easier to lead on the field and easier to plan the patterns. Conversely, changes to the team often made it a bigger challenge.'

At 14st 2lb and 6ft tall, Mourie was always prepared to shed blood for his team, especially on foreign soil. He was noted for his fitness levels, undertaking marathon-type training to keep his edge. But he was a creator as well as a destroyer as a flanker. He had an uncanny knack of anticipation, could tackle superbly and was the ideal link between forward and backs in scoring movements. He took a pragmatic approach to his position. If the needs of the All Blacks were such, he would happily switch from open to blindside.

*GREAT PROMISE: A youthful Graham Mourie scores for Wellington as they beat the touring England team, 25–16, in 1973*

But Mourie had a mixed relationship with the New Zealand public. His unavailablity in 1980 (for financial reasons) and 1981 (conscience reasons) caused some followers to grumble. In later years a few of his former team-mates took swipes at him.

Mourie recalled to the author that in 1980 he had just bought a farm. His team-mate, Andy Dalton, was in a similar situation, and so were others. The players were still amateur but the demands on them were escalating. The international rugby scene was in a transitional situation. More and more tests were being played, sometimes two series in a home season and then a tour overseas at the end of the year.

Unlike many other All Blacks through history, Mourie told the author 'no-one fronted up with the money to pay for a temporary worker on the farm while I was away,' said Mourie. 'It was a simple case of not being able to afford to always tour.'

He also declined to play against the touring Springboks in 1981.

'I felt the situation in South Africa was wrong, that it was wrong for rugby and wrong for New Zealand,' Mourie recalled.

For that momentous series, Andy Dalton successfully took over the captaincy. But such was Mourie's mana, he was asked, by coach Peter Burke, to captain the team to tour Romania and France at the end of the year. Dalton, mindful of the potential for a split in the team or among the selectors, had gone to Burke and said he would be happy to tour under Mourie again. In research for this book, both Dalton and Burke confirmed to the author that this was the case, but Mourie said he recalled only that 'the players' had been content for him to return.

'Some senior players wanted me back. If they thought I had deserted the ship it certainly wouldn't have happened like that.'

*FIELDS OF DREAMS: Graham Mourie often saved his best for Europe, playing 11 of his 21 tests in Britain and France*

Mourie had begun his All Black career by leading the second All Black team of 1976 to Argentina under coach Gleeson. It was unbeaten, devising brilliant tactics to counter the Argentinians' lineout height.

When the British Lions toured in 1977 Mourie played in the last two tests, being instrumental in the series-clinching try when he freed the ball up for Lawrie Knight to score in the fourth test.

He became the All Black captain at the end of that year for the tour of France and would retain the leadership, when available, right through to his retirement in 1982.

The big French pack dominated Mourie's team in the first test. But Mourie, Gleeson and others devised clever tactics, including short lineouts and speed from phase to phase to wear out the French and win decisively, 15–3, in Paris.

Mourie missed the 1978 series at home against Australia through injury (though he was a reserve for the final test). But he then led the All Blacks on their first Grand Slam tour of Britain.

The closest encounter was the 13–12 win over Wales. Andy Haden earned the derision of the Welsh with a spectacular dive from a lineout. He said the inspiration for the tactic

had come from Mourie. But the match-winning penalty had actually come from an infringement by Geoff Wheel on Frank Oliver further up the same lineout.

It is extraordinary that when Mourie led the 1978 team, four previous All Black touring sides had been undefeated in their matches with the Home Unions. But through various circumstances, none had managed to pull off the Grand Slam.

Of that achievement, Mourie said his side had been unexceptional in terms of physique and skills compared to other All Black teams. 'But they put everything on the line every time they took the field. The attitude was tremendous on and off the field,' Mourie recalled to the author in 1999.

But Mourie's team was brought back down hard to earth in 1979. The year proved a battle. Though Mourie would score his first test try, against France, that series was drawn. The Bledisloe Cup was lost in Australia. Then the All Blacks returned to Britain again at the end of the year. Scotland was well-beaten, 20–6, but England was only overcome 10–9.

Mourie was unavailable for the series in

Australia in 1980 but led the team for a third tour in as many years to Britain. It was the Welsh centenary. Mourie was in outstanding form as the Welsh were subdued, 23–3. He rates that All Black side as the best of his tenure.

The lyrical former Welsh flyhalf wizard and then commentator Cliff Morgan said of Mourie after his try in the match: 'I do not mind going to my maker because today I saw, from Graham Mourie, the greatest loose forward display the world could ever wish to see.'

Mourie played in the series against Scotland in 1981 but was unavailable, on conscience grounds, for the series against the touring Springboks. On the end of year tour, after missing the test against Romania because of injury, Mourie led the All Blacks to wins in both tests in France.

He bowed out of test football at the end of 1982 after leading the All Blacks to a hard-fought 2–1 series victory over Australia in New Zealand. He returned to France for a club season.

Mourie had played for Wellington in 1972–74 while studying at Victoria University and was in the Wellington side that briefly held the Ranfurly Shield in 1974. He was also introduced to the open-side flank position by NZ Junior and later All Black coach, Watson, in 1973 and was in the side that beat the All Blacks that year. In 1976 he had missed the chance to make the All Black team to tour South Africa because of injury

Mourie was noted for his ethical stands. In 1981 he had declined to play against the Springboks. The following year, in a move intended to highlight the hypocrisy of the 'shamateurism' of the era, Mourie made it public he had accepted payment for his book, thereby declaring himself a professional.

But he kept in contact with the game. He was involved in a number of ventures after his retirement, including work with West Nally, the marketing body for the 1987 World Cup. He returned to farming in Opunake, Taranaki, and club coaching. Mourie was linked with John Hart's unsuccessful 1994 bid to oust Laurie Mains as All Black coach. His star began its ascent again in late 1997 when he became Wellington's coach and, after a strong 1999 season, he was appointed to coach the Hurricanes with Bryan Williams. The Hurricanes just missed the play-offs this year. There are some who say Mourie would one day make a fine All Black coach.

## Graham Neil Kenneth Mourie (Taranaki)

**Captain in 19 tests, 15 wins and four losses**
v. France 1977 (1, 2),
v. Ireland, Wales, England, Scotland 1978
v. France 1979 (1, 2)
v. Australia 1979 (1)
v. Scotland, England 1979
v. Wales 1980 (1)
v. Scotland 1981 (1, 2)
v. France 1981 (1, 2)
v. Australia 1982 (1, 2, 3)

**Born:** September 8, 1952, Opunake.

**Position:** Flanker.

**Represented NZ:** 1976–82 – 61 matches (21 tests).

**Points for NZ:** 64 – 16 tries.

**First-class record:** Wellington 1972–74 (University); Taranaki 1975–82 (Opunake); North Island 1976–80, 82; NZ Trials 1974, 75, 77–79, 81, NZ Juniors 1973–75; NZ Colts 1972; NZ Universities 1972, 73.

**High school:** Opunake High First XV 1968, New Plymouth Boys' High First XV 1969, 70.

**Selector/coach/administrator:** Coached the Opunake (renamed Coastal) club in Taranaki; unofficially assisted the Auckland team in the 1980s as a forward coach; 1994 stood unsuccessfully for NZ selector; 1998–99 Wellington coach; 2000 coach (with Bryan Williams) of Hurricanes Super 12 team.

**Miscellaneous:** His biography, *Graham Mourie – Captain* (with Ron Palenski, Moa), was published in 1982. In a move intended to highlight the hypocrisy of the 'shamateurism' of the era, Mourie made it public he had accepted payment for the book, thereby declaring himself a professional.

**Other:** When Mourie captained the second All Black team to Argentina in 1976, he also met his wife. They later divorced. He now lives in Wellington with his partner, Shona, and their four children, Kohia, Rewa and twins Tai and Moana.

**Occupation:** Worked for West Nally, the marketing body for the first World Cup in 1987; Taranaki farmer; professional rugby coach.

# FRANK OLIVER

## *Frank could have been Grand Slam captain*

ONE OF New Zealand rugby's best kept secrets is that Frank Oliver was asked by coach Jack Gleeson to captain the 1978 All Black team that became famous for achieving New Zealand's first Grand Slam.

It has long been assumed Graham Mourie, who would lead the All Blacks, when available, from 1977 through to 1982, was an obvious selectors' choice as captain of Gleeson's ground-breakers.

But that is not so, according to Oliver.

He had established himself as an All Black test lock since the latter stages of the 1976 All Black tour of South Africa. He already had a wealth of captaincy experience, having led Southland, then Otago, the South Island, the New Zealand Colts and New Zealand Under 19 during his breakthrough into representative rugby.

In 1978 he was asked to captain the All Blacks in the series against the touring Wallabies. He led New Zealand to a 2–1 series victory.

Mourie had been the All Black captain for the first time on the tour of Italy and France the year before. This side had the same leadership – Mourie, Gleeson and manager Ron Don – as had led the second 1976 All Black side to Argentina.

But after appearing in seven of the nine matches, Mourie returned to France for the northern season and played for the Paris University club. Because of a back injury he was not available for the home series, although he was a reserve for the final test.

The management of the All Blacks had changed too. Russ Thomas, who would take some of the kudos for organising a trouble-free Grand Slam tour, was the new manager.

Why then did Oliver turn the chance down? 'In retrospect, it was the worst thing I ever did. It could have led to other things,' said Oliver told the author in 1999.

Oliver said he sensed it was best for the team if the captaincy be handed back to Mourie – in the same way Andy Dalton handed it back to Mourie after leading the All Blacks to their 1981 series win over the touring Springboks.

'I chose not to take it on – there was also the fact many of the team were going to be the younger players coming through from the Argentinian tour of 1976, whereas my team-mates from the 1976 South African tour were getting old and some had been dropped. There was potential for some division.'

But Oliver is proud to recount he played his part in assisting Mourie and the management on that tour. 'I got out of the 'back of the bus' and moved up to be with the younger players. I helped control the thing.'

Oliver was never concerned at filling the big shoes of the great All Black captains. 'It always came naturally. I'd done it so many times from a young age in so many teams that it was never a burden to do it like it was for some All Blacks,' he said.

He had impressed as a likely future All Black right from the beginning of his provincial career with Southland in 1969. His first All Black trial was in 1970, the year the All Blacks toured South Africa under coach Ivan Vodanovich. But it was to take him seven more seasons, until the All Blacks next toured South Africa in 1976 under JJ Stewart, for him to claim his first All Black jersey.

Oliver had established himself as a strong test contender by the end of that tour. He displaced Hamish Macdonald as Peter Whiting's locking partner for the fourth test and retained his place

*EARLY DAYS: Frank Oliver on the charge for Southland against the touring Irish in 1976*

against the 1977 British Lions and on the tour of Italy and France later that year.

Oliver played in all four internationals on the Grand Slam tour. Much has been made over the years of Andy Haden's theatrical leap out of the lineout in the final moments of the Welsh international. The Welsh blamed Haden's unsportsmanlike action for the referee, Roger Quittenton, awarding a penalty that Brian McKechnie converted into the winning 13–12 victory.

But in fact it was Frank Oliver, at No 3 in the same lineout, who unwittingly played the critical part in the drama. At the same time Haden, at No 5, threw himself out of the line, Welsh lock Geoff Wheel jumped off the shoulder of Oliver. This was the offence that Quittenton observed and acted upon, not Haden's antics.

Much was made of Haden's effort but constant television re-runs of the sequence proved Quittenton's decision was correct and that the Welsh had only themselves to blame for their unfortunate loss.

But Oliver formed a crucial part of a grand 'tight five' on that tour that also included

Haden, Gary Knight, Bill Bush, Brad Johnstone and Dalton in the internationals, supported by Mourie, Leicester Rutledge and Gary Seear.

In 1979 Oliver appeared in the two domestic tests against France, although a back injury forced him from the field in the first test. Oliver's form was affected by the injury and he did not gain selection for the 1979 tours to Australia and to England and Scotland, and the 1980 Australian tour. However, it was a broken thumb – 'I kept re-breaking the thing when doing my job of cutting and planting trees' – that affected his early 1980 season.

But he returned to his best form for Manawatu and the North Island to reclaim his black jersey against Fiji that year. He then toured in the side that played the Welsh centenary match in 1980.

In 1981 Oliver, his career winding down, was recalled from Australia, where he was to play in a festival game, to play the second test at Wellington against the Springboks. Graeme Higginson had broken an ankle at training. The All Blacks had won the first test, 14–9, but would bow to the Boks in the second, 12–24.

*POWERHOUSE DISPLAY: Frank Oliver (with ball) would force his way into the test team with consistent powerhouse form on the 1976 tour of South Africa*

The young Gary Whetton was then brought in to replace Oliver and partner Haden in the third and final test at Auckland, won 25–22 in the final moments.

Oliver was not a big lock by modern standards. He stood 1.91m (6ft 3in) and weighed 106kg (16st 11lb) at his heaviest. But as the 1976 *Rugby Annual* stated, he supplied 'the basic, low driving, hard rucking approach'.

He also had a high work rate and was extremely strong in the upper body after years of 'running around the bush with a chainsaw' while a forestry contractor.

'The men I marked as a lock were usually bigger than me and they all had their different strengths,' said Oliver in 1999. 'It was like that in South Africa, for instance. But I was 27 by then and had played heaps of provincial and trial rugby. I knew my way around a rugby field, so it wasn't too hard to fit into what the All Blacks wanted.'

But Oliver's courage was legendary. In France in 1977 he played the second test match with broken ribs. Any forward who has played rugby while recovering from cracked ribs would testify to how excruciatingly painful it is. The ribs are wrapped with adhesive tape around the torso so they cannot move far on impact.

Oliver told the author he'd suffered three broken ribs and had a fourth one cracked in a game against a French Selection, the fifth game of the tour. 'I was given a pain-killing jab before the game. I knew I could push straight but I got hit from the kick-off and actually fainted for a few seconds. I got up again and got going. But I had to have another painkiller at halftime and felt nothing for a day later.'

In 1979, again against the French, he was 'tickled up in a ruck' by a French boot in the back. The blow pinched a nerve, he found he couldn't stand, let alone run, and had to leave the field for the only time in his career. 'They were not too particular where they put their feet sometimes,' said Oliver of the French.

Unlike some All Blacks, Oliver said he enjoyed all four of the All Black coaches he played under.

'JJ Stewart was the first, in 1976. He was a very caring and intelligent man with a dry sense of humour. Jack Gleeson was quiet and a good thinker. I had a bit to do with him when I moved to Manawatu late in 1979, just before he died.

'Eric Watson was another dry bugger. You used to want to play for him so badly. And then there was Peter Burke, who'd been my NZ Under 19 coach. He called me in to fill in for the 1981 test against South Africa, but I really only had one training run under him …'

The professional rugby era has meant Oliver has gained a second lease of life as an international rugby traveller. He coached the Wellington Hurricanes for four seasons (1996–99) and was assistant coach to Gordon Hunter with the Auckland Blues in 2000.

'It's nice to meet some of these men again. People such as John Williams, the Bok lock back in 1976, and Ray Mordt, the winger who is now into coaching,' said Oliver.

'The old feelings can still be stirred, but we are all too old to go to war again,' he laughed.

There was even be a glint in the eye of Oliver when his and Hunter's Blues team took on might of the Hurricanes this year. Oliver had lost the Hurricanes' job to his former captain, Graham Mourie. So the friendly sparring continues.

Oliver's son, Anton, is the All Black hooker.

## Francis James Oliver (Otago)

**Captain in three tests, two wins and a loss** v. Australia 1978 (1, 2, 3)

**Born:** December 24, 1948, Dunedin.

**Position:** Lock.

**Represented NZ:** 1976–81 – 43 matches (17 tests).

**Points for NZ:** 8 – 2 tries.

**First-class record:** Southland 1969–76 (Marist), 1977 (Waiau); Otago 1978, 79 (Tokomairiro); Manawatu 1980–83 (Marist); South Island 1972, 74, 75, 77, 79; North Island 1980, 81; NZ Trials 1970–72, 74–77, 79, 80; NZ Juniors 1969, 70; NZ Services 1968, 72.

**High school:** Lawrence District High School, First XV 1963–65.

**Selector/coach/administrator:** Coached Galwegians club, Ireland 1993; coached NZ Under 19 team in 1994, of which a son, Anton, was captain; coached Manawatu 1995-97; coached Central Vikings 1997, 98 (NPC 2nd division winner); coached Wellington Hurricanes (Super 12) 1996, 97, 98; assistant coach Auckland Blues (Super 12) 2000.

**Miscellaneous:** A son, Anton, All Black hooker 1997–2000; another son, Brent, played for Otago B, the Central Vikings and NZ Universities. A brother, Paul, represented Otago 1974–76, 78–80; South Island 1976; NZ Juniors 1975, 76; NZ Colts 1973; NZ Universities 1975–77.

**Occupation:** Professional rugby coach. Formerly policeman, then forestry contractor, fisherman and foreman.

# DAVE LOVERIDGE

## Trapper's persistence was a quality above all others

THE FOOD-poisoning that doomed Laurie Mains' All Blacks on the eve of the 1995 World Cup final was not the first occasion such an occurrence has affected the New Zealand team.

In 1980, on the All Blacks' Australian tour led by Dave Loveridge, the All Blacks suffered food-poisoning *en masse* to such an extent that victory was impossible.

Instead, the underrated Wallabies, who had won the first test, 13–9, but bowed to the All Blacks in the second in Brisbane, 9–12, after the famous try sparked by Bruce Robertson and completed by hooker Hika Reid, went on to take the series with a resounding 26–10 win in Sydney.

Like the 1995 Johannesburg incident, there was conjecture that the All Blacks had been nobbled by bookmakers attemping to make the big 'killing'.

Loveridge nowadays can add little to the debate. But he is sure the Wallabies of that series did not get the credit they deserved.

'They were a strong team and had us struggling through the series. Instead, people said the All Blacks were no good. Yes, we could have been better, but other All Black teams that toured Australia would have struggled with these Wallabies, I am sure,' said Loveridge.

Loveridge was in his third year as an All Black – and had only recently established himself as the side's No 1 halfback after years of competition with Manawatu's Mark Donaldson – when he was chosen to captain the All Blacks in the absence of his Taranaki team-mate, Graham Mourie.

His own form dropped away but he fought

ALL CLASS: *Dave Loveridge's slight build and late start at the top belied a classy halfback who would be rated among the best ever by sound judges before he retired*

back to play a key role in the memorable win in the Welsh centenary test at the end of 1980.

*NO FAIR WEATHER FOOTBALLER: Years of yeoman service for Taranaki gave Dave Loveridge all the skills to run an international game, especially in the most adverse of weather conditions*

It was as a fighter against adversity that Loveridge might best be remembered. His long career at first-class level was typified by courage and persistence.

Typical was the way he battled back from a medial ligament operation on his left knee, suffered at the start of the 1984 season. Most critics believed the injury had ended his career for he was aged 33. Instead, Loveridge built his body back to full fitness and played the last of his 24 tests against Argentina in Buenos Aires in 1985.

But that was one of many adversities or obstacles to be overcome. Recognition came slowly. He had played six seasons of representative football before he got the All Black call at the age of 26.

His fans had watched in horror in 1977 when he was driven off New Plymouth's Rugby Park in an ambulance during the Taranaki-British Lions match after a serious leg injury. He would also win out in the long-running rivalry with Donaldson, battle back from the self-doubt that occurred with the unsuccessful captaincy stint, watch his beloved province be demoted from

first division, suffer concussion and other injuries, and even the disappointment of the cancellation of the 1985 tour of South Africa.

Loveridge's slow career start belied the fact that here was a classy player. His mastery of the halfback's skills were such he seldom played a bad game. Besides being a fast and elusive runner, especially astute at the blindside break, he had an exceptional pass and could convert even the most atrocious wet-weather lineout ball to quality possession for his backs. He was deceptively strong, could read the game well and thus chose his options intelligently. He could kick a team out of trouble or onto attack and was a determined defender.

'Mark Donaldson and I practised the basics a lot,' Loveridge told the author in 1999. 'Halfback is such a pivotal, decision-making position. The key is knowing when to use what weapon in your artillery. Being aware of what is happening around you and what you're going to do next comes with experience. But you have to try to be proactive, not reactive.

'The key to my success in the long-term was

*FIRING AWAY: Dave Loveridge gets his backs away against Scotland on the 1979 tour. Watching are Andy Haden, John Spiers, Graham Mourie and Murray Mexted. The All Blacks won 20–6.*

that I realised you had to work hard to achieve.'

Loveridge may have reached his peak in the 1983 series against the British Lions. Normally cautious critics were heard to say he 'might be our best ever'.

In the second test against the Lions, Loveridge scored a fine try to help his side to a 9–0 lead at the interval. However, the All Blacks then turned into a stiff Wellington southerly wind and the Lions must have been confident they could win. Instead, Loveridge took charge of the game, whipping a committed pack to do his bidding and running the blindside to maintain possession.

'It was just a day for playing the old tramlines,' the modest Loveridge recalled in 1999. 'I've always been of the opinion the blindside is where the opposition are most vulnerable.'

'Trapper' Loveridge gained his nickname from a Taranaki team-mate, former All Black prop Ash Gardiner. With long hair the fashion of the times, Gardiner reckoned the young halfback resembled a 'drowned rat' and then adapted it to 'Rat Trapper' and then 'Trapper'.

A bank transfer had taken Loveridge to Auckland – where he played two matches for the representative side in 1973 – after early rugby life with the Inglewood club and Inglewood High School.

But he returned to Taranaki to become a pig farmer and immediately became the provincial halfback. His rise was steady. He made the New Zealand Juniors against Romania in 1975, was a reserve for the tests against the 1978 Wallabies and played for the North Island.

Jack Gleeson chose him for his first test against Wales on the Grand Slam tour of 1978, after Donaldson had to withdraw because of injury. He had a fine debut in a match that went down in history for the way the All Blacks' Brian McKechnie kicked the winning points in injury time when Wales were penalised in a lineout that involved the infamous Andy Haden 'dive'.

Donaldson bounced back for the tests against England and Scotland, but Loveridge was rewarded with the Barbarians match berth.

He led New Zealand to wins over Hugo Porta's touring Argentinians in 1979, showing brilliant form. At the end of the year, on the tour to Scotland and England, he got the nod from new coach, Eric Watson, thus ending Donaldson's reign.

In the test against Scotland, after scoring earlier in the game, Loveridge pulled off an outstanding, try-saving tackle on the pacy fullback, Andy Irvine, with the score at only 10–3. He was injured in the tackle but immediately produced a blindside break which enabled Stu Wilson to score. Then he left the field.

When the All Blacks beat England, 10–9, a fortnight later, John Fleming got the only try, from a kick placed high by Loveridge.

In 1981 Loveridge played all eight tests of that year. His outside backs had a field day in some of those tests, especially against Scotland. In the stupendous on-field battle that rivalled the distracting off-field antics in the series-deciding third test at Eden Park, Loveridge suffered a bad concussion when trying to stop the powerful Springbok winger, Ray Mordt, from scoring his third try.

It was a particularly bad year injury-wise, even by Loveridge's standards. He had also suffered concussions at club and provincial levels. But he was passed fit enough to take his place on the tour to Romania and France at the end of the year and had another fine tour.

The Wallabies toured in 1982 and Loveridge was halfback in the three tests. In 1983 he was an integral part of the 4–0 whitewash of the Lions and in the one-off win over Australia in Sydney.

Loveridge suffered the knee ligament injury early in 1984 and missed the rest of the season. But he returned for 1985, was reserve for three domestic tests (two against England and one against Australia) and was named in the side to tour South Africa. On the replacement tour to Argentina he replaced David Kirk for the second test.

Standing 1.75m (5ft 9in) and weighing 75kg (11st 12lb), Loveridge played 54 games for the All Blacks between 1978 and 1985.

He ended his career in 1986 when he toured South Africa with the Cavaliers and later that year went to England to play for the Harlequins club.

He had long been known on All Black tours for his sense of humour and reckoned Stu Wilson had 'taught me well'. He believed 'the ice had to be broken and the tension melted down' on those long bus and plane trips. He recalled how the 1979–80 coach, Eric Watson, had 'had a way with the humour, especially the forwards and especially the front row, whom he used to turn around at halftime and tell them which way to run.'

Throughout his career Loveridge maintained he 'never saw Andy Haden fall out of that lineout against Wales back in 1978. It wasn't until after the game that someone explained it all to me.'

But when Loveridge dived over for one of his nine All Black tries he could sometimes be heard to say it was Haden who'd taught him how to dive like that.

Work on the farm helped Loveridge's strength. Unlike today's All Blacks, he never did weight-training. 'I remember sitting down with Barry John in a Llanelli bar on a tour. He said he'd never done any. Most players relied on skill and agility and practised hard.'

Loveridge is still a Taranaki pig farmer, married to Janine and with three children aged 22, 19 and 17. He still coaches the Inglewood senior team. His bad luck with injuries hasn't deserted him either. In 1998 he dislocated a shoulder after slipping over on the farm.

## David Steven Loveridge (Taranaki)

**Captain in three tests, one win and two losses**
v. Australia 1980 (1, 2, 3)

**Born:** April 22, 1952, Stratford.

**Position:** Halfback.

**Represented NZ:** 1978–83, 85 – 54 matches (24 tests).

**Points for NZ:** 36 – 9 tries.

**First-class record:** Auckland 1973 (University); Taranaki 1974–86 (Inglewood); NZ Juniors 1975; North Island 1978, 79, 85; NZ Trials 1977–82, 85; IRB Centenary 1986.

**Selector/coach/administrator:** Coach of Inglewood senior team in 1988–90 and 1998–2000; NZRFU staff coach 1997–2000.

**High school:** Inglewood High School, First XV 1969.

**Other:** Involved in rugby commentating on Taranaki radio in 1990s.

**Miscellaneous:** A book, *Master Halfback*, by Ron Palenski (Moa), was published in 1985.

**Occupation:** Pig farmer.

# ANDY DALTON

## Dalton proved a handy man in a crisis

APART FROM the unbeaten Buck Shelford, Andy Dalton was the most successful All Black captain of all time. But he might have given all those victories away for the chance to lead the All Blacks, on the field, in the first World Cup in 1987.

Dalton won 15 of the 17 tests he led the All Blacks. He played 58 games for New Zealand, including 35 tests, between 1977 and 1985.

But in 1987, after a season's absence through injury, Dalton was chosen to lead the All Blacks at the inaugural World Cup in New Zealand. A hamstring injury on the day the team assembled cruelly prevented Dalton from playing in the tournament, his hooking position being filled by Sean Fitzpatrick and the on-field captain's role by David Kirk. He remained the captain though and had an important role behind the scenes.

This was another 'character-building' setback for Dalton. Early in his career there had been plenty of others. He could not make the senior team at Lincoln College, Canterbury, and did not play senior rugby regularly until he was 23. As an All Black he lost his test place to John Black, Peter Sloane and Hika Reid. As captain of the All Blacks which beat the Springboks in 1981, Dalton then handed the reins back to his former skipper, Graham Mourie. Much later he would be floored by a cowardly punch (thrown from behind Dalton's back by Northern Transvaal's Burger Geldenhuys as the hooker was running across field) that broke his jaw early in the 1986 tour of South Africa by the rebel Cavaliers.

In spite of such adversity Dalton became New Zealand's most capped hooker and one of its most revered captains.

Recalling his slow start to senior rugby, Dalton told the author the experience was character-building. 'It made me more determined. I realised I wasn't as naturally gifted as some other players and that I had to do it the hard way. That was how it always was,' he said.

But Dalton quickly made up ground when he shifted to Counties and came under the eye of provincial coach Barry Bracewell and later Hiwi Tauroa.

'It was a terrific environment to learn in, with Bruce Robertson, Bob Lendrum, Peter Goldsmith, Mac McCallion and all the other stars Counties had in those days. I'd love to see that backline operating in today's game. They would be sensational. But then the whole team played a wonderful style of football.'

Dalton was the first of the modern-era All Black hookers to throw the ball into lineouts. He set the standard for all his successors because his accuracy was exceptional. Only 5ft 10in tall and 14st 9lb, Dalton was not only technically sound, but a well-rounded tight-loose forward suited to the changing needs of the position.

Dalton's reputation was ensured after only his first test. On the 1977 tour of France, after the first test defeat, Dalton was given his chance in the second test by coach Jack Gleeson. With the All Blacks brilliantly employing hit and run tactics, Dalton's pinpoint throwing allowed Andy Haden and Lawrie Knight to dominate the short lineouts. The team shocked the huge French pack and pulled off a famous victory.

He held his place for the home series against Australia and on the Grand Slam tour of 1978. But after the home series against France in 1979, Black won the position in Australia. Dalton (Murrayfield) and Sloane (Twickenham) shared the tests on the England-Scotland tour that year.

*HAPPINESS IS: Geoff Old and Andy Dalton can feel pleased with themselves. They've just helped beat the touring Springboks in the infamous 'flour-bomb' third test at Eden Park, Auckland in 1981, to take the series*

Dalton and Sloane were unavailable for Australia in 1980. Reid had a sensational tour and kept Dalton out of the Welsh centenary test team, the final time he would do so.

Dalton was to prove an admirable replacement for Mourie against the Boks. His calm authority was in stark contrast with the madness that occurred outside the test stadiums. After the series, he told coach Peter Burke that Mourie should be returned as captain for the tour of Rumania and France.

The 1981 series was probably the sweetest of many career highlights for Dalton. 'It was a terrific kick to beat the Boks. But it was also difficult. Protesters had come out to my farm and clubrooms had to be guarded by security. I was disgusted by some of the things that happened. Given that the tour was a lawful activity, it certainly opened my eyes to the lengths some people will go to get their views across,' Dalton said.

When Mourie retired at the end of 1982

Dalton led the All Blacks over the next three seasons. Victories over the British Lions, France, England and Australia at home, and Australia away followed. Farming commitments prevented him from touring England and Scotland (1983) and Argentina (1985).

Dalton was chosen as All Black captain for the 1985 South African tour, which was cancelled. He was a prime mover in the organisation of the Cavaliers tour in 1986.

In 1999, recalling the circumstances of the Cavaliers' tour, Dalton said simply: 'It should never have taken place.'

'But the interim injunction that halted the 1985 All Black tour was an injustice that has given me misgivings about our legal system and political interference ever since,' said Dalton. 'It was poorly handled by the NZRFU lawyers. It was also a difficult time because of my relationship with Ces Blazey [the NZRFU chairman] and others.'

Dalton called the Cavaliers' tour 'the most

*NO SHORTCUTS: Is Andy Dalton (extreme right) taking the long route and Andy Haden (extreme left) the short route as the 1979 All Blacks do laps at practice during the tour of England and Scotland?*

professionally organised tour' he ever made. Though he knew he wouldn't play again on tour, Dalton stayed with the team after the injury.

Known as one of the front row 'Geriatrics' by the mid-1980s, Dalton was summed up by fellow 'Geriatric', John Ashworth: 'The best captain I have had was Andy Dalton. He was on top of everything. He knew all the requirements and could bridge all the different groups that make up a side. He could get a lot out of his players and still be at ease in the position.'[1]

Explaining the phenomenon of the 'Geriatrics', which seemed to strike a chord with the game's followers, Dalton said he, Ashworth and Gary Knight were all farmers.

'We got along well together, on and off the field. We had a respect for each other's rugby abilities, which had grown over many years of touring. We'd all had to work hard to make our place in the All Black test front row and then to stay there. None of us were 'flashy' players, so that gave us another bond. And we didn't see why, despite the media interest in our ages, we should give the big time away while we were doing a good job.'

Dalton's All Black coach in 1983–84, Bryce Rope, was frank in his admiration for the 'Geriatrics'.

'I used to say to them: 'You know the front row requirements better than me or anyone. Play this test like you did the last one, only better!' That was my team-talk to those three. They used to laugh, but it was right.'

'One great thing that came out of the 1981 Springbok tour was a very special bonding of these forwards, who had survived tremendous pressure and adversity both on and off the field,' Rope told the author. 'That pack had been through so much together. They were like a machine. You don't try to tamper with something as good as that.'

Of his wretched luck on the eve of captaining the All Blacks in the first World Cup in 1987, Dalton said the hamstring injury that ended his career was 'really self-inflicted'.

Coach Brian Lochore had been delayed on a flight to Auckland and Dalton was running the team's first practice.

'We were playing touch footie and I was refereeing it. The hammie went. It tore even more badly when I tried to stretch out a couple of days later. I still hoped to play in the tournament, but after the Argentina game Brian Lochore said that Sean Fitzpatrick would play the rest of the games.'

But like a rugby version of tennis' non-playing captain, Harry Hopman, Dalton was able to contribute to the cup-winning effort. 'I was still very much part of the team. I think David [Kirk] was struggling a little with some of the off-field requirements and I was able to help him.'

Dalton's mixed luck continued in other areas of his game. He was in Counties' Ranfurly Shield-challenging teams seven times, for two draws and five losses by less than eight points.

As coach of Counties from 1989–91 he could reasonably have expected a little more luck also. But Dalton said the pre-professional environment was frustrating. 'Some excellent players came through, but there were also the downsides. Some players had to be baby-sat. They always had their hand out, they had to be transported to and from training and even have their boots organised for them,' he said.

Would he coach again? 'If the circumstances were right. The idea of being a fulltime coach does appeal.'

Dalton holds firm ideas on the professional era. The president of the New Zealand union in 1999, he spoke up publicly about the urgent need for today's young professionals to have advice and gain lifeskills for life after rugby.

While a few great players could 'guarantee' huge long-term incomes, the majority had to think beyond rugby as their sole employment.

'I am convinced it would benefit many of these players if they had personal mentors during and after rugby,' he said.

The NZRFU, especially Sir Brian Lochore and Jock Hobbs, had done a good job with the contracts for players, he said. 'But it would help if there were some clauses that demanded the players look at life after rugby,' Dalton said. 'They need to have a fallback position when their rugby is over.'

Dalton's father, Ray, was an All Black, in 1947 to Australia, and as vice-captain of the ill-fated 1949 side that toured South Africa, losing the series 4–0. A brother, David, an engineer who lives in Norway, has played rugby for that country and still plays there.

Dalton recently married for the second time, to Eileen. He has two children, Kate (20) and Hamish (17) by his first wife Pip. He runs a New Zealand-based hazardous waste disposal company with a staff of 76 and farms in Bombay, south of Auckland. He keeps fit by attending a gym several times a week.

Dalton was on the special six-man NZRFU panel which helped choose the new All Black coaches at the end of 1999.

---

### Andrew Grant Dalton (Counties)

**Captain in 17 tests, 15 wins and two losses**
v. South Africa 1981 (1, 2, 3)
v. Romania 1981 (1)
v. British Isles 1983 (1, 2, 3, 4)
v. Australia 1984 (1, 2, 3)
v. England 1985 (1, 2)
v. Australia 1985 (1)

**Born:** November 16, 1951, Dunedin.

**Position:** Hooker.

**Represented NZ:** 1977–85.

**Points for NZ:** 12 – 3 tries.

**First-class record:** Counties 1975–85 (Bombay club); North Island 1976–82; NZ Trials 1978, 81–84; Counties-Thames Valley 1977; IRB Centenary 1986.

**High school:** Selwyn College 1st XV 1968, 69.

**Selector/coach/administrator:** Coach of Counties 1989–91. President NZRFU 1999–2000.

**Miscellaneous:** Dalton's father, Ray, represented New Zealand 1947 and was vice-captain of the 1949 All Blacks in South Africa.

**Occupation:** Formerly a farm advisory officer, now a company manager and director.

---

1 *The Geriatrics,* Lindsay Knight, Moa, 1986.

# STU WILSON

## *Stu was only captain who led from the wing*

STU WILSON is the only player ever to have captained the All Blacks in a test from the wing.

Wilson was a brilliant, intuitive three-quarter who became known as the 'ultimate' finisher of attacks by the All Blacks.

He built an All Black test try-scoring record of 19 tries from 34 tests – a record which held until broken by John Kirwan in 1988. He was also deservedly known as a player who could play well in losing teams.

So it was ironic that Wilson, after eight triumphant years in the All Blacks, was called on to lead a very inexperienced New Zealand team on one of its ultimately less successful tours – thus earning himself, undeservedly, a cross to bear for some years to come.

'It was an experience I didn't particularly enjoy and I doubt if the All Black selectors will ever choose a winger to lead the All Blacks again,' Wilson told the author in 1999.

The 1983–84 All Black coach Bryce Rope told the author in 1997 he was sure the selectors had asked Wilson about the captaincy before appointing him.[1]

But Wilson is just as adamant the subject was probably not handled as it should have been. 'It might have been mentioned to me. But I was never given the opportunity to seriously discuss it or turn it down. No-one actually said, 'you're going to be captain'. Besides, even as a senior player, your position was never guaranteed, so you didn't go against the selectors' wishes.

'But there were other senior players, such as Murray Mexted, Mark Shaw and others, who should have been ahead of me for the job. If the selectors had looked at the harmony within the team, they would have realised that.

'I had to do a complete U-turn in becoming captain. It was not my style. I was there as a support figure. I could add a bit of humour when it came to the morale of the team.

'The ordinary player doesn't realise just what's involved in being captain. All the off-field, day-to-day and week-to-week decision-making with the management. It takes a lot of time and there was even inexperience in the management of that team.

'On top of that I had to play every game and lead from right out there on the wing when many of our problems were happening in the tight exchanges up front – all eight tour games. By the England test I was gone. I announced my retirement after that tour.'

Retrospective vision is a fine thing. But Wilson and Rope are nowadays unanimous that Mexted should have been the skipper. 'He was an absolutely outstanding player who had the style to carry off the PR duties and the black-tie dinners in Britain,' said Wilson.

So Wilson joined the Taranaki fullback, Joe O'Leary, as the only players to have captained New Zealand in a test from the wing or fullback in All Black history. O'Leary did the job in 1913. These statistics demonstrate how unsuitable the All Black coaches and selectors consistently reckoned the outside-back positions were for overall leadership.

Rather than trying to run a struggling team, Wilson's greatest footballing asset was an ability to visualise how an attacking move might evolve – and how he could complete it.

'I guess the secret of my success was knowing when a try was on,' Wilson told the author in 1999. 'By the time the ball got through two pairs of hands I knew if it was going to be good for me.'

'I liked to hit the line hard and often tried to change my angle so that, when I received the

*TRIPLE TREAT: Master finisher Stu Wilson dots down for one of his three tries against Scotland in the second test at Eden Park, Auckland. The All Blacks won 40–15*

ball, I was already inside or outside my marker.'

Wilson said his style of game depended hugely on the men inside and around him. Playing for Wellington, and at various times for the All Blacks, were Bernie Fraser, Allan Hewson, John Dougan, Jamie Salmon and Richard Cleland. Others he found conducive to bringing the best out of him were All Blacks Bruce Robertson and Bill Osborne.

'Bruce would say, "where do you want the pass to hit?" Well, what more could a winger ask for? He was a dream to play outside.'

A speedster standing 1.83m (6ft) tall and 82kg (13st), Wilson had the balance and quickness of foot and brain to beat the best-organised defences. He was not an aggressive player in the way his soul-mate, Berrnie Fraser, bristled power and aggression, but a highly-skilled technician who played the angles.

Among the many memorable tries Wilson scored was the second-test try in Paris which broke the Frenchmen's hearts when the Jack Gleeson-Graham Mourie-led All Blacks toured there in 1977. Wilson can recall the try like it was yesterday.

'It was at the first lineout after halftime. Mourie took a quick throw-in to Lawrie Knight, who tapped it down to Mark Donaldson at halfback. The ball rocketed out to Doug Bruce, who miss-passed Billy Osborne and out to Bruce Robertson. He struck through their line, turned them around, and then threw an overhead pass to me on the left wing. I cut back on the diagonal to score under the bread basket.'

The ultimate adrenaline rush? 'Oh, God yes. *Parc des Princes*! You're just the last one in the chain. But that's what they picked me for. To finish it off. That's when you know you've done your job.'

'I can still remember walking back to halfway. Those huge French players like Gerard Cholley and Jean Imbernon. They were run off their feet and they knew it.'

In the 1981 season Wilson was probably at his peak. He played in eight tests and scored eight tries. Several of those tries were rarities.

Against Scotland at Eden Park in the second test, the first of three Wilson tries came from yet another example of the way he could cut back against the flow of play. Later that season, against South Africa in the first test, he got the ball from broken play 40m out and nearest the left-hand touchline, only to carve his way through the tourists to score to the right of the posts. In the third test, after Allan Hewson made one of his well-timed entries into the backline, Wilson finished the attack with a superb effort.

Wilson's Wellington team was also at a peak, winning the NPC for the second time in his career and the Ranfurly Shield. It would defend the shield four times the following year. The capital's faithful supporters were usually well rewarded by the antics and accomplishments of Wilson, Fraser and Hewson in particular.

Wilson marvels at the way he and the other Wellington All Blacks excitedly flew to Wellington to play Manawatu the day after the third test against South Africa in 1981.

'We had just come out of a war zone in Auckland – both on and off the field. We were tired, sore and a little hung-over. I laced up the same boots from the day before and ran out onto Athletic Park,' he reminisced.

'The park was full and it was a lovely Sunday afternoon. We beat Manawatu and went on to take the championship. I think Mex, Hewie and Bernie all scored that day. You thought nothing of it – it was what you did then. It was wonderful. And it was back to work on the Monday ...'

Wilson had the ability to shine in a losing team. His All Black captain, Mourie, would say of him: 'When the team was down, as occasionally it was, it was Wilson who inspired the rest with his efforts to lift the workrate.'

An example was his play in the 1978 third-test loss to the Wallabies. Wilson was the All Blacks' best player, scoring a try and creating another.

Wilson's cheerful, 'funny man' image always played a big part in his rugby, on and off the field. His team-mates cherished his humour and even the pre-match build-ups and half-time talks were said not to be sacred ground for him. If he believed that opportunities were going begging in the backs because they were not receiving good possession, he would 'send a message to the forwards, asking if the ball was still made of leather because we hadn't seen it for so long?'

He also experienced the 'try starvation' that occasionally hit even the great attacking players. In 1983, his last year, he had gone 19 months without scoring a test try. But then he scored in the third test against the Lions to equal Ian Kirkpatrick's record. A fortnight later, in the fourth test, he extended the record with the second three-try bag of his great career.

Wilson played 85 games for the All Blacks, scoring 50 tries. In 199 first-class matches he scored 106 tries.

A big influence on Wilson's early development was his coach, Roger Dee, in the Wairarapa College First XV from 1970 to 1972. Wilson was a boarder and thrived on the

culture that ensued. After one school game, against Dannevirke High, he recalls Dee quietly commenting: 'Well played, Wilson. You could be an All Black one day.'

Wilson broke into big rugby after representing Wellington Colts in 1973 and 1974. In 1976 he scored 16 tries in 15 games for Wellington and won a place in the New Zealand Colts, the North Island and the All Black tour to Argentina where he played at centre in both unofficial tests.

He was named one of the five players of the year in the *Rugby Almanack* for 1976. An ankle injury halted progress for much of 1977 but he made the All Black team to France and did not disappoint.

Wilson went on to make tours to the UK in 1978, Scotland and England in 1979 and 1983, Australia and Wales in 1980, Romania and France in 1981 and played in one-off series against the Wallabies in Australia in 1979 and 1983.

At home he was involved in the series against Australia in 1978 and 1982, France in 1979, Scotland and South Africa in 1981 and the British Lions in 1983.

Wilson and his partner, Bev, live on the North Shore, Auckland. He has two daughters, Kristy and Livvy.

## Stuart Sinclair Wilson (Wellington)

**Captain in two tests, a draw and a loss**
v. Scotland, England 1985

**Born:** July 22, 1954, Gore.

**Position:** Three-quarter.

**Represented NZ:** 1976–83 – 85 matches (34 tests).

**Points for NZ:** 200 – 50 tries.

**First-class record:** Wellington 1973, 74, 76–83 (Wellington College Old Boys); North Island 1976, 77, 79, 82; NZ Trials 1978–81, 83; NZ Colts 1976.

**High school:** Wairarapa College, First XV 1970–72.

**Other:** A book about Wilson and Bernie Fraser, called *Ebony and Ivory*, was published by Moa in 1984. Wilson and Phil Kingsley-Jones have also written four rugby joke books (Moa).

**Miscellaneous:** Played cricket for Wellington at Rothmans (Under-23) level. Wilson worked as a sports broadcaster for 89FM and TV3 in the early 1990s. In 1999 he hosted the *One-Eyed Rugby Show* on Radio Pacific and has written a rugby column for *Truth* for 15 years.

**Occupation:** A former bar proprietor in Auckland, he has been a real estate salesman on Auckland's North Shore since 1997.

*(left) FAST AND FURIOUS: Stu Wilson props inside the hapless Scottish defence in 1981, with Andy Jefferd, Bruce Robertson and Graham Mourie in hot pursuit*

1 *The Power Behind the All Blacks*

# JOCK HOBBS

## *Fond memories don't include Nantes*

THE ALL Black captaincy, and rugby in particular, has provided Jock Hobbs with many salutary lessons.

A successful All Black captain in 1985 and 1986 and a key member of Canterbury's great Ranfurly Shield team of the early 1980s, Hobbs might ruefully recall two incidents in his rugby life which stand out for their negativity.

Hobbs was captain of the All Blacks when they lost the second test against France at Nantes in 1986 under coach and former fellow All Black skipper Brian Lochore. After an excellent tour and strong first test win, the All Blacks were savaged in the second test.

'Remember Nantes' became the catchcry of the All Blacks the following year as they built towards a triumphant first World Cup victory over the French in the final at Eden Park, Auckland.

But tragically for Hobbs, he would play no part in that. He was injured playing for Wellington against Auckland early in 1987, made a very slow recovery and finally heeded a specialist's advice to retire after a series of head injuries and concussions throughout his career.

Another reversal for Hobbs came in 1996, a decade after his retirement from the game. He had been elected to the NZRFU Council in 1995, and, only just into his thirties, he would have the briefest stay, approximately eight months.

With his old coach Lochore, he bore the brunt of the union's negotiating with players in a bid to head off the emergence of the professional World Rugby Corporation in 1995. A lawyer, he is generally regarded as the person who 'saved the All Blacks' from defecting after WRC had signed up dozens of international players from all the leading rugby countries.

*(left) JOCK HOBBS: A career of ups and downs*

'We had to act quickly,' Hobbs told the author in 1999. 'We had to retain the players because the WRC went after both international and provincial players. And we had to establish the contracts and systems for professional rugby.'

In 1999, in *Matches of the Century*, by Don Cameron, the author called Hobbs 'Rugby's Man of the Century' for this work.

'Hobbs bore an incredibly heavy workload, for he was among the first to realise that if the All Blacks went to WRC then all the great work of the previous 95 years of the 20th Century would have been wasted,' Cameron wrote.[1]

But an NZRFU board replaced the council in 1996 and, seemingly with harsh ingratitude by delegates, Hobbs was not elected.

Hobbs however sees these blows and others that can affect a sporting, professional or business career as character-building. 'You have your goals,' he told the author. 'Sometimes they don't work out and you have to re-set them. But you don't give up.'

After playing his first game for Canterbury he badly broke his arm, requiring a plate to be inserted. The following year he broke the arm again, but continued playing for Canterbury with the use of an arm guard. The next season, the first with Alex Wyllie as coach, he was dropped. Missing selections were other unpleasant parts of rugby that had to be accepted, he said.

Hobbs never seriously aspired to be an All Black in his formative years. He was a better cricketer than footballer at Christ's College, playing with future New Zealand representative Vaughan Brown, and Robbie Deans. Later, the Christ's First XV, containing the Deans brothers, Robbie and Bruce (both future All Blacks), Brown, Hobbs, Joe Leota and other excellent players, would dominate the

*BRAVE HEARTS: Jock Hobbs (with ball) powers through England's defence in the 1985 series, won by the All Blacks, 2–0. Back-up comes from Murray Mexted, John Ashworth, Gary Knight and Andy Dalton*

Christchurch secondary school championship.

'It is so much easier to perform better and gain higher selection if you're playing in a good team,' said Hobbs. 'When Alex Wyllie took over Canterbury and built a team through hard work and skills, it propelled many players forward. With the Ranfurly Shield Canterbury suddenly went from having no All Blacks to fielding about nine of them.'

Hobbs was first chosen for the All Blacks in 1983, replacing the retired Graham Mourie, who had filled a flanker's role since 1977 and had come to be regarded by many astute judges as New Zealand's greatest captain.

'Graham Mourie's shoes were big all right. I never pretended I was going to fill them in the way he had,' explained Hobbs. 'I'll never forget that first test at Lancaster Park against the Lions. I was so nervous. I can remember being in the team bus on the way to the game and seeing my parents walking to the game near the park. And being in the changing room with all those great All Blacks with years of experience and success. Then it was out on to the park, where we walloped the Lions. It was like sitting in the front seat of a Rolls-Royce!'

Hobbs played in all four tests against the Lions in a series won by New Zealand 4–0. He also played against Australia and went on the tour of Scotland and England under All Black coach Bryce Rope.

In 1984 Hobbs played the two home tests against France and in the three tests in Australia. When All Black captain Andy Dalton was unavailable, Hobbs led the All Blacks on a tour of Fiji in 1984.

In 1985, under new All Black coach Lochore, he was chosen for the aborted tour to South Africa.

'I wasn't as devastated as some other All Blacks, who had extended their careers for this one last 'Everest' of rugby,' Hobbs said. 'We went to Argentina instead. That might have seemed a poor substitute for some. But for me it was a marvellous country to visit and the Pumas were strong.'

Under Hobbs' leadership the All Blacks won the first test, 33–20, with John Kirwan in brilliant form. But they could not prevent the remarkable Hugo Porta from kicking Argentina to a 21–21 draw in the second test.

In 1999 Hobbs was one of the All Blacks to 'recant' on his decision to join the ill-fated Cavaliers' tour of South Africa in 1986. He appeared on the television progamme, *Legends of the All Blacks*, to say he regretted his decision.

'It was a difficult decision at the time,' he told the author. 'My initial inclination was to turn it down. Later I decided to go. There was no pressure from the other players but inevitably there was a strong sense of loyalty towards them. But that was just one of several issues involved.

'Of course, the concerns lingered while on tour. But I have never been involved with a more committed team. In fact, we overtrained and probably needed to relax more. On reflection, I often wonder if we were ever going to achieve what we set out to do – to beat South Africa in a series.'

Cavaliers' captain Dalton had his jaw broken early in the tour and Hobbs took over for the 'tests' and other big matches. What followed on their return for the Cavaliers was a two-test suspension by the NZRFU. Hobbs regained his test place for the last two tests against the touring Wallabies but not the captaincy, which was retained by David Kirk after the brilliant 'Baby Black' victory over France at Christchurch before the Australian tour.

However, after the Wallabies took the series by two tests to one (12–13, 13–12, 22–9), Hobbs was reinstated to the leadership for the tour of France. The series was shared 19–7, 3–16.

'Until Nantes and the second test, we had had an outstanding tour,' recalled Hobbs. 'We were a young side and had not been expected to win the first test. But we were physically crushed at Nantes – that's all I can say. We went into the test with injuries and then lost Buck Shelford, who was such an important part of our pack. It was a bit of a casualty ward at the finish.'

Hobbs said he liked to put that tour 'in context'. It had 'always interested me' that the 1977 tour of France, when Graham Mourie's All Blacks had reversed the 13–18 first test loss with a brilliantly conceived 15–3 win in the second test, was 'regarded as a resounding success when ours wasn't.'

'It was a very important tour for it provided the platform for the leadup to the World Cup a few months later,' said Hobbs.

But cruelly, Hobbs would play no part in the World Cup. History shows the brilliant Michael Jones emerged to fill Hobbs' role and Andy Dalton, again the appointed All Black captain, would give way to David Kirk because a hamstring injury prevented him from playing in the tournament.

Hobbs said the head injury that ended his career early in 1987 was a culmination of similar injuries going back to his school days.

'I didn't feel well for a long time after the Wellington-Auckland match in which it happened. A neurosurgeon told me in the strongest terms I should stop playing. But naturally, I was torn between that and making the cup squad. Time ticked along and even after more than a month I was not feeling well. My prospects of being selected were dropping, so I had a talk with 'BJ' (Lochore), reflected on the situation and then decided to call it quits.

'It was a disappointing finish to my career. It was a stop-stop situation – I was out of the World Cup reckoning and there would be absolutely no more football for me.'

Life after the All Blacks has not slowed much for Hobbs. He quickly became a successful coach of the University club and was Wellington club coach of the year in 1988. His coaching of NZ Universities and administrative work followed.

Nowadays, married to Nicky, a sister of the Deans brothers, with four children, Emily, Michael, Penny and Isabelle, aged between 14 and five, Hobbs is a successful businessman and no longer practises as a barrister.

He is a director and majority owner of Sports Network Ltd, a sports distribution company among whose products is Mizuno, until recently supplier to the All Blacks. He is also managing director of Strategic Capital Investments Ltd and chairman of Strategic Property Group Ltd. Hobbs recently completed an MBA from Henley College, England.

But the old bogy of injuries still haunts him. He has had to undergo two operations on his right hip and will need a full hip replacement in time. It limits his sporting pursuits to walking, tennis and golf.

## Michael James Bowie ('Jock') Hobbs (Canterbury)

**Captain in four tests, two wins, one draw and a loss**
v. Argentina 1985 (1, 2)
v. France 1986 (1, 2)

**Born:** February 15, 1960.

**Position:** Loose forward.

**Represented NZ:** 1983–86 – 39 matches (21 tests).

**Points for NZ:** 52 – 13 tries.

**First-class record:** Canterbury 1979–86 (Christchurch club); Wellington 1987 (University); NZ Trials 1983; South Island 1984–85.

**Selector/coach/administrator:** Coach University club, Wellington (1988–91) and NZ Universities (1992, 1994–95). Member of NZRFU Council 1995.

**Miscellaneous:** Awarded MNZM for services to sport in 1996.

**Occupation:** Chairman/director of various private and public unlisted companies.

1 *Matches of the Century,* Don Cameron, Wilson & Horton 1999.

# DAVID KIRK

## *The only All Black captain to win World Cup final*

DAVID KIRK, linked to coach Brian Lochore's era through their triumphant victories in the first World Cup tournament, experienced the full range of emotions as an All Black.

His kissing of the World Cup became perhaps the best-remembered image of New Zealand sport in the decade of the 1980s. Kirk remembered the euphoria when he said: 'I remember feeling like 'We've done it. We knew we could do it. We haven't let anyone down'. We were the best team in the world.'

Lochore fondly recalled Kirk had 'not only played brilliantly throughout the tournament, but captained the team extremely well on the field. He was the sort of personality New Zealand rugby needed.'

Kirk's less than strapping build and boyish good looks, combined with undoubted intelligence and forthrightness in dealing with problems that had arisen in the years before the 1987 World Cup, provided the image New Zealand rugby urgently needed at the time. The game had suffered deeply since the horrendously divisive 1981 Springbok tour. He possessed charisma aplenty for young and old, male and female, and became one of the most recognised sportsmen of the era.

But Kirk's time with the All Blacks had not always produced such a sense of satisfaction.

He had begun his All Black career in 1983, as understudy to Andrew Donald on the tour of England and Scotland, under coach Bryce Rope. He was still the understudy on the tour of Australia and Fiji in 1984.

Less known was Kirk's differences with his Otago coach, later the All Black coach, Laurie Mains, who preferred the more rugged (and eventual 1986 All Black) Dean Kenny as halfback, and wanted Kirk to play on the wing if selected. Kirk had refused to co-operate.

'I still wonder about that, especially the clash of ethics and meeting the coach's wants,' explained Kirk in 1999.

'Was my stand selfish? I felt there were several much better wingers in Otago than me. But primarily I felt that if I lost focus on the halfback position I was doing myself a disservice. I had already played for the South Island and New Zealand at halfback. It was important for me to keep going, to gain exposure. History shows I was vindicated.'

After moving from Otago to Auckland, he established himself and finished the 1985 season with four caps. He had made his test debut against England at Lancaster Park.

The enforced cancellation of the tour to South Africa soured that season however. Instead, the All Blacks toured Argentina. But after teaming with debut first five-eighth Grant Fox for a handsome win in the first test, Kirk was dropped for Dave Loveridge for the second test, dominated by the extraordinary boot of Hugo Porta and resulting in a draw.

'I was very disapppointed at being dropped and felt it was unfair,' recalled Kirk. 'But looking back, I can now see the Argentine tour was a last hurrah for a number of the players who had served the All Blacks so well.'

In early 1986, Kirk declined to be involved with the Cavaliers' tour of South Africa. He said he would have toured with the official All Black team, but not with an unofficial one. He also had to protect his Rhodes Scholarship to

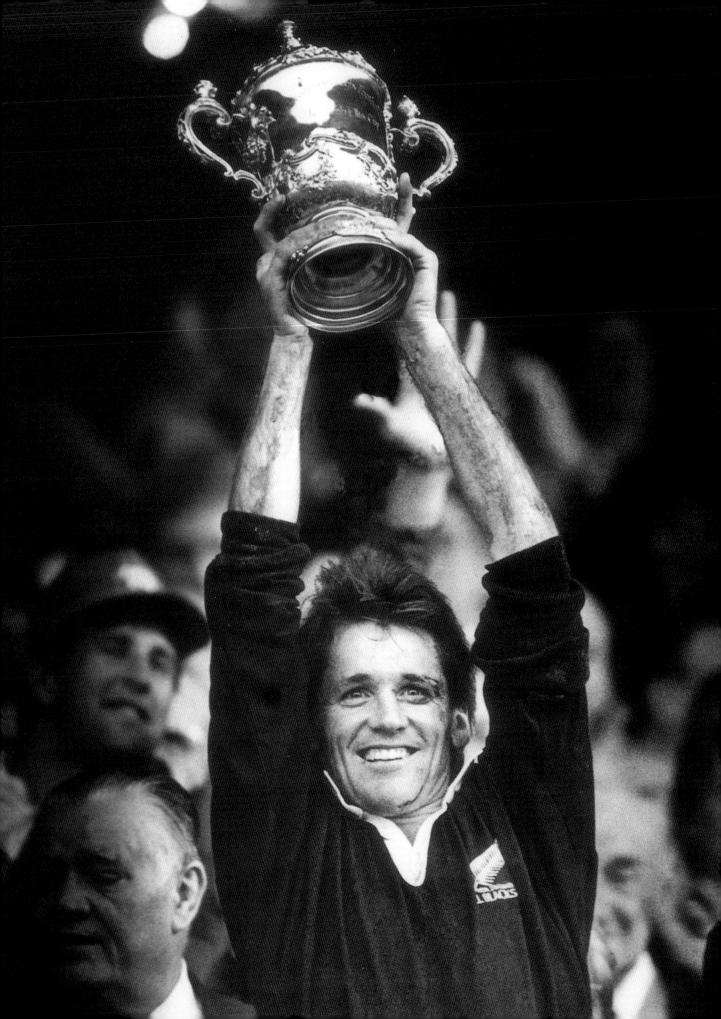

Oxford, which he would ultimately postpone until after the 1987 World Cup season.

'I think my opinions and my attitude toward sporting contacts with South Africa had matured and changed over the period of the year,' he would state.

The Cavaliers returned to face a two-test ban. Kirk thus became the Auckland and All Black captain. With only four players with test experience, Kirk led the 'Baby Blacks' to a fine victory over France.

'I think the French in their hotel must have been laughing like hell and thinking what a cakewalk they would have,' All Black coach Lochore recalled to the author in 1997.

It is part of the New Zealand game's folklore that Lochore was able to calm his young charges down in their build-up to the test on Lancaster Park to prepare a game plan that would beat the French. It was another David and Goliath story.

'Rugby being the game it is, giving as much as you can is often enough. And it was against France,' said Kirk.

The fairytale came to an end a week later when the Wallabies, under Alan Jones, scraped to a one-point win, 13–12, in Wellington in the first of a three-test series against Australia. Lochore felt some of the 'Baby Blacks' were already anticipating the threat to their positions from the Cavalier players.

So it proved when nine ex-Cavaliers were reinstated for the second test, with Kirk retained as captain for the series. The All Blacks scraped home, 13–12, but lost the third test, 9–22.

Lochore said in 1997 there had been no great split among the selectors over the choice of 'Baby Black' or Cavalier, though there were some long discussions. He also did not detect any rancour among the players over the new team.

However, though it was not made public for some years, by the time of the third test in Auckland, Lochore became aware of resentment between the two factions over who had the greater right to wear the black jersey at that time. Kirk was one target of some ex-Cavaliers.

*(left) HAPPINESS IS: David Kirk became the 'face' of New Zealand rugby after this triumphal pose was beamed around the world. The occasion is his acceptance of the first World Cup*

Jock Hobbs replaced Kirk as captain for the late-1986 tour of France. Rumours of antipathy towards Kirk reached their peak on the French tour. Kirk was to reveal in his 1997 book, *Black and Blue*, that he had gone back to his hotel room and cried after one nasty confrontation with team-mates on that tour.

Of the 1986 season, Kirk told the author in 1999 that the All Black selectors had made some questionable decisions.

'The first was retaining so many of the old guys after the Cavaliers had returned. The team and its style and tactics actually went backwards at that point.

'Their second bad decision was leaving me as captain in those circumstances. I was in an invidious situation. They were virtually setting me up to fail. But then it would have been difficult, from the public persective, for them to have dropped me after the Baby Blacks' triumph. And having put me through that, shouldn't they have retained me as captain for the tour of France?'

But Kirk again demonstrated his character at this point. Instead of becoming demoralised, his play in France was impressive, particularly in the first test, and he was a first-choice player when Lochore and his fellow selectors sat down to plan the World Cup campaign.

The World Cup provided many highlights for Kirk. With the captaincy thrust back on to him when skipper Andy Dalton pulled a hamstring at practice soon after the All Blacks assembled, Kirk lifted his game to a new level. His pace, passing, running and kicking were excellent and his tackling put to rest any lingering doubts about his robustness. Kirk scored four tries in the pool games and then produced a 'blinder' in the final against France.

His support work was rewarded with a try from a pass from Michael Jones and later he initiated the try which finally broke the French. Kirk had dipped under tacklers at a ruck and burst 40m upfield, from where No 8 Wayne 'Buck' Shelford recovered the tackled ball and sent John Kirwan flying to the corner for one of New Zealand's most famous tries.

However, after the cup tournament, Kirk would captain New Zealand to beat Australia and play only three matches for Auckland before injury and retirement from this level.

The *Rugby Almanack* said: 'He showed excellent qualities of leadership and did more to restore the popularity of rugby than any other individual has done in recent years.'

Kirk then left All Black rugby at the peak of his powers to take up a Rhodes Scholarship at Oxford University. He was 26. He had played 34 matches for the All Blacks, including 17 tests, and had scored 17 tries. He had led the All Blacks in 10 tests, for eight victories and two losses.

David Kirk's life after the All Blacks has seen a myriad of change. He married Brigit Aitcheson in 1989 and the couple have three sons, Hugo, Barnaby and Harry. A medical doctor when he went to Oxford, Kirk changed careers dramatically by studying economics, politics and philosophy. He worked in London for an American business management consultancy but came back to New Zealand in an ultimately unsuccessful attempt to gain a National party parliamentary nomination.

Kirk worked for the Prime Minister's Office from 1992–95 and then joined the corporate sector with Fletcher Challenge (Energy 1995–97 and Paper 1998–99).

Kirk played in two Oxford-Cambridge fixtures while on scholarship. He coached the Wellington rugby team with mixed success during 1993–94. Wellington finished fifth in the NPC in 1993, missing the semi-finals by a whisker, and was seventh in 1994.

'Wellington has continued to struggle to keep itself in the top group,' noted Kirk to the author in 1999. 'One of my accomplishments with the team was to improve Wellington's profile and establish a more professionally organised structure, with fitness programmes and buildups. This has been broadened and one hopes Wellington is on the verge of a breakthrough.'

He continued to have a peripheral role in rugby during 1997–1999 as an author of two rugby books and was a weekly rugby columnist with the *Sunday Star-Times*. He moved to Sydney in late 1999. Primarily because of his business career Kirk holds no ambitions to coach again in the professional era.

Kirk is one of only three All Black test captains to have won a Rhodes Scholarship to Oxford University, the others being Chris Laidlaw and George Aitken.

## David Edward Kirk
## (Auckland)

**Captain in 10 tests, 8 wins and 2 losses**
v France 1986 (1)
v. Australia 1986 (1, 2, 3)
v. Italy, Fiji, Argentina, Scotland, Wales, France (World Cup) 1987
v. Australia 1987 (1)

**Born:** October 5, 1960, Wellington.

**Position:** Halfback.

**Represented NZ:** 1983–87 – 34 matches (17 tests).

**Points for NZ:** 68 – 17 tries.

**First-class record:** Otago 1982–84 (University); Auckland 1985, 86 (University); South Island 1982–84; North Island 1986; NZ Trials 1983, 85.

**High school:** Wanganui Collegiate, 1st XV

**Selector-coach:** Coach, Wellington, 1993–94.

**Other:** Wrote autobiography, *Black and Blue* (Hodder Moa Beckett) 1997.

**Miscellaneous:** One of only three All Black test captains to have won a Rhodes Scholarship to Oxford University, the others being Chris Laidlaw and George Aitken.

**Occupation:** Formerly a medical doctor, Kirk has worked for a business management consultancy in London, the New Zealand Prime Minister's Office from 1992–95 and then Fletcher Challenge (Energy 1995–97 and Paper 1998–99). He moved to Sydney in late 1999 as the company's chief operating officer, Australasia.

# WAYNE 'BUCK' SHELFORD

## *When the 'perfect' record was not good enough*

WAYNE 'BUCK' Shelford is the only long-term unbeaten All Black captain. Shelford had won 13 tests and drawn another as captain of the All Blacks between 1988 and 1990, when he was sensationally dropped by coach Alex Wyllie before the series against Australia.

Only a few months earlier, on the 1989 tour to Wales and Ireland, Shelford had been in tremendous form. The British had no doubts he was the best No 8 in the world.

But his demise had come after unconvincing form by Shelford and the All Blacks against Scotland in the domestic tests of 1989.

Shelford had played 48 games for the All Blacks, including 22 tests, from 1985. He was unbeaten in 33 consecutive games. He had captained the team on unbeaten tours to Japan, Australia and Canada, Wales and Ireland, and in home tests against Wales, France, Argentina, Australia and Scotland.

The All Blacks were undefeated in 48 matches and 21 tests during his period, a world record run.

The Wyllie–Shelford combination brought a level of fitness, commitment and sophistication that was unmatched by opponents. It contained the greatest try-scorer the All Blacks had produced, John Kirwan, and the greatest points-scorer, Grant Fox, as well as a host of champion players.

Such was the sophistry of this team that its lineout calls, for instance, sometimes could contain a reference to where the referee was standing, so that the players knew whether they should risk 'stretching the rules' and get away with it.

There had never been a test rugby team as

*BODY ON THE LINE: Buck Shelford was an inspirational captain whose sides never lost a test*

dominant as the All Blacks under Wyllie and Shelford. When it won by 15, it was regarded as a close-run result. Closer scores were a rarity.

Gary Whetton was made captain, but the All Blacks, though they usually won, were never

able to regain their former potency in the build-up to and during the 1991 World Cup. Three games into Whetton's tenure, after beating the Wallabies in the first two tests, the unbeaten sequence would be broken with the third-test, 21–9 loss at Athletic Park, Wellington.

Meanwhile, Wyllie's All Black coaching record for all matches would reach 58 wins, five losses and a draw from 64 games by the end of 1991. This gave him an overall success rate of 90.6%, bettered among his predecessors by only Fred Allen (97.3%), Jack Gleeson (92.3%) and Neil McPhail (90.7%).

Apart from Shelford and Joe Stanley, Wyllie had stuck faithfully to his trusted squad and test XV, who repaid him with excellent results. In the aftermath of the 1991 World Cup campaign, it seems he should perhaps have dropped other players instead, or also, at least to give them a shake-up.

Shortly after he was dropped as captain in mid-1990, Shelford's book was published. Shelford, speaking before the axing, had said that though both Wyllie and John Hart were outstanding coaches, he related better to Wyllie 'because Alex is so straight and to the point.'[1]

'There is no nonsense and you are left in no doubt about what he wants and expects. You always know his intentions, his plans, and where you fit in the All Black scheme of things. I find his up-front manner refreshing.'

'There are a lot of Aucklanders in the All Blacks and at times they have made it clear they don't want to alter their provincial tactics. However, they can't argue because the All Blacks, under Grizz, are unconquered.'

Shelford also said the power of the Auckland team rubbed off on to the All Blacks. 'It was inevitable. Gary Whetton, Grant Fox, Alan Whetton called the shots ... Everyone was used to getting everything they wanted.'

'None of this would have mattered, but by 1990 the politics had taken over from the rugby ... It was most noticeable in the fitness. Players were not putting in the hard graft. The basic attitude at training was 'a short time's a good time.''

Time would show the sacking of Shelford had left the All Blacks short on two major counts. They were without their supremely combative No 8, who had established a huge psychological

*(left) HAKA PARTY: Buck Shelford leads by example as the All Blacks warm up for another victory under his leadership*

advantage over every test rival he had met. Zinzan Brooke would take until the mid-1990s to grow fully into the role. But the most crucial loss was the quality of leadership. Whetton would prove an adequate onfield general, but inadequate behind the scenes. Shelford's focus, discipline, integrity and simplicity of operation would be sadly missed – as the record book from the time of his leaving the team still shows.

Shelford told the author in 1997 that when Wyllie dropped him, he unwittingly abandoned the one person who stood between Wyllie's World Cup success and the disunited, cynical and eventually ignominious mess the campaign became.

'At the end of the day, I was probably Grizz's biggest ally – if only he had talked to me,' said Shelford, who to this day believes a 'player conspiracy' led to his demise.

Shelford's style was to lead by example. His physique (6ft 2in, 16st), legendary strength and courage enabled him to breach the advantage line from set piece plays consistently. His determination and low body position enabled him to break tackles. He was the perfect No 8 for the era – with the mobility and skills to support or set plays up for his backs, or mix it in the tight, as required.

His fitness level was always of the highest. It enabled Shelford to complete arduous schedules, whether with the All Blacks, leading his beloved fledgling province, North Harbour, from third to first division, or the Maoris, Combined Services or NZ Sevens.

Shelford's toughness would become legendary as the seasons rolled around.

'His quickness to take the law into his own hands would have been harshly judged in rugby's more recent years, but there was no question he was one of the great forwards to play for New Zealand.'[2]

Shelford's star had begun to rise when the North Harbour union came into being in 1985. He had played for Auckland from 1982–84 while with the North Shore club. When the Harbour union was formed, Shelford stayed with the club and became the North Harbour captain as it rose from third to second to first division in the NPC.

That same year, 1985, Shelford made the All Blacks for the first time, chosen for the tour of South Africa that did not take place because of a court injunction. Instead, he toured Argentina with the All Blacks, playing in four of the matches.

Shelford was one of the Cavaliers who toured South Africa in 1986. After their return and a two-test stand-down period imposed by the NZRFU, Shelford faced the first major disappointment of his career when he could not play in the second test against the touring Wallabies because of injury. But he toured France at the end of the year and played in both tests.

The first test was won handsomely but in the second test, at Nantes, the All Black underwent a baptism of fire that would show why he had the character to become the greatest No 8 in the world. He had three teeth knocked out, was concussed and had a testicle ripped out of the scrotum. He said he did not know of the injury until after he left the field.

By now the dominant player in his position, Shelford was a star, among many, of the All Blacks' World Cup-winning effort in 1987. He played in five of the six matches and was instrumental in helping John Kirwan to the try that finished the French challenge in the final, after recovering loose ball from a long run by captain David Kirk.

Shelford was part of the team that demolished the Wallabies for the Bledisloe Cup a month later and then, with Kirk's retirement, was captain of the team that toured Japan, playing in all five matches.

After this point, with new coach Wyllie at the helm and Shelford leading on-field, the All Blacks had one of the greatest periods in their proud history.

Shelford's leadership helped send the Welsh home after two hidings in 1988, followed by a 2–0 series win in Australia. France and Argentina were 'manhandled' in 1989 and the Welsh and Irish teams trounced. Shelford had appeared at his majestic best as he helped pound Wales, 34–9, and scored one of the three tries that subdued Ireland, 23–6, on the tour at the end of that year.

It was said Shelford was carrying an injury against Scotland early in 1990. Shelford always denied this. However, the team struggled. It won the first test comfortably enough, 31–16, but was behind 12–18 at halftime in the second, before scrambling home 21–18.

Shelford spent five years playing-coaching in Italy and England between 1991–95. 'I still wanted to play football. I was still really enjoying it. But by 1995, after another 120 or so games, I knew it was time to give it away,' Shelford said.

Since 1998 he has coached North Harbour,

developing a promising young side. He also has a hotel in Silverdale, north of Auckland, where he lives with his wife Joanne, daughter Lia and son Eruera.

## Wayne Thomas Shelford (North Harbour)

**Captain in 14 tests, 13 wins and a draw**
v. Wales 1988 (1, 2)
v. Australia 1988 (1, 2, 3)
v. France 1989 (1, 2)
v. Argentina 1989 (1, 2)
v. Australia 1989 (1)
v. Wales, Ireland 1989
v. Scotland 1990 (1, 2)

**Born:** December 13, 1957, Rotorua.

**Position:** No 8.

**Represented NZ:** 1985–90 – 48 matches (22 tests).

**Points for NZ:** 88 – 22 tries.

**First-class record:** Auckland 1982–84 (North Shore); North Harbour 1985–91 (North Shore); North Island 1985; NZ Trials 1985, 87–91; NZ Emerging Players 1985; NZ Colts 1978; NZ Maoris 1982, 83, 85, 87–90; NZ Combined Services 1979, 81, 83, 85; Wasps 1985, 86; North Zone 1987–89; NZ XV 1991; NZ B 1991.

**High school:** Western Heights High School, Rotorua; 1st XV 1973–74.

**Selector/coach/administrator:** Former captain-coach in Italy and for Northampton club, England; coach North Harbour 1998–2000.

**Miscellaneous:** Brothers Dean and Darryl played for NZ Combined Services and Bay of Plenty respectively. An uncle, Gordon McLennan, was an Otago representative and All Black triallist. Another uncle, Jack McLennan, played for Otago. All Black flanker (1981, 83–85) Frank Shelford is a second cousin.

**Occupation:** Hotelier and professional rugby coach.

1 *Buck, the Wayne Shelford Story,* with Wynne Gray, Moa, 1990.

2 *The Encyclopaedia of New Zealand Rugby*

# GARY WHETTON

## *Era of triumphs ends with World Cup demise*

GARY WHETTON was one of the most successful captains in the All Blacks' long history.

He was also 'beyond dispute one of New Zealand's best performed locks of any era.'[1]

Whetton faced the ultimate rugby challenge when, aged 21, he was called upon to lock the All Black scrum and mark Springbok colossus Louis Moolman in the deciding third test of the remarkable 1981 series against South Africa. He passed the test and went on to play 11 great seasons for the All Blacks, eventually breaking the 55-test All Black record held by Colin Meads.

But although Whetton played through the most golden of All Black eras, his tenure as captain ended in failure, frustration and probably some bitterness. The failure was that he could not lead the All Blacks to triumph in their defence of the World Cup in 1991. The frustration came in the change of coaching guard that followed and the bitterness in that he never got the opportunity, after a wonderful career, to 'go out on my terms'.

Whetton had been an integral part of an All Black team that had fashioned the greatest sequence of wins in a century of the national pastime. From the triumphs of the 1987 World Cup under Brian Lochore through almost the next three years under the coaching of Alex Wyllie and the captaincy of Wayne 'Buck' Shelford, the All Blacks would be unbeaten.

Whetton had assumed the captaincy of the almost unbeatable Auckland team in 1988. Its players increasingly dominated the All Black ranks in those years. He led the All Blacks in one game on the Australian tour of 1988 and was the vice-captain on the tour of Wales and Ireland, leading the side in five tour matches.

The All Black selectors dropped their bombshell after the Scottish home series in 1990 and replaced Shelford as captain with Whetton for the Australian series. The selectors said Shelford's form and an injury were behind their decision. But a furore that divided the nation followed and Whetton became a victim of this sentiment. He would find himself under great pressure for the remainder of his career from the fans who sought to 'Bring Back Buck'.

After convincingly securing a home series win over Australia, the All Blacks dropped the third test, 9–21, thus ending a 50-match winning sequence. Two losses to Selection XVs followed on the French tour at the end of 1990, though the test series was won emphatically to secure Whetton's hold on the captaincy.

He therefore retained the leadership through to the 1991 World Cup. By the time of the quarterfinal against Canada in that tournament he had reached his 56th test, surpassing Meads' mark of 55 tests set 20 years earlier.

But he would play only two more – the losing semifinal against Australia, the eventual winner of the World Cup, and the play-off for third place against Scotland. He would therefore end his time as All Black captain with the fine record of 12 victories from 15 tests.

The new All Black coach, Laurie Mains, did not select Whetton for a trial in 1992, the message being he did not require the great lock's services for his tenure. Whetton was chosen for a World XV that played Mains' All Blacks in the third of the centenary series in 1992 and completed the season for Auckland.

*STANDING UP: Gary Whetton received a lot of flak when he took over the captaincy but claimed he'd never sought the job*

'It definitely made it harder to leave the All Blacks – not being able to go out on your own terms after such a long career,' Whetton told the author in 1999.

'It was difficult in that first year, watching the All Blacks struggle in 1992. I realised I had to get out of New Zealand.'

So Whetton moved to France and the Castres Olympique club. Instead of looking to wind down his career, he went on to help win the French club championship final, an unusual distinction for a New Zealand player. 'I never thought I'd experience the highs again, but we did and it rounded off my career beautifully.'

There is still a trace of disappointment when Whetton recalls the All Black captaincy issue of 1990.

'All the conspiracy theories are rubbish from my perspective. I never asked for the job. It was thrust upon me,' said Whetton.

'I didn't need or deserve all that baggage that came with the job when Buck was dropped. I believe the All Black management didn't stand up when it happened. Instead they ducked for cover and left me to take most of the flak. Here were three powerful selectors who made the decision and then allowed it all to fester. Yes, I was very disappointed.

'But it should be remembered Buck was dropped on form as a No 8. I didn't replace him. Zinzan Brooke did. Then the selectors looked for a captain and asked me to do the job.'

The hardest challenge of his career, perhaps outranking his debut match, was leading the All Blacks against the Wallabies at Lancaster Park, Christchurch, in his first test as captain.

'The controversy over Buck's dropping made the test build-up a tremendous challenge. But the team responded and got behind me. I think we saw it as the only way to battle our way out of the mess.'

Whetton's philosophy regarding captaincy is simple. 'In the end it comes down to only one thing, especially in a country like New Zealand – winning!

'I played with some tremendous and very successful captains, such as Andy Dalton, probably the best of them all, and Graham Mourie and Buck Shelford. But at the end of your career, you're remembered for your winning record.'

Those captains, plus Auckland coaches John Hart, Maurice Trapp and Bryan Williams, and Andy Haden, had helped develop his leadership style through his development years.

Whetton had been little known outside Auckland when chosen to make his All Black debut and replace an injured Frank Oliver for the third test of 1981. But playing alongside his mentor, Haden, he turned in a fine performance in the pressure-cooker atmosphere of Eden Park to taste sweet victory.

'It was a huge baptism of fire,' recalled Whetton to the author in 1999. 'The coach and skipper just said "do your job". Louis Moolman was a man-mountain, a legend. I can still remember his yellow eyes, like a lion. He just gave me the evil eye when we ran on. I recall he whacked me two or three times but I just got up and kept on going. I guess it was the adrenalin pumping. I was so naive I didn't think about being scared.

*LOCKING PARTNERSHIPS: Gary Whetton formed outstanding locking teams with Andy Haden and then Murray Pierce*

'I often wonder how I got through it all – I hadn't even won my Auckland blazer at that stage. We won and it set my career alight. If we had lost, I might have been a one-test wonder.'

Whetton had unusual abilities for a lock. Blessed with an awsome physique of 1.98m (6ft 6in) in height and weighing 110kg (17st 4lb), he was seldom bested in the tight exchanges and the lineouts. But it was his pace and ball skills in the loose which sometimes left defenders gasping.

'As the game evolved during my career I changed with it,' Whetton said of the extra dimensions he developed in his style of play. 'If I came into rugby today, they'd probably play me on the wing like Jonah Lomu,' he jested.

Whetton's twin brother, Alan, also had a long career with the All Blacks, making the side three years after Gary and ending at the same time with the World Cup of 1991. He

represented New Zealand 1984–91, in 65 matches, including 35 tests, and scored 26 tries.

'It was often a comfort to have your twin brother with you in the All Blacks and the Auckland teams,' said Whetton. 'When it comes to the highs, you share them with the whole team, but with the lows like injuries, non-selections and other reversals, we were able to share them as brothers.'

Sibling rivalry was never a problem. Gary made the All Blacks three years before Alan. 'We both knew he just needed the right break and he'd get in too – that's how it panned out.'

The brothers went to Auckland Grammar. Gary played soccer until the fifth form and they only made the First XV, coached by Graham Henry (nowadays the Welsh coach), in their final year at school.

That was 1977 and after steady progress through the colts' grades, Gary had become a regular member of the Auckland team in only 1981, several months before he got the call to represent his country. That call came after a sound game against the Boks for Auckland.

So began a fabulous locking partnership with Haden that also served the All Blacks until 1985 and Auckland until 1986. But the old warhorse, Haden, was initially not enamoured with the young pretender. The pair were involved in an altercation in a club game between Grammar and Ponsonby early in the 1981 season. Haden was sent off and missed a test against Scotland because of the subsequent suspension.

Whetton went on at the end of 1981 to tour Romania and France and play the three tests. But he felt the keenness of healthy competition when Graeme Higginson kept him out of two tests against Australia in 1982. He battled back and gave an outstanding performance in the decisive third test victory, however.

His growing confidence was apparent in his fine series against the British Lions in 1983, won by the All Blacks 4–0. But a knee injury while playing for a World XV in South Africa that year ruled him out of the test against Australia and also the tour to Scotland and England at the end of 1983.

He was an integral part of the All Black team which beat France in a home series in 1984. On the tour of Australia he struggled to find form as the All Blacks lost the opening test but came back to his best to master the Wallabies' Steve

Cutler as New Zealand took the second and third tests and the series.

Whetton was joined by Murray Pierce in the first test against England in 1985. They would play together in a record 25 tests up until 1989, when Pierce would retire. However, Whetton was dropped for the first test in Argentina (on a tour that replaced the stymied South African tour) in 1985. He returned to partner Haden in the second test after an injury to Pierce.

Like all the Cavaliers who had toured South Africa, Whetton was forced to sit out a two-match ban when he returned. He missed the one-off French test and the first test against the touring Australians. But then began a run of 40 consecutive tests that would prove his great durability and consistency. He was a key member of the All Blacks' remarkable unbeaten sequence from 1987 to 1990 and thus one of the most dominant players on the world scene.

Tests at home included the last two tests against the Wallabies in 1986, the World Cup matches of 1987, Wales in 1988, France, Argentina and Australia in 1989 and Scotland and Australia in 1990. Tours were to France in 1986 and 1990, Australia in 1987 and 1988, Japan in 1987 and Wales and Ireland in 1989.

Auckland was also the dominant province during Whetton's long golden run. Its successes included its record hold on the Ranfurly Shield and seven national championship titles between 1982 and 1990. Whetton had led the virtually unbeatable Auckland team since 1988.

Whetton had only four locking partners during his 11-year run and 58 tests with the All Blacks, such was the stability of the team. They were Haden (12 tests), Albert Anderson (four), Pierce (25) and Ian Jones (17).

Nowadays, Whetton owns a financial services company and lives in Auckland with his wife, Jane, and their three sons, William, Jack and Louis. He coaches William's team with the North Harbour Marist club and enjoys occasional coaching work for the NZRFU at colts level.

## Gary William Whetton (Auckland)

**Captain in 15 tests, 12 wins and three losses**
v. Australia 1990 (1, 2, 3)
v. France 1990 (1, 2)
v. Argentina 1991 (1, 2)
v. Australia 1991 (1, 2)
v. England, United States, Italy, Canada, Australia, Scotland (World Cup) 1991

**Born:** December 15, 1959.

**Position:** Lock.

**Represented NZ:** 1981–91 – 101 matches (58 tests).

**Points for NZ:** 36 – 9 tries.

**First-class record:** Auckland 1980–92 (Grammar); North Island 1982–84, 85; NZ Trials 1982, 89–91; NZ Colts 1979, 80; North Zone 1987, 88.

**High school:** Auckland Grammar.

**Miscellaneous:** Gary Whetton's twin brother, Alan, represented NZ as a flanker from 1984–91 in 65 matches, including 35 tests, scoring 26 tries.

**Occupation:** Formerly manager corporate affairs, Fisher & Paykel; now owner of financial services company Gary Whetton & Associates Ltd.

1 *They Led the All Blacks,* Lindsay Knight (Rugby Press), 1991.

# SEAN FITZPATRICK

## *Testing times pushed Fitzy on to remarkable record*

SEAN FITZPATRICK holds the world record as a rugby test captain, with his 39 victories in 51 tests being perhaps the most remarkable statistic in this book.

But the records don't stop there. Fitzpatrick, 34 when he retired, played 92 tests for the All Blacks and scored 12 test tries. He played 63 tests in succession. In all games for the All Blacks, he played 128 times over 12 years, 62 as captain, and scored a total of 20 tries.

Fitzpatrick played his first test with Joe Stanley in 1986 and made his last tour with Stanley's son, Jeremy, in 1997. He saw vast changes to the game during that time. He had begun in the 'shamateur' days, when there was only a mythical world crown, and ended after playing in three World Cups and when professionalism ensured top players could accumulate great wealth. The rules had been changed to transform the game.

But his winning habit as All Black captain was learned the hard way. He found the job difficult at first when new coach Laurie Mains appointed him in 1992. But after mixed results through to 1994, Fitzpatrick's team set the rugby world alight at the 1995 World Cup. Under new coach John Hart in 1996 and 1997 his leadership and the results kept getting better.

'Yes, I struggled when first appointed captain,' Fitzpatrick told the author in January, 2000. 'And it wasn't a position I had sought.'

'But in the end that kind of a beginning became a blessing because I worked much harder at it. I was always conscientious about doing my very best, of trying to involve everyone and ensuring there were no cliques in the team. The change in the side in this respect from 1991 to 1992 was significant.'

'I had been fortunate with captains – Andy Haden and Gary Whetton with Auckland, and David Kirk, Buck Shelford and Whetton with New Zealand. Shelford was exceptional because he commanded so much respect from the opposition. He had a mana, a presence about him,' said Fitzpatrick.

'They all had qualities I sought to bring to my own leadership but there were also a few traits I didn't like which I rejected.'

'Players must have confidence to speak to you as a captain. When I first arrived on the scene, I was told to shut up and listen. The oldies didn't encourage comment from newcomers. Nowadays the new guys can contribute but must earn the respect of their peers.'

As he began his 12th season as an All Black in 1997, Fitzpatrick, who'd only left the field twice during 83 tests, was seen as nearly indestructible. A century of test appearances – achieved by only France's Philippe Sella and Australia's David Campese – was within his sights.

Until late 1997, a long line of test understudies such as Hika Reid, Ian Abercrombie, John Buchan, Warren Gatland and Graham Dowd had come and gone, with only one international appearance between them – and that was as a replacement prop for Craig Dowd. Norm Hewitt had fared only a little better, until the end-of-year British tour, when Fitzpatrick's injury worsened. Although Hewitt and the young 'pretender', Anton Oliver, were playing well, they could not match Fitzpatrick's leadership, all-round ability, head for the big occasion and uncanny knack of scoring tries.

But it is estimated Fitzpatrick had by then packed down in 7500 scrums, at least 25,000

*FIRST SERIES WIN: Sean Fitzpatrick acknowledges the All Blacks' supporters during the triumphant 1996 tour of South Africa*

rucks and mauls and thrown the ball into 5000 lineouts during his first class career. His body had begun calling for respite. When the end came, it came quickly.

After leading the All Blacks to victory in the Tri-Series again, Fitzpatrick had surgery on a chronic knee injury and missed most of Auckland's NPC campaign. On the British tour he made only two replacement appearances. The knee kept swelling up. He said he'd give it the summer to settle down and reassess the situation. But the injury failed to respond to treatment and rest and he announced his retirement in April 1998.

He therefore threw the plans of the coach, Hart, awry. The 1999 World Cup had seemed an increasingly possible goal that he, Hart and the rest of New Zealand had started to consider as the sprightly 'veteran' continued to play superb rugby, refreshed from the new goals possible with the advent of the professional era. Hart

had often stated age was not the primary criteria in deciding when an All Black should be dropped. The old All Black hands, Frank Bunce, Zinzan Brooke and 'Fitzy', were also helping to coach the side. Hart in fact made his captain an offer to become assistant coach.

This intriguing development emerged at the end of 1997 and left Fitzpatrick with a dilemma.

'John asked me after the second test against England on the 1997 tour. I obviously thought hard about it. But he needed a prompt answer, whereas I needed time to see if my knee was going to come right. So I told him I still wanted to play, if possible,' Fitzpatrick said.

'In hindsight, especially after what occurred in 1998, it has made me wonder. Could I have made a difference? I might have been able to help them through that tough period. Then again, was it too early to be coaching the players I had been playing with? I just don't know ...'

*HAPPY HOOKER: Sean Fitzpatrick enjoys the wide-open spaces during his side's record-breaking tour of South Africa in 1996*

Such a coaching appointment would have been unprecedented in modern times. It would have rivalled the case of Jimmy Duncan, New Zealand's first official test captain in 1903 and first official New Zealand team coach in 1904. It would have bettered the record of Bob Stuart, captain of the All Blacks in Britain and France in 1953–54 – a tour that Fitzpatrick's father, Brian, was on – who was co-opted two years later as All Black forward coach against the touring Springboks of 1956.

The world record holder for hookers' test appearances always seemed destined to play top football. His father was an All Black five-eighth in the early 1950s and his family gave him strong support.

He toured overseas with Auckland in 1984 but could not crack the top team because of errant lineout throwing. He was still not Auckland's No 1 by 1986, when he was chosen as the reserve hooker for the side that would beat France at Lancaster Park, Christchurch, and become known as the 'Baby Blacks'. This game gave Fitzpatrick his first big break because the first-choice hooker, Bruce Hemara, had to withdraw because of injury.

A pause came when Hika Reid replaced him for the last two tests against Australia in 1986, when the suspended Cavaliers, who had toured South Africa against NZRFU wishes, were reintroduced and moulded with the 'Baby Blacks'.

But Fitzpatrick quickly re-established himself on the tour of France, playing both tests. This would begin a sequence of 63 consecutive tests, only broken when he stood down for the 1995 World Cup pool game against Japan.

By 1987 Fitzpatrick had leapfrogged Reid and was deputy to Andy Dalton, All Black captain for the first World Cup. When Dalton was injured before the first game, Fitzpatrick got all six cup games. He scored two tries in the Bledisloe Cup walloping the All Blacks gave the Wallabies soon afterwards. He was set to stay.

But who would have believed he would still be there 10 years later? He rode above the tide of mediocrity that finally caught up with Alex Wyllie's team in 1990–91 and kept getting better. Although an element of gamesmanship crept into his game in the early 1990s, he left most of that phase behind him as he matured into the national leadership role.

If ever there was a time he was tempted to

quit the game, it was after the 1991 World Cup campaign. Fitzpatrick was so depressed at the outcome he decided to retire. He threw his boots away, but his wife Bronwyn wasn't convinced. 'Wait until you see how you feel after the holidays,' she said.

When new coach Mains phoned in January Fitzpatrick was indeed rearing to go. He underwent a crash fitness course. An earlier incident had been one of his tussles with Australia's Phil Kearns. Fitzpatrick had taunted Kearns on the Wallaby's debut in 1989. A year later, the tables had turned. After scoring a clinching try in the Athletic Park test, Kearns made his famous gesticulation to Fitzpatrick. What did he say? 'He invited me to a barbecue next time I was in Sydney.'[1]

But now Kearns and the Wallabies were 'No 1'. Fitzpatrick used this as motivation as he pounded his way to a new fitness level that was surely the turning point in the triumphant second half of his long career.

Mains would give Fitzpatrick the captaincy of the All Blacks when his first-choice skipper, Mike Brewer, couldn't play because of injury at the 1992 trial in Napier. Fitzpatrick's early leadership was not distinguished. He seemed unable, in the way of a Whineray, a Mourie, a Dalton or a Leslie, to make mid-game tactical changes when the opposition nullified 'Plan A'.

But although the pair had their difficulties with some indifferent results in 1992–94, Mains was never tempted to return to Brewer, and Fitzpatrick's improved generalship kept pace with the All Blacks' own varied, faster and often sensational game through 1995–97.

As the achievements grew, it became difficult to recall the consistently excellent Fitzpatrick having a poor game. But there was one. In the second test, at Athletic Park, Wellington, against the British Lions in 1993, he had a shocker. The test was lost too, 7–20. He admitted it was his worst game. 'I gave away two penalties which Gavin Hastings kicked, and, at a crucial time, I knocked on, creating the try-scoring chance Rory Underwood was looking for.'

But after much media criticism, his coach spoke out strongly on his behalf. 'A great player like Sean should not be subjected to such vitriol,' said Mains. 'How could you condemn

*BLEDISLOE GLORY: Sean Fitzpatrick holds the Bledisloe Cup aloft at Eden Park after leading his All Blacks to another victory over the Wallabies*

him on one performance after all the great rugby he had played?'

Another 'low' at Athletic Park was the incident in 1994 with Johan le Roux, the Springbok prop who bit him on the left ear. It would haunt both players for years to come.

But the biggest disappointment came when Fitzpatrick's All Blacks lost the final of the 1995 World Cup. The build-up through 1995 had been handled brilliantly and the All Blacks had slipped into South Africa largely unheralded. Then they produced their 'demolition derbies', reaching new heights of attacking excellence, right through to the final. Eighteen All Blacks were affected by food poisoning on the eve of the final against the Springboks. Fitzpatrick and the Brooke brothers were not poisoned and he declined to use the occurrence as an excuse for the loss.

'The South Africans had worked us out,' he told the author. 'They were hungry for their first World Cup. It is possible the result would have been the same even if we hadn't had our problems leading into the final.'

According to Fitzpatrick, it was about three hours after the final that he made his momentous decision to soldier on as an All Black. He could see that this All Black team was going to become a great power. The team therefore made light of the tragedy when they unleashed their dynamic brand of rugby on the Wallabies and in the second test on the tour of France at the end of 1995.

With the change from Mains to Hart in 1996, critics wondered if the new coach might try a new captain. Instead, he retained the entire team intact, adding the superb running of Christian Cullen from the back to supply even more potency. Among the string of victories over the next two years was the 1996 series win in South Africa – the first in almost 70 years of trying.

Mains and Hart were two very different characters. What were their strengths?

'Laurie's greatest expertise was as a forward coach. He was superb technically in how to get his message across. He trained us hard and had the forwards superbly drilled. He got rid of all the cliques and the new-old orders and created a very close team environment,' said Fitzpatrick. 'Players trusted Laurie because he was honest.'

'John's strengths were man management and the excitement he added to the All Blacks. It's in the way the team was portrayed. It helped take the pressure off the players when they knew they had the support of the public.'

'John's best years were 1996–97, when he had players who weren't afraid to disagree with him. In 1998 he didn't have the confidence in the older players to make the right decisions and decisions were increasingly made, during a game, off the field.'

And how competitive was Fitzpatrick? South Africans said he was a master of gamesmanship. The Australians wouldn't argue with that. But while he was ordered off the field at least three times in club football and was cited after an Auckland-Otago match and given a one-match suspension, his international record sheet remained clean.

Among the comments when he retired were:

Kearns: 'I can't imagine too many other players matching that record [of 92 tests]. His retirement is sad but good news for Australia. For once we won't have to play a test with two referees.'

Uli Schmidt, the former Springbok hooker: 'He isn't very well liked here in South Africa. Actually, to be honest, a lot of people hate him. They don't like the dirty tricks he brought into the game. He would hold on to players after the ball was cleared … But I admire him for what he's achieved. His all-round play was excellent.'

Craig Dowd, All Black prop: 'In a physical sense, his greatest quality was that he was so incredibly strong … like a third prop, one of the best scrummagers in the game. He served his apprenticeship with Richard Low and Steve McDowell and then, in turn, taught us.'

Tom Lawton, former Wallaby hooker: 'I don't think the world will see another player like him.'

Mains: 'He certainly possessed that indefinable X factor. When the going was tough Fitzy was always there. He exemplified that rare player who blended composure and competitiveness.'

Hart: 'I don't think people outside the All Blacks can fully appreciate the tremendous impact he has had on New Zealand rugby …'[2]

Nowadays, Fitzpatrick is into the second year of a three-year contract with the NZRFU as a consultant. Four key areas of his employment are the Institute of Rugby and the Rugby Academy, the players' association, the All Blacks and the sponsorship by adidas. He works for Coca-Cola in market development and Air New Zealand in promotions. He also does speaking engagements. All these activities are handled through his company, called Katika. His business manager is former All Black Andy Haden.

Would he take up coaching and perhaps win the All Blacks' job some day? Fitzpatrick was reticent to commit himself on the subject. 'I am doing a couple of coaching papers at the Institute of Rugby this year though,' he concluded.

Fitzpatrick lives in Auckland with Bronwyn and their daughters, Grace and Eva.

## Sean Brian Thomas Fitzpatrick (Auckland)

**Captain in 51 tests, 39 wins, 11 losses and a draw**
v. World XV (1, 2, 3), Ireland (1, 2), Australia (1, 2, 3), South Africa 1992; British Isles (1, 2, 3), Western Samoa, Australia, Scotland, England 1993; France (1, 2), South Africa (1, 2, 3), Australia 1994; Canada, Ireland, Wales, Scotland, England, South Africa, Australia (1, 2), Italy, France (1, 2) 1995; Western Samoa, Scotland (1, 2), Australia (1, 2), South Africa (1, 2, 3, 4, 5) 1996; Fiji, Argentina (1, 2), Australia (1, 2, 3), South Africa (1, 2) 1997

**Born:** June 4, 1963, Auckland.

**Position:** Hooker.

**Represented NZ:** 1986–97 – 128 matches (92 tests).

**Points for NZ:** 90 – 20 tries.

**First-class record:** Auckland 1984–97 (University); Auckland Blues 1996, 97; NZ Colts 1983; NZ XV 1992; North Island 1995; North Island Universities 1984; NZ Universities 1984, 85; NZ Trials 1986, 87, 89–95; North Zone 1988; Barbarians 1985, 87, 94, 96, 97; Harlequins 1995.

**High school:** Sacred Heart College, First XV 1980–81.

**Miscellaneous:** His father, Brian, played 22 times for the All Blacks from 1951–54; Fitzpatrick's biography, *Fronting Up*, was published in 1994, while a second biography, *Turning Point*, was published in 1998.

**Occupation:** Marketing consultant for Coca-Cola, promotions with Air New Zealand, NZRFU consultant, public speaker.

1,2 *NZ Rugby Monthly,* June 1998, Bob Howitt.

# PAUL HENDERSON

## *All hail the world-record holder*

I T IS doubtful if New Zealand has produced many loose forwards as durable as the former Southland and Otago flanker, Paul 'Ginge' Henderson – even though injury was his constant companion as an All Black.

Henderson made his first-class debut for Southland back in 1983 and when interviewed by the author for this book in 1999 was still playing serious rugby. He was with Malone, a second division club in Northern Ireland, after playing for the MTN Falcons in Johannesburg, South Africa in 1998.

It is fair to say Henderson was not often a first-choice test player. He managed only seven tests in an All Black career extending through seven years from 1989 to 1995 and including two World Cup campaigns.

But when one considers his competition for an All Black loose-forward place – ranging through players such as Michael Jones, Mike Brewer, Wayne Shelford, Zinzan Brooke, Alan Whetton, Arran Pene, Jamie Joseph and Josh Kronfeld – it is understandable.

It is also unlikely Henderson would ever have been elevated to the august ranks of All Black test captaincy under the old pre-World Cup system.

But conversely, Henderson showed he had that special quality reserved for All Black captains by leading his side to the near-perfect

*KAMIKAZE PILOT: Paul Henderson guided the All Blacks to one of their more remarkable victories when they beat Japan in the 1995 World Cup*

*NEAR-PERFECT: Paul Henderson managed only seven tests in an All Black career that extended from 1989 to 1995. But when his big chance came, his leadership helped produce the near-perfect rugby game*

game – a world record 145–17 victory over hapless Japan at the 1995 World Cup.

Henderson told the author he never wanted the captaincy that day. 'In the lead-up to that game I believed Zinzan Brooke, who was recovering from an achilles heel injury and hadn't played in the earlier cup matches against Ireland and Wales, would lead the team,' Henderson said.

'But Zinny said he just wanted to concentrate on getting through his first cup game by playing his own game. I didn't want to do it and actually tried to steer our coach, Laurie Mains, away from the subject when he approached me. But Laurie was cunning. All he said to me was, 'Are you up to it?'

'In the game itself the mistake level from the first to the 80th minute was almost nil. I was one of only two guys who made an error. But the funny thing is I've never actually watched that match on video.'

Henderson had a strong background of rugby achievement when young. Two brothers and his father all played for Southland. He was selected in the NZ Secondary Schools' side in 1981 but the team did not play because of protests at the Springbok tour that year. After making a strong impression as a perpetual-motion open-side flanker with the national schools' team in 1982 Henderson made his debut for Southland against the touring British Lions in 1983.

But he had to play seven seasons of first-class rugby before he got the All Black call. Injury was to be a key word in Henderson's career. It ended two of his All Black tours. But it also allowed him to join two other All Black touring parties after original selections were ruled out:

- He was chosen for the 1989 tour to Wales and Ireland but after three games he was injured and had to return home.
- When his Otago team-mate, Mike Brewer, was ruled medically unfit to travel to the 1991 World Cup, Henderson was his replacement.
- Injury cut short Henderson's tour of Australia and South Africa in 1992.
- But in 1993 Henderson was added to the All Black side after Michael Jones was forced out through injury before the team left.

However, Henderson also successfully toured France in 1990 and Argentina in 1991 and played in the three centenary tests of 1992 as well as the first test against Ireland that year.

But it was a freak injury that threatened to end Henderson's career in 1990 after the All Black trials in Palmerston North. He received a cut above any eye in the game. The wound flared up suddenly on the flight back to the South Island.

'I really wondered if I was going to die, such was the swift reaction to a toxin and the huge swelling,' Henderson recalled. 'The cut was to the left eye but I couldn't see out the right eye either because of the swelling.'

'The doctors managed to kill the bug with antibiotics but it was touch and go for a while.'

Henderson said his rugby longevity is due to his natural fitness, the fact he 'never got stale like other players because I moved from Southland to Otago and back to Southland, and then the advent of full professionalism in 1995.

'It's been a hell of a ride. Only now do you look back and think about all the high times and the low ones. When you're younger, in the midst of it, you tend to be more blasé as it flashes by.

'But I know what it means to be an international rugby player. I have been with guys in Britain – rich men – who said they'd have given everything away to have been good enough to be chosen for England.'

'I'm fortunate to have experienced both the amateur and the professional eras,' Henderson said. 'But I do think the game has lost a little of its honesty – caused by its transition into a business no doubt.'

Henderson said he was 'still playing because I enjoy it enormously. I also want to secure the financial future for my wife and family.' He and wife Susan have three children, aged seven, six and three.

## Paul William Henderson (Southland)

**Captain in one test**
v. Japan, 1995 World Cup

**Born:** September 21, 1964, Bluff.

**Position:** Flanker.

**Represented NZ:** 1989–93, 95 – 25 matches (7 tests).

**Points for NZ:** 21 – 5 tries.

**First-class career:** Southland 1983–86 (Invercargill), 92–97 (Marist); Otago 1987–91 (Dunedin); Otago Highlanders 1996; NZ Colts 1983, 84; South Zone 1987, 89; NZ Trials 1990–93, 95; South Island 1995; NZ Divisional XV 1993, 95; NZ B 1991.

**High school:** Southland BHS.

**Miscellaneous:** Twin brother David played for Southland, South Island XV and the Divisional XV; older brother Peter played for Southland and Otago; father D.B. Henderson played for Southland and was reserve when Southland won the Ranfurly Shield from Taranaki in 1959.

**Occupation:** Was professional rugby player-coach overseas in 1999; owns deer farm in Southland.

# JUSTIN MARSHALL

## Marshall's captaincy role came 'just in time'

TAINE RANDELL, the captain of the All Blacks through a difficult transitional period of rebuilding in the late 1990s, would surely have envied the start made by his predecessor, Justin Marshall, as All Black captain in 1997.

Marshall was unbeaten in four tests as leader on the tour of Britain and Ireland at the end of that year.

As with many others, he got the job only because of injury to another. Sean Fitzpatrick, who began as captain in 1992, had built a great record through the 1995–97 seasons. But on the tour he was halted by a knee injury that would soon afterward end his career.

Marshall therefore led the All Blacks to impressive victories over Ireland 63–15, Wales 42–7, and England 25–8, before the All Blacks were ambushed by a determined England team in the second test at Twickenham to scrape to a 26–26 draw.

So Marshall joined a small but illustrious group of All Black halfbacks who have led New Zealand in tests from this ideal pivot position between back and forward over the past century – captains such as Freddie Roberts, Teddy Roberts, Frank Kilby, Pat Vincent, 'Ponty' Reid, Chris Laidlaw, Dave Loveridge and David Kirk.

His tenure as captain was almost certainly considered by All Black coach John Hart as a caretaker role. Randell was being groomed for the task and he would take over for what would prove a fateful 1998 season. Though Marshall would have his own problems in overcoming injury that year, he must have been grateful the added burden of leadership no longer remained on his shoulders.

But while he had the job Marshall was

LUCKY LEADER: Justin Marshall considered himself fortunate to have such an experienced team around him on the unbeaten 1997 tour

appreciative of the state of the well-oiled 'black machine' he had inherited from Fitzpatrick.

'I was quite lucky to captain a side that had so much experience and players such as Zinzan Brooke to guide me if I wasn't making the decisions required,' said Marshall.

*CARETAKER ROLE: Though a youngster himself, Justin Marshall's time as captain was seen as caretaking the job while Taine Randell was groomed for the long-term leadership*

But it was not all smooth going. In the first England test of 1997 at Old Trafford, for instance, Marshall was felled by a disgusting roundhouse blow from behind by the England lock and future captain, Martin Johnson.

'I don't remember it, ' Marshall said. 'It shook me up a bit and my jaw was aching and one of my ears was ringing for a long time.

'But I just tried to settle down and do the basics and gradually I was able to get back into the game.'

The second test provided the ultimate leadership challenge. England shook the All Blacks and bolted to a large lead by halftime. Marshall's men fought back well, but it was a day when several potential try-scoring movements were muffed as evidence of staleness was to be seen. In the end, the 26–26 draw was a fair result. England had squandered a seemingly unbeatable lead but the All Blacks were just not good enough on the day to put their hosts away in the final stages.

'It was a frenzy at the start and it wasn't until the second half we started to get our game

right,' said Marshall. 'But I felt it was an achievement to battle back like that.'

'It had been a tough year. But we were strongly motivated to win. Some of our passes didn't stick, but England must have felt cheated all the same.'

Marshall is a powerfully-built halfback who thrives on sniping runs to link with his loose forwards and cross the gain line. He also plays an exceptional cover-defensive game.

He had made his debut for Southland in 1992 at the age of 18 and played for the New Zealand Under 19 and Colts sides through to 1994. He played for the New Zealand Divisional team and toured Argentina with the New Zealand Development team in 1994.

Southland gained promotion to the First Division of the NPC in 1995 but Marshall had already made the move to Canterbury, where his career blossomed. His partnership at provincial and All Black levels with first five-eighth Andrew Mehrtens proved outstanding.

Marshall's 1998 injury woes were not the first he had experienced. In 1994 he had to pull out of Southland's NPC programme because of a chronic groin injury. 'It was serious,' recalled Marshall. 'I had to leave the field several times at halftime and then had to quit altogether. There was talk of a two-year rest from the game and even a plate in my pelvis. I couldn't even get out of bed at times over a four-to-five-month period.

'Then Canterbury's coach Vance Stewart got in touch. Graeme Bachop had gone to Japan. He organised a visit to Dr David Burke in Christchurch and from there it was to see a Sydney specialist who had treated people like the rugby league star, Ricky Stuart, for the same problem.

'I went with Angus Gardiner, who also had groin problems. After a lot of treatment over several months I gradually came right.'

Coach Laurie Mains took Marshall on the All Blacks' tour of Italy and France at the end of 1995 and he played a major role in the side's outstanding second test win over France after displacing incumbent halfback Stu Forster.

He cemented his place as the All Blacks' No 1 choice under new coach John Hart. In the outstanding 1996 season he played in all 10 tests and all 12 in 1997. Marshall was voted NPC player of the year in 1996 and contributed to Canterbury's NPC title win in 1997.

When Fitzpatrick could not take his place, Marshall captained the All Blacks in the opening British tour match of 1997 against Llanelli. He retained the leadership for each of the tests.

Marshall also played a role in the Canterbury Crusaders' back-to-back Super 12 titles in 1998 and 1999. He suffered a chronic achilles heel injury early in the 1998 competition which ended his participation. He made a remarkable recovery from the injury to be fit enough three months later to take his place in the All Blacks for the majority of their programme. However, the All Blacks suffered a dreadful year, with five test losses in succession, and Marshall became the target of the critics. 'I had strived to make a full recovery. But the match fitness, especially for tests, meant I was one or two yards off the pace,' admitted Marshall to the author in 1999.

Marshall's rise to the top coincided exactly with the advent of full professionalism. The 1995 All Black tour was the first time the All Blacks had been officially paid. With the advent of Super 12 in 1996, top players' payments trebled and quadrupled.

'It couldn't have come at a better time for me,' said Marshall. 'I love the environment. It is something you only dreamed about previously and I realise how lucky I have been.'

Marshall and Mehrtens enjoy a good relationship off the field. 'Yes, we're good mates,' said Marshall. 'We enjoy similar activities, such as golf.'

Interestingly, in a 1999 interview Marshall said the pair had never managed to play a game together for their club, Christchurch High School Old Boys.

'That was the big plan when I came up from Southland in 1995, but then he made the All Blacks that winter and didn't play club football. In fact, the three or four games I played for the club in 1995 are the only ones I have managed in the five years I've lived in Christchurch.'

## Justin Warren Marshall (Canterbury)

**Captain in four tests, three wins and one draw**
v. Ireland, Wales, England (1, 2), 1997

**Born:** August 15, 1973, Gore.

**Position:** Halfback.

**Represented NZ:** 1995–99 – 46 matches (39 tests).

**Points for NZ:** 100 – 20 tries.

**First-class record:** Southland 1992–94 (Woodlands); Canterbury 1995–2000 (HSOB); Canterbury Crusaders 1996–2000; NZ Colts 1993; NZ Divisional team 1993; NZ Development teams 1994; NZRFU President's XV 1996; Harlequins 1996; NZ Barbarians 1996.

**High school:** Gore High School.

**Miscellaneous:** Nephew of 1958 All Black fullback Lloyd Ashby.

**Occupation:** Professional rugby player.

# TAINE RANDELL

## Tumultuous beginning may bring dividends

TAINE RANDELL was picked out as All Black captaincy material by two New Zealand coaches, but eventually became the victim of the penchant for control by one of them. A third All Black coach declined to continue with Randell as his onfield general, but other good judges say he may one day return as the captain.

At the end of 1999 Randell – New Zealand's fourth-youngest captain when appointed – had passed Sir Brian Lochore's mark of 18 tests and was equal with Graham Mourie's mark of 19 tests in charge of the team.

In the space of only two years Randell had only Sean Fitzpatrick (51 tests) and Sir Wilson Whineray (30) in front of him.

But New Zealand's loss to South Africa in the play-off for third and fourth at Cardiff in the World Cup made Randell's hold on the captaincy tenuous. It followed the All Blacks' resounding semifinal defeat at the hands of France and with it the hopes of the nation that the team would regain the cup after a 12-year wait.

These reversals signalled the end of All Black coach John Hart, who resigned. New coach Wayne Smith declined to comment on the

FUTURE MAPPED OUT: Taine Randell had looked a future All Black captain from the days when he used to lead national school and colts teams

*BORN AGAIN: Although Taine Randell has lost the captaincy, it is possible he could again lead the All Blacks*

captaincy over many off-season months of conjecture. But in late May 2000, when the new All Black squad was announced, Canterbury Crusader Todd Blackadder was named as the captain.

Randell was retained in the All Black squad, where it was expected he might be utilised as a blindside flanker. Blackadder and Randell are good friends and Randell pledged to give the new captain his full support.

Interestingly, this pair and Justin Marshall all made their All Black debuts in the same match – against Italy A at Catania in October 1995. They were the last three All Black test captains.

The All Black coach Laurie Mains had brought Randell into the team on that end-of-year to Italy and France. He played two matches at No 8 and two on the flank. The following year, under Hart, he was given the task of captaining the midweek team on the tour of South Africa. He made his test debut in 1997 at No 8 when he replaced the injured Zinzan Brooke for the game against Fiji. When Michael Jones was injured, Randell moved to the blindside, where he played in 11 more tests that year. He completed such a fine season the *New Zealand Rugby Almanack* named him one of its players of the year.

Longtime All Black captain Fitzpatrick was unable to captain the side in the tests in Britain at the end of 1997. Instead, halfback Marshall was captain. However, this move by Hart was seen as an interim move while he groomed Randell for the job. When Fitzpatrick announced his retirement in early 1998, Randell was appointed.

But after the trauma of 1998 – when Randell led the All Blacks in five consecutive test

*SETTING EXAMPLE: Taine Randell on the burst against Tonga in last year's World Cup. His side struggled at first but won 45–9*

losses, the worst record since the All Blacks played their first test almost a century ago – it became widely known he would have liked to give up the captaincy. However, after two months of encouragement with his Otago coach, Tony Gilbert, and the team that won the 1998 NPC, Randell's state of mind improved to the point where he felt he might like to continue in the national job.

By February of 1999, Hart knew this. He could have immediately declared his support for Randell and announced he was to continue as the leader. Instead, he chose to keep silent. The implication was Hart was seriously mulling over other candidates.

The influential *NZ Rugby Monthly* caused a stir when it announced it had replaced the cover of its May edition because its cover story had to be 'spiked'. The story had involved Randell and the state of the All Black captaincy.

Its then associate editor, John Matheson, would state later that on May 8, 1999, Randell had met with Hart, Peter Sloane and Gordon Hunter at Christchurch's Centra Hotel. Randell was told he was still a serious contender for captain. But, according to Matheson, Randell told him he had left the meeting with the distinct impression longtime All Black Robin Brooke was the preferred option at that time.

What happened after that is unknown. Brooke was later part of an unprecedented Auckland Blues outfit that rejected its coach, Jed Rowlands. Brooke had been the captain of the team. Hart then saw the potential for embarrassment in continuing with the Brooke option. There was another suggestion, emanating from Palmerston North, that Anton

Oliver had been offered the captaincy about the same time.

Randell was eventually retained as captain. But how much had the rebuff affected his confidence? The All Blacks made a good recovery during 1999, winning the Tri-Nations series, but stumbling badly to Australia at the end of that competition. They were installed as favourites by the bookies for the World Cup. But the ravings by the British press that this was the best All Black side to leave New Zealand shores were highly debatable – as history proved, they were an insult to the great teams of years gone by.

However, Randell's belated re-appointment was one of a number of poor judgments by Hart in the cup campaign. It has emerged that under Hart the World Cup All Blacks were unable to express themselves.

'His captain seemed incapable of making any decisions on the field ... not because of any failings in his leadership ability but because Hart was intent on pulling the strings from the sideline,' stated Matheson.

'As a result, Hart's All Blacks lacked strong on-field leadership. As a player, why would you look to Randell for leadership when you knew he had no power? It was a ridiculous scenario.'[1]

In an editorial in May this year, Matheson backed Randell's retention. His justification was as follows:

'Despite not being able to captain the side the way he wanted to, because of John Hart's insistence that he control things, Taine took all of the critics, fair and square on his young shoulders.

'He concedes Hart originally selected him for the captaincy because the coach knew he could control a younger player rather than someone like Ian Jones or Robin Brooke. But he fronted for the job, did the best he was allowed to do and, as a result, a young man of steel has emerged from the All Black ashes.

'With the strings no longer being pulled by John Hart, Taine is his own man.'

Randell recalled the great contrast in his early and later years as an All Black when interviewed by the author this year.

'I had been nurtured at the beginning. But in 1997 I got my big break and really enjoyed the year. We achieved a mighty record and it was wonderful to be learning from Fitzy and Zinny [Brooke],' Randell said.

'In retrospect, our performances did begin to tail off at the end of the year, but we put it down to a long, hard year.'

Randell said he 'wasn't too worried about any captaincy aspirations' as 1998 came into being. But he was thrust into the captaincy job and would finish the year with a horror start for one so talented.

'Yes, we got on that losing streak and couldn't get off it. It is such a fine line – because we didn't lose them by much and actually could have won some.'

But Randell also reasoned the slump was caused by 'the loss of several key players and leaders, the fact the guys needed a break after an endless amount of football, and because other international sides had improved.'

Randell said he enjoyed the job but the high public profile the captaincy involved may have been a strain for the young man. However, as with Whineray, Fitzpatrick and a host of other All Black captains, he had done the 'hard yards' learning how to lead.

Remarkably, Randell is only 25. He celebrated his birthday, on November 11, at the end of the World Cup – on the same day his grandfather died and Hart walked away from another attempt at the All Black coaching job.

It is possible Randell could yet again be the All Black captain. In a less stultifying atmosphere than Hart's All Black environment became, Randell's style and his ability to make the essential mid-game decisions that mark the great leaders from the rest could blossom. He has proved he can handle the pressure when leading Otago and the Highlanders.

It is therefore interesting to compare Randall's two years as leader with the first three years of Fitzpatrick, who most remember as a great captain. Randell's captaincy record was 11 victories and eight losses. In 1992, his first season, Fitzpatrick lost three tests from nine, in 1993 two from seven and in 1994 he lost three and drew one from six tests. So from 22 tests he had lost six and drawn one. Some critics at the time called for coach Mains' head but seemed to forget about Fitzpatrick.

Indeed, Fitzpatrick told the author he believed Randell would be a better captain for the hard lessons he had learned at the head of the All Blacks.

On this basis, Randell's best years of leadership may lie ahead. But All Black captains, once relieved of the burden, seldom return as captains. Just one example is Ian Kirkpatrick, who went on to many more fine years of service for the All Blacks, but was never asked to lead New Zealand in a test again after 1973.

Randell had long looked a future All Black leader. From his days at college he had often led the teams he played for. After representing New Zealand at secondary school and under 17, Randell made his debut for the Otago representative side at only 17 in 1992. He played for the New Zealand Colts for three years, the last two as captain.

When introduced to the Otago team its loose forward contingent included All Blacks Arran Pene, Jamie Joseph and Josh Kronfeld. They taught him well and by 1994 he was a regular member of the side.

Randell told the author his position preference was for the blindside.

'Yes, that's what I prefer. But I don't mind. It really depends on the team's requirements and what the coach decides. I don't mind openside either.'

But what about the flexibility of using him in several positions in a match – something suggested by the critics before and during the World Cup but an option that Hart, through his selection of the squad, never contemplated? Substitution rules now make such options attractive.

'In certain games, that has got a place. With big, driving players like Filo Tiatia, Isitolo Maka and Paul Miller at No 8, the value in this tactic has been shown.'

Randell, who has degrees in law and commerce, is a part-owner of a computer games shop in Dunedin. He holds business aspirations when his playing days are over. He recently built a house on St Clair Beach.

'I'm sure I'll finish my rugby career in Otago. After that, I've absolutely no idea,' said the Hawkes Bay born-and-bred Randell.

---

## Taine Cheyenne Randell (Otago)

**Captain in 19 tests, 11 wins and eight losses**
1998: v England (1, 2), v Australia (1, 2, 3)
v South Africa (1, 2)
1999: v Samoa, v France, v South Africa (1, 2),
v Australia (1, 2)
World Cup: v Tonga, v England, v Italy,
v Scotland, v France, v South Africa

**Born:** November 5, 1974, Hastings.

**Position:** No 8 or flanker.

**Represented NZ:** 1995–99 – 41 matches (31 tests).

**Points for NZ:** 55 – 11 tries.

**First-class record:** Otago 1992, 93 (University), 1994–2000 (Dunedin); Otago Highlanders 1996–2000; NZ Colts 1993–95; NZ Trials 1996–98; NZ Colts Black 1995; North Otago Invitation XV 1996; NZ Maori 1996; Barbarians 1996–97.

**High school:** Lindisfarne College, First XV 1989–91.

**Miscellaneous:** Completed LLB and BCom at Otago University.

**Occupation:** Professional rugby player; part-owner of computer games shop.

---

1 *NZ Rugby Monthly,* John Matheson, November 1999 edition.

# TODD BLACKADDER

## Blackadder's 'escape acts' could no longer be ignored

TODD BLACKADDER hails from the tiny but celebrated Glenmark club in North Canterbury. It has been a powerhouse in country rugby and is the club that produced Alex ('Grizz') Wyllie, a tough All Black loose forward who played 210 games for Canterbury, was captain in more than 100, including two Ranfurly Shield eras, and then went on to coach Canterbury and the All Blacks through some of their most successful eras.

Blackadder is now part of the new Wayne Smith-inspired All Black era. Wyllie is a legend in the area. But Wyllie never captained the All Blacks in a test match.

Of his choice of Blackadder as his on and off-field general for 2000, All Black coach Smith simply said: 'Captains need the ability to lead by example, the ability to inspire everyone around them.'

Smith and fellow selectors Tony Gilbert and Peter Thorburn had also relied on an NZRFU report made by Sean Fitzpatrick, a former All Black captain, on the qualities a captain needed.

To the many thousands who have flocked to Lancaster Park to watch the Crusaders battle to three consecutive Super 12 titles – although the crowds have yet to be treated to a home final – Blackadder is the hard-nosed, uncompromising leader of 15 warriors.

'He is a leader who inspires his players by his

*INSPIRATIONAL LEADER: With three Super 12 titles as captain of the Canterbury Crusaders, Todd Blackadder had shown an ability to lead by example and inspire all around him*

unquenchable appetite for doing the hard work. To him, the bangs and bruises, the bumps and blood are accepted and expected from men wearing the red-and-black colours of Canterbury ...'

'Off the pitch, Blackadder is a different person; ever modest, always honest, sometimes humble, even soft-hearted. He has a good woman behind him in Priscilla, his wife, and he is very much a family man – a doting dad to his daughter Shinae [now 9] and son Ethan [now 8].'[1]

It has been well-documented that the responsibilities of All Black captaincy extend far beyond the public gaze. Blackadder had a fine preparation for the national job because of the way he learned to cheerfully handle the fanatical but well-meant adulation of the Canterbury rugby public.

The Blackadders have had to make sacrifices. They have done so without complaint. A typical example was when Canterbury hosted the NPC final against Counties-Manukau at Lancaster Park in 1997.

'Four days out ... Blackadder was whisked to Auckland in the morning to join rival captain Errol Brain in a television promotion. He was back in time for a quick bite and a spot of dishwashing before a media interview at his Rangiora home. Then it was a drive to town to be the guest on an hour-long radio sports programme.'[2]

The demands on his time have often been long and hard, but Blackadder does not complain. 'I actually don't mind because I know I'm doing it on behalf of the team and that's all part of the job description. It helps

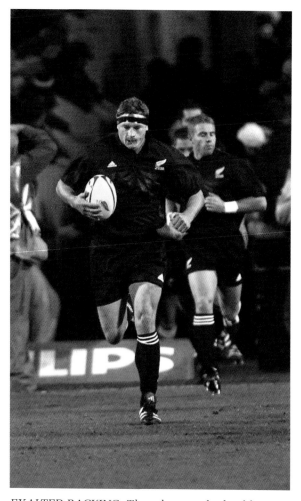

*EXALTED BACKING: Though some doubted his ability to play at international level, Todd Blackadder had the public backing of former All Black captains such as Colin Meads, Sir Wilson Whineray, Jock Hobbs, Buck Shelford and Andy Leslie*

take the pressure off the other guys. What can be annoying is the 30 to 40 calls a day.'

The story is told that, after being selected for the All Black tour of South Africa in 1996, he sat at the dining table for four hours accepting congratulatory calls while the tea went untouched.[3]

Priscilla Blackadder said: 'Now it's his only job and that's the advantage of professional rugby. Before that he was courier driving then racing off to rugby training. Sometimes the kids might not see him for three or four nights.'[4]

The Blackadder reputation of being 'an ordinary Joe Blow' was illustrated by this 1998 description by then Christchurch journalist Shayne Currie.

'A stroll up Todd Blackadder's Rangiora driveway puts a few myths to rest. Forget the glitzy, media-generated image of professional rugby players – the flash cars and bleached hair styles, the cellphones and spa pools.

'Lying in the garden is a rugby ball and nearby a child's bike, left collapsed in a heap. There's a set of golf clubs at the door, but they're not quite Greg Norman specials.

'And out the back is the man himself, and not on a deckchair, sipping on a Steinlager and negotiating his next sponsorship deal.

'Todd Blackadder is doing Real Work, chopping firewood with the help of daughter Shinae. It's entirely in keeping with his rugged, durable personality – the no nonsense, man of the land and ready-to-bleed-for-my-province image.

'Tonight he leads the Crusaders against the Highlanders ... his opposition captain is good friend Taine Randell, a man he shares many common bonds with – they made their All Black debuts together, both are contenders for the All Black captaincy ...

'People like to build this rivalry up, but at the end of the day we are more concerned about what we are doing than what they are doing,' Blackadder said of Randell and the Highlanders.

'Everyone gets on. Most rugby players are good mates with all the guys in the other team. When you run out there, they are the opposition, but after the game we have a beer together. That's just life and New Zealand is probably a little bit too small to dislike (one another).'

But none of the media expectation sits easily with Blackadder. For one thing, he was not even thinking about leading the All Blacks in a test.

'I don't set those goals. I want to play well, week in, week out. Whatever happens, happens. A lot of those things are out of my control. The only thing I can control is myself.' Does he fit into the John Hart style? 'That's up to John Hart. It's not what I say. Selectorial matters are out of my control, basically.'[5]

But Blackadder's record as Canterbury and Crusaders captain finally had to swing the All Blacks' job his way this year. He had dragged the Crusaders up from last place in 1996 to sixth in 1997. They drew with semifinalist Natal and lost by one point in controversial circumstances to eventual champion Auckland.

He was a blindside flanker then and it was his inspirational tackling that set the example for a team which established a reputation for the best defensive record in the competition. At the end of 1997 came the NPC championship title for Canterbury. It beat Counties-Manukau 44–13 in the final, after twice beating Auckland, then still regarded as one of the strongest provinces in the world.

'Blackadder's "Honest Abe" style of leadership and his willingness to put his body on the line in foraging for the ball and bolstering the defensive screen earned him the admiration of rugby regulars and recognition from the wider community. It was hardly a surprise when he was named Canterbury's player of the year.'[6]

He is in fact the only player in its 26-year history to have won the award twice.

Durability is another word closely attached to the Blackadder legend. His grand total of first-class matches by the end of the Super 12 series this year was 217 matches, including 47 tries and 230 points. He has been replaced only four times in those matches, which makes him one of the most durable players in the modern game.

When he led his side to its third successive Super 12 championship earlier this year Blackadder had played 60 matches for the Crusaders, 51 of those games as the captain. Each total more than any other player in the competition.

But it was also the style of the Crusaders' success that caught the imagination of the nation. Apart from their start to the Super 12 this year, the Crusaders have always struggled.

In 1998 they won only one of their first four matches, but then produced nine victories on the trot to pip the Auckland Blues for the title.

In 1999 it took wins in their last four matches to allow them to scrape into the top four. They then won their semifinal and the final away to clinch the title again.

This year it took a stupendous defensive effort – after being outplayed by 168–34 in the ruck and maul count – and a superb 42m penalty into a stiff breeze at the end by Andrew Mehrtens, to scrape home 20–19 over the much-favoured Brumbies in the final.

Unlike the domination shown by the Auckland Blues in the early years of the Super

12, Blackadder's Crusaders have become renowned for their escape acts. These include the final-minute win in the 1998 final at Eden Park, the 1999 escape at Pretoria when Mehrtens dropped a goal, the big 1999 win over the Cats at Nelson after being down 6–31, this year's comeback win over Queensland at Brisbane, and of course this year's final act at Canberra.

But there has been one common denominator in all of these: Blackadder. His side's comebacks have been so frequent it must amount to more than good fortune, as some critics in the north first claimed.

'When the tide's running in your favour it's not difficult for anyone to be a captain,' said Crusaders coach Robbie Deans earlier this year.[7]

'It's when things run against you that the need for good leadership kicks in. If you've got leadership qualities they're shown when your side is under pressure and that's where Todd has excelled.'

Team-mates talk about their captain's 'remarkable composure on the field.'

Veteran journalist Lindsay Knight wrote that what made Blackadder special was hard to pinpoint exactly. He didn't have the academic background of other successful All Black captains such as Wilson Whineray, David Kirk or Graham Mourie. Or the aggressive leadership of captains such as Buck Shelford and Sean Fitzpatrick. But until Blackadder, there hadn't been a captain with the same combination of dignity and modesty since Brian Lochore.

'He's also a natural diplomat, as was shown in his victory speech after the 1998 final at Eden Park,' said Knight. 'Even in the euphoric moment Blackadder remembered to thank not only the Canterbury public but those in other parts of the Crusaders' region – Nelson Bays, Marlborough, West Coast, Buller, Mid-Canterbury and South Canterbury.'[8]

At Canberra this year, giving the victory speech, Blackadder abbreviated that to thanking those from 'Timaru to Cape Farewell.'

Deans pointed out that while Blackadder had not been to an institution of higher learning, he rated his natural intelligence and common sense.

'He's a good thinker and if he set his mind on academic pursuits he'd achieve there too. As a person, his great quality is consistency. He's a

*TRIPLE CROWN: Todd Blackadder made his All Black debut in the same game as two other future All Black captains*

great people person. He commands respect but also gives respect.'[9]

Blackadder was first chosen for the All Blacks by coach Laurie Mains for the tour of Italy and France in 1995. It was the first professional tour by New Zealand and he played in four matches. He made his debut against Italy A at Catania on October 25, 1995 in the same match as two future All Black captains, Justin Marshall and Taine Randell, also made theirs.

Blackadder was one of the first chosen for the 1997 All Black tour of the UK, particularly for his leadership abilities. He became the 121st player to captain the All Blacks on that tour.

He has played for the All Blacks every year since 1995, but never on a regular basis until this year.

Blackadder did not appear to harbour any bitterness for the way he was tried as a test forward in 1998 and then quickly discarded. He was allegedly suffering from shin splints at the time he played the tests against touring England.

The controversy that took over the nation, especially earlier this year, was whether Blackadder could command a test place on his playing ability – a prerequisite for an All Black captain. There were many who subscribed to Hart's view that he did not. That he as not quite big enough for a test lock and not quick or agile enough for a loose forward.

But his commanding form throughout the Super 12 – and the lack of consistency among his chief rivals – put the issue beyond doubt.

New Zealand's greatest lock – and a former test captain – Colin Meads was one who backed Blackadder being given the opportunity to lead the All Blacks at test level. So did other former All Black test skippers such as Whineray, Jock Hobbs, Shelford and Andy Leslie.

Leslie would have seen similarities between Blackadder's situation and his own. A great leader of Wellington, Leslie was ignored for a decade. He finally got his chance in 1974 amid dire warnings from former All Blacks he 'wouldn't be up to it physically.' But Leslie led the All Blacks back to near the top of international rugby over the next three years.

But another former test captain believed Blackadder would struggle in lineouts in tests. In justifying the selection, Thorburn, the third national selector, pointed out there were far fewer lineouts these days, that 'lifting' meant any height disparity was negated, and that Blackadder's high workrate in all other phases made him far more valuable overall than would the specialist lock of yesteryear. Blackadder stands 1.93m tall and weighs 114kg.

Another experienced rugby journalist, Christchurch's Bob Schumacher, said Blackadder's elevation to Canterbury's captaincy in 1996 by the then coach Vance Stewart was 'an inspired choice.'

Schumacher believed Blackadder had shed much of his early shyness with the media and in speaking to audiences and now seemed to enjoy the work.

'He's not a pretentious person. He's not a fan of formal dinners. He'd rather spend time with his mates at a barbecue with a few beers.'

Knight believed that, 'Maybe that's why New Zealand has fallen in love with this guy ... he's one of us.'[10]

Blackadder always wanted to play for Canterbury as a boy. He grew up during one of the province's great shield eras from 1983-86 and idolised players such as Deans [his coach with Canterbury and then the Crusaders in recent years]. 'To finally pull on that jersey was certainly a highlight,' Blackadder said.

But Blackadder spent his late teenage years in Nelson Bays, working on a dairy farm. He is a life member of the Collingwood club. He played for the club in 1989–90, helping it to the Nelson-Bays senior B championship in 1990. Blackadder played nine matches for Nelson-Bays that year and also made the New Zealand Under 19 and NZ Divisional sides that year.

Every New Year Blackadder returns to help sell raffles for the club, which runs a hamper raffle around the motor camps of the area during the busy tourist-holiday maker season. He also bestowed Collingwood with official custodial status of all his representative jerseys, which are now on show at the club during weekends. Although Blackadder moved away from the area a decade ago, Collingwood feels justified in claiming him as its 'first All Black captain'.

## Todd Julian Blackadder (Canterbury)

**Captain in 2 tests, 2 wins***
2000: v Tonga
v Scotland

**Born:** September 20, 1971, Rangiora.

**Position:** Lock and loose forward.

**Represented NZ:** 1995–2000 – 17 matches (4 tests).

**Points for NZ:** 15 – 3 tries.

**First-class record:** Nelson-Bays 1990 (Collingwood); Canterbury 1991–93 (Belfast), 1994–2000 (Glenmark); NZ Colts 1991, 92; NZ Divisional XV 1991; NZ Development 1994; NZ Trials 1993, 94, 96–98; NZ A 1997, 99; NZ XV 1993; Canterbury XV 1995; Canterbury Crusaders 1996, 97; Hawkes Bay Invitation XV 1996

**High school:** Rangiora High School 1st XV, 1988.

**Miscellaneous:** The scar on Blackadder's face – it has been called a 'Nike logo' – is not an old rugby injury but the result of a car accident in younger days.

**Other:** Non-rugby interests include motor sport and jet boating.

**Occupation:** Former farm labourer, drainlayer, courier driver, now professional rugby player.

* As at June 25, 2000

1, 2, 3, 4 Bob Schumacher, *The Press*, October 24, 1997.

5 Shayne Currie, *The Press*, April 24, 1998.

6 John Brooks, *The Press*, December 27, 1997.

7, 8, 9, 10 Lindsay Knight, *NZ Rugby World*, May 2000

# CONCLUSION

## HIGH STANDARDS SET EARLY AND SELDOM DIMINISHED

What conclusions be gained from this study of the evolution of the All Black captains?

We have been able to learn much more about what drove these often exceptional men to countless victories in the black jersey.

The highest standards were set right from the first time a New Zealand team was assembled in 1884 and the All Blacks have seldom fallen below those benchmarks.

No other rugby nation has a record comparable with the All Blacks, although South Africa did hold supremacy for many years. Other countries' captains and coaches were often heard to comment that 'You never meet a poor All Black team.'

But long departed captains would roll over in their graves to learn of the slipping standards of the All Blacks recently, especially the unprecedented five test losses in succession in 1998.

All Black captains have long used the term that 'defeat is not an option'. That motto was created through generations of capable leaders, through their dedication and personal and financial sacrifice. Sadly, more recently, defeats have been called wake-up calls by the coach, while the opposition had outpassioned the All Blacks. It is an intolerable situation that must be addressed by the new regime.

## SO WHO WAS THE GREATEST CAPTAIN?

All Black captains have accumulated fabulous records over the years. While Sean Fitzpatrick is the latest, and greatest in many peoples' opinion, his tenure needs to be matched up against the likes of Sir Wilson Whineray, Sir Brian Lochore, Graham Mourie, Andy Dalton and Buck Shelford.

This is the elite group of all the All Black captains. But how one goes about sorting out just who is the greatest becomes fraught with danger as the subjective and sentimental attributes intermingle with the objective.

Whineray had a fabulous record. Only five losses in 30 tests over seven years as captain. His tenure was the longest of all. In that time his team beat every rugby-playing nation. They lost one series, narrowly, in South Africa in 1960. Conversely, he could call on the support of a vast nucleus of test-hardened players, thus reducing the need for crucial leadership decisions in many tests. The rules of the day also allowed him to control games far more easily. However, there is plenty of evidence to show Whineray could and did make tactical decisions that proved criticial. He was also very young when he took the job. Whineray's was the first truly long-term tenure and it set the benchmark that others have strived to meet.

Mourie is perhaps the next most revered captain. He had only four losses in 19 tests. His tenure was also long – six years from 1977 to 1982. Circumstances conspired against Mourie's leading New Zealand more often. The game was in a transitional period when the players' financial situation was not keeping up with the rapidly increasing annual test programme. With a heavy domestic programme and an end-of-year tour overseas the norm, Mourie, a farmer, sometimes had to cry off touring. But have the All Blacks ever had a better tactician? The stand-out feature of his tenure was the way he was credited with devising brilliant and often original tactics to drive his All Black teams. In an era of much less stability within the All Black ranks than other great captains, when his teams often struggled, and the scores were close, Mourie usually pulled something out of the hat. It was noticeable that when Mourie was unavailable for some tours or series, the All Blacks' success rate sometimes dropped.

Lochore is a sentimental favourite with many followers, perhaps because he has continued to work for the game for three decades since his playing days. His record was outstanding – in 18 tests the only three losses were in the 1970 series in South Africa. Fred Allen is often called the greatest of our coaches, being unbeaten in his tenure. Lochore, except when injured, was captain throughout Allen's reign. We can only surmise that if Allen had stayed as coach, instead of quitting at the end of 1968, Lochore might have improved his South African record. He led the All Blacks on their finest post-war tour to that point – the 1967 tour of Britain. But like Whineray, he was supported by a fabulous group of long-term All Blacks. And like Whineray, he could not quite find the answers in South Africa.

At the end of his career, Lochore showed his true mettle. With everything to lose and in semi-retirement, he answered the call to help the All Blacks, one more time, against the Lions.

Dalton is the dark horse in any discussion on the great captains. He may be remembered as a a sort of caretaker captain. But his record was outstanding – 15 wins from 17 tests. His victims included the 1981 Springboks and the 1983 Lions. And if he had been able to play in the six World Cup matches of 1987, he would almost have matched the great Whineray's record of wins. As it is, he bettered both Lochore and Mourie for success. Conversely, Dalton's run in the mid-1980s was achieved through the help of a vastly experienced forward pack, and most of his matches were at home.

Shelford is another sentimental favourite – and fairly so. He was unbeaten from 14 tests, his only blemish being a draw. His team played played sublime rugby for three years until his shock sacking, based on lack of form, in 1990. Many of his victories were very one-sided. Shelford led by example and had established a huge psychological advantage over all his international rivals when the end came. Conversely, he had the advantage of leading New Zealand's greatest wave of talented players since the 1960s.

That brings us back to Fitzpatrick and more scrutiny. Fifty-one tests for 39 wins over six years is easily the most prodigious All Black captain's test programme in history. There were also 11 losses and a draw, most of those coming during his difficult early tenure in 1992–93. During 1995 under Laurie Mains and then the first two years of John Hart's era, Fitzpatrick led a side that set new standards in consistency in international rugby. He became the first All Black captain to win both one-off (1992) and long (1996) series in South Africa, as well as be unbeaten in a series against South Africa in New Zealand (1994). His 79% success rate did not match some of his predecessors though. He was aided by a vastly experienced nucleus by the end of his era. The jump New Zealand gained on competing nations in quickly bedding in professionalism from 1995 was a significant bonus for the captain.

## THE SECOND-LEVEL CAPTAINS

The author has a second-level group of All Black captains. It consists of Tom Ellison, Dave Gallaher, Cliff Porter and David Kirk. This quartet did not quite reach the status of the elite group, because they did not achieve as much.

Ellison was New Zealand's first official tour captain and, as we have learned, was one of the great early contributors to the New Zealand teams' tactics, high standards and perhaps the inventor of the wing-forward position. It was Ellison who first spoke out about biased refereeing and the need for out-of-pocket expenses for touring All Blacks. He was captain in 1893; professionalism became official in 1995. So Ellison was more than a century ahead of his time.

Gallaher is another sentimental favourite, especially in the north. He set a benchmark in 1905 for all who followed.

But consider Porter. The 1924 Invincibles' captain's own benchmark season after season was the nurturing his players. We have wonderful evidence to show Porter's prime interest on several tours was always the welfare of his men.

Kirk joins this illustrious quartet because of his success in captaining the All Blacks to the first World Cup. Expectations at the subsequent three cup tournaments have been equally as high. The favourites in 1991 and 1999, New Zealand fell at the semifinal hurdle, while in 1995 a less heralded side submitted the final in extra time after 18 of the side had been food poisoned on the eve of the game. As Brazil has found in soccer, World Cups are difficult to win, even for the best. As the rugby's world of countries grows, a second title for the All Blacks might prove just as elusive.

## THEY ALSO SERVED US WELL

The third group of the more illustrious All Black captains contains Billy Stead, Maurice Brownlie, Peter Johnstone, Andy Leslie and Gary Whetton.

Stead was unbeaten as a captain and in an amazing 42 games as an All Black. He led New Zealand both before and after the more celebrated Gallaher, but proved a faithful lieutenant on the first great tour. Brownlie led the All Blacks on their first great trek of South Africa and emerged with a tied series. Completely unappreciated at the time, his achievement would not be improved on until Sean Fitzpatrick's era 60 years later. Johnstone was also unbeaten and helped lead the recovery New Zealand so badly needed after the despair of the 1949 whitewash in South Africa. Leslie also led a grand recovery from a trying time. Whetton, much maligned after displacing Buck Shelford and then losing the 1991 World Cup semifinal, nevertheless completed one of the best winning records of any All Black captain – 12 wins from 15 tests.

## IS THIS MEASUREMENT FAIR?

Like the All Black coaches, the All Black captains are inevitably judged on their win–loss record.

But there are other methods that can be used to measure success. These can include the style of rugby played during the captain's era; whether he had to work with his coach to develop a largely youthful or inexperienced group of players; and the age, experience and remaining potential of the players in the squad when coach and/or captain retires.

Close analysis of the great All Black periods reveals not only a close captain-coach relationship in many cases. It also shows a nucleus of outstanding players who have coincidentally emerged to play under or within that partnership. This inner elite provides the stability on which the All Blacks of that era are built. Fringe players will come and go, but the nucleus soldiers on.

An outstanding example of the nuclear theory was the All Blacks in the 1960s. They never lost a series between 1960 and 1970. The partnerships of first Whineray–McPhail and then Lochore–Allen were built on the skilful mass provided from players such as Colin Meads, Ken Gray, Kel Tremain, Don Clarke (until 1964), Chris Laidlaw, Ian MacRae and Bruce McLeod. Hundreds of test caps were collectively accumulated by the team. Provided standards did not slip, reputation alone would have been a benchmark opposing sides dreaded to face.

## AND ARE COMPARISONS FUTILE?

True comparisons between captains, coaches or players of differing eras are largely futile?

Today's professional giants would destroy All Black sides of the past. Perhaps. The advantages of the modern players, built over a century of evolution, seem obvious.

But this author does not fully concur. If a game could be played in rugby's Valhalla, what rules would be used? The skills required in much earlier times were often quite different from today's game. So the score might be a lot closer than we think.

Champions of one era would surely be champions in another. It is not hard to imagine Bert Cooke, the first player to reach 100 first-class tries and perhaps the greatest footballer ever to lace up boots, quickly catching on to the requirements of the modern game. He would be as effective as today's Christian Cullen, on attack and defence.

Or that Colin Meads or Maurice Brownlie could comfortably foot it with today's forwards. Given the same training and nutritional aids, they would in fact prove superior to many.

So would Billy Wallace, Charlie Seeling, George Nepia, Fergie McCormick, Tiny White, Peter Jones, Sid Going, Bob Scott, Kevin Skinner, Ken Gray, Mark Nicholls and a host of other great players of the past.

The subject of comparisons in rugby is an enjoyable but inevitably inconclusive one.

How do we measure the worth of some tenures?

Some captaincy tenures seem far more worthy of accolades than others. How do we measure Bob Duff's two tests and two victories in 1956 to lift the 'world crown' from South Africa after 35 years of trying, for instance? The feat uplifted the national spirit to a level perhaps incomprehensible to the modern generation.

Compare that with Paul Henderson's quiet satisfaction at a job well done in the 1995 World Cup. He led the All Blacks to a massive world record, guiding a near-perfect performance, over Japan.

Many other captains' roles were just as brief and not as notable. But they all find their place in the tapestry that is the All Blacks unmatchable test record.

## LEADERSHIP IN OTHER FIELDS

It is not really surprising so many All Black captains have gone on to become leaders in other fields after their playing careers wound down. Leadership is clearly a quality that asserts itself in every walk of life.

Having proven themselves in the toughest field of all, sometimes being ambitious, but almost always retaining the ability towards sound decision-making, many captains find their niche later in life.

Two recently were knighted. We can look to the evidence of Sir Wilson Whineray and David

*HAIL THE ORIGINALS: The 1905 All Black 'Originals' wore their uniforms at training. The leather on their jerseys was said by some British critics to be one of the reasons they were often so difficult to tackle*

Kirk in corporate business, John Graham in education and business, Bob Stuart in agricultural economics, Ron Elvidge in medicine and Chris Laidlaw in diplomacy and politics, to name a few.

It probably more naturally followed that a number of the captains became All Black selectors and even coaches. They include Duncan, Gallaher, Stead, Allen, Stuart, Duff and Sir Brian Lochore.

Others became coaches at provincial and Super 12 level – Dalton, Kirk, Shelford, Mourie, and Oliver. And still others coaches overseas – Andy Leslie and Laidlaw. Some even became NZRFU councillors or administrators, such as Hobbs, Meads and Dalton.

WHY SOME WIN OFTEN AND SOME DO NOT
We have seen how a good number of All Blacks became the captain at the end of their careers. Some were successful. And some were not. Young readers may find it ironical that Colin Meads, regarded by modern-day followers as the 'greatest' of the many hundreds of All Blacks through history, did not end his 15-year All Black career with a series win. But in analysing his situation, and the period of turmoil All Black rugby was entering into, we may have more sympathy.

WHAT DOES IT TAKE TO BE AN ALL BLACK TEST CAPTAIN?
Fred Allen, the undefeated former All Black

coaching great, told the author in 1997 he was never in doubt about raising Lochore to the captaincy. 'It was my decision to make and it was the one least expected by my fellow selectors, Des Christian and Les George. I could not go past Lochore,' he said.

'It was the integrity and the quiet dignity of the man. Whineray had it. The army had taught me about the qualities of leadership and Brian had what I always looked for – strength of character, the capacity to provide discipline by example. He had a resilience. He would have been a leader of men in any field.'

### WHY WOULD YOU TURN DOWN THE DREAM JOB?
Some chose not to do the captain's job. Others tried it, then asked to bow out. It was worthwhile to record, as this book has done, that there have been instances of players who could have been All Black captains but who chose, for the overall good of the team, not to do so.

Frank Oliver and Andy Dalton, both in Graham Mourie's era, chose not to take the leader's role when it was offered. In Oliver's case, the opportunity never arose again. However, Dalton had already led the All Blacks and would do so again when Mourie's career came to an end. But it begs the question – just how good a record could have have had?

### WHAT DO HIS PLAYERS EXPECT OF THEIR CAPTAIN?
A questionnaire taken of the All Blacks would reveal they prize most highly in their captain his honesty, integrity, good organisation on and off the field, an ability to relate well with them, an excellent technical knowledge, an harmonious relationship with the coach and the manager, a clear sense of direction, and preferably as much test experience as possible.

### ADJUSTING TO THE ROLE
Fitzpatrick spoke about the adjustments an All Black had to make in his off-field life when appointed captain. Being captain meant rooming alone, which he initially found strange. But then he began to appreciate that it was important for a captain to have his space. He needed to think, to plan. The captain had to organise the days ahead.

This might seem logical to the reader but is not always easy for longtime All Blacks to make the adjustment. Stu Wilson, captain on one tour, spoke about the difficulties he had after seven years as one of the great comedians of All Black teams.

### UNEASY LIES THE CROWN ...
This study has pointed to the precarious life of the All Black captain. Their job description is simple: Deliver victories – or face the axe!

We have seen how intrigue has played a part in the elevation or dethroning of a few of the captains. But as with their troops, the team's commanders have often been felled by injuries. It was troubling to read of the times, long before modern medicine's arthroscopic surgery, when knee injuries, for instance, cut down the careers of great All Blacks at their peak. An example is Ces Badeley, chosen to captain the 1924–25 All Blacks but dropped as captain after the Australian leg of the campaign. The selectors decided his dicky knee might make him a non-playing leader on the great 'Invincibles' tour. And they were proved right.

Rusty Page had a similar problem on the 1935–36 tour, playing in only two games – the second and 21st of the 35 matches – and retiring immediately after the tour.

Sadly, there was certainly no chance that players struck down with such injuries could resurrect their careers in the way the 1987–98 All Black great, Michael Jones, did when surgeons rebuilt one knee and then some years later the other.

### ANOMOLIES OF LEADERSHIP
There have sometimes been inequalities and freakish anomolies in the performances of the All Black test captains.

Take Johnny Smith, the brilliant centre who captained the All Blacks in 1949. His team was very much the 'third XV' of All Black rugby since the leading group were in the process of losing a series, 4–0, to the Springboks in South Africa at the time.

Such occurrences don't happen nowadays, but then neither does the fact that Smith was in New Zealand, rather than South Africa, because of that country's racial policies.

### POSITIONS OF THE CAPTAINS
What is the best position to captain the All Blacks from? This question has raged for more

than a century. And after that amount of debate, all we can absolutely state is that fullback and wing are not the places to lead from.

There has only been one fullback and one wing captain the team in the test arena.

Easily the most popular place has been loose forward, where there have been a total of 21 captains. The inside backs come next, with 18. There having been nine halfbacks and nine first five-eighths.

There have also been five locks, four centres, three hookers and two props lead the All Blacks.

Clearly then, loose forward or the inside backs seems the place All Black selectors deem as most suitable to watch over and lead the team's performance.

But expediency, or when an outstanding individual comes to the fore, has sometimes caused the selectors to pluck men who spend their days buried in the tight to wear the purple.

MOST CAPTAINS

Up to the end of 1999, the most test captains have come from Canterbury and Wellington, with 10. Otago have had eight, Auckland seven, Taranaki four, Waikato three, Southland three, Hawkes Bay two, and one from South Canterbury, Manawatu, North Harbour, Counties, Poverty Bay, King Country, Wairarapa, West Coast and North Auckland.

Provincial representation of the All Blacks and their captains was much wider in former days.

RECOGNITION OVERDUE

Although this book is about the All Black test captains, it has also provided some details of all the captains who led the All Blacks against New South Wales, in the days when rugby was restricted to that state in the 1920s and 1930s. Since the Australian Rugby Union has now recognised these games as official tests, the author believes the New Zealand union should follow suit.

REMARKABLE STATISTIC

Perhaps the most surprising statistic to emerge from this book was the fact that slightly more All Black captains throughout history have come from South Island beginnings rather than the North Island. The figures are 23 from the south and 22 from the north.

Between 1929 and 1954, for instance, the All Blacks had 16 test captains of which only two, Jack Griffiths and Johnny Smith, were North Island-born.

The distribution of the All Black coaches through history is similarly surprising, but on this one the North Island comes out slightly ahead. Between 1937 and 1957, for instance, all the coaches were from the south.

The significance of these figures suggests that despite the huge population advantage enjoyed by the north, the south still holds much of the nation's rugby knowledge. This precious resource has traditionally been handed down through proud clubs and provinces on both islands.

The influence of Vic Cavanagh jnr was a prime example. Though never destined to become All Black coach, Cavanagh's methods were embraced directly by those who did, such as Dick Everest, Bob Stuart, Neil McPhail, Fred Allen, Eric Watson, and indirectly, in a later generation, by Alex Wyllie and Laurie Mains.

It is therefore of major importance that this fount of knowledge continues to penetrate New Zealand's rugby layers. Professionalism has been with us less than five years. As it takes a tighter grip, the elite academy systems are churning out our future stars. But how far down the chain will tradition and knowledge reach as club competitions, some 120 years of age, continue to struggle and wither?

A second problem is the state of the All Black captaincy. At the end of 1999 Randell, who was New Zealand's fourth-youngest captain when appointed, had passed Sir Brian Lochore's mark of 18 tests and was equal with Graham Mourie's total of 19 tests in charge of the team. In the space of only two years Randell had only Fitzpatrick (51 tests) and Sir Wilson Whineray (30) in front of him.

But how much actual leadership had he been allowed to assume? Critics observed that under John Hart he seemed incapable of making decisions on the field, seemingly because Hart was intent on pulling the strings from the sideline.

It seemed a sorry state – and one that critics of the All Black coaches holding too much sway had feared and expressed for many decades.

As new coach Wayne Smith heralded in a brave new era, the demarcation lines in the leadership roles of captain and coach urgently needed to be carefully re-drawn if All Black rugby was to return to its place in the sun. Todd Blackadder's leadership seemed to have allayed those fears.

The author's third and final concern in the new era is to see whether the type of 'intellectual' rugby player that took New Zealand to the top – and then found an outlet for leadership in some other field – will remain in the game. Can the future Whinerays, Daltons, Grahams, Stuarts, Hobbs', Mouries, Kirks and others still find a place in big rugby?

# ALL BLACK CAPTAINS VERSUS NEW SOUTH WALES AND QUEENSLAND

ALL BLACK captains led their teams against Australian opponents in matches that historically have not been classed as 'internationals'.

New Zealand's test programme proper did not begin until 1903, although the first New Zealand team under the auspices of the newly-formed New Zealand Rugby Football Union toured in 1893.

Before 1903, New Zealand's international programme had been inter-colonial matches played between 1884 and 1901 against New South Wales and Queensland, both in New Zealand and in Australia.

But between 1914 and 1929 – the year Australia achieved its remarkable 3–0 clean-sweep of the touring All Blacks – no fully representative Australian team was selected. World War I led to the demise of rugby in Queensland for many years and it was played, to any great extent, only in New South Wales. Victoria resumed inter-state matches in 1927 and Queensland in 1928.

In March 1999 the Australian Rugby Union

*This 1923 All Black team defeated New South Wales 38–11 in Wellington. Back row: Cliff Porter, Edward Stewart, Les McLean, Read Masters, Bob Tunnicliff. Middle row: T W Leslie (trainer), Ron Stewart, Jack Ormond, Les Cupples, Herman Morgan, Fred Lucas, J Taylor (masseur). Front row: 'Tuna' Swain (reserve), 'Bull' Irvine, 'Ginger' Nicholls (captain), Alf Griffiths (manager), 'Son' White, DG Fairbrother (reserve), 'Doc' Nicholls. In front: Lui Paewai, Bert Cooke (reserve), John St George (reserve)*

confirmed the status of all international matches played in Australia by New South Wales in the early 1920s as official test matches. It said NSW was effectively the Australian team.

Included in the ARU statistics were 15 matches against New Zealand. When this book was published the NZRFU had not reciprocated, leaving the record books of the two countries' performances differing.

We have included here details of all of the New Zealand captains against Australian state opponents because they make up such a large part of the early programme of the All Blacks and their predecessors.

These games were approached as 'test matches' by the New Zealand teams and the national selectors and coaches.

The author believes it is possible the NZRFU may eventually accord 'test status' to these matches. The captains were:-

WILLIAM MILLTON, 1884, V. NSW, THREE WINS
After seven years for Canterbury, Millton was chosen to lead New Zealand's first touring team, a party of 19 players chosen from Auckland, Wellington, Canterbury and Otago unions which won its eight games in Australia.

TOM ELLISON, 1893, V. NSW (2),
V. QUEENSLAND (2), FOUR WINS
Tom Ellison, considered a great pioneer of the game, led the first official New Zealand team to tour overseas. The side was unbeaten in its 11 matches, including three games against New South Wales and two with Queensland. Ellison did not play the third match against NSW.

ALF BAYLY, 1894, V. NEW SOUTH WALES, ONE LOSS
Outstanding utility back was the leading try-scorer on the 1893 New Zealand tour of Australia. He captained New Zealand to a 6–8 loss to New South Wales at Christchurch in 1894 in the first 'test' ever played in this country. Bayly led New Zealand on the 1897 tour of Australia and captained the North Island in the first inter-island match in 1894. Featured in an early rugby tragedy, when in 1899 'Barney' Armit's neck was broken when he tried to hurdle over Bayly's tackle in the Taranaki–Otago game. Armit died 11 weeks later.

DAVEY GAGE, 1896, V. QUEENSLAND, ONE WIN
Remarkable Maori utility back who played 68 matches on the NZ Native tour, was in the first

official New Zealand team and captained New Zealand against the touring Queensland side of 1896 in the only 'test' in Wellington, winning 9–0.

*JIM TILYARD: Beat off the favoured Charlie Brown as captain to lead the 1920 All Blacks to a clean sweep*

JIM TILYARD, 1920, V. NSW, THREE WINS
Jim Tilyard captained the All Blacks in all seven matches on their tour of Australia and two games at home in 1920. The side was unbeaten. Tilyard's appointment surprised some, since Charlie Brown, who had led the New Zealand Army team to South Africa the previous year, was favoured to get the job.

'MOKE' BELLIS, 1922, V. NSW, THREE 'TESTS',
WON ONE, LOST TWO
An 'automatic' selection for the All Blacks in the early 1920s, 'Moke' Bellis had toured Australia and played in all the tests against the 1921 Springboks before leading the team to Australia in 1922 and playing against New South Wales in New Zealand in 1923. His team, in which only 10 of the 24 players had represented New Zealand before, lost the series in 1923, 1–2. Weighing 14st

*MOKE BELLIS: A big wing-forward and 'automatic' choice in the early 1920s, his leadership in 1922 was not so successful and he would eventually lose out to the rising Cliff Porter*

4lb, Bellis was regarded as a big man in the positions he played in his era. Cliff Porter took the injured Bellis' place at wing-forward for the third 'test' of the 1923 series. Porter would go on to captain the 1924–25 'Invincibles' while Bellis would not gain selection.

## 'GINGER' NICHOLLS, 1923, 3RD 'TEST' V. NSW, ONE WIN

Halfback 'Ginger' Nicholls, brother of fellow All Blacks, Mark and 'Doc' Nicholls, led New Zealand to a big win in the third 'test' over the touring New South Wales team in 1923. The national selectors made many changes in the series as they sought to build a team for the 1924–25 tour to Britain and France. Nicholls played only one official test match – he had been a controversial selection ahead of provincial arch-rival Teddy Roberts for the first test against the 1921 Springboks. Standing 5ft 5in and weighing 9st 6lb, Nicholls was one of the smallest All Blacks.

## CES BADELEY, 1924 V. NSW, 1ST 'TEST', ONE LOSS

Ces Badeley was appointed captain of the 1924 All Blacks. He led the side on its preliminary tour to Australia but suffered a knee injury in the first game, against New South Wales, and did not play again on Australian soil. However, he had recovered enough to score two tries in the final build-up game, against Manawatu-Horowhenua. But after making the farewell speeches as the captain, it was announced Badeley had been replaced as captain by Cliff Porter. Against competition from Mark

Nicholls, Bert Cooke and Neil McGregor he played only two matches on the great tour, becoming the defacto back coach. Years later, Badeley said he understood the selectors had been concerned about his recurring knee injury and didn't want a non-playing captain.

## JIM DONALD, 1925, V. NSW, THREE 'TESTS', THREE WINS

Wing-forward Jim Donald led a New Zealand team to Australia in May, 1925. The NZRFU had declared members of the 1924–25 'Invincibles' team ineligible to tour.

In addition, Jimmy Duncan (1901 v. NSW at Wellington); Jimmy Hunter (1905 v. NSW, two 'tests' in Sydney); Teddy Roberts (1921 v. NSW at Christchurch); Jock Richardson (1923 v. NSW, 1st and 2nd 'tests' in NZ); Cliff Porter (1925 v. NSW at Auckland, 1926 v. NSW, three tests in Sydney, 1928 v. NSW, three 'tests' in NZ) all captained New Zealand in matches against New South Wales but are covered in their chapters elsewhere.

Pen portraits of the captains concerned are:-

**William Varnham Millton** – born February 10, 1858, Christchurch, died June 22, 1887, Christchurch; Forward; represented NZ 1884 (8 matches); 35 points (4 tries, 9 conversions); First-class record: Canterbury 1876, 78–84 (Christchurch club); delegate to CRFU 1881–86, secretary 1883–87; played cricket for Canterbury 1878–86, captaining the team against the Australian touring team in 1886; brother Edward was also member of the 1884 NZ rugby team; hero of passenger rescue from vessel *Melrose*, which was wrecked off Timaru in 1878; practised law in Christchurch; died of typhoid aged 29.

**Thomas Rangiwahia Ellison** – born November 11, 1867, Otakou; died October 2, 1904, Wellington; Forward; Represented NZ 1893 (7 matches); 20 points for NZ (2 tries, 5 conversions, 1 goal from mark); First-class record: Wellington (1885–89, 91, 92 (Poneke); NZ Native team on British tour 1888–89, scoring 113 points including 43 tries, and playing against Ireland, Wales and England; leading participant at first annual meeting of NZRFU 1893, introduced motion to adopt black jersey and silver fern for NZ team; published an early coaching manual in 1902; believed to be first Maori to enter legal profession, admitted as solicitor in 1891.

**Alfred Bayly** – born May 20, 1866, Waitara, died December 14, 1907, Wanganui; Centre who could play well at wing and five-eighth; represented NZ 1893, 94, 97 (19 matches); 22 points – 6 tries, one goal from a mark; First-class record: West Coast (North Island) 1882, Taranaki 1883, 85, 87–1901 (represented six different Taranaki clubs), North Isalnd 1894, 97; Taranaki RFU president 1899–1906, selector 1891–98, 1901, 1906; NZ selector 1901, 05; NZRFU president 1907 (died in office). Five brothers also represented Taranaki, including Walter, who played for New Zealand in 1894.

**David Richmond ('Pony') Gage** – born January 11, 1868, Kihikihi, died October 12, 1916, Wellington; Utility back; represented NZ 1893, 96 (8 matches), 6 points for NZ (2 tries); First-class record: Wellington 1887–89, 91, 92, 94, 96, 1901 (Poneke), Hawkes Bay 1890, 93, 97 (Pirates); Auckland 1895 (North Shore); North Island 1994; member of NZ Native team 1888-89, playing in 68 of the 74 matches in Britain after missing the early Australian section of the tour; was member of the first official NZ team in 1893 and the 1896 side that played Queensland; played 131 first-class matches; worked as native interpreter and later for Wellington City Council.

**James Thomas Tilyard** – born Waratah, Australia August 27, 1889, died November 1, 1966, Dannevirke; Five-eighth; represented NZ 1913, 20 (10 matches, 1 test); 20 points for NZ (4 tries, 2 conversions, 1 dropped goal); First-class record: Wellington 1908–11, 13–20 (Poneke) and Wanganui 1912 (Wanganui), 1921 (Wanganui & OB); North Island 1920; played as a halfback, five-eighth and three-quarter in 43 games for Wellington and 12 for Wanganui; made All Black debut at first five-eighth in the third test against Australia in 1913; represented Wellington at cricket 1907–08; a brother, Fred, had one game for the All Blacks, against New South Wales, 1st 'test' in Dunedin, 1923; another brother, Charlie, represented Wellington 1919, 20; Jim Tilyard's occupation was a labourer.

**Ernest Arthur ('Moke') Bellis** – born April 1, 1894, Palmerston North, died April 22, 1974, Taihape; Wing-forward and loose forward; represented NZ 1920–23 (20 matches, 3 tests); 27 points for NZ (9 tries); First-class record: Wanganui 1914, 20 (Moawhanga Huia), 1921–31

(Hautapu); North Island 1920–22; NZ Trials 1921, 24; NZ Services 1918, 19; his son, E.V. Bellis, represented Auckland and Wanganui before World War II; a grandson, Peter Bellis, played for Wanganui and became one of New Zealand's greatest lawn bowlers; 'Moke' Bellis was a butcher and then a farmer in the Taihape area.

**Harry Edgar ('Ginger') Nicholls** – born January 21, 1900, Wellington, died April 1, 1978, Wellington; Halfback; represented NZ 1921–23 (7 matches, 1 test); 3 points for NZ (1 try); First-class record Wellington 1917, 18, 20–23, 26 (Petone); North Island 1919, 22; NZ Trials 1921, 24; Wellington-Manawatu 1923; made provincial debut at 17 but faced rivalry with Teddy Roberts (1913–22 All Black); also toured NSW 1922 All Blacks; toured with 1924 'Invincibles' as correspondent after missing selection; father Syd Nicholls represented Wellington 1889, brothers Mark (1921–30) and 'Doc' (1923) played for the All Blacks, another brother, Guy, played for North Auckland 1929–30; 'Ginger' Nicholls was a Wellington City Council Transport Department employee.

**Cecil Edward Oliver Badeley** – born November 7, 1896, Auckland, died November 11, 1986, Auckland; Five-eighth; represented NZ 1920–24 (15 matches, 2 tests); 29 points for NZ (9 tries, 1 conversion); First-class record: Auckland 1916–28 (Grammar); North Auckland 1926 (Whangarei HSOB); North Island 1919–21, South Island 1922; NZ Trials 1921–27; toured Australia with 1920 All Blacks and played two tests against the 1921 Springboks, captain 1924 All Blacks to Australia; brother Vic was 1922 All Black; a publican.

**James George Donald** – born June 4, 1898, Featherston; Wing-forward; represented NZ 1920–25 (22 matches, 2 tests); 20 points for NZ (6 tries, 1 conversion); First-class record: Wairarapa 1917–30 (played for six clubs – Gladstone, Featherston Liberal, Featherston United, Masterton, Southern United and Greytown); North Island 1920, 21; NZ Trials 1921–27; Wairarapa-Bush 1921–30; first played for NZ on tour to NSW 1920, then in two tests against the Springboks in 1921; toured Australia in 1922 and again in 1925, playing in all eight games; younger brother Quentin represented NZ 1923–25; a farmer near Tauherenikau.

# THOSE WHO COULD HAVE LED BUT SERVED INSTEAD

## Saxton was one who was robbed

THERE ARE a number of All Blacks who would have captained the team in tests if circumstances had been different.

In modern times, for instance, Mike Brewer, the Otago loose forward, was long predicted to be a future All Black test captain in the late 1980s. But injuries several times hindered his career. He missed the 1991 World Cup campaign, for instance, when he failed a medical as the team departed for Britain.

When Laurie Mains took over as the All Black coach in 1992, it was an 'open secret' that Brewer was Mains' preferred choice. But again he was injured, allowing Sean Fitzpatrick to pick up the laurels and go on to lead the All Blacks in the most matches and claim the most victories in the history of the game.

Another player who was cruelly treated by circumstance was Charlie Saxton.

Readers may recall the recent adidas television advertisements which featured All Black captains such as Fred Allen, Wilson Whineray, Brian Lochore, Ian Kirkpatrick and 'Buck' Shelford pulling their All Black jersey

*ROBBED OF CHANCE: Charlie Saxton (right) who was robbed of the chance to captain the All Blacks in a test because of war, is shown with fellow 1948 Otago selectors (from left) Vic Cavanagh jnr, Arthur Marslin and Bill Duncan*

on. The new All Black major sponsor was obviously attempting to create a perceived linkage between itself and the heritage of the All Blacks.

Saxton led off the series. But he never captained the All Blacks in a test and the jersey he was wearing is his 1946 Kiwi Army jersey.

Saxton's All Black career, like so many others, was ruined by World War II. After the great Danie Craven called him the most outstanding halfback the Springboks had opposed on their series-winning 1937 tour – he met them playing for South Canterbury – Saxton became the brilliant halfback on the record-breaking All Black tour of Australia the following year.

His career was on the upward slope, for the All Blacks were being groomed for their second tour of South Africa in 1940. But the team never made it. Herr Hitler made sure of that. Most of the players spent 1940 and the next few years attending to more serious matters on Africa's deserts and elsewhere.

So it is interesting to surmise if Saxton was actually robbed of the captaincy laurels.

New Zealand's sole selector in 1938 and 1939 – the only time in history we have had a sole selector – was the great Ted McKenzie, brother of fellow All Black selector and coach, Norman, and of a famous All Black of the 1890s, William 'Offside Mac' McKenzie.

Ted McKenzie had been an All Black selector continuously since 1924 and had guided some great sides. He had the enormous responsibility of picking an All Black team to try beat the Springboks for the first time (the 1928 series had been tied, 2–2) on South African soil.

When war was declared in September, 1939, McKenzie was told by the NZRFU to submit his team to the union by December 31, 1939 – if the war was over by then.

So the team was never submitted and McKenzie did not divulge to anyone the names of the players he chose. Some have wished therefore that there had been more than one selector, since the chances of the team leaking out for posterity would have been greater.

But according to the late Winston McCarthy, the famed radio broadcaster and author, there was an occasion when Ted McKenzie bent on the subject of the 1940 team.

In 1946, in poor health and with only a few months to live, he used to visit Wellington for medical treatment. On one such occasion he spoke on the subject with Tom Morrison, a new NZRFU executive member that year and soon to become a highly successful All Black coach and later chairman of the union.

'I suppose you have wondered, like many others, whether you were in the team to go to South Africa in 1940? Well, you were – and so was your friend Charlie Saxton; in fact, I was going to recommend him as captain.'

Tom Morrison, naturally elated, said, 'Thanks, Mr McKenzie. Who else did you...'

But before he had finished the question he was interrupted with ... 'That's all you're entitled to know, Tom', and that was that, stated McCarthy in his book *Haka, the All Blacks' Story*.

# LAW CHANGES AND GAME DEVELOPMENTS

## *Were the All Black captains too clever for their own good?*

THE ALL Blacks and their captains and coaches evolved their styles through the decades, but were governed by the laws of the game that applied in their era.

By understanding the past, we can begin to understand the present and perhaps make some perceptive predictions about the future.

It would be difficult for the young, for instance, nurtured on the high-scoring rugby of the late 1990s, to be empathetic towards the rugby of the 1950s and early 1960s, when extraordinarily low scores and more frequent draws were the order of the day.

Apart from evolutionary factors such as ground conditions, player fitness/preparation and the social expectations of the day, the rules governed how the game could be played.

A feature of the rugby game, compared to some other sports, is the regularity with which the governing body was prepared to change or adjust the rules. While some law changes were effective in the short term, the continual changing indicates they often did not fulfill the intention.

Rugby's history and evolution is dotted with both innovators and coaches prepared to stretch the rules to their limit, sometimes with results far beyond what the law-makers, with their surgery, had envisaged. Some developments were positive and others negative. Some restrained the game's growth, while others emancipated it. For every coach who saw new possibilities for attack in a law change, there were dozens who sought for ways to close that option down.

Were the All Blacks sometimes too successful for their own good? Among IRFB changes were those to laws after years of All Black dominance in these areas. These concerned the banning of the 2–3–2 scrum in 1932, and the

disappearance of the marauding wing-forward as a consequence; the introduction of the maul in 1974 and the subsequent gradual disappearance of the ruck; and the introduction of higher value for tries, after the Don Clarke goal-kicking phenomenon through the 1950s and 1960s.

Some will argue these changes were not made to curb All Black success in particular. Perhaps they were coincidental? The ruck, for instance, was never popular with the British. No doubt New Zealand teams were vigorous at rucktime, sometimes overly so. The maul, which was a feature of the game mainly from lineouts in New Zealand, was the natural outcome of the demise of the standing tackle.

The increased value for a try, for instance, was a universally popular move. Scoring values had been the subject of great debate and change over many years. Ironically, today, with a differential of four points between a converted try and a penalty goal, we have witnessed the emergence of the 'professional foul', and the penalty try to combat it, to show us that law tampering remains a very inexact science.

As we shall read, the South Africans, who invented aggressive forward defence and re-invented scrum and lineout mechanics, could equally claim their dominance was softened by law changes from the powers that be.

EARLY OVERSEAS INFLUENCES ON NZ GAME
Rugby, in one shape or form, had been played in New Zealand for at least 20 years before the arrival of the British team in 1888 and the return of the NZ Native team in 1889, were to change the game beyond recognition.

The awful ploy of hacking – kicking the shins of the ball-carrier – had been legislated out of the game in 1871 (the same year the first international, between England and Scotland, was played). So hacking had a very short life in the New Zealand game. An 1877 law change in Britain had also required that players release the ball in the tackle. But the British team showed how back play could be more concerted and systematic, especially from the base of the scrum. Previously, New Zealand teams had played under the ruling that heeling from a scrum automatically put the forwards offside.

The winter after the British visit the Natives capped off their incredible 107-match tour of Australia, Britain and New Zealand by showing off their newfound skills and combinations with a successful sweep of their own country. They would disperse and influence the style of game as players, coaches and administrators to the highest level. Though the All Black Originals are generally credited with introducing specialist scrum positions to Britain, it was in fact the Natives who did so. It is described in Tom Ellison's book, published three years BEFORE the 1905 tour. The traditional method was 'first up, first down' in the front row, meaning that players filled the scrum positions as they arrived at a breakdown.

Up to that time, passing and running in a co-ordinated attacking movement did not exist in New Zealand rugby. Having obtained the ball, players just ran strongly until tackled. The art of scrummaging was to take the ball forward, not heel it back.

Ellison and William 'Offside Mac' McKenzie, two early New Zealand captains, and Jimmy Duncan, the first New Zealand test captain (1903) and the first officially-appointed test coach (1904), were to be a prime movers in the development of a more refined game in the late 1890s and early 1900s.

## 1905 ALL BLACKS

When the All Blacks first toured Britain 16 years after the Natives, the British were still playing the old scrum method. The All Blacks designated front, middle and backrow players and the front row, which consisted of two hookers rather than three front rankers, did not pack down until everyone was in position.

New Zealand played the 2–3–2 scrum and employed the wing-forward position, which was regarded as blatant cheating, through obstruction, by the British. The captain, Dave Gallaher, was a wing-forward. He fed the scrum

and would place himself between the ball and the opposition, alternately protecting his halfback or attacking the opposition's inside backs. After years of contention, the position would be outlawed in 1932 when the three-fronted scrum became compulsory.

The All Black backs introduced many successful plays and ploys that led to a huge number of points (976 for, 59 against, in 35 matches) scored. Skip and reverse passing, running against the line of attack, use of the blindside, running the fullback into the line, timing of a short pass to beat a man on his inside or a long lob pass to outflank him, the use of the short, recoverable kick or the centre kick to supporting players inside – these were some of the new tactics employed to break up defences. Hand-to-hand passing and short support among the forwards complemented the backplay. The emphasis was on combination and teamwork. The skill of the individual was a component of the whole.

The 'Originals' established the New Zealand tradition for teamwork over individual expression. British writers have commented down through the years of the ability of the Home Unions to produce brilliant backs who played as individualists. New Zealand has rather produced sound, competent, and from time to time, brilliant combinations.

British standoff halves seldom if ever ran with the ball. Their job was to move the ball away from the forwards and allow the three-quarters to use the space provided. This meant predictable play. The All Black halves often ran with the ball. A quarter of the team's 243 tries were scored by players whom New Zealand called their 'five-eighths'.

In another of his coaching books, *Rugby – A Tactical Appreciation*, former All Black coach JJ Stewart described a photo, taken from high above the action, of a try scored by the 'Originals' which was most revealing of the pattern of the day. The winger is scoring in the corner. The play has come from a lineout, near the tryline, on the opposite side of the field. The All Blacks had won the lineout on the left-hand side of the field and moved the ball through all their backs to the right-hand side. Yet not one forward has left his lineout position! Cover defence, or forwards assisting their backs to defend, was therefore not yet a feature of the game. In those times backs defended against backs.

The All Black Originals of 1905–06 had revolutionised the game with their combinations and ploys, both back and forward.

The 1907 All Blacks had many of the Originals' stars fresh from the tour to Britain the year before. Interest in Australian rugby was at a peak, with crowds of more than 50,000 watching the All Blacks.

It was soon to change, with the 'All Golds' team that featured an Australian and New Zealand players touring Britain and the introduction of professional Northern Union (rugby league) into Australasia after the tour.

But for the moment, with the magic of the newly-coined nickname ringing out, Jimmy Hunter's All Blacks and rugby in Australia held centre-stage.

With a backdrop of the Sydney Cricket Ground, the 1907 team was:
From left: Stephen Casey, Jim O'Sullivan, Alex McDonald, George Spencer, John Hogan, Frank Mitchinson, Bill Cunningham, Henry Paton, Fred Roberts, Billy Wallace, Jimmy Hunter (captain), Edgar Wylie (manager), Frank Fryer, George Gillett, Ernie Booth, Alf Eckhold, Charlie Seeling, Simon Mynott, 'Massa' Johnston, Ned Hughes, 'Bolla' Francis, Jack Colman.

Apart from Gallaher, four players from the All Black 'Originals' – Billy Stead, Jimmy Hunter, Freddie Roberts and Alex McDonald – would go on to captain the All Blacks in tests up to World War I. Gallaher, Stead, George Nicholson and McDonald would also coach or co-coach the All Blacks at various stages through the next five decades and have lasting influence on the New Zealand game.

## UP TO WORLD WAR I

In the 30 years before World War I New Zealand had played teams in Australia, Scotland, Ireland, Wales, England, France, Canada and the United States, but had not yet played a South African team. It had played 127 such matches, winning 117, losing seven and drawing three.

New Zealand innovations were, understandably, copied by other countries. Apart from those mentioned above, such tactics included aggressive loose forward play, heeling from a loose scrum (which developed into rucking), the dribbling foot rush, and the emphasis on teamwork over individual considerations.

## THE GOLDEN TWENTIES

The All Blacks were undefeated on their 1924 tour of Britain and France and shared both the 1921 series against the Springboks in New Zealand and the 1928 series in South Africa. There was great depth at national and provincial levels.

It was an era when player-coaches abounded. Cliff Porter did the job on the 1924 tour and Maurice Brownlie in 1928. Jock Richardson was also an influential test captain on the Invincibles' tour. The McKenzie brothers, Norm and Ted, would hold tremendous influence at national and provincial levels through this decade, the 1930s and the 1940s.

Forward play continued to develop, with the 2–3–2 scrum providing the near-perfect platform for backplay of superb quality.

There was more specialisation in lineouts, the ball being required to be thrown five yards, jumping for the ball and techniques to obtain and retain it being developed.

A coaching manual from the 1930s praises the attacking abilities of the 1924 All Blacks. Its advice to backs is to stand very deep on attack, and, on getting the ball, to run as hard as possible down the field. This, the manual

claims, will force your marker to run up to you at full speed. Then the runner can sidestep or swerve and beat his man. It is emphasised that this cannot be done unless the marker is forced to run up at top speed and both backlines are deep. This pattern initiated from the 2–3–2 scrum and the uncertainty of who would win each scrum. There was a vast no-man's land between the two backlines. Although forwards, particularly the wing-forward, ran back on cover defence, there was no concept of aggressive, go-forward defence by forwards.

## INTENSIVE COACHING

Up until World War II, the only intensive, widespread coaching, similar to today's specialists, attempted in New Zealand was in Southland in the 1920s. It happened after the Maroons won the Ranfurly Shield from Wellington in 1920. According to the rugby historian, Morrie Mackenzie, in his 1969 book, *Black, Black, Black*, a wave of fervour swept the province and the *Southland Times* started a campaign for a professional coach. The Southland union duly advertised the job and Ernie 'General' Booth, a member of the 1905 All Black 'Originals', was appointed. It was then pointed out that a paid professional coach was against the rules of rugby, but this problem was 'disposed of'. There were other practical difficulties. The Star club, for instance, was coached by Billy Stead and preferred it that way. Booth's best work was done in the schools and with the representative team. Southland BHS, coached by Booth, produced several All Blacks, including Rusty Page and Bert Geddes, and a crop of representative players.

## THE 1930s AND 1940s

Evolving from the old 'have it down' requirement that the ball carrier had to release the ball when held and his progress stalled, the law required that when a tackle had been made, the next player to play the ball must do so with the foot. So before a player could pick the ball up, run with it, pass it or kick it, it had to be played with the foot (a requirement which lasted until 1959).

This amendment led to the development of rucking and dribbling. The ruck came about when two or more players drove over the ball, and laid it up for the halfback. It became a highly sophisticated tactic in New Zealand rugby for many years, perfected in the Cavanagh era by the southern provinces in the 1940s and exported north in the 1950s. In the early 1950s, Canterbury, in particular, converted the dribbling aspect into vigorous driving with the ball at foot. The aim was the keep momentum going after a tackle, suck in the opposition forwards, and when the momentum stopped, feed the ball to the backs. Rucking would become less prevalent with the dropping, in 1959, of the requirement to play the ball and the ball carrier no longer having to release the ball when held (leading to the maul from 1974 onwards).

Dribbling became a valuable skill under the play the ball requirement. Rather than play it with the foot and pick it up, players toed it on, under control, after the tackle, as individuals or in packs. The skill level of the best dribblers, especially under the heavy, muddy conditions prevalent, was impressive and oppressive. The trick was in keeping the ball close to the toe, so that defenders could be intimidated not to fall on the ball. Dribbling's heyday was the 1930s and 1940s.

The 2–3–2 scrum and the wing-forward position were outlawed by the IRB in 1932. Since 1901 all New Zealand's opponents had played the 3–2–3, 3–4–1, 3–3–2 or 2–3–2 scrum. Once other countries began to specialise in scrum positions, rather than the 'first there, first down' principle, there was little advantage to New Zealand in the 2–3–2 formation. Since the resumption of international rugby after World War I the New Zealand scrum had been under increasing pressure in test matches. It was the wing-forward position that opposing nations hated.

The limitations of the 2–3–2 scrum were exposed on the 1928 tour of South Africa, when the All Blacks found it hard to win scrum ball. They experimented with the 3–2–3 scrum, but regressed back after a reversal and without perseverence. On the 1937 Springbok tour of New Zealand, five years after the law changes, New Zealand's conservatism and inability to adapt to the new scrum were severely tested, with dire results. It was still possible for a team to call a scrum instead of a lineout, and this the Boks did continuously. Even on the 1949 tour of South Africa, the All Black inadequacies against an even more sophisticated Springbok formation, were again exposed.

The period also saw a continuation of the development of backplay, right through to the late 1940s. Most of the international teams of the twenties and thirties had gifted backs and back combinations. The literature and tradition of this period confirm that fine backs proliferated in the British Isles, South Africa, Australia and New Zealand.

The influential All Black captains of the period included Frank Kilby, Jack Manchester, Ron King and 'Brushy' Mitchell. They worked in growing harmony with All Black coaches such as Billy Wallace, Vinny Meredith, Jim Burrows, Alex McDonald and Norm McKenzie. Mark Nicholls, a New Zealand selector in 1936–37, also had strong influence.

## WORLD WAR II

World War II inevitably stunted rugby. International games were discontinued. Although rugby was played by the troops overseas, particularly by New Zealand in North Africa, it was too spasmodic and too uncertain to be more than a holding action for the game. Rugby's development halted during those years, so that the game the All Blacks were playing in 1947 was the same game they played in 1939.

## FATE OF THE FORTY-NINERS

New Zealand sent a team to South Africa in 1949 with high hopes of playing expansive rugby. Its game was based on getting to the loose ball, securing possession from the ensuing ruck and providing opportunities for its backline to score tries. But it was quickly to discover its pre-war concepts were outmoded by an entirely different game. Rugby moved into the 'modern' era.

South African rugby was not affected by the war to anywhere near the same extent as the other rugby-playing nations. Its game had progressed. South Africa had long based its game on the winning of the set pieces, lineouts and scrums, from which the flyhalf dictated play, keeping opponents pinned in their own half, and an accurate goal-kicker converted subsequent scoring chances.

But this time the South Africans produced two new, powerful concepts – a new-style 3–4–1 scrum and an entirely new method of lineout strategy. The South African scrum formation meant the hooker did not bind in the traditional sense, but bound very loosely so that he could throw his feet and body towards the mouth of the scrum. The locks assisted by not pushing on the hooker, but on their props. By swinging in this position, holding onto his tighthead prop with just a handful of jersey at the collar, the hooker could be almost prone and closer to his halfback's feed at the moment of contact with the ball.

The scrum was resolved very quickly. A wide 'side' channel was created between the loosehead prop and the flanker, who packed at a wider angle. The channel was between one leg of the prop and the flanker. Sometimes the halfback had difficulty getting back in time to retrieve the possession, such was the speed of delivery.

A more significant factor was that, barring accidents, it became impossible for the opposing hooker to get near the ball. The terms 'tighthead' and 'loosehead' came into the rugby terminolgy. Gone was the aspect of uncertainty about who might win the scrum. Its instant result was that the backline in the team not putting the ball into the scrum stood up in flat defensive mode, while the other backline stood even deeper than before in attacking mode.

The 1949 All Blacks encountered the South African lineout technique of blocking. The two players at front and back of the designated jumpers, usually No 3 and No 5, would move across the line of touch and place themselves between their jumper and the opposition. The law did not at that time require space between the two lineout formations, so the ploy was within the law and very effective. The only way to counter this advantage to the Boks was to do likewise. The lineouts became a melee of blocking bodies, and very physical compared to what they had been.

Another South African lineout innovation in 1949 which would alter world rugby and stifle traditional backline attack for several decades, was the activities of its No 8. The traditional New Zealand No 8 was a tight-loose player, expected to cover-defend behind his backline and support it on attack. He was part of the lineout.

But the South African No 8s all stood out beyond their lineout, opposite the first and even the second five-eighth. They did not corner-flag, but ran aggressively at the opposition backline, which had won with the ball from the lineout.

Their activities were devastating. Five-eighths often received the ball at the same time these big, powerful No 8s arrived.

Again, the laws allowed for this to happen. There was no compulsion to be part of the lineout, as there is (as a result of those tactics) in today's game. Players getting offside were allowed a reasonable chance to get back onside before being penalised. So, for example, if a flanker or No 8 left a scrum, a ruck or maul or lineout early (before the ball had emerged), he was given leeway to get back onside by retiring. The laws, which also said that only a member of the team playing the ball could be offside, therefore allowed the No 8 to head for the opposing five-eighth from the moment the winger threw the ball into the lineout.

There might seem to be a number of counters to this tactic – standing deeper, running halfbacks, forwards retaining the ball, use of the short side. But these counters are even more easy to negate. The All Blacks devised the tactic of taking the ball to the ground to form a ruck. But the referees did not often allow the ruck and possession was lost. It was also very hard work, with little gain. The total effect was horrendous.

The 1949 tour ended the playing career of Fred Allen, the only influential All Black captain of the 1940s. That tour was also to end an era among the coaches. The long careers of Alex McDonald and Norm McKenzie would end as a new broom swept changes into the 1950s.

## CHANGES IN THE 1950s
Aggressive forward defence now became universal. After the tour, New Zealand rugby at all levels quickly adopted these South African scrum and lineout tactics. The consequences of these South African innovations were that the game worldwide underwent enormous changes in a very short space of time.

The All Blacks would be more closely guided by coaches from this time on. The coaches who would craft the new game would include Tom Morrison, Arthur Marslin, Bob Stuart, Dick Everest and later Jack Sullivan. There would be irony in the fact that Sullivan and Morrison, two of New Zealand's most exciting attacking pre-war backs, would be at the forefront of this new style that sometimes led to the stifling of backplay and initiative. Influential captains of the decade included

Peter Johnstone, Bob Stuart, Bob Duff and a young Wilson Whineray.

The loose trio became far more influential on the game. Backs were closely hounded by these marauders, as well as their immediate markers. The term 'advantage line' became increasingly important in tactics. This imaginary line was the point of restart at set play. It had always existed, but now took on new meaning. If a team in possession could be contained or forced into error behind it, the defending team had done well. Likewise, to take the ball over the gain line meant one's forwards did not have to go back and momentum could be maintained.

Defending backs were able to stand level with the scrum mouth in those days, not behind the hindmost feet of the scrum. Backlines therefore stood deeper. Those with the skill or aspirations to attack could still succeed spectacularly by moving the ball wide and having the fullback in, for the extra man or overlap. But as defensive patterns became more sophisticated and disciplined, such attacks proved less productive.

The new philosophy could be clearly seen in the play of the All Blacks in Britain and France in 1953–54, during the 1956 Springbok tour of New Zealand and in the 1959 British Lions tour of New Zealand. The principal tactic was to attack only from rucks, not set plays – and to ensure your forwards were always going forward.

The ruck law required players to be on their feet and the ball on the ground. A player held with the ball had to release it, for it to go to ground. The holding players had to allow him to do that. They could not grab the ball and start their own forward motion. Any runner, being tackled, had to release the ball and move away. This loose ball was the seed of the ensuing ruck. There could be no mauls.

There was a lot of kicking from set play by inside backs. The plan was that this would allow their forwards to go forward to the broken play phase. From the resulting ruck possession it was hoped to find opposition backs absent (caught up in the ruck) or disorganised. Accurate tactical kickers and running forwards who could handle were much prized. The backs had become very much the supporting players to the dominant forwards. There were a lot more scrums and lineouts than today, which

might seem to make the prospects dull. But some brilliant players, exciting rugby and entertaining teams emerged.

## SCRUM LAW CHANGES AND CONSEQUENCES

Law makers could see that the modern scrum techniques had removed the unpredictability from this phase. Backlines stood up in flat defence and flowing backline attack from scrums had all but disappeared. Law makers moved almost annually to change the scrum. Coaches and players had to be very adaptable. Resourceful as ever, the best of them just as quickly devised ways to gain advantage or to defeat the intentions of the law makers.

The law makers legislated many times on the put-in, where the ball must bounce, how many feet it must pass, how hookers must bind, how other positions must bind, the turning of the scrum, number of players in the scrum etc.

All attempts have failed. The reason is simply that in the positioning of the front rows, the meshing of the heads inevitably means one team is going to have the loosehead and its hooker closer to the put-in. It is incredible that until 1949 players, coaches and administrators failed to appreciate that, or the advantages and limitations of it.

Though they still make frequent scrum law changes, including significant adaptions in 1996, administrators have given up on the unpredictability factor. Teams base their scrum tactics around ensuring their loosehead ball is quality possession, while the defending team tries to damage the quality of the ball won by its opponent by exerting extreme pressure.

## CHANGING PERCEPTIONS IN TACTICS

Not many tries were scored in matches in the 1950s and 1960s. Game outcomes tended to depend on goals kicked, especially as the primary tactic was to play the game in their half, wait for points and not to make mistakes.

However, this did not curb the public interest in big rugby. Its appetite seemed insatiable. Major rugby grounds all over the world expanded to accommodate the need. There was still a lot of drama. A 6–3 score in a test or a Ranfurly Shield match did not produce a call for expansive action by the crowd. It wanted the game tied up and safely won.

But this was at the top level. For players of all abilities it was not as much fun as it might have been. The law makers realised that backlines had to be given more space to operate. The momentous law changes of 1963 provided this.

## WATERSHED WAS 1963

Wilson Whineray was easily the most influential All Black captain of the 1960s, a decade in which the All Blacks never lost a series between 1960 and 1970. He set the platform for captains such as John Graham, Brian Lochore and Colin Meads to follow. The stand-out All Black coaches of the 1960s were Neil McPhail and Fred Allen. They would be aided by these law amendments.

The lineout changes, and the offside requirements, of 1963 by the IRB meant the two backlines would be 20 yards (10 yards back from each lineout formation) apart until the lineout was over. Loose forwards off the back of the lineout were restricted. The team throwing in decided where the last man would stand and thus the length of the lineout.

But the game did not go back to the way it had been played before Hennie Muller. The dynamism of the loose forward trio had become all but irresistible. Loose forwards, hunting as a unit, had changed the game forever. They were now more restricted, but no law could completely stifle their speed, skills and intentions.

Loose forward philosophy became more scientific in the 1960s and beyond. Though each position became more specialised, especially the openside loosie, their role as a unit expanded. Increasingly, they were the highly-skilled attacking supporters of their backs. But their original role, to disrupt the opposition's inside backs from all set phases, also became more sophisticated. New Zealand would lead the world in producing, *en masse*, this type of player and developing his role in the game. However, the other countries, particularly South Africa, were not too slow in following.

Scrum law changes at this time helped provide more opportunities for inside backs. Previously, the offside line was the ball (e.g. as the ball was moved back through the scrum, that was the offside line). Halfbacks were under considerable pressure. They could receive the ball at the same time as an opposing halfback and his two flankers if the scrum ball was too slow.

The new offside line was the hindmost feet of the scrum. Only the defending halfback could

advance past that point. Flankers had to stay bound until the scrum was over, unless they stepped backwards, behind the hindmost foot of their scrum.

The new laws worked. But at the same time, they encouraged the development of new tactics and game styles that were not envisaged.

## THE NEW SCRUM TACTICS

Scrum ball was still produced quickly. So the flankers, though they had to remain bound, then went about their jobs much as before. But if scrum ball could be slowed, flankers would not be able to anticipate when they would leave the scrum. Slow ball became desirable sometimes. Another law change allowed the No 8 to detach and pick up the ball and pass or run. Halfbacks became more adroit at spoiling their opposite's possession. The 1971 British Lions produced the scrum tactic of delivering the ball on the right-hand side of their No 8's feet, thus preventing the opposing halfback from getting near it.

The Lions also showed that flankers might as well push. The sustained scrum push, with long, drawn-out scrums, resulted. Now New Zealand teams had to practise their scrummaging. Long, hard hours had to be devoted to the scrum's setting and dynamics. Scrum machines appeared. Push-over tries became part of the tactics. In spite of a vast improvement in All Black scrumming, particularly from coaches Bob Duff and JJ Stewart, the short time for preparation for home series tests still held terrors.

When the Lions toured New Zealand again in 1977, they reduced the All Blacks to the ignominious, but still legal three-man scrum tactic at one point.

All Black captains who guided test sides through this testing period included Meads, Ian Kirkpatrick, Andy Leslie, Tane Norton and Graham Mourie. The coaches included Ivan Vodanovich, Duff, Stewart, Jack Gleeson and Eric Watson. But overall, the decade of the 1970s progressed with remarkably steady improvement for the All Black team.

## THE ARRIVAL OF THE MAUL

The term 'maul' had not been part of rugby's terminolgy since the last century. But in 1974 a sentence appeared in the law books which stated that 'a maul ends a tackle' and went on to define what a maul was. It is unclear why the change was made, but appears to have been a British initiative.

However, it was to alter the game considerably. As with previous changes, it would eventually lead to the development of the most negative of modern rugby's trends, killing the ball; which would mean even more drastic rule surgery in the early 1990s to free the game up again. Safety, at scrum, ruck and maul, had also been foremost in the minds of the legislators, as they strove to eliminate serious injuries among developing players, throughout the 1980s.

The maul, in short, meant the player with the ball no longer had to release it when surrounded by players and held. It would lead to long, drawn-out pushing and pulling, with ball unseen by players and spectators. The law makers could not have foreseen this, or what it spawned – such as the rolling maul, the pile-up or the changes in tactics that would all emerge.

The most influential All Black captains of the 1980s included Mourie, Andy Dalton, Jock Hobbs, David Kirk, Buck Shelford and Gary Whetton. The All Black coaches confronted by these developments made light of them and the 1980s was New Zealand's most consistently successful decade. The coaches were Peter Burke, Bryce Rope, Brian Lochore and Alex Wyllie.

Rugby had virtually returned to its pulling-pushing style in the 19th century, if not quite to the Eton Wall Game. The solution then had been, as stated earlier, for players to be required to 'have it down'. Not to do so meant being hacked (kicked on the shins) in pre-referee days, and penalised in the twentieth century. In the 1990s, it would mean a possibly even worse result – the loss of possession.

THE GAME OF TODAY
All Black rugby saw three coaches, Alex Wyllie, Laurie Mains and John Hart, in charge in the 1990s, and each played their role in the evolutionary process. The game has altered considerably in that comparatively short time.

Today's game plan will inevitably centre upon retaining possession and maintaining continuity. Though the games played by the All Blacks and the Super 12 teams, in particular, have been spectacular, the concepts of contestability and unpredictability have been

further eroded. Lifting in lineouts and the new tackled ball rule requiring support players remain on their feet when claiming the ball, have resulted in two out of the three great sources of possession becoming more predictable. The lineout situation is similar to the 'loosehead' of our scrums.

In June, 1997, the IRB produced the Cape Town Charter criticising the predictability of ruck-maul possession, in particular, and seeking more consistency from referees. Written by Syd Millar, an experienced law-maker and former great player, captain and coach, it stated how it hoped the modern game would be played. The move brought a perhaps too-strong barrage of criticism from New Zealand's leading coaches, enamoured with the game's new free-flowing impetus.

The situation had worsened by 1999, when ever-strong defensive patterns had taken the game out of balance. Australia, undoubtedly the finest team, won the World Cup with an incredibly efficient defensive style. But the predictability factor would indeed be looked at by special IRB laws experts at the end of 1999 and the situation improved.

Additionally, while the changes have already led to the introduction of more streamlined forwards (and fewer behemoths), the need for bigger, stronger backs in most positions may not be so welcome. This trend had been on the move, particularly out on the wings, since the late 1980s. But the need for stronger backs, faced by, or delivering the more frequent bone-jarring, head-on tackles during the continuity phases of possession, seems obvious. The attrition rate, especially on loose forwards at the tackled ball phase, and combined with the demands of the new professional schedule, is another factor being fully tested in both hemispheres.

The designated runner, usually strong forwards but occasionally big wingers, has been with the game for several decades (remember 'Willie Away'?), used to take a defender out of the backline after the ensuing ruck, rather than to elude him. But it is now a far more frequently used tactic, as teams pursue the ideal of perhaps a dozen tackled-ball phases won. The range of refereeing interpretations of what is then allowed, ball on or near the ground, is enormous and obviously one of the concerns to the IRB.

The advantage line's importance is now greater than ever. Teams are seldom prepared to chance a ploy, in the interests of long-term gain, behind that line. This has produced the strong head-on marking described above. Retention of the ball is everything. Kicking, for re-possession, has largely been eliminated, while to become isolated as the ball-carrier is the fate most feared of all. Midfield backs seek the welcoming embrace of their own forwards, running on the tangent, with ever more frequency, rather than send the ball out to unsupported three-quarters.

Teams have moved swiftly to negate the advantages of the new lineout lifting laws. The midfield becomes cluttered soon after the ball has been spectacularly taken off the top of the lineout and delivered to the dive-passing halfback. Counters to this type of anticipatory defence have so far included the equally spectacular eight-or-more lineout drive, based on the ball winner, and moving at an irresistable and high rate of knots.

Conversely, the new scrum rules, requiring all hands to remain on deck, have seen tries scored directly from set scrums, especially on the blindside, where the well executed move can be impossible to defend.

The All Blacks under John Hart cut a virtually invincible swathe through international rugby in 1996 and 1997, but then the impetus petered out. Teams that succeeded in beating them, such as Australia, South Africa and France, did not attempt to copy the All Blacks' methods. Instead, they devised new tactics and set new standards. History always told us that sooner, rather than later, they would.

# NEW ZEALAND'S
# INTERNATIONAL RECORD

NEW ZEALAND'S test programme proper did not begin until 1903, although the first New Zealand team under the auspices of the newly-formed New Zealand Rugby Football Union toured in 1893.

Before 1903, New Zealand's international programme had been inter-colonial matches played between 1884 and 1901 against New South wales and Queensland, both in New Zealand and in Australia.

But between 1914 and 1929 – the year Australia achieved its remarkable and only 3–0 clean-sweep of the touring All Blacks – no fully representative Australian team was selected. World War I led to the demise of rugby in Queensland for many years and it was played, to any great extent, only in New South Wales.

Victoria resumed inter-state matches in 1927 and Queensland in 1928.

We included all of the matches played by New Zealand against its Australian state opponents because they make up such a large part of the early programme of the All Blacks and their predecessors. In March 1999 the Australian Rugby Union confirmed the status of all international matches played in Australia by New South Wales in the early 1920s as official test matches. It said NSW was effectively the Australian team. Included in the ARU statistics were 15 matches against New Zealand. When this book was published the NZRFU had not reciprocated, leaving the record books of the two countries' performances differing.

**1884:** Tour to Australia – NZ beat NSW, 11–0, 21–2, 16–0.

**1893:** Tour to Australia – NZ beat NSW 17–8, lost 3–25, won 16–0; beat Queensland 14–3, 36–0.

**1894:** NSW tour to NZ – NZ lost to NSW 6–8.

**1896:** Queensland tour to NZ – NZ lost to Queensland 0–9.

**1897:** Tour to Australia – NZ beat NSW 13–8, lost 8–22, won 26–3; beat Queensland 16–5, 24–6.

**1901:** NSW tour to NZ – NZ lost to NSW 3–20.

**1903:** Tour to Australia – NZ beat Australia 22–3.

**1904:** Great Britain tour to NZ – NZ won 9–3.

**1905:** Tour to Australia – NZ beat NSW 19–0, drew 8–8.

**1905:** Australia tour to NZ – NZ lost to Australia 3–14.

**1905–06:** Tour of British Isles – NZ beat Scotland 12–7, beat Ireland 15–0, beat England 15–0, lost to Wales 0–3.

**1907:** Tour to Australia – NZ beat Australia 26–6, 14–5, drew 5–5.

**1908:** Anglo-Welsh tour to NZ – NZ won 32–5, drew 3–3, won 29–0.

**1910:** Tour to Australia – NZ beat Australia 6–0, lost 0–11, won 28–13.

**1913:** Tour to USA and Canada – NZ beat All America 51–3.

**1913:** Australia tour to NZ – NZ beat Australia 30–5, 25–13, 16–5.

**1914:** Tour to Australia – NZ beat Australia 5–0, 17–0, 22–7.

**1920:** Tour to Australia – NZ beat NSW 26–15, 14–0, 24–13.

**1921:** South Africa tour to NZ – NZ lost 5–13, won 9–5, drew 0–0.

**1921:** NSW tour to NZ – NZ lost 0–17.

**1922:** Tour to Australia – NZ beat NSW 26–19, lost 8–14, lost 6–8.

**1923:** NSW tour to NZ – NZ won 19–9, 34–6, 38–11.

**1924:** Tour to Australia – NZ lost to NSW 16–20, won 21–5, won 38–8.

**1924:** Tour to British Isles, France and Canada – NZ beat Ireland 6–0, beat Wales 19–0, beat England 17–11, beat France 30–6.

**1925:** Tour to Australia – NZ beat NSW 26–3, 4–0, 11–3.

**1925:** NSW tour to NZ, – NZ won 36–10.

**1926:** Tour to Australia – NZ lost to NSW 20–26, won 11–6, won 14–0.

**1928:** Tour to South Africa – NZ lost to South Africa 0–17, won 7–6, lost 6–11, won 13–5.

**1928:** NSW tour to NZ – NZ won 15–12, 16–14, lost 8–11.

**1929:** Tour to Australia – NZ lost to Australia 8–9, 9–17, 13–15.

**1930:** British Isles tour to NZ – NZ lost 3–6, won 13–10, 15–10, 22–8.

**1931:** Australia tour to NZ – NZ beat Australia 20–13.

**1932:** Tour to Australia – NZ lost to Australia 17–22, won 21–3, 21–13.

**1934:** Tour to Australia – NZ lost to Australia 11–25, drew 3–3.

**1935:** Tour of British Isles and Canada – NZ beat Scotland 18–8, beat Ireland 17–9, lost to Wales 12–13, lost to England 0–13.

**1936:** Australia tour to NZ – NZ beat Australia 11–6, 38–13.

**1937:** South Africa tour to NZ – NZ won 13–7, lost 6–13, 6–17.

**1938:** Tour to Australia – NZ beat Australia 24–9, 20–14, 14–6.

**1946:** Australia tour to NZ – NZ beat Australia 31–8, 14–10.

**1947:** Tour to Australia – NZ beat Australia 13–5, 27–14.

**1949:** Tour to South Africa – NZ lost 11–15, 6–12, 3–9, 8–11.

**1949:** Australia tour to NZ – NZ lost 6–11, 9–16.

**1950:** British Isles tour to NZ – NZ drew 9–9, won 8–0, 6–3, 11–8.

**1951:** Tour to Australia – NZ beat Australia 8–0, 17–11, 16–6.

**1952:** Australia tour to NZ – NZ lost 9–14, won 15–8.

**1953–54:** Tour to British Isles, France and Canada – NZ lost to Wales 8–13, beat Ireland 14–3, beat England 5–0, beat Scotland 3–0, lost to France 0–3.

**1955:** Australia tour to NZ – NZ beat Australia 16–8, 8–0, lost 3–8.

**1956:** South Africa tour to NZ – NZ beat South Africa 10–6, lost 3–8, won 17–10, 11–5.

**1957:** Tour to Australia, – NZ won 25–11, 22–9.

**1958:** Australia tour to NZ – NZ beat Australia 25–3, lost 3–6, won 17–8.

**1959:** British Isles tour to NZ – NZ won 18–17, 11–8, 22–8, lost 6–9.

**1960:** Tour to South Africa – NZ lost 0–13, won 11–3, drew 11–11, lost 3–8.

**1961:** France tour to NZ – NZ won 13–6, 5–3, 32–3.

**1962:** Tour to Australia, – NZ beat Australia 20–6, 14–5.

**1962:** Australia tour to NZ – NZ drew with Australia 9–9, won 3–0, 16–8.

**1963:** England tour to NZ – NZ won 21–11, 9–6.

**1963–64:** Tour to British Isles, France and Canada – NZ beat Ireland 6–5, beat Wales 6–0, beat England 14–0, drew with Scotland 0–0, beat France 12–3.

**1964:** Australia tour to NZ – NZ beat Australia 14–9, 18–3, lost 5–20.

**1965:** South Africa tour to NZ – NZ won 6–3, 13–0, lost 16–19, won 20–3.

**1966:** British Isles tour to NZ – NZ won 20–3, 16–12, 19–6, 24–11.

**1967:** Australia tour to NZ – NZ beat Australia 29–9.

**1967:** Tour to British Isles, France and Canada – NZ beat England 23–11, beat Wales 13–6, beat France 21–15, beat Scotland 14–3.

**1968:** Tour to Australia – NZ beat Australia 27–11, 19–18.

**1968:** France tour to NZ – NZ won 12–9, 9–3, 19–12.

**1969:** Wales tour to NZ – NZ won 19–0, 33–12.

**1970:** Tour to South Africa – NZ lost 6–17, won 9–8, lost 3–14, lost 17–20.

**1971:** British Isles tour to NZ – NZ lost 3–9, won 22–12, lost 3–13, drew 14–14.

**1972:** Australia tour to NZ – NZ won 29–6, 30–17, 38–3.

**1972–73:** Tour to British Isles, France and North America – NZ beat Wales 19–16, beat Scotland 14–9, beat England 9–0, drew with Ireland 10–10, lost to France 6–13.

**1973:** England tour to NZ – NZ lost 10–16.

**1974:** Tour to Australia – NZ beat Australia 11–6, drew 16–16, won 16–6.

**1974:** Tour to Ireland, Wales and England – NZ beat Ireland 15–6.

**1975:** Scotland tour to NZ – NZ won 24–0.

**1976:** Ireland tour to NZ – NZ won 11–3.

**1976:** Tour to South Africa – NZ lost 7–16, won 15–9, lost 10–15, 14–15.

**1977:** British Isles tour to NZ – NZ won 16–12, lost 9–13, won 19–7, 10–9.

**1977:** Tour to France – NZ lost 13–18, won 15–3.

**1978:** Australia tour to NZ – NZ won 13–12, 22–6, lost 16–30.

**1978:** Tour to British Isles – NZ beat Ireland 10–6, beat Wales 13–12, beat England 16–6, beat Scotland 18–9.

**1979:** France tour to NZ – NZ won 23–9, lost 19–24.

**1979:** Tour to Australia – NZ lost to Australia 6–12.

**1979:** Tour to Scotland and England – NZ beat Scotland 20–6, beat England 10–9.

**1980:** Tour to Australia – NZ lost to Australia 9–13, won 12–9, lost 10–26.

**1980:** Tour to Wales – NZ beat Wales 23–3.

**1981:** Scotland tour to NZ – NZ won 11–4, 40–15.

**1981:** South Africa tour to NZ – NZ won 14–9, lost 12–24, won 25–22.

**1981:** Tour to Romania and France – NZ beat Romania 14–6, beat France 13–9, 18–6.

**1982:** Australia tour to NZ – NZ beat Australia 23–16, lost 16–19, won 33–18.

**1983:** British Isles tour to NZ – NZ won 16–12, 9–0, 15–8, 38–6.

**1983:** Tour to Australia – NZ beat Australia 18–8.

**1983:** Tour to Scotland and England – NZ drew with Scotland 25–25, lost to to England 9–15.

**1984:** France tour to NZ – NZ beat France 10–9, 31–18.

**1984:** Tour to Australia – NZ lost to Australia 9–16, won 19–15, 25–24.

**1985:** England tour to NZ – NZ won 18–13, 42–15.

**1985:** Australia tour to NZ – NZ beat Australia 10–9.

**1985:** Tour to Argentina – NZ won 33–20, drew 21–21.

**1986:** France tour to NZ – NZ won 18–9.

**1986:** Australia tour to NZ – NZ lost to Australia 12–13, won 13–12, lost 9–22.

**1986:** Tour to France – NZ won 19–7, lost 3–16.

**1987:** 1st World Cup – NZ beat Italy 70–6, beat Fiji 74–13, beat Argentina 46–15, beat Scotland 30–3, beat Wales 49–6, beat France (final) 29–9.

**1987:** Tour to Australia – NZ beat Australia 30–16.

**1988:** Wales tour to NZ – NZ won 52–3, 54–9.

**1988:** Tour to Australia – NZ beat Australia 32–7, drew 19–19l, won 30–9.

**1989:** France tour to NZ – NZ won 25–17, 34–20.

**1989:** Argentina tour to NZ – NZ won 60–9, 49–12.

**1989:** Australia tour to NZ – NZ beat Australia 24–12.

**1989:** Tour to Wales and Ireland – NZ beat Wales 34–9, beat Ireland 23–6.

**1990:** Scotland tour to NZ – NZ won 31–16, 21–18.

**1990:** Australia tour to NZ – NZ beat Australia 21–6, 27–17, lost 9–21.

**1990:** Tour to France – NZ beat France 24–3, 30–12.

**1991:** Tour to Argentina – NZ beat Argentina 28–14, 36–6.

**1991:** Tour to Australia – NZ lost to Australia 12–21.

**1991:** Australia in NZ – NZ beat Australia 6–3.

**1991:** 2nd World Cup – NZ beat England 18–12, beat USA 46–6, beat Italy 31–21, beat Canada 29–13, lost to Australia (semi-final) 6–16, beat Scotland (play-off for 3rd) 13–6.

**1992:** World XV in NZ – NZ lost to World XV 28–14, won 54–26, 26–15.

**1992:** Ireland tour of NZ – NZ beat Ireland 24–21, 59-6.

**1992:** Tour to Australia – NZ lost to Australia 15–16, 17–19, won 26–23.

**1992:** Tour to South Africa – NZ beat South Africa 27–24.

**1993:** British Isles tour of NZ – NZ won 20–18, lost 7–20, won 30–13.

**1993:** Australia in NZ – NZ beat Australia 25–10.

**1993:** Western Samoa tour of NZ – NZ beat W. Samoa 35–13.

**1993:** Tour of Scotland and England – NZ beat Scotland 51–15, lost to England 9–15.

**1994:** France tour to NZ – NZ lost to France 8–22, 20–23;

**1994:** South Africa tour to NZ – NZ beat South Africa 22–14, 13–9, drew 18–18.

**1994:** NZ in Australia – NZ lost to Australia, 16–20.

**1995:** Canada tour to NZ – NZ beat Canada 73–7.

**1995:** 3rd World Cup – NZ beat Ireland 43–19, beat Wales 34–9, beat Japan 145–17, beat Scotland 48–30, beat England 45–29, lost to South Africa (final) 12–15.

**1995:** NZ beat Australia 28–16 at Auckland and 34–23 at Sydney.

**1995:** Tour to Italy and France – NZ beat Italy 70–6, lost to France 15–22, beat France 37–12.

**1996:** Western Samoa tour of NZ – NZ beat W. Samoa 51–10.

**1996:** Scotland tour of NZ – NZ beat Scotland 62–31, 36–12.

**1996:** Tri-Nations Series – NZ beat Australia 43–6, beat South Africa 15–11, beat Australia 32–25, beat South Africa 29–18.

**1996:** Tour to South Africa – NZ beat South Africa 23–19, 33–26, lost to South Africa 22–32.

**1997:** Fiji tour to NZ – NZ beat Fiji 71–5.

**1997:** Argentina tour to NZ – NZ beat Argentina 93–8, 62–10.

**1997:** NZ beat Australia 30–13, Tri-Nations Series – beat South Africa 35–32, beat Australia 33–18, beat South Africa 55–35, beat Australia 36–24.

**1997:** beat Ireland 63–15; beat England 25–8, beat Wales 42–7; drew with England 26–26.

**1998:** beat England 64–22, beat England 40–10; lost to Australia 16–24, lost to South Africa 3–13, lost to Australia 23–27, lost to South Africa 23–24, lost to Australia 14–19.

**1999:** beat Samoa 71–13; beat France 54–7; beat Soth Africa 28–0; beat Australia 34–15; beat South Africa 34–18; lost to Australia 7–28. World Cup: beat Tonga 45–9; beat England 30–16; beat Italy 101–3; beat Scotland 30–18; lost to France 31–43. lost to South Africa 18–22 (play-off for 3rd and 4th).

# BIBLIOGRAPHY

*Lochore, An Authorised Biography*, Alex Veysey, Gary Caffell and Ron Palenski, Hodder Moa Beckett, 1996.

*They Led the All Blacks*, Lindsay Knight, Rugby Press, 1991.

*Super Sid*, Bob Howitt, Rugby Press, 1978.

*Mexted – Pieces of Eight*, Alex Veysey, Rugby Press, 1986.

*Boots 'n all*, Andy Haden, Rugby Press, 1984.

*High Flying Kiwis*, Mark Taylor, Rugby Press, 1988.

*Colin Meads All Black*, Alex Veysey, Collins, 1974.

*The Art of Rugby Football*, Tom Ellison, Geddis and Blomfield, 1902.

*Pathway Among Men*, Jim Burrows, Whitcombe and Tombs, 1974.

*All Black Magic*, Terry McLean, Reeds, 1968.

*Battling the Boks*, Terry McLean, Reeds, 1970.

*The Boot*, Don Clarke and Pat Booth, Reeds, 1966.

*Listen, It's a Goal*, Winston McCarthy, Pelham Books, 1973.

*Makers of Champions – Great New Zealand Coaches*, Joseph Romanos, Mills Publications, 1987.

*One Hundred Great Rugby Characters*, Joseph Romanos and Grant Harding, Rugby Press, 1991.

*I, George Nepia*, George Nepia and Terry McLean, Reeds, 1963.

*The Tour of the Third All Blacks*, 1935, Charlie Oliver and Eric Tindill, Sporting Publications, 1936.

*The Bob Scott Story*, Bob Scott and Terry McLean, Herbert Jenkins, 1956.

*Fergie*, Alex Veysey, Whitcoulls, 1976.

*Men in Black*, RH Chester and NAC McMillan, Moa, 1978.

*Centenary – 100 Years of All Black Rugby*, RH Chester and NAC McMillan, Moa, 1984.

*Shield Fever*, Lindsay Knight, Rugby Press, 1986.

*The Visitors, The History of International Rugby Teams in New Zealand;* RH Chester and NAC McMillan, Moa, 1990.

*The Encyclopaedia of New Zealand Rugby*, RH Chester and NAC McMillan, Moa 1981; 1998 edition, Ron Palenski.

*New Zealand Rugby Almanack* (various editions), Arthur Carman, Arthur Swan and Read Masters, Sporting Publications.

*New Zealand Rugby Almanack* (various editions), RH Chester and NAC McMillan, Moa.

*Rugby Annual* (various editions), Bob Howitt, Moa.

*Mud in Your Eye*, Chris Laidlaw, Reeds, 1973.

*The Fourth All Blacks, 1953–54,* John Hayhurst, Longmans, 1954.

*Rugby Greats,* Volumes One and Two, Bob Howitt, Moa, 1975 and 1982.

*Kirky*, Lindsay Knight, Rugby Press, 1979.

*Haka! The All Blacks Story*, Winston McCarthy, Pelham Books, 1968.

*New Zealand Rugby Legends,* Terry McLean, Moa, 1987.

*Graham Mourie Captain*, Ron Palenski, Moa, 1982.

*Loveridge – Master Halfback,* Ron Palenski, Moa, 1985.

*The Complete Rugby Footballer*, D Gallaher and WJ Stead, Methuen, 1906.

*With the All Blacks in Great Britain, France, Canada and Australia, 1924–25*, Read Masters, Christchurch Press, 1928.

*With the All Blacks in Springbokland 1928*, MF Nicholls, LF Watkins, 1928.

*Round the World With the All Blacks 1953–54*, Winston McCarthy, Sporting Publications, 1954.

*The Battle for the Rugby Crown*, Terry McLean, Reeds, 1956.

*Famous Fullbacks*, Joseph Romanos, Rugby Press, 1989.

*All Blacks in Chains*, JM Mackenzie, Truth, 1960.

*On With the Game*, Norman McKenzie, Reeds, 1960.

*Football is 15*, Gordon Slatter, Whitcombe and Tombs, 1970.

*On the Ball,* Gordon Slatter, Whitcombe and Tombs, 1970.

*The Geriatrics*, Lindsay Knight, Moa, 1986.

*Ebony and Ivory*, Alex Veysey, Moa, 1984.

*Willie Away,* Terry McLean, Reeds, 1964.

*New Zealand Rugby Football Union,* Archive Interviews (various), 1990.

*New Zealand Rugby Museum Newsletter* (various), Bob Luxford.

*Forerunners of the All Blacks*, Greg Ryan, Canterbury University Press, 1993.

*History of New Zealand Rugby Football*, Volumes 1–4, Vols 1 & 2 by AC Swan; Vols 3 & 4 by RH Chester and NAC McMillan.

*Straight From the Hart,* Paul Thomas, Moa Beckett, 1993.

*Grizz the Legend*, Phil Gifford, Rugby Press, 1991.

*Laurie Mains*, Bob Howitt and Robin McConnell, Rugby Press, 1996.

*For the Record, The Allan Hewson Story*, Ian Gault, Rugby Press, 1984.

*Black Magic*, Graham Hutchins, Moa, 1988.

*Beegee, the Bryan Williams Story*, Bob Howitt, Rugby Press, 1981.

*Old Heroes, the 1956 Springbok Tour and the Lives Beyond*, Warwick Roger, Hodder and Stoughton, 1991.

*All Blacks Tour 1963–64,* Andrew Mulligan, Whitcombe and Tombs, 1964.

*Rugby in My Time,* Winston McCarthy, Reed, 1958.

*Springbok and Silver Fern,* Reg Sweet, Reed, 1960.

*Great Days in New Zealand Rugby,* Terry McLean, Reed, 1959.

*All Blacks Versus Springboks,* Graeme Barrow, Heinemann, 1981.

*Trek Out of Trouble,* Noel Holmes, Whitcombe and Tombs, 1960.

*Beaten by the Boks,* Terry McLean, Reed, 1960.

*All Black Magic, The Triumphant Tour of the 1967 All Blacks,* Terry McLean, Reed, 1968.

*Up Front, The Story of the All Black Scrum,* Graeme Barrow, Heinemann, 1985.

*The Best of McLean,* Terry McLean, Hodder and Stoughton, 1984.

*Between the Posts, A New Zealand Rugby Anthology,* edited by Ron Palenski, Hodder and Stoughton, 1989.

*Danie Craven on Rugby,* Danie Craven, Beerman Publishers, 1952.

*Springboks Down the Years,* Danie Craven, Howard Timmins Ltd, 1956.

*Buck, The Wayne Shelford Story,* Wynne Gray, Moa, 1990.

*McKechnie, Double All Black,* Lynn McConnell, Craigs Publishers, 1983.

*Out of the Ruck, A Selection of Rugby Writing,* edited by David Parry-Jones, Pelham Books, 1986.

*Fred Allen on Rugby,* Fred Allen and Terry McLean, Casswell, 1970.

*Rugby on Attack,* Ron Jarden, Whitcombe and Tombs, 1961.

*They Missed the Bus,* Kirkpatrick's All Blacks of 1972–73, Terry McLean, Reed, 1973.

*Cock of the Rugby Roost,* France-New Zealand 1961, Terry McLean, Reed, 1961.

*Kirwan – Running on Instinct,* Paul Thomas, Moa, 1992.

*Inga the Winger,* Bob Howitt, Rugby Press, 1993.

*The Game, the Goal – The Grant Fox Story,* Alex Veysey, 1992.

*Brothers in Arms – The Alan and Gary Whetton Story,* Paul Lewis, Moa, 1991.

*Iceman – The Michael Jones Story,* Robin McConnell, Rugby Press, 1994.

*Fronting Up – The Sean Fitzpatrick Story,* Stephen O'Meagher, Moa Beckett, 1994.

*Magic Matches, Great Days of New Zealand Rugby,* Graham Hutchins, Moa, 1991.

*After the Final Whistle,* Spiro Zavos, Whitcoulls, 1979.

*Winter of Discontent, the 1977 Lions in NZ,* Terry McLean, Reed, 1977.

*Grant Batty,* Bob Howitt, Rugby Press, 1977.

*Kings of Rugby, the British Lions 1959 New Zealand Tour,* Terry McLean, Reed, 1960.

*Springboks at Bay,* Maxwell Price, Longmans, 1956.

*Rugger, the Man's Game,* EHD Sewell and OL Owen, Hollis and Carter, 1950.

*The Fourth Springbok Tour of NZ,* RJ Urbahn and DB Clarke, Hicks Smith and Sons, 1965.

*Now is the Hour, the 1965 Springboks in NZ,* AC Parker, Whitcombe and Tombs, 1965.

*The Bok Busters,* Terry McLean, Reed, 1965.

*Rugby Triumphant,* Don Cameron, Hodder and Stoughton, 1981.

*Battle of the Giants,* CO Medworth, Reed, 1960.

*All Blacks Retreat From Glory,* Don Cameron, Hodder and Stoughton, 1980.

*All Black Power,* Terry McLean, Reed, 1968.

*Red Dragons of Rugby,* Terry McLean, Reed, 1969.

*Goodbye to Glory, The 1976 All Black Tour to South Africa,* Terry McLean, Reed, 1976.

*Rugby and be Damned, All Blacks' Tour of South Africa 1970,* Gabriel David; Hicks, Smith and Sons Ltd, 1970.

*Tour of the Century, the All Blacks in Wales 1980,* Keith Quinn, Methuen, 1981.

*The Mighty Lions,* John Reason, Whitcombe and Tombs, 1971.

*The Encyclopaedia of World Rugby,* Keith Quinn, Shoal Bay Press, 1991.

*New Zealand Rugby Skills and Tactics,* Ivan Vodanovich technical editor, Lansdowne Press, 1982.

*Great Rugby Players,* David Norrie, Hamlyn, 1980.

*Otago Rugby Football Union Annual* 1956

*Rugby in Blue and Gold,* Dave McLaren

*Record of Otago Rugby 1882–1940,* A C. Swan

*Rugby Players Who Have Made New Zealand Famous,* R.A. Stone

*The Pride of Southern Rebels,* Sean O'Hagan, Pilgrims South Press, 1981.

*Great Men of New Zealand Rugby,* Tillman.

*Winters of Revenge,* Spiro Zavos, Penguin, 1997.

*Change of Hart,* Paul Thomas, Moa Beckett, 1997.

*The Canterbury Rugby History,* Larry Saunders, 1979.

*Black, Black, Black,* J.M. Mackenzie, Minerva, 1969.

*Inside the All Blacks,* Robin McConnell, Harper Collins, 1998.

*Ka Mate! Ka Mate!* Spiro Zavos, Viking, 1998

*The Visitors,* Chester and McMillan, Moa, 1990

*The Power Behind the All Blacks, the Untold Story of the All Black Coaches,* by Paul Verdon, Penguin, 1999

# INDEX

Numbers in **bold** type refer to photographs.

(overleaf) SUMMIT MEETING: Twenty-one All Black test captains got together in Wellington in August, 1984. Standing, from left: Ron King, Bob Stuart, Wilson Whineray, Fred Allen, Rod McKenzie, Peter Johnstone (rear), Archie Strang, Ian Clarke, Kevin Skinner, John Graham, Ron Elvidge, Beet Algar (at 92 the oldest living All Black, though not a former test captain), Bob Duff, Graham Mourie, Ian Kirkpatrick (rear), Kel Tremain, Colin Meads, Tane Norton. In front: Ponty Reid, Dave Loveridge, Stu Wilson and Andy Leslie.